The Strange History of the

AMERICAN QUADROON

The Strange History of the

American Quadroon

 FREE WOMEN OF COLOR
IN THE REVOLUTIONARY
ATLANTIC WORLD

Emily Clark

THE UNIVERSITY OF NORTH CAROLINA PRESS   *Chapel Hill*

This book was published with the assistance of the Tulane University School of Liberal Arts and the Thornton H. Brooks Fund of the University of North Carolina Press.

All rights reserved. Designed by Sally Fry and set in Adobe Caslon Pro by Rebecca Evans. Manufactured in the United States of America. The paper in this book meets the guidelines for permanence and durability of the Committee on Production Guidelines for Book Longevity of the Council on Library Resources.

The University of North Carolina Press has been a member of the Green Press Initiative since 2003.

Library of Congress Cataloging-in-Publication Data
Clark, Emily, 1954–
The strange history of the American quadroon : free women of color in the revolutionary Atlantic world / Emily Clark.
pages cm
Includes bibliographical references and index.
ISBN 978-1-4696-0752-8 (alk. paper)
1. Racially-mixed women—Louisiana—New Orleans—History—19th century. 2. New Orleans (La.)—Social conditions—19th century. 3. Sex symbolism. I. Title.
HQ1439.N65C53 2013
305.0890509763'35—dc23
2012042539

17 16 15 14 13   5 4 3 2 1

THIS BOOK WAS DIGITALLY PRINTED.

For Callie Winn Crawford and Sylvia R. Frey,
WITH GRATITUDE AND LOVE

Contents

Illustrations

The Strange History of the
AMERICAN QUADROON

Evolution of a Color Term and an American City's Alienation

Let the first crossing be of a, pure negro, with A, pure white. The unit of blood of the issue being composed of the half of that of each parent, will be $a/2 + A/2$. Call it, for abbreviation, h (half blood).

Let the second crossing be of h and B, the blood of the issue will be $h/2 + B/2$ or substituting for $h/2$ its equivalent, it will be $a/4 + A/4 + B/2$, call it q (quarteroon) being ¼ negro blood.

—Thomas Jefferson, 1815[1]

Travelers have long packed a bundle of expectations about what they will encounter when they visit New Orleans. Long before jazz was born, another presumably native-born phenomenon drew visitors to the Crescent City and preoccupied the American imagination. The British traveler Edward Sullivan observed succinctly in 1852, "I had heard a great deal of the splendid figures and graceful dancing of the New Orleans quadroons, and I certainly was not disappointed."[2] Sullivan's fellow country-woman Harriet Martineau provided more-disapproving intelligence on New Orleans quadroons some fifteen years earlier: "The Quadroon girls of New Orleans are brought up by their mothers to be what they have been; the mistresses of white gentlemen."[3] Frederick Law Olmsted observed of the city's quadroon women just five years before the outbreak of the Civil War that they were "one, among the multitudinous classifications of society in New Orleans, which is a very peculiar and characteristic result of the prejudices, vices, and customs of the various elements of color, class, and nation, which have been there brought together."[4]

The Civil War did not much alter advice to visitors about New Orleans quadroons. The "southern tour" in a guidebook published in 1866 includes New Orleans quadroons in its itinerary. Admitting that "the foregoing sketch of society and social life in New Orleans, I need hardly remind my reader, was penned long before the late rebellion had so changed the aspect of every thing throughout the South," the entry reassures its readers that they may nonetheless expect to encounter survivals of the quadroon in the postbellum city. "The visitor will, however, be surprised as well as delighted at the extent to which the manners and customs of 'the old regime,' are still perpetuated among the descendants of the early settlers in the Crescent City."[5] Twenty-first century travel literature upholds the practice of enticing tourists to New Orleans with tales of the quadroon. "The quadroons (technically, people whose racial makeup was one-quarter African) who met here were young, unmarried women of legendary beauty," a popular travel website explains. "A gentleman would select a favorite beauty and, with her mother's approval, buy her a house and support her as his mistress," the entry continues, concluding with a guarantee that traces of this peculiar tradition could be found only in one place in America. "This practice, known as plaçage, was unique to New Orleans at the time."[6]

Passages like these give the impression that New Orleans was the sole place in America where one could encounter beautiful women produced by a specific degree of procreation across the color line, women whose sexual favors were reserved for white men. The reality was, of course, more complicated than that. Women whose racial ancestry would have earned them the color term quadroon lived everywhere in nineteenth-century America.[7] Today, the most well known of them is undoubtedly Virginia-born Sally Hemings, who bore her owner, Thomas Jefferson, seven children. Sally Hemings was the daughter of white planter John Wales and an enslaved woman he owned named Betty Hemings. Betty was the daughter of an enslaved woman named Susannah and a white slave-ship captain named John Hemings. Sally Hemings came to Monticello as the property of Thomas Jefferson's wife, Martha Wales Skelton, who was, like Sally, the daughter of John Wales.[8]

Sally Heming's ancestry qualified her as a quadroon under Thomas Jefferson's own rubric, but when he sat down in 1815 to clarify to an acquaintance the legal taxonomy of race in his home state of Virginia, he did not take the living woman best known to him as his example. Instead, he eschewed the vivid register of language and enlisted the symbolic representation of algebra to illustrate the genetic origins of the physical and legal properties of the woman who bore most of his children and was his deceased wife's half sister. In a virtuosic and bizarre display of what one scholar has called a "calculus of color," Jefferson presented a tidy mathematical formula to define the race and place of the quadroon. The complicated, messy identity and status of Sally Hemings were tamed by the comforting discipline of symbolic logic. Flesh and blood, love, shame, and fear were safely imprisoned within the cold confines of mathematics. Unnamed, Sally Heming's mother was reduced to $a/2 + A/2 = h$ (half-blood). Sally herself was $a/4 + A/4 + B/2$. "Call it q (quateroon) being ¼ negro blood," Jefferson instructed (see Figure 1).[9]

This formulaic representation renders race as a kind a chemical compound comprising elements that act on one another in ways that multiply, mix, or cancel one another out to produce predictable results. Just as the combination of the elements of hydrogen and oxygen in the proportions represented by the formula $2H_2 + O_2 = 2H_2O$ will always produce H_2O—water—Jefferson's calculus of race was meant to be precise, immutable, reliable, knowable. With detached precision, Jefferson produced theoretical mulattos and quadroons devoid of the untidy human elements of desire and power that destabilized the living expressions of his mathematical calculations. He may have been driven to abstraction by the disturbing situation of his own reproductive life, but larger historical currents probably played as important a role in his recourse to symbolic logic.

More than two decades before he drafted the chilling equations of 1815, Jefferson produced his well-known observations on race in *Notes on the State of Virginia*. The black people Jefferson references in *Notes* are not abstract symbols but corporeal examples, their differences from "whites" mapped on their bodies and projected onto their sensibilities.[10] The observations in *Notes* are evocative, almost sensual passages, dense with palpable detail. Here, race is human, organic, expressive, a thing whose qualities can be described, but whose essence cannot be defined. Race slips the porous boundaries of words and threatens to overwhelm with its immeasurable meaning. Jefferson's calculus of 1815, by contrast, imprisons race within the abstract forms and structures of mathematics, subjecting it to universal rules that prescribe and predict comforting certainties that can be anticipated, managed, even controlled.

The dissonance between Jefferson's qualitative disquisition on blacks in *Notes on the State of Virginia* and his algebraic calculations of 1815 begs questions about more than the incongruities in the mind and life of one man. It points to a widespread and enduring tension in the American imagination over the symbolic expression and meaning of race that intensified and accelerated with the outbreak of widespread, violent slave rebellion in the French sugar colony of Saint-Domingue in 1791. Jefferson's own disquiet over the events that convulsed Saint-Domingue for the next thirteen years is clear in his correspondence, public and private. He spared his daughter Martha Jefferson Randolph none of his fearful assessment in the early let the 1st crossing be of a. pure negro, with A. pure white. the Unit of blood of the issue being composed of the half of that of each parent, will be $\frac{a}{2} + \frac{A}{2}$ call it, for abbreviation. h (half-blood)

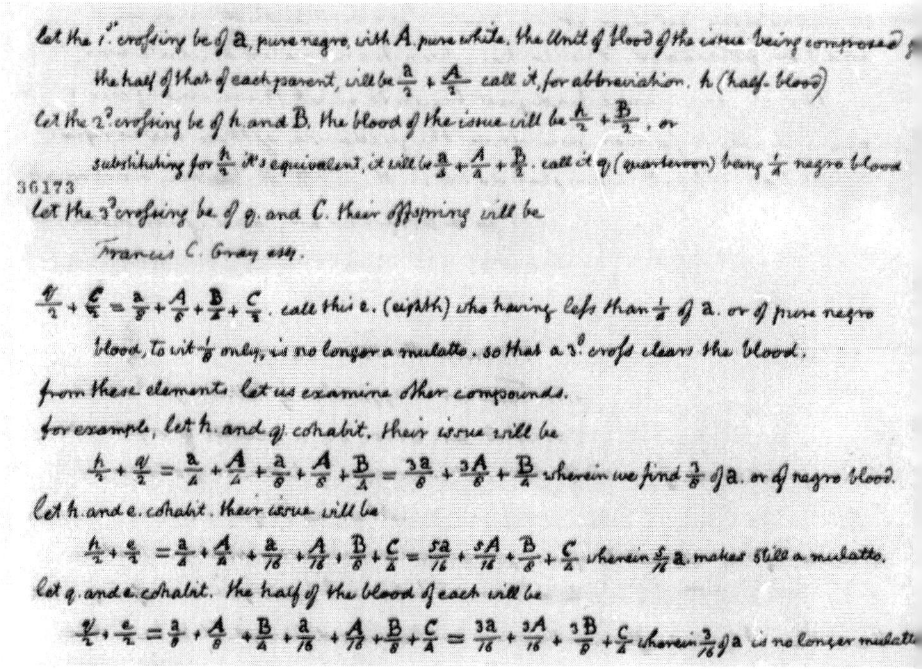

let the 2^d crossing be of h. and B. the blood of the issue will be $\frac{h}{2} + \frac{B}{2}$, or

substituting for $\frac{h}{2}$ it's equivalent, it will be $\frac{a}{4} + \frac{A}{4} + \frac{B}{2}$. call it q (quarteroon) being $\frac{1}{4}$ negro blood

36173

let the 3^d crossing be of q. and C. their offspring will be

Francis C. Gray esq.

$\frac{q}{2} + \frac{C}{2} = \frac{a}{8} + \frac{A}{8} + \frac{B}{4} + \frac{C}{2}$. call this e. (eighth) who having less than $\frac{1}{4}$ of a. or of pure negro blood, to wit $\frac{1}{8}$ only, is no longer a mulatto. so that a 3^d cross clears the blood.

from these elements let us examine other compounds.

for example, let h. and q. cohabit. their issue will be

$\frac{h}{2} + \frac{q}{2} = \frac{a}{4} + \frac{A}{4} + \frac{a}{8} + \frac{A}{8} + \frac{B}{4} = \frac{3a}{8} + \frac{3A}{8} + \frac{B}{4}$ wherein we find $\frac{3}{8}$ of a. or of negro blood.

let h. and e. cohabit. their issue will be

$\frac{h}{2} + \frac{e}{2} = \frac{a}{4} + \frac{A}{4} + \frac{a}{16} + \frac{A}{16} + \frac{B}{8} + \frac{C}{4} = \frac{5a}{16} + \frac{5A}{16} + \frac{B}{8} + \frac{C}{4}$ wherein $\frac{5}{16}$ a. makes still a mulatto.

let q. and e. cohabit. the half of the blood of each will be

$\frac{q}{2} + \frac{e}{2} = \frac{a}{8} + \frac{A}{8} + \frac{B}{4} + \frac{a}{16} + \frac{A}{16} + \frac{B}{8} + \frac{C}{4} = \frac{3a}{16} + \frac{3A}{16} + \frac{3B}{8} + \frac{C}{4}$ wherein $\frac{3}{16}$ of a. is no longer mulatto

FIGURE I. Jefferson's racial algebra. Thomas Jefferson to Francis Gray, March 4, 1815. Courtesy of the Library of Congress, American Memory.

months of the violence. "Abundance of women and children come here to avoid danger," he told her in November of 1791, having written to her earlier that the slaves of Saint-Domingue were "a terrible engine, absolutely ungovernable." He gave full vent to the enormity of his fears to his colleague James Monroe two years later. "I become daily more and more convinced that all the West India Island will remain in the hands of the people of colour, and a total expulsion of the whites sooner or later take place," he wrote in the summer of 1793. "It is high time we should foresee the bloody scenes which our children certainly, and possibly ourselves (south of the Potomac), have to wade through and try to avert them." Later that year he wrote to Governor William Moultrie of South Carolina to warn him that "two Frenchmen, from St. Domingo also, of the names of Castaing and La Chaise, are about setting out from this place [Philadelphia] for Charleston, with design to excite an insurrection among the negroes." These men were neither former African captives nor French émigrés dedicated to the cause of racial equality, but the products of sexual relations between the two. "Castaing," Jefferson advised Moultrie, "is described as a small dark mulatto, and La Chaise as a Quarteron, of a tall fine figure."[11]

Jefferson and his contemporaries did more than worry about the Haitian Revolution and the mixed-race people who seemed bent on spreading it. They acted with new urgency to insulate themselves from the threat of slave rebellion and racial reordering in the Atlantic world by means of policy and ideas. The revolution in the French colony of Saint-Domingue that culminated in the establishment of the slave-free black republic of Haiti in 1804 produced a new urgency in attempts to define and manage race throughout the Atlantic world. Race was the basis for the system of chattel slavery that fueled the Atlantic economy. If it could not be imaginatively codified and its mechanism understood, manipulated, controlled, slavery was imperiled. Jefferson's algebra was one of a range of symbolic strategies Americans deployed in response to racial anxieties magnified by the Haitian Revolution. The American quadroon was another. Both were equally fanciful reductions of a complex reality.

The term *quadroon* was primarily descriptive for most of the eighteenth century, a color term applied to people whose genetic makeup was imagined to have been one-fourth African.[12] Spanish and Spanish colonial artists began to attach qualitative meaning to the color terms in the second half of the eighteenth century in a genre known as *casta* painting. *Casta* paintings comprise multiple panels, usually in multiples of four, in each of which a man and woman of different races are shown with their child or children. Each scene is labeled with the color terms for the racial taxonomy being depicted. For example, a panel portraying a Spanish man and a black woman with their child is labeled "de Español y Negra: nace Mulata." Such couplings between people imagined as occupying racial extremes were rendered in pejorative ways. As one scholar has noted, "The message is clear: certain mixtures—particularly those of Spaniards or Indians with Blacks—could only lead to the contraction of debased sentiments, immoral proclivities, and a decivilized state" (see Figure 2).[13]

Médéric Louis Élie Moreau de Saint-Méry, a jurist and naturalist from the French Antilles, betrayed his anxiety over the uncontrollable nature of interracial procreation in a spectacularly detailed 1796 racial taxonomy that provides twenty combinations that produce a quadroon (see Figure 3).[14] Elsewhere, he portrayed mixed-race women as dangerous beauties who seduced French men away from their proper loyalties and paved the way for the overthrow of the plantation regime in Saint-Domingue.[15] Other late eighteenth-century writers likewise gendered the term *quadroon* and linked it to irresistible beauty. In his 1793 account of Surinam, John Gabriel Stedman succumbs to the powerful charms of a "young and beautiful Quadroon girl" and fathers a son on her.[16]

At the end of the eighteenth century, Americans imagined the beautiful, seductive quadroon as a foreigner in the Caribbean who did not occupy American territory. In fact, of course, the quadroon was already well established in the bosom of the young republic under circumstances such as those at Monticello.[17] This homegrown American quadroon was unacknowledged, however, both literally and figuratively. She, like Sally Hemings, remained in the shadows for nearly two centuries while Americans developed a complex symbolic strategy that kept her at an imaginative distance from the nation's heart and heartland. When the Haitian Revolution drove thousands of mixed-race women from the Caribbean to American shores, the figure of the quadroon supplied something more accessible than algebraic abstraction to neutralize the threat embedded in mixed-race people. The foreign female of color who migrated to the United States from the blood-soaked shores of Haiti could be mastered and controlled by white American men. This fantasy of sexual triumph supplied an antidote to the terror inspired by the image of Haiti's virile black men poised to export their war on slavery to the American mainland.

The émigré quadroon offered other advantages in the symbolic management of America's mixed-race population. She was more easily contained

FIGURE 2. Andrés de Islas, *De Español y Negra: nace Mulata*, 1774. From Ilona Katzew, *Casta Painting: Images of Race in Eighteenth-Century Mexico* (New Haven: Yale University Press, 2004), 116. Courtesy of the Latin American Library, Tulane University.

Les 20 combinaiſons du Quarteron offrent depuis 71 juſqu'à 96 parties blanches & depuis 32 juſqu'à 57 parties noires.

QUARTERON.

Venu du Blanc & de la Mulâtreſſe .	.	.	. 96	32
——— Quarteron avec la Quarteronne	.	.	. 96	32
——— Sang-Mêlé avec la Mulâtreſſe	.	.	. 95	33
——— Quarteronné ———————	.	.	. 94	34
——— Mamelouc———————	.	.	. 92	36
——— Blanc avec la Marabou .	.	.	. 88	40
——— Métif avec la Mulâtreſſe .	.	.	. 88	40
——— Sang-Mêlé avec la Marabou	.	.	. 87	41
——— Quarteronné ———————	.	.	. 86	42
——— Mamelouc ———————	.	.	. 84	44
——— Blanc avec la Griffonne .	.	.	. 80	48
——— Métif avec la Marabou .	.	.	. 80	48
——— Quarteron avec la Mulâtreſſe	.	.	. 80	48
——— Sang-Mêlé avec la Griffonne	.	.	. 79	49
——— Quarteronné———————	.	.	. 78	50
——— Mamelouc ———————	.	.	. 76	52
——— Blanc avec la Sacatra .	.	.	. 72	56
——— Métif avec la Griffonne .	.	.	. 72	56
——— Quarteron avec la Marabou	.	.	. 72	56
——— Sang-Mêlé avec la Sacatra	.	.	. 71	57

FIGURE 3. Moreau de Saint-Méry's racial taxonomy. From Médéric Louis Élie Moreau de Saint-Méry, *Description Topographique* . . . (Philadelphia, 1797), 84. Courtesy of the Latin American Library, Tulane University.

and controlled than her domestic counterpart could be. The endemic American quadroon was geographically pervasive, but a limited range could be imaginatively imposed on the invader, quarantining the threat she posed. Anxiety over the destabilizing potential of procreation across the color line was assuaged if America ignored its own interracial population and practices, preoccupied itself with the migrant quadroon, and found a way to cordon off the newcomer from the rest of the nation. When the Haitian Revolution first drove the quadroon from the Caribbean to the United States, she surfaced in Philadelphia and created quite a stir. By the 1810s, however, she had migrated away from the city so closely associated with America's founding and attached herself to a site comfortingly located on the geographic margins of the young republic: New Orleans.

Sequestering the quadroon figuratively in the Crescent City shaped American identity and historical narrative in subtle but powerful ways, effectively turning New Orleans into a perpetual colonial space in the national imagination. The subjection of eroticized women of color by white men is one of the key mechanisms and metaphors of colonialism. Historians and theorists have disputed the view of colonialism as a project limited to the empires of Europe and Asia, exposing the colonial enterprises of the United States not only in overseas sites such as the Philippines but within the nation's continental borders. Native Americans and Mexican-descended inhabitants of the American West and Southwest are now widely recognized as the objects of episodes of domestic colonialism. In such instances, "mainstream" America defined itself and its values against an "other,"—usually a feminine, colored other. Slavery and racism, too, fit easily into the concept of domestic colonialism.[18] The nation's symbolic use of the figure of the quadroon has produced yet another instance of domestic colonialism, rendering New Orleans an internal alien barred by this presumably exceptional feature of its past from claiming a comfortable berth in the national historical narrative.[19]

The acceptance of New Orleans as exceptional and its exclusion from the normative common history imagined to have been shared by the rest of America paradoxically secure some of the most prominent building blocks of American exceptionalism. The presumption that the history of New Orleans and its quadroons is unique diverts the gaze of the rest of the nation away from its own unattractive Atlantic past, allowing it to remain firmly fixed on less-troubling founding scenes played out on the Mayflower and in Independence Hall. Americans have used the figure of the quadroon for more than two centuries not just to explain and explore race but to delineate an American past and polity that is as sanitized—and as unsatisfying—as Thomas Jefferson's equation. The pages ahead tell the intertwined stories of the quadroon as symbol, the flesh-and-blood people this symbol was supposed to represent, and New Orleans, the city long imagined as America's only home to both.

CHAPTER ONE
The Philadelphia Quadroon

> It is rumoured that a race of real Quadroons is like to be produced
> in the Northern Liberties, through the expert management of the
> delicate certificate Doctor, and one of his sweet-scented brother-in-
> laws. From the nature of the copartnership, carried on between those
> sentimental worthies; the connoiseurs are all in a quandary, much
> altercation is like to arise in settling the point of consanguinity.
>
> —*Spirit of the Press* (Philadelphia), 1807[1]

The cryptic notice that opens this chapter appeared on the front page of Philadelphia's *Spirit of the Press* in the fall of 1807. The charged words of the item—an attending physician, partnership, consanguinity—all vaguely point to the birth of racially mixed progeny, "a race of real Quadroons."[2] But the words do not make much sense, unless one imagines some mad doctor undertaking a living demonstration of the salutary benefits of interracial breeding among the artisans and laborers who populated Philadelphia's Northern Liberties district. A contemporary item in another Philadelphia paper offers the key to decoding the cipher. "Is the Quadroon party forming to support the intended *protégé* of Mr. Dallas?" asked the *Democratic Press*. "Were the intrigues of Dr. Leib at Lancaster last winter connected with the formation of the Quadroon party?"[3]

The significance of the names Dallas and Leib in the same paragraph is arcane but clear. Michael Leib was the leader of the radical faction of the Pennsylvania Democratic Republican Party, known as the Philadelphia Democrats, and Alexander Dallas was among the most prominent members of a rival group of more-moderate party members. The two groups had been sparring in Philadelphia's partisan press for years, but the impending election of 1808 brought the factionalism to an ugly climax. This episode is generally seen as a turning point in the ideological evolution of the Democratic Republicans who came into power with the election of Thomas Jefferson in 1800.[4] But the piquant emergence of the quadroon on the pages of Philadelphia's newspapers that year revealed a less nobly conceived anxiety that stalked the city's popular imagination: Haiti. Labeling a rival political faction "Quadroons" contributed nothing to the debate over the relative merits of unfettered popular democracy. But it did ignite the popular passion that was becoming essential to early national politics by conjuring for white Philadelphians a cluster of festering resentments and potent fears born of their city's close connections to the new black republic.

The eruption of Philadelphia's quadroon press war in 1807 has virtually disappeared from American historical consciousness. And while Philadelphia's deep entanglement with colonial Saint-Domingue and the black republic that succeeded it in 1804 is slowly being rescued from obscurity, it remains powerfully overshadowed by the city's star role in the American Revolution.[5] Yet, Philadelphia's negotiation of its relationship with Haiti is important for understanding the ideas and forces that shaped the early American republic after the seminal drama that unfolded in Independence Hall in the summer of 1776. The ugly rhetoric that spilled across the pages of the Philadelphia press in 1807 testifies to the limits of the American popular and political imagination on the matter of abolition and racial equality. Haiti showed the young United States what it might become. It was an image that fascinated many in the young republic in the 1790s with the possibilities of its example. By 1807 it represented what was to be avoided as the United States forged its nationhood. This chapter uncovers the intricate and overlapping histories of Philadelphia and the new black republic that explain why and how the image of the quadroon communicated so immediately and viscerally to Philadelphians.

Philadelphia was a boomtown in the 1790s, with a burgeoning population and a robust commercial economy. With a population of 28,500 in 1790, it was the young republic's largest city and served as its national capital during this last decade of the eighteenth century. It was also the nation's largest port, its waterfront crammed with commercial vessels that plied the waters of the Atlantic and Caribbean, bringing wealth to a growing cadre of merchant capitalists. The French sugar colony of Saint-Domingue played a major part in the port's success. In 1789, nearly 20 percent of the vessels arriving in Philadelphia from foreign harbors arrived from Saint-Domingue. Seven years later, at the height of the fighting in the Caribbean colony, the figure had jumped to more than a third.[6] The enslaved labor force that worked the fabulously productive cane fields of the "Pearl of the Antilles" provided a major market for Pennsylvania flour. Philadelphia bottoms also carried New England cod, timber, and other building supplies to the island colony. In return, thousands of tons of Saint-Domingue sugar, molasses, and coffee were unloaded at the city's docks, where wealthy Philadelphia merchants, foremost among them Stephen Girard, took consignment of the cargoes.[7]

The lives of hundreds of less famous Philadelphians were directly implicated in the Saint-Domingue trade as well. More than 300 different captains led voyages to and from the island over one four-year period in the early 1790s, each one of them, along with every member of their crews, bringing home with him not only welcome family income but news and perspectives that shaped the city's consciousness. Even Philadelphians far removed from maritime commerce were touched by Saint-Domingue and its affairs. Carriage makers George and William Hunter, whose extravagantly decorated coach, the "Eagle Car," was a highlight of Philadelphia's Grand Federal Procession of July 4, 1788, built a thriving business in the 1780s and early 1790s by catering to the tastes of wealthy Dominguan planters.[8] When Saint-Domingue was swept into the French Revolution in 1789, and subsequently rocked by the slave rebellion that became the Haitian Revolution, Philadelphians were not neutral spectators. "Events on the island were noteworthy, and problematic," notes one historian, "because they disrupted a situation ripe with advantage."[9] Indeed. A Philadelphia newspaper published a letter in November 1791 from a merchant in Cap Français advising that there was "no demand for provisions of any kind, and our market is overstocked with all kinds of American produce." Some 25,000 barrels of American flour and 1,500 barrels of pork, destined to feed the slaves who were now burning the sugar fields of the northern plain of Saint-Domingue, languished in Cap Français warehouses.[10]

Commerce riveted many Philadelphians to the news from Saint-Domingue, but others watched just as intently for an altogether different reason. While Philadelphia merchants wrung their hands over their rotting flour and pork, not to mention the annual production of 40 million pounds of sugar produced by the burned plantations that would not be transported in their bottoms that year, others were quietly jubilant. For the hundreds of Philadelphians who remained in slavery, the "situation ripe with advantage" could be exploited to precipitate a veritable epidemic of freedom. All Philadelphians had an undeniable interest in how the revolutionary movement played out in Saint-Domingue, though they were hardly unified in their aspirations for it.

The positions of the embattled Dominguans themselves were even more diverse and deeply, violently, divisive. Wealthy planters, known as *grands blancs*, were ideologically sympathetic to the monarchy of the *ancien régime*, but other circumstances weakened their loyalty to French sovereignty. They chafed under the constraint of the *Exclusif*, which prohibited trade between French colonies and other empires and nations, and they feared that the egalitarian republicans in France would press for the reform or abolition of the forced labor that fueled Saint-Domingue's economy. American planters had shown them the advantage of taking control of their destinies, and the outbreak of revolution in France in the spring of 1789 produced just the disordered circumstances that made a grab at independence auspicious for Dominguan plantation masters. *Petits blancs*, small planters, overseers, artisans, and petty traders of French descent, were sympathetic to the republican cause of the revolutionaries but were generally unenthusiastic about the ideology of racial equality promoted by some of the radicals in the movement. As long as the French Revolutionary movement remained moderate on racial equality, *petits blancs* favored remaining a French colony. Altogether there were just over 30,000 whites of both types. Free people of color, or *gens de couleur libres*, numbered some 28,000 and generally cast their lot with the republicans, hoping for full and unequivocal recognition of equal political and social rights. As denizens of the first republic in the Western Hemisphere, Philadelphians had a natural sympathy for the Dominguans, black and white, who sided with the republican cause, but their trade relied on the success of the plantations belonging to the *grands blancs*.[11] All in all, in the first year of the French Revolution, many Philadelphians, especially merchants and others who stood to profit by an increased commerce with Saint-Domingue, saw expanded opportunity in the prospect of an independent Saint-Domingue.[12]

The enslaved laborers of Saint-Domingue complicated Philadelphia's position when those in the colony's most important sugar-plantation region, the Northern Province, rose in rebellion in August of 1791. Numbering about a half million and constituting 90 percent of the colony's population, the enslaved, once roused to revolt, constituted a potentially insurmountable threat to the colony's plantation regime. The republicans who now controlled France had no interest in shoring up the independence-minded *grands blancs*, but they did hope to put down the slave rebellion and restore the colony's profitable plantation economy. In a bid to win the support of the *gens de couleur* against the slave forces, the ruling French National Legislative Assembly granted them equal rights in a decree issued on April 4, 1792. A few months later, in June, the French revolutionary government sent 6,000 troops and two Revolutionary Commissioners, Léger-Félicité Sonthonax and Étienne Polverel, to enforce the decree, establish the revolutionary government, quell the violence unleashed by the slave uprising, and persuade the enslaved rebels to return to the cane fields to restore the colony to its former productivity.[13]

Philadelphians whose livelihoods were tied to the fortunes of Saint-Domingue saw the arrival of Sonthonax and Polverel as a generally hopeful development. Still others were positively inspired by it. France's decision to enforce the decree of April 4 roused those in the city who had long worked for the end of slavery in Pennsylvania and, by the 1790s, for the radical proposition of universal abolition in all of the young American republic. Slavery arrived in Pennsylvania within three years of the colony's founding in 1681, and by the 1740s, 15 percent of its manual labor force and domestic servants were enslaved, rising to 20 percent by the 1760s. In the 1760s as many as 500 enslaved people debarked in Philadelphia annually, many of them directly from Africa, and by the middle of the decade enslaved men and women made up about 8 percent of the total population of the city of 18,000. With the influx of Irish and German indentured servants during the Seven Years' War, Philadelphia developed a preference for Euro-descended servants and wage laborers, and, aided by growing distaste for the sale of human chattel, the slave trade all but vanished there.[14] Thus, when Pennsylvania was the second state to pass abolition legislation in 1780, "An Act for the Gradual Abolition of Slavery," it was decidedly closing a door on something that had played a significant part in its colonial history without taking a step that would radically affect is current economy. Moreover, the act did not free slaves outright but prohibited the entry of new slaves into the state and dictated that children born to slaves after passage of the act would be free.[15]

The 1780 act, which left thousands of people in Philadelphia enslaved, fell far short in the eyes of Pennsylvania's antislavery activists, who established the Pennsylvania Abolition Society (PAS) in 1784 to press for more-sweeping reform. Partially successful in passing more legislation restricting slavery and slave trading in Pennsylvania in 1787, the PAS was stirred to a new round of debate on the future of slavery in the young American Republic with the outbreak of the slave rebellion in Saint-Domingue. The April 4 decree widened the discussion beyond the immorality of bondage to the more radical consideration of racial equality. Events in Saint-Domingue made it possible in Philadelphia's public sphere to discuss and imagine an American republic that extended the full promise of the Revolution to all.[16]

Just as events in Saint-Domingue had engendered this progressive turn in debates over slavery and racial equality, so too did they gradually conspire to produce a conservative reaction in the mid-1790s. On the island, France's April 4 decree and the arrival of its emissaries Sonthonax and Polverel infuriated not only the *grands blancs* who still hoped to preserve their racial and economic privilege, along with their sugar plantations, but other whites in the colony as well, including *petits blancs* and many white soldiers and sailors. Interracial violence rocked Saint-Domingue's principal city, Cap Français, in the last months of 1792, often pitting free black troops loyal to Sonthonax and Polverel against white troops incensed at the commissioners' pronouncement that the April 4 decree authorized the command of free black officers over white soldiers. While the commissioners attempted to quell what one historian has dubbed a race war in the northern city of Cap Français, trouble of another kind bloomed in the western and southern parts of the colony. There, *grands blancs* alarmed by the commissioners' commitment to imposing the April 4 decree and their support of the free black militia in their conflicts with white soldiers in Cap Français allied themselves with the British, against whom the French had just declared war, with the ultimate aim of achieving independence. The commissioners were forced to leave the tinderbox that Cap Français had become to take on the treasonous planters of the west and south of the colony who had agreed to submit to British sovereignty to preserve their racial privilege. Although Sonthonax and Polverel managed to bring the western and southern districts to heel, they had to exert destructive force to do so. The colonial capital of Port-au-Prince was subdued only after the commissioners' forces launched a devastating naval bombardment against it.[17]

In the absence of the commissioners, the environment in Cap Français deteriorated. Whites from the surrounding countryside trickled into the city in increasing numbers. Seeking security from the rebel slave forces emboldened by the diversion of Sonthonax and Polverel to the west, many began to plan their departure, at least temporarily, from the colony. The war with Britain made their immediate escape impossible and their waiting unpleasant. British privateers effectively cut the city off from trade, and supplies of food and other necessities dwindled. American merchants, who had continued to send their ships to the colony, were now trapped by the embargo and discouraged by the inhabitants who had fled their plantations. They began to contemplate abandoning the colony, too. Stephen Girard's brother, Jean, wrote to his sibling in Philadelphia that "as I arise from my bed I begin to cudgel my brains for some means of getting away safely and without loss from St. Domingo which I regard as a doomed land." As winter turned to spring in 1793, commercial ships congregated in Cap Français harbor waiting until it seemed safe to form a convoy under the protection of the French naval vessels that bided their time with them. The French sailors aboard the ships, some of whom had been in the Antilles for two years with steadily decreasing access to food and other basic supplies, were among the unhappiest of those waiting to leave Cap Français. Trapped sweltering and hungry on their ships in the late spring of 1793, they were themselves on the brink of rebellion.[18]

François Thomas Galbaud du Fort, newly appointed governor general of the colony, sailed into this unhappy scene in early May 1793 and proceeded, by most accounts, to make it worse by escalating a power struggle with Sonthonax and Polverel into armed combat. The commissioners made their way to Cap Français from the west, already advised by their agent in the city that Galbaud was reassessing decisions they had previously made and reviving interracial conflicts that the commissioners had taken pains to suppress. Upon their arrival, they determined that Galbaud had overstepped his authority and transgressed theirs, and pressed Galbaud to resign his post and return to France. The governor general did resign and was escorted to one of the French naval vessels, the *Normand*, where he was to remain until such time as the convoy set sail. But Galbaud had second thoughts about going quietly. Aboard the *Normand* he was persuaded by some of the commissioners' white opponents to rally the disgruntled French sailors to his side and launch an attack from the harbor on the commissioners and their free black allies. On June 20, Galbaud led a force of some 2,000 against the commissioners and their free black troops. Fighting continued for two days, culminating in the outbreak of a devastating fire. By June 23 most of the city of Cap Français had burned to the ground, and Galbaud's forces had been defeated. He and 10,000 refugees fled to Baltimore in a convoy of 120 ships.[19]

The commissioners had vanquished Galbaud, but the destruction of Cap Français was a high price to pay, and another mortal threat lay on their doorstep. Saint-Domingue occupied only the extreme western part of the island of Hispaniola. Spain controlled the rest and planned to exploit the disorder in Saint-Domingue to gain control of the entire island. Like Britain, Spain sought and found allies among those disgruntled by the French revolutionary government's concessions to free people of color: those who remained enslaved in the colony. The rebel slave forces, which sought universal freedom and equality under the command of the black

General François-Dominique Toussaint Louverture, joined the Spanish and set their sights on capturing the rich plantation district of the northern plain around Cap Français.[20]

In the wake of the destruction of Cap Français, the remnants of the regular French troops, left without leadership or protection, went over to the Spanish and to Louverture. On August 29, little more than two months after the catastrophe in Cap Français, Louverture made clear his primary cause with a declaration at Camp Turel addressed to the blacks of Saint-Domingue:

> Brothers and friends, I am Toussaint Louverture; perhaps my name has made itself known to you. I have undertaken vengeance. I want Liberty and Equality to reign in St Domingue. I am working to make that happen. Unite yourselves to us, brothers, and fight with us for the same cause.[21]

Sonthonax acknowledged with a formal proclamation made the same day that his free black troops were no match for the army of slaves longing to be free led by Toussaint, declaring, "All the blacks and mixed-race people now enslaved are declared free to enjoy all the rights attached to the status of French citizens."[22] Five months later, free black Dominguan delegates to the French National Convention helped push through a more sweeping measure. "The enslavement of blacks throughout the colonies is abolished," it decreed, and, "all men domiciled in the colonies, without distinction of color, are French citizens and enjoy all the rights provided by the constitution."[23]

Philadelphians followed each of these turns of events closely in their newspapers, where firsthand accounts from American ships' captains and merchants began appearing in print in early July, within weeks of the conflagration in Cap Français.[24] By August about 600 of the 10,000 refugees who had fled with Galbaud had arrived in the city, where they regaled any who would listen with their melodramatic version of events.[25] Sonthonax and Polverel, they wailed, "called to their assistance the twenty-five thousand black 'brigands,' by whose means this opulent city has been burned, and who obtained from the commissioners their liberty, as a reward of these meritorious services."[26] Philadelphians, informed by both their republican sensibilities and their concerns about the outlook for commerce with the colony, did not immediately ally themselves to the refugees' cause. Led by John Nicholson, John Wachsmuth, and James Vanuxem, merchants whose fortunes were deeply entwined with Saint-Domingue, Philadelphians reached deep into their pockets to provide food, clothing, and shelter for some of the men, women, and children who "escaped by swimming from fire and sword, naked and in want of everything." They stopped short, however, of joining the refugees in their outrage at their usurpation by the radical republicans Sonthonax and Polverel and their new ally, Louverture. "Some among them," observed an account read into the minutes of a meeting held in Philadelphia's Philosophical Hall in August 1793 to organize refugee relief, "may have by their guilt drawn the misfortunes they feel on their own heads."[27]

The limits of Philadelphia's sympathy were shaped in newspaper stories that indicted the alliance between the British and the *grands blancs* for months following the razing of Cap Français. "Many of these aristocrats have thrown off the mask, and there is not a species of slander but they vomit forth against the French republic," proclaimed a correspondent from Baltimore in late August.[28] An account first published in a New York newspaper held up the specter of a British-controlled Saint-Domingue with its publication of correspondence addressed to the governor of Jamaica by the *grands blancs* of the southern settlement of Jérémie. "Permit us to address you at a time of universal joy—at a time when the English and French of this dependency are one people. The arrival of troops and other succours from his Britannic Majesty guards our property, and delivers us from the oppressive load of a war." In what must have struck the Philadelphians as particularly galling, the *grands blancs* of Jérémie borrowed from the American Revolutionary lexicon, calling themselves the "Council of Safety" and averring in an echo of American patriot rhetoric that the "inhabitants of St. Domingo, not having it in their power to apply to their lawful sovereign to deliver them from the tyranny that oppresses them, sue for the protection of his Britannic Majesty, offering to him the oath of fidelity."[29] The account by the former mayor of Môle St. Nicolas, a settlement in the west of the colony, was published in Philadelphia in November, reporting that, "A considerable number of the inhabitants of the parishes adjoining the Mole eagerly came to partake of the disgrace and infamy with which the inhabitants were covered, by taking the oath of allegiance to his Britannic Majesty."[30] Newspapers published similar accounts of the submission of the antirepublican French to the British through the end of 1793, sometimes including the inflammatory language of the oath the English reputedly administered to the Dominguans: "I swear to shed even the last drop of my blood in support of the British flag at St. Domingo, to fight until death against all Frenchmen, bearing arms against the King of England, and to perish rather than to acknowledge the French Republic."³¹

Philadelphians found the *grands blancs'* alliance with the British ideologically repugnant, but their primary concern remained the outlook for commerce with the colony. Before the burning of Cap Français, *Dunlap's American Daily Advertiser* assured readers in early June 1793 that the "last letters received by Citizen Genet . . . contain the most satisfactory particulars respecting the tranquility which the Colony enjoys since the surrender of Port au Prince" by "men who stirred up by the British government, had formed the design of delivering the Colony to that power."³² The Cassandras "who have spread a notion through the United States, that American Vessels carrying provisions to the French part of St. Domingo, might run the risque of being seized there with their cargoes" were simply "inveterate enemies to France," according to the article. "The Citizens of the United States, may on the contrary rest assured," the report continued, "that they shall always receive from the National Commissioners and public functionaries in that Colony, the protection which they have a right to expect for themselves and their property, and that they shall be duly paid for all such articles as they may supply the Colony with."³³ Refugees from the Cap reversed such glowing assessments in the pages of the same newspaper, predicting doom for trading interests under the triumvirate of Sonthonax, Polverel, and Louverture. French officials in Saint-Domingue and the United States, foremost among them French Ambassador to the United States Edmond-Charles Genêt, sought to discredit refugee narratives of events and reassure Philadelphians about the prospects for the speedy restoration of peaceful and profitable commerce. "We feel how essential it is," Polverel and Sonthonax wrote in a letter to Genêt that was published in English translation in Philadelphia's *National Gazette*, "that the United States, infested as they are by emigrants from St. Domingo, should learn the truth of events thro' the agents of the republic."³⁴

Some Philadelphia newspapers published opinions that reached beyond a concern for trade and disgust with the *grand blanc* alliance with the British. The *National Gazette* proclaimed in October that it was "a gross error to believe in the maintenance of slavery in St. Domingo. Let the proprietors undeceive themselves; already it exists no more." Nor were the *grands blancs* who fell to the violence of the black troops of Louverture to be pitied. "Can the annihilation of a cruel, vicious, aristocratic people, enemies to the French Republic, be a crime?" the *National Gazette* asked.

"No! No!" it responded. "Those blood-suckers of the people who have never done anything for the Republic, who know nothing but gold, and pollute the land of liberty," these traitors to republican ideals "ought already to have manured with their infectious bodies the ground which has been exhaulted for them, and upon which they still breathe."[35] The *General Advertiser* and the *Pennsylvania Gazette* both published reports of the French Society of the Friends of Liberty and Equality on the results of their subscription to aid "the unfortunate situation of the French citizens who were forced by the conflagration at Cape Francois and the destruction of the means of subsistence in that part of the French colony of St. Domingo, to seek an asylum in the United States, where they are now labouring under the pressure of the greatest indigence." The society pointedly noted, however, that it did "not in any manner approve of the conduct of the greatest number of the colonists," noting that "their prejudices and their aristocracy of colour, not less absurd and prejudicial to mankind than that of the heretofore French nobles, have been the principal cause of all the evils which now assail them."[36]

Philadelphians grudgingly provided immediate financial relief to the refugees but were not prepared to welcome them as permanent members of their community. "It is certainly very fortunate," wrote a correspondent to the *General Advertiser* in July 1793, "for the unhappy fugitives from Cape Francois, who are reduced to the greatest want, to find through the humanity of the citizens of the United Sates, and of the French societies, the most immediate relief in their multiplied distresses." Like many others, however, this citizen "wished that something permanent be proposed and adopted by the United States." The solution he proposed was to settle the refugees in rural New York on land that the Oneida Indians had supposedly forfeited under the terms of the bogus Stanwix treaty.[37]

Settling groups of French refugees in the American hinterland was not an altogether novel idea. A number of wealthy French investors speculated on property in rural Maine and upstate New York early in the 1790s with the plan to sell it off to those fleeing the revolutionary violence and uncertainty in France and its colonies. But the only one of these initiatives to bear fruit was a settlement organized in the weeks following the Cap Français crisis and sited in northeast Pennsylvania. Founded by two Frenchmen, the "Asylum" was financed by two Philadelphia merchants with commercial ties to Saint-Domingue, Robert Morris and John Nicholson.[38]

There was more than a hint of quarantine in the scheme advanced by the anonymous correspondent to the *General Advertiser* and that underwritten by Morris and Nicholson. The young American republic craved protection from the amorphous bundle of threats that the refugees carried with them. Some feared the aristocratic tendencies of the elite among the refugees, others the proclivity for violent rebellion in the name of a democracy far more radical than most Americans were willing to embrace. When yellow fever broke out in Philadelphia in the late summer of 1793, many were convinced that the contagion had come in the hold of a ship transporting cargo and people from the ill-fated island.[39] Linked so closely in time to the arrival of the refugees, it would have been surprising if Philadelphians had not yoked the ravages of the epidemic to the hapless Dominguans. Yet perhaps most pervasive and insidious of all the fears aroused by the refugees' arrival was the less tangible threat posed by those who may have brought with them a commitment to racial equality and the universal abolition extended by Louverture, Sonthonax, and Polverel in the aftermath of the Cap Français catastrophe. The Dominguans came from a place that had vaulted far beyond Pennsylvania's 1780 Act for the Gradual Abolition of Slavery. And there was more. They modeled in their intimate lives a radical blindness to color that challenged Philadelphians to contemplate a more revolutionary reordering of established hierarchies than even universal abolition promised.

When the refugee convoy arrived in the United States in the summer of 1793, its passengers carried more than news of death and pillage: they brought gossip. In the tense days between the arrival of Sonthonax and Polverel in Cap Français and Galbaud's ill-fated assault on the commissioners, a contretemps in the realm of etiquette exacerbated the distrust between the men. Galbaud, in an effort to establish his status as primary official in Cap Français, sent word to the commissioners upon their arrival from the west that he wished to welcome them with a reception at his lodgings. Sonthonax and Polverel, perhaps to deny Galbaud the role of host in a city they considered ostensibly under their authority rather than his, spurned the invitation with vague excuses about the heat and other plans. Those plans turned out to be a grand reception of their own at which they feted the free people of color who had not only been their staunch allies in battle against the treasonous *grands blancs* of the western and southern districts but the companions of their intimate lives.

Critics of the commissioners were appalled by the guest lists of the parties they had given since their arrival the year before. "You cannot imagine these orgies, called patriotic fêtes," an outraged white colonist reported in his memoir of the period. At these events, "the women of color, proud of having become the idols of the day, were given the leading place."[40] Both of the commissioners took free women of color as mistresses after coming to Saint-Domingue in 1792, and Sonthonax eventually married a woman of mixed race. The commissioners' free black partners were almost certainly present at the fete the men organized on June 19, 1793, and many of the eighty other invitees were free women of color who had recently been granted their freedom. Many of these women were married to free men of color, but others had chosen white partners. Galbaud's wife had refused to receive "all the concubines in the city as part of her society." Galbaud did not insist that she do so, signaling to the free black population that as an official of the republic he was bound to uphold the letter of the April 4 decree, but as an individual he continued to recognize a racial hierarchy. By throwing their own party with its defiantly mixed guest list, Sonthonax and Polverel signaled to Galbaud that his rejection of the new racial order was as transgressive as was his pretension to power.[41]

Along with the stories of the new social prominence of free women of color and their intimate association with the French commissioners who had abolished slavery in Saint-Domingue, a small number of such women came in the flesh to Philadelphia, where they aroused curiosity, fascination, and fear. Médéric Louis Élie Moreau de Saint-Méry, a prominent Dominguan who took up residence in Philadelphia before the Cap Français refugee influx, complained that "the French colored women live in the most obnoxious luxury in Philadelphia, and since this luxury can only be provided by the French and by former French colonials, the contrast of their condition with the misery of the mass of their compatriots is revolting."[42]

Moreau de Saint-Méry's observations suggest that amorous adventures with free women of color were the exclusive vice of Francophone men, but John Murdock's play *The Triumphs of Love*, staged in Philadelphia in 1795, suggests that Anglo-Philadelphians also courted these women. Early in the play, a character named Trifle confesses to his Quaker friends that he is in love "over head and ears, by all that is charming in woman; deluged, inveloped, swallowed up in the great gulf of love," with "one of those called people of colour," who has come to Philadelphia from Saint-Domingue. One of his friends quite clearly shares Trifle's attraction to the "soft, such sweet, languishing, melting, dissolving looks" of her color and begs Trifle to tell him where he can find "this yellow piece of perfection."[43]

The Cap Français crisis of 1793 was a turning point in Philadelphia's relationship to Saint-Domingue. Before it, the city's rewarding commercial links with the colony, its sympathy with the republican ideology embraced by the French Revolution and, for some, the potential of Saint-Domingue to point the way toward racial equality and abolition throughout the Atlantic world fostered a sense of common purpose and a shared future for the American city and the island colony. That expectation was fractured after 1793. For many white Americans, the destruction of Cap Français amidst bitter interracial violence and the rise of the black general Toussaint Louverture turned the revolution in Saint-Domingue into a cautionary tale of slave rebellion and free black agency run amok. Saint-Domingue could no longer be effectively evoked as a source of inspiration for Philadelphians who backed the cause of universal abolition and full racial equality. Sensing the change in popular opinion, the Pennsylvania Abolition Society stepped back from its energetic advocacy for universal abolition and softened its once-radical rhetoric.[44]

At the same time, merchants began to reassess the wisdom of concentrating so much of their attention on the beleaguered colony. Trade continued, but unpredictability and risk were the rule. A cargo of "eleven hogsheads of sugar, three bales of cotton, and eight casks of claret," rescued by an American bottom from two ships that had been abandoned near Cap Français, made its way onto Philadelphia's wharves in the summer of 1793.[45] But such chance bonanzas were no substitute for stable trade. By late autumn, merchants were hedging their bets on the future of Saint-Domingue. The owners of the brig *Columbia* advertised the sale of a cargo of mahogany, cotton, and coffee landed from Saint-Domingue in late November 1793 at the same time that they offered the vessel for sale or charter.[46] Those merchants who continued to believe in the commercial prospects of the colony must have been discouraged by the report of a Baltimore merchant published in the *Pennsylvania Gazette* in 1795. American merchants were sending an "immense influx of every article, as well as of our own produce, as that imported from every part of the world," to Saint-Domingue. "Who the adventurers have expected were to consume it," he continues, "is hard to conjecture," since "the white people are all gone."[47]

Even if buyers were to be found, getting cargos to Saint-Domingue proved increasingly difficult. Late in 1794, the United States normalized trade with Britain with Jay's Treaty, infuriating the French, who were still at war with Britain. In retaliation, the French unleashed their privateers in the Caribbean on American shipping.[48] American commerce with Saint-Domingue thus was doubly imperiled by unstable markets and conditions in the colony and by the depredations of authorized French privateers on the high seas. Shortly after taking office in 1798, President John Adams responded with an embargo that banned U.S. commerce with France and French colonies. Toussaint Louverture, now the leader of Saint-Domingue and eying independence from France, understood that trade with the United States was crucial to Dominguan survival and sought rapprochement with the United States on his own. Late in 1798, Louverture dispatched an emissary, Joseph Bunel, to the U.S. capital in Philadelphia to ask the Adams administration to lift the embargo and provide diplomatic support to his government as it sought independence from France.[49]

Adams, who believed that "independence is the worst and most dangerous condition they can be in, for the United States," was not immediately sympathetic to the proposals that Joseph Bunel brought to Philadelphia, but the members of his administration who treated with Bunel in the last days of 1798 were supportive.[50] There is no evidence that they were influenced in their deliberations by opposition to slavery and admiration for the hopes of the black general for the foundation of a black republic. Rather, it is almost certain that they were favorably inclined because of their hopes to retain the loyalty of the Philadelphia merchants who had been their natural allies in Federalist economic policy. Robert Morris, a signer of the Declaration of Independence who helped finance the Revolutionary War, remained a staunch Federalist supporter.[51] But Stephen Girard, the French-born leader of Philadelphia's Saint-Domingue trade, was moving toward the Republicans in the wake of the XYZ Affair and the passage of the Alien and Sedition Acts earlier in 1798.[52] Lifting the embargo and supporting an independent Saint-Domingue in its quest for peace and the restoration of its plantation economy were actions calculated to appeal to America's merchant elite, particularly those in the nation's largest port who had invested heavily in cultivating the Dominguan trade in the early 1790s. Bunel's mission to Philadelphia met with success. Following a meeting with Secretary of State Thomas Pickering and other members of the administration just after Christmas in 1798, he closed the negotiations with President Adams himself in January. On February 9, 1799, Adams signed the bill authorizing trade with Saint-Domingue and diplomatic relations with the government headed by Toussaint Louverture. Both matters were to proceed at the president's discretion.[53]

The expectation of the merchants was that the lifting of the embargo and America's soft support for Dominguan independence would usher in a new trade boom. Louverture had ended slavery but he had every intention of reviving the island's vibrant sugar economy with a labor force of *cultivateurs*, former slaves who remained bound to the plantations they had served before the rebellion. The new black regime sought to reassure Americans that it was not racist. "The Americans are good whites, and we will not go to war with them," a prominent Dominguan assured Richard Yates, a New York merchant who reported on conditions in Saint-Domingue to Secretary of State Thomas Pickering in the spring of 1798.[54]

Edward Stevens was dispatched as consul general of the United States to Saint-Domingue within weeks of the passage of the February act of Congress lifting the embargo and arrived in Cap Français in April 1799. Over the next eighteen months he kept up negotiations with Louverture, securing promises of safe passage for U.S. shipping and, in turn, helping Louverture secure supplies to suppress the insurrection of André Rigaud, his rival in the southern districts of the island. In a telling passage in one of his dispatches to Secretary Pickering, Stevens admitted that American merchants seemed hardly to have broken stride in their trade with the colony during the embargo. "Notwithstanding the rigorous Laws enacted in America, to prevent Vessels from sailing to French ports, and the Vigilance of American Cruizers," Stevens observed, "the Flag of the United States is seen as frequently in every part of this Colony, as it was before the prohibiting Act was passed." If they wanted to continue to claim the loyalty of the American merchant community, Adams and the Federalists had little choice about their Saint-Domingue policy.[55]

The merchants of Philadelphia would have been pleased to know the details of Stevens's dispatches. There were 10 million pounds of coffee waiting to be exported from Jérémie in the extreme west of the island in the summer of 1799, and in the autumn of 1800 the prospects of a return to full production in regions disrupted by Louverture's war with Rigaud were bright. "The Cultivators of the South have been recalled to their respective Plantations, the various civil Administrations reorganised, and the most effectual Measures adopted for the future Peace and good order of that Department," Stevens reported ebulliently. "Agriculture and Commerce begin to revive."[56]

The Adams administration's support of Philadelphia traders' interests in Saint-Domingue were insufficient, in the end, to woo many of them away from the Democratic Republican camp of Thomas Jefferson in the election of 1800. Their defection had as much to do, however, with local politics and differences over breadth of political participation as it did with international trade policy. A Federalist clique known as the Junto had maintained an iron grip on Pennsylvania politics since the mid-1780s.

Well connected and unapologetically elitist, the Junto looked for ways to minimize the electoral impact of Philadelphia's growing cadre of artisans, retailers, and modest traders on state and national politics. They also hoped to avoid sharing power with wealthy, accomplished men who did not share their deep roots in pre-Revolutionary power structures—men such as the French-born merchant Stephen Girard and his lawyer, Jamaican-born Alexander Dallas. Dallas, Girard, and a number of other Philadelphia merchants including Andrew Pettit and Andrew Bayard, made common cause with the artisans and shopkeepers who supported the Democratic Republicans to elect Thomas Jefferson president and sweep the Federalists from office in Pennsylvania.[57]

Jefferson initially maintained the Adams administration's tacit support of Toussaint Louverture's regime in Saint-Domingue, but he did so reluctantly. His ambivalence toward slavery is well known. While a member of the Congress of Confederation in 1784 he developed a plan for the western territory that banned slavery there after 1800. His draft constitution for Virginia would have made all children born to enslaved mothers after December 31, 1800, free.[58] But when 1800 arrived, his home state of Virginia was traumatized by the rebellion of an enslaved Richmond blacksmith named Gabriel Prosser. The event seemed to confirm white southern fears that Saint-Domingue's slave revolt was destined to spread to the shores of the United States.[59]

Jefferson's challenge after his election lay in determining how best to prevent the contagion of black rebellion. Louverture's regime had assured the United States that it would not only refrain from attempting to spread abolition to the American mainland, but that it would fight any efforts to do so that emanated from rival factions in Saint-Domingue. Jefferson's alternative was to side with Napoleon's brother-in-law, Charles Leclerc, who had been dispatched with an enormous expeditionary force to Saint-Domingue to wrest control from Louverture, reestablish slavery, and restore the lucrative sugar production of the colony.[60] Tenche Coxe, a powerful Pennsylvania political figure who had shifted his allegiance from the Federalists to the Republicans in the 1800 election, reminded Secretary of State James Madison of the risk that lay in siding with Leclerc late in 1801. Once he had reclaimed Saint-Domingue for France and restored slavery there, Leclerc might send "a large detachment of republican blacks from St. Domingo to Louisiana," where they would precipitate "the sudden emancipation of the blacks there." Leclerc knew, Coxe observed, that it would be far easier to secure the reintroduction of slavery into Saint-

Domingue "by sending the most warlike to Louisiana."[61] But Leclerc failed. When the French force was defeated and finally evacuated from Saint-Domingue at the end of 1803, the only remaining threat to American slavery was the black government of the island. Jefferson bowed to the pressure from his fellow planters and denied American support to the newborn Republic of Haiti in 1804.[62]

Philadelphia Republicans with longstanding and substantial commercial ties to Saint-Domingue were dismayed by Jefferson's about-face in 1804 and continued to hope for a softening in his position.[63] Most Philadelphians, however, had not shared their view since the mid-1790s. The willingness to contemplate intimate and enduring ties between the city and Saint-Domingue that was allegorized in the love affair between the Quaker and the Dominguan woman of color in John Murdock's play of 1795 was gone. It waned in no small measure because of the continuing violence in Saint-Domingue and fears about its contagion. A black woman was arrested in Philadelphia in 1796 for setting fire to her master's house, confirming for some white observers the reality of a rumored conversation among a mixed group of Dominguans and American blacks about "torching the urban centers of slaveholding America from north to south." A subsequent rash of arsons in northern cities doubtless played a part in Pennsylvania governor Thomas Mifflin's request to President Adams that he be allowed to prohibit the debarkation of any "French negroes" in his state in the summer of 1798 when another large wave of Dominguan refugees began arriving in Philadelphia.[64] Philadelphians' fears about the eruption of Dominguan-inspired violence in their own streets seemed to be confirmed in 1804 when a crowd of several hundred blacks marked July 4 and 5 by forming themselves into armed military formations, electing officers, and marching through the streets "damning the whites and saying they would shew them St. Domingo."[65] The following year, when Philadelphians gathered in front of Independence Hall to celebrate July 4, an angry cadre of whites drove the free blacks from the festivities with a nasty verbal assault.[66]

Demographic and economic changes in Philadelphia at the beginning of the nineteenth century exacerbated the turn against people of African descent, grafting onto the existing fears of rebellion a potent class antagonism. In the closing years of the eighteenth century, the black population of Philadelphia swelled as its own free colored population grew through natural increase and as blacks from the slave states sought refuge there. White wage laborers and artisans resented what they believed to be the increased competition produced by this demographic shift.[67] At the opening of the nineteenth century, Philadelphia racism spilled beyond the ideologically reasoned contours and fears of insurrection that had characterized it in the 1790s. It became a charged popular resentment that yoked the specter of Saint-Domingue to the economic and political frustrations and aspirations of the city's white workers. This development revealed itself in the events and language that marked the fracturing of Thomas Jefferson's party in Philadelphia. The stage was set for the quadroon to make her surprising appearance in the City of Brotherly Love.

Jefferson's election in 1800 launched a vigorous national debate in the young republic over the direction democracy should take, one that seems to have generated more heat and vitriol in Philadelphia than nearly any place else. On one side were those who favored a radical version that sought to eradicate all traces of privilege and hierarchy from the political process and government, opening up not only the franchise but appointments and election to government office to a much broader spectrum of the population. Without such reforms, the entrenched elites would exercise their power "to enable the *merchants, the few* to ride in their carriages and wallow in luxury" while the "government [wa]s supported by draughts on the industry of the people at large."[68] This radical position particularly appealed to the same artisans and laborers who felt themselves threatened by the growth of Philadelphia's black population. Merchants and professionals who had allied themselves with the Democratic Republicans against the Federalists in the 1790s sought a more moderate realization of democratic principles, one that protected and nurtured American commerce without magnifying the role of the federal government. Many of them, either directly or indirectly, were long involved in trade with Saint-Domingue. They were certainly not colorblind, but their position on Toussaint Louverture's cause and relations with the black republic that he founded put them at odds with developing popular opinion in their own party.[69]

In Philadelphia, the differences between these two camps evolved into a full-blown political battle. The putative leader of the radicals, who called themselves the Philadelphia Republicans, was William Duane, who became editor of the *Aurora* in 1798. Duane was a powerful personality who succeeded in making the *Aurora* "the most widely read Jeffersonian organ in the nation."[70] Duane drew on his success to pressure Jefferson into turning incumbents out of appointed offices and replacing them with men previously shut out of power. Joining Duane in this campaign was Dr. Michael Leib, the son of a tanner who made his home in the socially unpretentious Northern Liberties neighborhood in Philadelphia. Together they sought to unseat a cadre of socially and economically powerful Democratic Republican officeholders who had once been their allies in the assault on the Federalists that culminated in Jefferson's triumphant election to the presidency.[71]

The most prominent of the radicals' targets was a man they had, ironically, supported in the 1799 gubernatorial election, Thomas McKean. Thanks in part to Duane's vigorous electioneering in the pages of the *Aurora*, McKean was swept into office in 1799 by a stunning margin of 9,000 votes over his Federalist rival, James Ross.[72] McKean had impressive bona fides in state and national politics, but he was a relatively new ally of the Democratic Republicans. He signed the Declaration of Independence, served on the Continental Congress until 1783, helped draft the Articles of Confederation, and served Pennsylvania's state constitutional convention. A lawyer with a keen interest in jurisprudence, he served as chief justice of Pennsylvania from 1777 until he was elected governor in 1799. In the early 1790s, McKean was a committed Federalist who believed in an independent judiciary and a strong executive branch. He jumped ship and joined the Democratic Republicans in 1796. Historians generally attribute McKean's political realignment to a "friendship for France and hatred for England" strong enough to lead "him to sit at the banquet table with Genet" and push him "to consort with Pennsylvania radicals in denouncing the Jay treaty."[73] The origins of McKean's international politics have lain unexamined, but even a cursory investigation exposes the role of his intimate connections to Saint-Domingue interests in Philadelphia.

Thomas McKean's brother-in-law was merchant Andrew Bayard, and his eldest daughter, Elizabeth, married Bayard's partner, Andrew Pettit, in 1791. Pettit and Bayard owned the schooner *Industry*, which was making trips from Philadelphia to Cap Français about every three months at the time of the wedding. Pettit remained involved in Dominguan affairs, serving prominently with fellow merchant James Vanuxem on Philadelphia's committee to oversee relief to the refugees from Cap Français in the summer of 1793.[74] Thomas McKean undoubtedly retained an antipathy toward the British and amity toward the French as a legacy of his participation in the American Revolution, but the interests of his family reinforced and renewed alignments that other Federalists easily relinquished. It is no coincidence that he switched his allegiance to the Democratic Republicans in 1796 on the heels of Jay's Treaty, a Federalist initiative that disadvantaged and exasperated Philadelphia merchants with Dominguan connections like his son-in-law's.

Despite accepting the support of the radical wing of the Pennsylvania Democratic Republicans led by Duane and Leib, McKean's loyalties remained tethered to older alliances. He was not an enthusiastic supporter of Leib's 1799 campaign for Congress and was certainly sympathetic to, if not directly involved in, the organization of a more conservative group of Democratic Republicans that gathered at the Rising Sun Tavern to strategize the election of a more moderate candidate.[75] Duane and Leib outmaneuvered the moderates; Leib was elected; and the radical element among the Democratic Republicans held the reins in Pennsylvania politics for the next two years despite McKean's elevation to the governorship. The uneasy peace that marked this division of power was shattered in 1802 when a Philadelphia tinsmith-turned-merchant named Thomas Passmore brought suit against McKean's son-in-law, Andrew Pettit, and his partner, Andrew Bayard.

Thomas Passmore was a prosperous self-made man who identified much more comfortably with men such as tanner's son Michael Leib than with the privileged Pettit and Bayard, who insured his brig, *Minerva*, for a voyage in 1801. The ship was still close to home when it sprang a leak off of New Brunswick, New Jersey, where Passmore abandoned it, subsequently filing a claim for his loss with Pettit and Bayard. The underwriters refused to pay the claim, Passmore filed suit against them, and the court found in Passmore's favor. When Pettit and Bayard filed an appeal after the deadline for doing so had passed and the court agreed to hear their appeal, Passmore may well have thought that privilege and family connections were at work to protect the son-in-law of the former chief justice and present governor of Pennsylvania. In a fit of enraged frustration, Passmore drafted a screed about the "quibbling underwriters," in which he accused his insurers of delaying tactics and declared Bayard "a liar, a rascal, and a coward." He then proceeded to post his indictment prominently in a coffeehouse, an action that exposed him to libel charges. Instead of filing separately for libel, Pettit and Bayard attached Passmore's public attack on them to their appeal of the original judgment. When the case went to the Pennsylvania Supreme Court, the attorney for Bayard and Pettit argued that Passmore's public libel should be considered with the rest of the case and that it constituted a contempt of court. Passmore refused to apologize to Bayard and Pettit and the court found him in contempt, sentencing him to thirty days imprisonment and a fine. Early in 1803, having served his prison term, Passmore petitioned the state assembly to impeach the judges who had found him in contempt, charging that they had exercised arbitrary power in their refusal to grant him a trial by jury for the libel charges.[76]

Radical Democratic Republicans in the Pennsylvania assembly, including Michael Leib, were happy to oblige Thomas Passmore. For several years they had fixed on the state judiciary, with its preponderance of Federalist and moderate Democratic Republicans, as a lingering seat of aristocratic power that was dangerous to the making of the democratic republic they envisioned. Leib and his ally Duane backed a plan to call a constitutional convention to, among other things, dismantle the English common-law framework of the Pennsylvania judiciary and replace it with a system in which the power of the legal system was distributed beyond the circle of wealthy and influential men who had controlled it since Independence.[77] The assembly voted articles of impeachment against the three judges, and the trial commenced early in 1805. Judges Edward Shippen, Jasper Yeates, and Thomas Smith were acquitted, but the vote of thirteen to eleven exposed the deep rift between the radical and moderate Democratic Republicans.

The Passmore incident has long served as a window onto the nature of the bitter ideological battles that plagued the party of Thomas Jefferson in the first decade of the nineteenth century. It certainly illuminates the issues and the players in the contest over the nature of democracy as it played out in early national Pennsylvania. But it does more. The dramatis personae on one side of the Passmore case were all implicated, some directly, some more tenuously, in Philadelphia's relationship with the West Indies, especially Saint-Domingue. This is the back story to this political imbroglio, and it is worth teasing out its details.[78]

Andrew Bayard and Andrew Pettit had been in profitable partnership for more than a decade when Passmore pressed his claim against them. In 1800 they were underwriters, but in the early 1790s they were merchants whose schooner *Industry* regularly plied the waters to Cap Français.[79] Pettit and Bayard were among the merchant elite in Philadelphia for whom the "revolutionary qualities of circumstances in St. Domingue, be they French or Haitian, were of secondary importance to their immediate implications, which could be measured in the thousands of tons of goods that arrived in Philadelphia from St. Domingue."[80] Their fortunes were made in Saint-Domingue and could grow larger if their nation normalized relations with the new Republic of Haiti.

Thomas Passmore's trading activity, by contrast, was very modest in 1803 and mostly confined to domestic markets. He prospered as a tinsmith in post-Revolutionary Philadelphia, but he could never have entered the ranks of ship owners with the profits of his trade alone. Passmore, like a number of other Philadelphia artisans, became a capitalist thanks to financing provided by the Bank of North America, founded by Phillip Morris at the close of the Revolutionary War. When he took on Pettit and Bayard, Passmore's tin lamps, lanterns, canisters, and signal horns were sold domestically, outfitting the Lewis and Clark expedition in 1803, for example. His ill-fated brig, *Minerva*, got no further than New Brunswick, New Jersey, with her cargo.[81] When Thomas Passmore went up against Pettit and Bayard, he was a provincial parvenu confronting the cosmopolitan bluebloods of Philadelphia's commercial aristocracy, whose fortunes in the early 1800s were still very much tied up in commerce with Saint-Domingue.

The lawyer that Pettit and Bayard chose to represent them was a man who was no stranger himself to the West Indies, Alexander J. Dallas. Born in Jamaica in 1759, Dallas grew up in Edinburgh and London before returning to Jamaica in 1780, where he was admitted to the bar. His Philadelphia-born wife suffered ill health in Jamaica, and in 1783 he moved his family to her hometown, signing citizenship papers a mere ten days after he arrived. Dallas was admitted to the Pennsylvania bar two years later but was more politician than advocate. He ultimately served as treasury secretary as well as acting secretary of war and acting secretary of state under James Madison, but most of his political career played out in Pennsylvania, beginning when the Federalist governor Thomas Mifflin named him secretary of the commonwealth in 1791, a post he held for a decade. Despite his indebtedness to Mifflin, Dallas was among the founders of the Democratic Republican Party in Pennsylvania and, with Thomas McKean, one of the leaders of the conservatives who opposed the more radical positions taken by Duane and Leib. When Dallas did step away from politics to practice law, he represented some of the most prominent of the Philadelphia merchants engaged in trade with Saint-Domingue. He was Stephen Girard's lawyer, as well as Pettit and Bayard's.[82]

Pettit, Bayard, and Dallas all had direct ties with the West Indies that marked them as the segment of Philadelphia's merchant community that remained friendly to Saint-Domingue even after it abolished slavery and submitted to the leadership of the black revolutionary Toussaint Louverture. They were marked as well by association with objects of popular opprobrium that were linked to the island. Pettit and Bayard conducted business amicably with Joseph Bunel, the merchant planter dispatched to the United States by Toussaint Louverture in 1798 to parlay with President John Adams in an attempt to restore U.S.-Dominguan trade relations disrupted by the quasi-war with France. Many Philadelphians were wary of Bunel simply because he represented a black regime, but just as many if not more would have been disturbed by his domestic arrangements. Bunel was married to a black woman.[83]

Joseph Bunel wed Marie Françoise Mouton in Saint-Domingue prior to his mission to Philadelphia, perhaps at the behest of Louverture, who insisted on formalizing the life partnerships of those closest to him with the Catholic sacrament of matrimony. Marie, a Creole born on the island, kept her residence in Saint-Domingue to look after her successful clothing business in Cap Français but made trips back and forth to Philadelphia, where the couple were described in an 1802 newspaper article as "Bunel, a white man, and his wife, a negress."[84] Marie moved her residence to Philadelphia early in 1803, just in time for the eruption of the Passmore case.

Marie Bunel continued her career as a merchant in Philadelphia, achieving such success that she was able to acquire a farm outside the city to which she could retreat in the summers. She had a black hand to work under the farm's manager and an indentured domestic to serve her at the city residence she shared with her husband. Joseph, meanwhile, nurtured trade relations, keeping Philadelphia merchants informed of conditions on the island, encouraging them to maintain commerce with the new black republic of Haiti, and engaging himself in lucrative shipping activity in the first months of Haitian independence. Leaving Marie behind in Philadelphia, he sailed to Haiti in the summer of 1804 with a commercial cargo on which he made a very handsome profit, and in subsequent months commissioned three more ships to bring goods to Haiti, including a large shipment of gunpowder. Bunel traveled back and forth between Philadelphia and Haiti for the next three years, but sailed back to Cap Haïtien for good in 1807, leaving his wife behind in charge of their substantial business in Philadelphia until she, too, returned to Haiti in 1810.[85]

Joseph Bunel's marriage to a black woman mirrored his loyalty to the black Republic of Haiti. In the early and mid-1790s, when Philadelphia's trade with Saint-Domingue made merchants such as Pettit and Bayard rich, there was still space in the popular imagination for such connections. But by the turn of the nineteenth century, as we have seen, both of Bunel's choices were generally regarded as unnatural in Philadelphia, especially by the laboring and artisanal classes who constituted the radical wing of the Democratic Republicans. Pettit, Bayard, and their lawyer, Alexander Dallas, were unattractive to this constituency not only because of their wealth, privilege, and political conservatism but because of their associations with the intimate racial disorder of Saint-Domingue.

When the enmity between the radical and conservative Democratic Republicans of Pennsylvania degenerated into acrimonious partisan war in the aftermath of the Passmore case, the figure of the black woman emerged as a charged rhetorical device, replacing a more neutral, learned term that would not have resonated nearly as powerfully with the radicals' constituency. The conservative faction headed by McKean and Dallas had been labeled the Quids, a shortened version of *tertium quid*, "a third something," shortly after its emergence in the election of 1799. Duane's *Aurora* was the primary vehicle for attacking the Quids, but the currency of the label probably reached its height with the publication of a vitriolic and gossipy anonymous pamphlet titled *The Quid Mirror* that was published after the radical Democrats failed to defeat McKean in the election season of 1805. It dubbed Thomas McKean a "law maniac" who was "evidence of one of Fortune's frolics," condemned Alexander Dallas as a sycophant who "courted and flattered every man who could relieve him," and declared of U.S. Senator George Logan that "the utmost extent of his genius goes not beyond catching grasshoppers." But it was in the portrait of William Bache, the brother-in-law of Dallas's daughter, that *The Quid Mirror* tapped into a vein of popular antipathy that radical Democrats would exploit by giving the Quids a new name. Bache "kept a seraglio of sable concubines," the pamphlet informed its readers, and by "grimace and monkey tricks he strives to put honour, honesty and truth out of countenance."[86] Bache's intimate commerce with women of color had transformed him, according to *The Quid Mirror*, into the likeness of the creatures to which people of African descent were popularly compared. Thomas Jefferson famously opined that orangutans were attracted to black women.[87] William Bache was merely a Quid in 1806, but in 1807, as the radical Democrats unleashed a new assault on the faction, he and his political fellow travelers were rechristened the Quadroons.[88]

Shifting from the esoteric Latin label that merely described the birth order of the rival political faction to one that was so viscerally evocative of illegitimacy and contamination was a stroke of genius. Lest anyone be uneducated in the rich negative connotations of the term *quadroon*, the radical Philadelphia Democrats elaborated the connections they wished to draw between the unnatural, racially tainted bastardy of people labeled quadroons and the political faction they hoped to defile with the label. "A new party is said to be forming in Pennsylvania, which are designated by their leader or founder, from a *Creole* epithet—Quadroons," the radical Democrats announced, accusing the rival faction of the invention of their own insulting label. The Quadroon faction was a danger to democracy because it was the product of a hidden and hypocritical alliance, the radical Democrats' notice explained: "They are only the successors in *fact* and *form* of the *third party* or quids and consist of the same materials, pursue the same measures, affect the same public spirit and disdain of federalism, with which they secretly combine."[89] The radicals cast the Pennsylvania Quadroons as the spurious issue of Republicans and Federalists, and "the foul hatchings of this detestable combination," the radicals warned, would fatally corrupt and destroy democracy in the young republic.[90] The label allowed the radicals to tap into potent sexual and racial imagery in ways that ranged from civilized innuendo to blatantly crude parries such as the one that dubbed a Quid leader "Mr. Scratch'em," the "baboon chairman of the New-market quadroon meeting" who was "*up a tree*" (see Figure 4).[91]

Political figures accused in the radical press of being Quadroons felt themselves compelled not only to reject affiliation with the hybrid faction but with the defamatory connotations of its label. "Jacob Shearer, Esq, one of the *bright* representatives of Philadelphia county, has told us, that he is no *quadroon*."[92] The racial calumny against Shearer intended in the double entendre "bright" would have been clear to Philadelphians in 1807. "Bright" had been used to describe light-skinned people of mixed African and European descent in Pennsylvania since at least 1788. But in the fall of 1807, in a move that may have been calculated to magnify the impact of the quadroon epithet, the radical Democrats' house organ published sensational testimony from a Maryland court case that named the white father of a "bright mulatto child."[93] In retaliation, the Quids tried to tar radical Democratic leader Leib with his own brush, suggesting that he had abandoned his principals and become, himself, a Quadroon. The Quid party's principal newspaper pointed out that, as "Dr. Leib has, heretofore, invariably urged the necessity of rotation in office," Pennsylvanians should

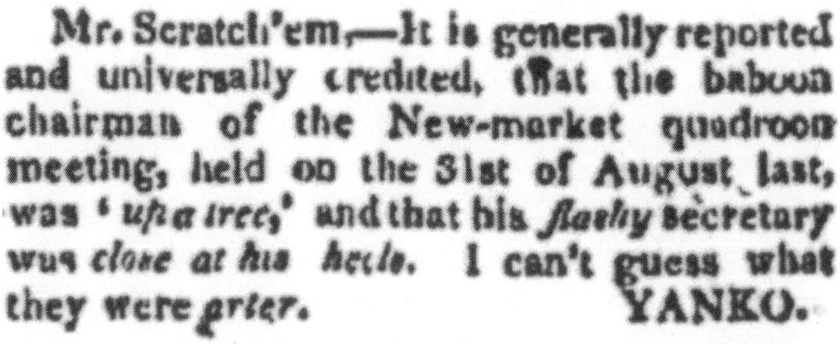

Mr. Scratch'em,—It is generally reported and universally credited, that the baboon chairman of the New-market quadroon meeting, held on the 31st of August last, was 'up a tree,' and that his *flashy* secretary was *close at his heels.* I can't guess what they were after.   YANKO.

FIGURE 4. "Mr. Scratch'em." This satirical notice explicitly links one of Philadelphia's political factions to racist imagery tied to Saint-Domingue/ Haiti. From *Tickler* (Philadelphia), September 5, 1810, 3.

"no longer doubt his attachment to a rotation of *principles* . . . That he has turned Quid or Quadroon."[94]

THE QUADROON PRESS WAR was at its height for only a few months in the fall of 1807. It is easy to overlook it as a spasm of colorful invective, but Philadelphia's long association with Saint-Domingue and the deep entanglement of the leaders of the moderate Democratic Republicans with its affairs make it worth a careful second look. Neither the sordid realities of the southern planter's household nor the intimate life of Thomas Jefferson conjured the quadroon political trope in Philadelphia. A potent public threat especially apparent there did: the specter of infectious sedition and social disorder raised by the Haitian Revolution. Although the figure of the quadroon appeared in Philadelphia again from time to time until 1813, another dramatic episode in Haitian history would transport the quadroon safely away from Philadelphia and other parts of America and site her on the nation's margins.[95] When 9,000 black and white refugees of the Haitian Revolution found their way en masse to New Orleans in 1809, the locus of the Haitian peril and the evocative trope of the quadroon followed them. Haiti was at the heart of the quadroon's migration to American shores when she appeared briefly but dramatically in early national Philadelphia, and again when she took up permanent residence in New Orleans.

CHAPTER TWO

From *Ménagère* to *Placée*

A[u]guste Tessier . . . se propose de donner Bal deux sois par semaine aux femmes de couleur libres, ou les hommes de couleur ne seront pas admis.

(Auguste Tessier proposes to give a ball two evenings each week for free women of color to which men of color will not be admitted.)

—*Moniteur* (New Orleans), November 23, 1805

Auguste Tessier was not among the Saint-Domingue refugees to settle in Philadelphia and complicate its politics. Like many others, he chose New Orleans instead.[1] As one fellow Dominguan emigrant observed, "one finds there the same habits, as well as frenchmen [*sic*] who know more or less who you are, either personally or by reputation, and who share more or less the same culture."[2] When he introduced a novelty into the popular dancing tradition of his adopted city during the social season of 1805, however, Tessier changed the culture of New Orleans. At the balls organized by Orleanians in the 1790s, white men who fancied a dance with a free woman of color had to compete for their favors with men of African ancestry who shared the crowded dance floor. Tessier's balls featured the Dominguan tradition of excluding men of African descent to give white men an unobstructed opportunity to court women of color.[3] His innovation, coupled with the plight of the Haitian refugees who settled in New Orleans, would cast a long shadow over the city's reputation and history. The arrival of Haitian refugees in Philadelphia shaped the politics of a city and a state for a decade or so. Their appearance in New Orleans was more far reaching and longer lasting, supplying the nation with a narrative that neutralized the threat of the black republic at the same time that it serviced white male fantasies of intimate mastery. In New Orleans, the avatar of Haiti was transformed from a bloodthirsty, rebellious black army into a feminine seductress who submitted willingly to white male control. This chapter reconstructs the origins and mechanics of this transformation, a sleight of hand that preserved the peace of mind of the American slave republic.

THE LARGEST SINGLE WAVE of Dominguan refugees comprised the 10,000 who fled the destruction of Cap Français in the summer of 1793. They and other migrants of the 1790s distributed themselves among several cities along the eastern seaboard of the United States. Philadelphia, as we have seen, became home to perhaps 2,000, but significant numbers also settled in New York, Boston, Baltimore, Norfolk, and Charleston.[4] The demographic impact of this first cohort was widely distributed, and they and the revolution they fled had a decisive yet diffuse influence on the politics of the young American republic, seeding a nimbus of fear about the contagion of black rebellion.[5] Only in Philadelphia, in the figure of the quadroon, did Haiti and its refugees function with specific symbolic power in the political discourse. Additional refugees arrived in the United States following the withdrawal of British troops from the western and southern provinces in 1798, and again with the defeat of Leclerc's expedition and the evacuation of French troops from Saint-Domingue in 1803. Only a second massive emigration in 1809 came close to duplicating the size of the 1793 exodus. Like the earlier migration, it was triggered by cataclysmic events, but this time 9,000 refugees converged on a single destination in the United States: New Orleans.[6]

The 9,000 who made for New Orleans in 1809 did not arrive directly from Haiti but from Cuba, where they had formed a large, concentrated refugee colony in the eastern part of the island. The evacuation of the British from Saint-Domingue in 1798 and the fear and chaos that followed the withdrawal of the French in 1803 propelled thousands of Dominguans to seek sanctuary in the vicinity of eastern Cuba's principal city, Santiago. There was already a refugee community there, and the Spanish colonial government, interested in fostering staple crop agriculture in this underdeveloped part of Cuba, encouraged the tide of newcomers to settle in. The Dominguans literally put down roots, acquiring on favorable terms large plots of land that they quickly developed into coffee plantations, increasing Cuba's annual coffee harvest from 8,000 to 300,000 arrobas within three years. Their spectacular productivity was not enough to protect them, however, from the continuing vicissitudes of global politics. After Napoleon invaded Spain in 1808 their position became precarious, and on March 12, 1809, the colonial government in Cuba issued a proclamation that spawned vigilante committees throughout the island to investigate resident Frenchmen and expel those they thought dangerous. Few Dominguans escaped the dragnet, which operated with energetic efficiency.[7]

Nearly all of those ejected from Cuba made for New Orleans. To the degree that the migrants themselves participated in determining their destination, the city's French colonial origins would have made it a congenial choice. As the refugee Pierre Collet explained, "I thought I saw in Louisiana the place that would offer the most advantages to a poor colonist forced to flee, because, first of all, they [Louisianans] speak the same language." In New Orleans, the refugee would be at home in other ways as well. There would be no unpleasant adjustment from the torrid tropics to the icy winters of Philadelphia or New York. "Its climate," Collet noted, "is not unlike our own."[8] Such affinities and similarities, however, were not the deciding factor when an improvised flotilla of Cuban, French, and American sloops and schooners set sail from Santiago de Cuba in the spring of 1809. It was instead almost certainly the human property the migrants hoped to bring with them that made Louisiana their favored destination.

As one historian has pointed out, the refugee colony in Cuba was "solid ground for white resistance."[9] Many of the whites who would flee from Saint-Domingue to the Spanish colony in 1803, and some of the people of color, ignored the general abolition of 1794 and continued to claim ownership of human chattel.[10] Their coffee plantations in the western and southern districts of Saint-Domingue were built on the labor of enslaved men and women. With workforces averaging from fifteen to thirty laborers, they did not approach the scale of exploitation of the great sugar plantations of prerevolutionary Saint-Domingue, but the inhuman architecture of the slave system remained central to their economic strategy. The refugees of 1809 might not be able to reestablish themselves as planters yet again in Louisiana, but they knew that if they could successfully assert ownership of any domestic and field laborers they managed to bring with them from Cuba they would find a ready market waiting for them. In Louisiana, the migrant Collet believed, "What's left of our Negroes is worth a lot more money, and they are more easily rented."[11]

He was right. Louisiana's appetite for bound labor was the highest of any place in the United States and its territories in 1809, a hunger paradoxically fed by the demise of Saint-Domingue's sugar monoculture. Sugarcane grew in southern Louisiana, but its semitropical climate brought occasional frosts that made the crop just unpredictable enough to stymie widespread commitment to growing cane. Those who did experiment with sugar found it difficult to sell their product. What Louisiana produced could not compete either in price or quality with the avalanche of white crystals that poured from the ports of Saint-Domingue. The Haitian Revolution's disruption of Dominguan sugar production was a deus ex machina for Louisiana planters. The opening in the market, together with the development of an improved refining process, transformed sugar planting from a foolhardy gamble to a guaranteed path to riches. By the mid-1790s Louisianans with capital began buying out the small planters around them, assembling the large parcels of land demanded by the greedy cane. The same planters, whose success with cane depended as much on labor as on land, waited impatiently for the ships carrying human cargo into the city's port, turning New Orleans into a thriving slave market second only to Charleston's. When the United States began enforcing the abolition of the international slave trade in 1808, the labor-hungry planters had to rely on the domestic trade that brought workers sold away from plantations in Virginia and Maryland. The supply was never enough to satisfy the burgeoning market, and the Anglophone laborers habituated to wheat and tobacco cultivation in more temperate climes were not ideal candidates for the Louisiana cane fields. Nor did the rural upper South provide the skilled domestics sought by the port's booming hospitality industry. The refugees who sailed toward New Orleans in the spring of 1809 were right in thinking that their 3,000 French-speaking captive laborers, accustomed to work in the tropics or skilled in the domestic arts, were the most valuable currency they could carry into their new refuge.

There was a hitch. The act adopted by Congress in 1807 "to prohibit the importation of slaves into any port or place within the jurisdiction of the United States" applied unambiguously to Louisiana. The incoming passengers who were labeled *criados* (servants) by the Cuban port officials who recorded their departure could be admitted to American territory as free people. If they were recognized upon their arrival as chattel by the American authorities at the mouth of the Mississippi, however, they were slaves who ran afoul of the ban. The American officials in New Orleans apparently never entertained the possibility that the general abolition of slavery in Saint-Domingue in 1794 applied to the people claimed as property by the refugees. When William C. C. Claiborne, U.S. governor of the Territory of Orleans, was advised on May 15, 1809, by the commander of the fort at the mouth of the Mississippi that "a vessel from St. Yago, with a number of French passengers and thirty six slaves, is now near this City," he did not hesitate to assign the thirty-six *criados* who had sailed from Santiago a label that returned them to bondage. In the same letter, which was addressed to Secretary of State Robert Smith, he signaled a ready concession to the interests of the region's planters, some of whom he was related to by marriage. "The difficulties which the Law of the U. States oppose to the introduction of these slaves into the Territory," he wrote, "have induced a number of very respectable and humaine Citizens, to address to me a Petition (to admit the slaves), which I have now the honor to enclose you." As he penned his missive, Claiborne was under the impression that permission was sought for the entry of a relatively small number of enslaved people. "It is stated to me," he advised Smith, "that the whole number of French families from Cuba, who propose to take refuge in this Territory, may probably be accompanied by from 250 to 300 slaves," purportedly representing "the few faithful domesticks who had accompanied them in their misfortunes."[12]

Before Claiborne could send his letter and the planters' petition on its way, the French consul in New Orleans, François Desforgues, rushed into the governor's office "to inform, that within 10 days, there would probably arrive here about two thousand French from St. Yago, & that at least six thousand more from Havanna, might be expected in three or four weeks." He confirmed reports that Claiborne had received the day before that thousands of refugees were at the mouth of the river. "I really fear that so great and sudden an Emigration to this Territory, will be a source of serious inconvenience and embarrassment to our own Citizens," the governor wrote.[13]

Claiborne could do little to control the flood of humanity making its way to New Orleans. The refugees were carried in vessels owned and captained by a diverse cadre of entrepreneurs who improvised an evacuation without guidance from any national government.[14] Captains Rodriguez, Ramires, Lopez, Le Floche, Meunier, and Petit joined Captains McDonald, Watts, and Hopkins sailing schooners and sloops named *Carmen*, *Le Sauveur*, and *Polly*, among others. With group passports from Cuban port officials in hand, they set out without invitation for the mouth of the Mississippi. Each ship paused at Fort Plaquemine downriver from New Orleans to register its cargo and passengers and then, beginning on May 15, began to put in at New Orleans. Claiborne instructed the commander at Fort Plaquemine to detain some of the vessels to modulate the flow of refugees into the city's hostels and boardinghouses, but that measure did little to stem the tide. *Nuestra Señora Del Carmen* was followed by Captain McDonald's schooner, *Louisa*, on the 16th. On the 18th, the *Colline*, *Petite Marie*, *L'Esperance*, and *Tomassa* put into the city's port, followed on the 22nd by the *Clervo*, *Polly*, *Dispatch*, and *Clarissa*. This initial flotilla emptied some 1,026 men, women, and children onto the streets of New Orleans in the space of a week. The resources of the city of approximately 10,000 were immediately strained.[15] "These unfortunate People are for the most part without resources, and must depend upon the Benevolence of this society for the means of present support," Claiborne observed to Secretary of State Smith. "A supply of provisions has been forwarded to those now in the River," he continued and, with a note of dismay, admitted that "like relief will have to be afforded such as may hereafter arrive."[16]

Claiborne's worries were more than material. "I fear," he wrote privately to Thomas Jefferson on May 17, "that the misfortunes of Spain and her Colonies will give to this *Territory* an encrease of population, which may retard the growth of the true American Principles."[17] Several days later, Claiborne reported local opposition to offering sanctuary to the Dominguans. "The expediency of refusing them an Asylum has been suggested," he reported to the secretary of state. "I regret to see a space in our Society filled with a foreign Population, which I hoped would have been occupied by native Citizens of the U. States," Claiborne confided. But the governor acknowledged the conventions of "hospitality and indulgence which humanity and courtesy require" and overrode both his own and others' anxiety.[18]

Like others before him in the northern port cities, Claiborne harbored a vision of refugees passing swiftly through New Orleans en route to settlement in sparsely populated rural areas. He wanted to believe the heads of the white families who arrived at his doorstep on May 20, who told him "that having been obliged to make great sacrifices of their property in Cuba, their pecuniary means were limited; too much so, to continue in this City." Instead, they assured the anxious governor, "that as well from necessity as choice, they should retire to the interior of the Territory as soon as possible." In the meantime, Claiborne continued to slow the pace of arrivals by "a short detention of the several Vessels at the Fort at *Plaquemine*." He ordered the commander of the fort "to permit their departure from *thence* at such periods, as may prevent this City from receiving at the same moment, a too great influx of visitants, and to give time to those previously arrived to disperse and retire to the Country."[19]

Claiborne's creation of the Fort Plaquemine bottleneck slowed the disgorgement of refugees in the port, but the governor was powerless to address the obstacle that kept them tethered to the city. The human property the free Dominguans brought with them remained on the ships tied up at the dock, forbidden to disembark by the Congressional act ending the international slave trade. Without what was for many their only potential financial asset, the refugees considered themselves stuck. Public opinion on the advisability of allowing a large number of "French Negroes" into Louisiana was ambivalent. Many feared they would infect American soil with the contagion of Haitian rebellion, but other factors weighed in favor of their admission. The sooner the refugees were able to take possession of their human property, the sooner the city would be relieved of the burden of providing for them. And in the process, the city's hungry slave market would be able to take advantage of a labor windfall. On balance, Orleanians and their governor favored admission of the enslaved workers. Claiborne could hardly request the suspension of the law himself, but he helped those who could by implicitly endorsing their petition to Washington.[20]

The illegal human cargo remained aboard the vessels tied up at the harbor, where any insurrectionary contagion they might be carrying was more or less effectively quarantined for the time being. But they were not the only source of potential trouble. "Among this mass of Emigration, there will doubtless be found some excellent Citizens; But I fear," the governor confessed, "there will also be many, who can alone be ranked among the worthless class of community. Of that class, New Orleans has already its full complement."[21] Claiborne may have been thinking of a criminal element, but there was another "class of community" aboard the vessels bound for the city that was already numerous and problematic in New Orleans: free people of color.

The first vessel to debark refugees in Louisiana, the schooner *Nuestra Señora Del Carmen*, captained by A. V. Rodriguez out of Santiago de Cuba, carried twenty-seven free people of color along with seventy-two whites and thirty-two enslaved people. Three days later, free people of color made up two-thirds of the schooner *La Colline*'s passenger list, with eighty-three free people of color easily outnumbering thirteen enslaved persons and thirty-four whites. By July 8, when Claiborne's deputy sent a summary report on the refugees to the Department of State, some 1,369 free people of color had debarked, making up roughly a third of the 4,282 arrivals.[22] Migrants continued to arrive during the rest of the summer, and eight ships made the round trip at least twice, almost always bearing large numbers of free people of color. The *Nuestra Señora Del Carmen* returned to Santiago and brought another seventy-one refugees to New Orleans in June, more than half of them free people of color. Most of the 300 passengers on the large ship *Arctic* on the first of its two rescue voyages were slaves, but more than seventy were free people of color. The more diminutive sloop *Polly* made three trips in quick succession, transporting well over a hundred free people of color on its single deck.[23]

The first cohort of free colored refugees numbered 1,369, of which 608 were adult women and 178 adult men. The demography of the schooner *Swiss*, which arrived in late May of 1809, implies an explanation for the imbalance. The vessel bore thirty-two white men, ten white women, and six white children. Sailing with the forty-eight white people were fifty-eight free people of color, twenty-nine women, twenty-two children, and only seven fully grown men. Almost certainly the life partners of many, if not most, of the white men on the *Swiss* were among the free women of color on board.[24]

French-born Jean Moreu and men like him could well have been among those aboard the *Swiss*. Moreu, like many fellow refugees, settled in the Faubourg Ste. Marie in New Orleans, a part of the city best known early in the nineteenth century for the cheap lodging and nightlife it offered rowdy young flatboatmen at the end of their arduous voyages downriver. There, still living in a rented room about a year after his arrival, Moreu called in a notary to draw up a will that described the family he had brought with him to America. Marie Jeanne, a free woman of color with whom he had cohabited for twenty years, and the three mixed-race natural children he fathered on her were, he stipulated, his only heirs. He had nothing presently to bequeath them except the right to collect a debt owed him in Saint-Domingue. Entrusted with executing Moreu's last wishes was Joseph Saint Victor, his "old and good friend," who himself shared his life with a free woman of color and their six mixed-race children in another part of Faubourg Ste. Marie.[25]

Black men who might rise in bloody rebellion represented the most terrifying of the threats posed by the Dominguan influx of 1809, but the lopsided shipboard demography of the *Swiss* and the living arrangements of men like Moreu and Saint Victor stoked another fear.[26] A powerful discourse developed in prerevolutionary Saint-Domingue that portrayed free women of color as dangerous, sexually irresistible figures who seduced French men away from the attachment they should feel for French women and, by extension, France itself.[27] The formation of sexual partnerships across the color line that produced mixed-race children, known as *métissage*, was a widespread practice in many of France's colonies, especially those where French men greatly outnumbered French women. In Saint-Domingue, Michel-René Hilliard d'Auberteuil estimated in 1776 that for the 11,000 free men living in the colony's countryside, there were only 7,200 free women, 4,000 of them free women of color. The ratio was even more unbalanced in the cities, where there were 6,200 free women, 3,000 of them free women of color, for 13,900 free men. Even if there had been enough free white women to supply every free white man in Saint-Domingue with a wife, Hilliard d'Auberteuil observed that illicit sexual partnerships would prevail. "Marriages are rare in Saint-Domingue," he lamented. "The French workers who come here seeking their fortunes almost never marry; concubinage attaches them to white or black women by only the slightest of ties," a situation that left them free to pursue their money-making agendas uninhibited. The result, according to Hilliard d'Auberteuil's count, was that 7,400 white and free colored prostitutes and concubines outnumbered the 6,000 white and free colored married women in Saint-Domingue.[28]

During the first stage of its colonization of the Americas, metropolitan France was not anxious about *métissage*.[29] In fact, until the late seventeenth century, it supported an assimilationist policy that advocated the intermarriage of French men and Indian women to enlarge and implant a stable French presence in the Americas. The 1685 *Code Noir* regulating slavery in France's colonies even left a small space for legitimate marriages between French men and enslaved African women. Some French men did marry Indian and African women, but many more chose to conduct sexual relations with them outside of marriage. "In a colony where the number of white men is so much greater than that of white women, where most European men are condemned to bachelorhood by inevitable circumstances," explained Justin Girod de Chantrans in 1785, "they are agreeable to and satisfied with the favors of women of color."[30] Such behavior fed a chronic metropolitan grumble about "libertinage," but it was not until the middle of the eighteenth century that such complaints began to develop into a coherent ideology that linked theories of patriotism to sexual behavior in the colonies. At the same time that European powers fought a succession of wars among themselves, culminating in the expensive Seven Years' War of 1757–63, they saw their American possessions begin to develop economies and identities that attenuated colonial loyalties to the homeland. Colonists' drift away from marriage to European women, accompanied by a growing population of children of mixed ancestry, heighted metropolitan France's anxiety about its relationship to its colonies. Not least, *métissage* posed an obvious threat to race-based slavery, the fuel of the economic dynamo of which Saint-Domingue was the foremost exemplar. Metropolitan opinion prodded colonials themselves to think more systematically about the nature of their own identities. For those who sought to be recognized as fully European despite birth and continued residence in the colonies, *métissage* and a growing body of people of mixed African and European descent constituted a circumstance that could be counted against them in their bid to demonstrate their suitability for full membership in the European polity.[31]

In Saint-Domingue, where African-descended people outnumbered those of unmixed European descent by a ratio of nine to one, the anxiety about *métissage* was especially acute. It coalesced in 1750 in a treatise by Emilien Petit, a Dominguan native of French ancestry, entitled *Le Patriotism américain*. In it, Petit urged the strong promotion of marriage among the colony's whites, a campaign against partnerships outside of marriage, and a ban on marriage between French men and African-descended women. In the decades following Petit's intervention, instead of withering away through the growth of white intermarriage, the population of free people of color grew ever larger. In 1771, 18,418 whites outnumbered the colony's 6,180 free people of color by a ratio of nearly three to one. By 1788, on the eve of the Haitian Revolution, 21,813 free people of color approached demographic parity with some 27,723 whites.[32]

Contemporaries believed that this dramatic increase was the result of rising numbers of white men manumitting the children they fathered on enslaved African partners. "It is the concubinage of white men with black women that is the cause of there being so many free mulattos," Médéric Louis Élie Moreau de Saint-Méry explained succinctly. Historians have generally presumed the same.[33] A meticulous study of free people of color recently conducted by a Francophone historian, however, shows that the growth in the free colored population owed as much to the economic boom that characterized Saint-Domingue in the last third of the eighteenth century as it did to *métissage*. Forty-five percent of the manumissions in Port-au-Prince and 49 percent of those in Cap Français were of people classified as *nègre*, indicating unmixed African descent. Expanded opportunities to earn money in the colony's robust economy enabled enslaved people to buy their way out of bondage and made it easier for the newly freed to earn enough to liberate family members who remained enslaved.[34]

The practical reality that lay behind the growth of the free colored population proved no obstacle to the emergence of a stereotype that portrayed hypersexual mixed-race women as both the product and the cause of Saint-Domingue's compromised French identity. In the discourse that emerged in the 1780s and 1790s, the incontinence and libertinage of white men was replaced as the culprit of French degeneracy by the sexually powerful *mûlatresse*. Justin Girod de Chantrans produced a disquisition on free women of color in 1785 that served as a foundation for more elaborate treatments by the Baron de Wimpffen and Moreau de Saint-Méry published within months of each other in 1796. Girod de Chantrans explains phlegmatically in his work that women of African descent are "naturally more lascivious than Europeans," and that they consciously learned to amplify this advantage when they "collected and reserved to themselves all the pleasure (giving practices) of which they were capable."[35] By the mid-1790s, when Moreau de Saint-Méry and Wimpffen published their descriptions of the *mûlatresse*, the outbreak of the Haitian Revolution had cast in a new light the characteristics and practices that Girod de Chantrans had dispassionately enumerated a decade earlier.

Echoing each other in a nearly pornographic evocation of the free woman of color's sexual charms, Moreau de Saint-Méry and Wimpffen delineated with sensationalized hindsight the latent danger of the black seductress. "The whole being of a Mulatress is a book given to pleasure, and the fire of this Goddess burns in her heart until she dies," Moreau de Saint-Méry informed his readers. "The imagination cannot conceive of anything more inflamed that she has not felt, guessed, accomplished. To charm all the senses, to raise them to the most delicious ecstasies, to suspend them by the most seductive raptures: this is her only object of study." In Wimpffen's less artful description, women of color "have reduced voluptuousness to a kind of mechanical art, which they have carried to the highest point of perfection. In their seminaries," he confides, Aretino, the author of a bawdy Renaissance satire set in a brothel, "would be a simple and modest scholar!" Both men compared the women's sensibility to fire, but Wimpffen added fireworks to his description. "They join to the inflammability of niter, a petulance of desire," a dangerous mixture that "in despite of every consideration, incessantly urges them to pursue, seize, and devour pleasure, as the flame devours its aliment." Moreau de Saint-Méry closed his damning paean with a well-placed Classical reference to lend a civilized gloss to his erotic litany. "Not even the code of Paphos," the birthplace of the Greek goddess of love, Aphrodite, "knows all the secrets of the amorous pleasures" at the command of Saint-Domingue's enchanting *mûlatresse*. White men were in thrall to these women's seductive virtuosity, despite the threat it posed to the integrity of their French identities and loyalties.[36]

As if their lethal charms were not enough to threaten the stability of France's hold on its most valuable colony, *mûlatresses* further imperiled the colony by their unfettered love of sartorial luxury. Instead of investing in the built environment of Saint-Domingue or in its industry, they frittered away their money on "the most beautiful things that India produces, the most precious muslins, handkerchiefs, cloths and linens." These intrinsically beautiful fabrics they lavishly embellished with "rich lace, jewels, valuable in their multiplicity rather than their type." They were, Moreau de Saint-Méry observed, "so insatiable in their desire for these costly things that we see a fairly large number of mulattos in Saint-Domingue that could change their entire ensemble every day for a year."[37] In an essay on dance that he published at about the same time, Moreau de Saint-Méry produced an even more extreme example of the women's extravagant wardrobe. "At one of their balls, everyone wore taffeta, at another, everyone was in muslin, and at yet another all wore linen!" In 1785, Girod de Chantrans had suggested that instead of complaining about the prodigal expenditures on jewels and clothes, the French should view this behavior as a "voluntary tax which the metropole lays against the libertinage of the colonists."[38]

After the outbreak of the Haitian Revolution, the *mûlatresse* was portrayed in the discourse shaped by Moreau de Saint-Méry and Wimpffen as the shameless survivor of the tragedy she helped foment. "The French colored women live in the most obnoxious luxury in Philadelphia," Moreau de Saint-Méry observed during his temporary exile in the City of Brotherly Love between 1794 and 1798. This account was not published until the early twentieth century but almost certainly reflected the conversations among the white refugees who kept company with him at his Philadelphia bookshop. "Since this luxury can only be provided by the French and by former French colonials, the contrast of their condition with the misery of the mass of their compatriots is revolting."[39]

Moreau de Saint-Méry's observation that the exiled *mûlatresses* of Philadelphia were kept by white men gestures at another of the women's dangerous characteristics according to his rubric: their preference for white sexual partners. According to Hilliard d'Auberteuil, "they love white men, and disdain the mulatto."[40] Moreau de Saint-Méry reiterated this prejudice, with emphasis, "Mulatresses affect a strong disdain for mulattos, and the same at their balls, which resemble those of the whites." At these soirées, attired in their finest muslins, taffetas, or linens, they "wanted no others but the white men."[41] These seductresses set their lures specifically to entrap white men, and, Moreau de Saint-Méry cautioned, it was all part of an elaborate scheme to extract as much as they could from their white paramours while they reserved their true affections for men of their own race. "This disdain is merely feigned," Moreau de Saint-Méry warned. "Many prefer a mulatto, and secretly bed him" in the privacy of their own homes.[42]

Early national American readers had access to these lurid condemnations of free women of color even if they could not read French. Baron de Wimpffen's book was first published in English, and in 1808 native Philadelphian Leonora Sansay made an American contribution to the portrait of the Saint-Domingue *mûlatresse*. A former love interest of Aaron Burr, Sansay married a Dominguan refugee and returned with him to Cap Français in 1802. In 1808 she published *Secret History; or, the Horrors of St. Domingo*, an account of the state of the colony just prior to the triumph of black revolutionary forces.[43] Before the revolution, she informed her readers, the *mûlatresses'* "splendor, their elegance, their influence over the men, the fortunes lavished on them by their infatuated lovers, so powerfully excited the jealousy of the white ladies, that they complained to the council of the ruin their extravagance occasioned to many families." When the council responded by imposing sumptuary laws on free women of color, they "shut themselves up in their houses, and appeared no more in public." The disappearance of their best customers dealt such an economic blow to the colony's merchants that they persuaded the authorities to rescind the regulations, "and the olive beauties triumphed."[44]

The *mûlatresse's* bottomless appetite for luxury could have more dire consequences for white women than sartorial humiliation. It could rob them of the economic security their husbands were supposed to provide. Sansay tells of a refugee woman from Jérémie whose husband stayed behind in Saint-Domingue at the outbreak of the revolution to guard his possessions. She returned to the colony a few years later to find her husband "attached to a woman of colour on whom he lavished all his property." When the situation in Jérémie became intolerable, he sent his wife and daughter to safety in Cuba in one boat and "embarked with his mistress in another." Once in Cuba, he took a house in the country with his "favorite, leaving his family in town, and in such distress that they were often in want of bread." The man, Sansay accused, "was rich!" But instead of fulfilling the responsibilities of a husband, he "lavished on his mistress all the comforts and elegancies of life, yet refused his family the scantiest pittance." He went so far as to deny his daughter a dowry. After the daughter's selfless fiancé overlooked her poverty and married her, the girl, presumably weakened by shame and hardship, promptly died.[45]

The sexually precocious free woman of color appeared briefly, as we have seen, as the object of a besotted Philadelphia Quaker's affection in John Murdock's 1795 *Triumphs of Love*, hinting that the stereotype was established in some form in the American imagination before its exposure to the powerfully moralizing characterizations produced by Moreau de Saint-Méry, Wimpffen, and Sansay. Another English publication from the early nineteenth century reveals yet one more way that the imagined qualities of the Saint-Domingue *mûlatresse* were transported to American shores. The memoir of Pierre-Louis Berquin-Duvallon, a Dominguan refugee who lived in New Orleans from 1800 to 1802 before relocating to France, was published in English in 1806. In it, he portrayed the free woman of color in New Orleans as the twin of the Dominguan *mûlatresse* who had contributed to the undoing of white colonists like him. He found the free colored women in New Orleans marginally less objectionable than the free black men he encountered there, "but they come close with their propensity for libertinage, (and) their vanity." These women harbored a "hatred of whites in general and for white women in particular," but, as with the Dominguan *mûlatresse* described by Moreau de Saint-Méry, it was "a hate which is subordinated, however, to their personal interest, since a large number of them live in concubinage with the same white men, by virtue of greed more than by ties of sincere attachment." The English translation of Berquin-Duvallon played up the implicit warning to white men who might be tempted by the *mûlatresse*'s charms. In John Davis's freely edited 1806 version of Berquin-Duvallon, "Money will always buy their caresses," and, although they "live in open concubinage with the whites," they "are incited more by money than any attachment." Offering fatherly advice to his readers, the translator continued, "After all we love those best, and are most happy in the intercourse of those, with whom we can be the most familiar and unconstrained." The hearts of the *mûlatresses* of New Orleans, he insisted, "are with men of their own colour.[46]

Thomas Ashe, an Irishman who claims to have visited New Orleans in

1806, reprised and embellished the descriptions of Moreau de Saint-Méry and Wimpffen in his own portraits of the Crescent City's free women of color. Moreau de Saint-Méry's *mûlatresse* wore "rich lace, jewels . . . used in profusion," while on Ashe's, "the bosom is covered with solitaries, composed of every different kind of jewels." Wimpffen attested that "their favourite coiffure is an India handkerchief, which is bound round the head: the advantages they derive from this simple ornament are inconceivable." Ashe made it conceivable, and added gold and paste jewels for good measure: "Their most general head-dress is either a handkerchief of gold-gauze braided in with diamonds, or else chains of gold and pearls twisted in and out through a profusion of fine black hair, which produces a pleasing effect." Moreau de Saint-Méry's luxurious Indian fabrics, "the most precious muslins, kerchiefs, fabrics and linens," and his "rich laces" became in Ashe's account petticoats "ornamented at the bottom with gold lace or fringe richly tasselled" and "a cloak made of gauze, or some such light material, which hangs as a loose train to the ground, or is occasionally fastened to the side by a clasp of jewels."[47]

Ashe may or may not have actually seen the opulently dressed free women of color he described as strolling along the New Orleans levee in search of white men to support their expensive tastes. His descriptions are often wildly inaccurate and borrow freely from others' works, as did many other contemporary travel accounts. But by the time he sat down to write his book a year or so after he completed his travels he had access not only to Moreau de Saint-Méry and Wimpffen but to Berquin-Duvallon, who had transported the trope of the *mûlatresse* to New Orleans. Moreau de Saint-Méry was the first to convey the extravagant seductress beyond the boundaries of Saint-Domingue, where her natural habitat had been destroyed by the revolution, to American shores. But his sighting of the temptress in Philadelphia lay unpublished until the twentieth century. It was Ashe's fantastic account of her sartorial splendor that sensationalized her and fixed her in the popular imagination at a new site on the American mainland. The *mûlatresses*, their beauty enhanced by jewels and gold trimming from the tops of their heads to their slippers "of gold embroidery," had a new home.[48]

The arrival of the *mûlatresse* in New Orleans created expectations of titillation—or outrage—among all who ventured to the city in the wake of Ashe's publication, but it also made a more critical contribution to the American psyche. The presence of the *mûlatresse* in continental America was a threat to the sexual order that was emerging as central to forging a stable American polity. If America was to be exposed to the reverbera-tions of the Haitian Revolution, however, the *mûlatresse* was preferable to the alternative of unbridled black male violence. Directing the gaze of the American public toward the *mûlatresse* drew attention away from the more terrifying danger of the black rebellion that might escape the island's boundaries to far more devastating effect. Succumbing to the temptations of the *mûlatresse* was evil, but she was, in the end, a woman susceptible to the mastery of any white man who could satisfy her taste for luxury. Admitting the *mûlatresse* to American soil and minds represented a devil's bargain.

Leonora Sansay's *Secret History* captures the covenant proposed by the *mûlatresse* in the story of Zuline, a young free woman of color in Cap Français. During the violence of May 1793 that ended in the burning of the city, Sansay writes, "a Frenchman was dragged from his place of con-cealment by a ruthless mulatto, who, drawing his sabre, bade him pre-pare to die." The mulatto promised to spare his life in return for money, and the Frenchman, having none, persuaded him he could get as much as he needed from an American merchant who was his friend. While the Yankee merchant dickered with the armed mulatto and the Frenchman trembled with fear, "a young girl of colour, who lived with the Ameri-can, entered, and having learned the story, employed all her eloquence to make the mulatto relent." The girl "sunk at his feet, and pressed his hands which were reeking with blood," using the same charms that could be the downfall of vain white men for another purpose. "She was beautiful; she wept, and beauty in tears has seldom been resisted." She even "offered him, in addition to the sum proposed, all her trinkets," the things supposedly dearest to a *mûlatresse*'s heart. The mulatto relented, rejecting the baubles and the money, sparing the life of the Frenchman "for you alone, for to you I can refuse nothing. He shall be concealed, and guarded by myself till the moment of embarking" with the evacuating fleet. In return, the mulatto intended to take Zuline for his mistress. When the mulatto returned to collect his debt, the American merchant, revealed to be her lover, kept the rebel from claiming his ultimate prize. Zuline "was the means of saving many others, and the accounts I have heard of her kindness and generosity oblige me to think of her with unqualified admiration."[49]

Sansay's fable lays out perfectly the pivotal role the *mûlatresse* was to play as American consciousness came to grips with the Haitian Revolu-tion. The free woman of color was an insatiable consumer who seduced white men, including American white men, tempting them away from their proper roles as faithful husbands and fathers. The French discourse that cast the *mûlatresse* as a usurper of patriotic filiation applied equally to Americans. As Jan Lewis pointed out long ago, "marriage was the very pattern from which the cloth of republican society was to be cut." Only marriage properly fulfilled the prescription articulated in an American publication of the mid-1770s, enabling a man to experience the "endearing intercourse of friendship and communication of pleasure, the tender feelings and soft passions of the soul." No longer simply an ally of the state in establishing social order, marriage was the bedrock of a new variety of patriotism founded on affection. "In this happy state, man feels a growing attachment to human nature, and love to his country."[50] Lust for the *mûlatresse* perverted the course of patriotic married love, but it also offered a saving alternative to the rapacious and violent black rebel. Of the two invasive threats Haiti posed to the young American republic, the seductress was preferable, even welcome, despite her admitted evils (see Figures 5 and 6).

This literature prepared people to know what to expect and what to fear when thousands of Haitian refugees began pouring into New Orleans in 1809, whether native Orleanians or Anglo-Americans living far from the city's remote perch at the edge of the continent. The shipboard demographics of the free people of color were thus simultaneously comforting and disturbing. Among the initial swell of 4,282 refugees who arrived before July 18, 1809, free people of color comprised 608 women and only 178 men, accompanied by 583 children. Though vastly outnumbered by the 729 white men who arrived in the same cohort, the arrival of free men of color among the refugees was a particular worry, evoking fears of violent rebels like the treacherous mulatto in the tale of Zuline. Three years before the events of 1809 made such a threat plausible, the territorial legislature had already barred any free men of color from Haiti, from whom "serious inconveniences might arise." The same legislation took pains to make the gender aspects of the law clear, dictating that it would "not operate against women of color, nor against young people of that description, under fifteen years of age, who shall be supposed to have left the island above named to fly from the horrors committed during its insurrection."[51]

Governor Claiborne reproved the American consul at Santiago for allowing adult men of color to make their way to New Orleans, notifying him in the late summer of 1809 that "the males above the age of fifteen, have in pursuance to a Territorial Law been ordered to depart.—I must request you Sir, to make known this circumstance." Adult male immigrants

DESALINES.
huye del valor frances, pero matando blancos.

FIGURE 5. *Desalines* [*sic*]. This portrait of Jean-Jacques Dessalines, Toussaint Louverture's successor as commander of the Haitian revolutionary forces, is typical of popular images that portrayed the figure of the terrifying black Haitian male in the early nineteenth century. From Jean-Louis Dubroca, *Vida de J. J. Dessalines . . .* (Madrid: La Imprenta real, 1805). Courtesy of the Latin American Library, Tulane University.

COSTUMES

DES AFFRANCHIES ET DES ESCLAVES
des Colonies.

FIGURE 6. *Costumes des Affranchies et des Esclaves des Colonies.* Saint-Domingue's *mûlatresses*, portrayed as seductive, extravagantly dressed free women of color like the two facing forward in this engraving, posed a lesser threat than black male revolutionaries. From Nicolas Ponce, *Receuil des vues des lieux principaux de la colonie Francaise de Saint-Domingue* (Paris, 1791). Courtesy of the John Carter Brown Library, Brown University.

were illegal and feared, but Claiborne further implored the consul "also to discourage free people of Colour of every description from emigrating to the Territory of Orleans; We have already a much greater proportion of that population, than comports with the general Interest."[52]

By making it difficult, if not impossible, for adult free men of color to come to New Orleans and remain there, territorial authorities unwittingly increased the likelihood that its white male inhabitants would be drawn into relationships with free women of color. Of 308 children born to Dominguan free women of color between 1810 and 1812 some 101, fully a third, were born to mothers who could identify no father for the sacramental register. The significance of these figures comes into focus when compared with 58 children baptized by Orleanian free women of color during the same period. Only 22 percent of the children they brought to the baptismal font lacked a named father. The difference between the two groups underlines the obvious: refugee women through the ages have been and continue to be particularly vulnerable to sexual exploitation.[53] Some of those who arrived in New Orleans may have had sexual partners in Cuba who, for a variety of reasons, did not accompany them to Louisiana. In the case of free men of color, they were clearly prohibited, but other scenarios can also explain the unattached mothers who baptized children shortly after their arrivals. It is likely that many resorted to transitory relationships or even prostitution as an economic survival strategy. Some, like the widow Catherine Couvreur, were doubly vulnerable. A native of St. Marc, Couvreur gave birth to a son in April of 1810, indicating that she was either in the early stages of pregnancy when she made the voyage to New Orleans or conceived the child shortly after her arrival. Identified as the widow Fonteneau in the baptismal record of her son, Couvreur seems to have fallen into even more difficult circumstances two years later, when she gave birth to another son. There is neither an indication of the father's identity nor mention of her status as a widow in the baptismal record on this occasion. Such details suggest a slide into prostitution or impoverished cohabitation, circumstances that would have robbed her of the dignity of being recognized as a widow by the priest who registered her son's baptism.[54]

Some women seem to have made fleeting liaisons with one of the many unattached Anglophone Americans who came and went from New Orleans during this period. Maria Louise Peche, a native of St. Marc, bore a daughter in October of 1810 to John Trigg, a native of Kentucky. Whether Trigg was one of the rowdy "Kaintucks" who floated flatboats down the river and quickly spent their earnings on strong drink and women before making the arduous trek back upriver is impossible to know. In any event, Peche bore no more children to him or any other man before she died in 1814, leaving the toddler an orphan.[55] Maria Pedra Hibard of Jérémie identified John Harvey, a native of Boston, as the father of the daughter she bore in the spring of 1810. Four years later, Harvey stood in a different sanctuary in New Orleans with his wife, Prudence Oldner of Norfolk, to baptize a son, testimony to the transient nature of his relationship with Hibard. The father of Marie Catherine Oger's daughter was identified as "Joseph Haltt, American," in the child's 1812 baptismal record. Mother, child, and father all subsequently disappear from the record.[56] Charlotte Miranda seems to have found the difficulty of raising a child alone as a refugee too much to bear. When a trio of Haitian refugees brought her eleven-month-old son, Andre, to be baptized in 1812, no father was identified, and they testified to the priest that Miranda had returned to Haiti shortly after the child's birth.[57]

Theresa Sagory, a native of Môle St. Nicolas, was luckier than such women. Not long after her arrival in the city, she formed a stable relationship with Antonio Ignacio Silva, a native of the Azores who served as the chief pilot for New Orleans. He had come to the city as a twenty-year-old in the early 1780s and was a bachelor of fifty when the flotilla from Santiago de Cuba began arriving at the mouth of the Mississippi. It is hard to resist imagining that he somehow made the acquaintance of Sagory as he boarded the ship that had brought her from Cuba to guide it expertly upriver to the port. Their daughter, Maria, was born late in 1811, and the old bachelor acknowledged his paternity in her baptismal record. When their next child was born two years later, she was named after his mother, Rosa. Sagory bore Silva two more daughters in the next several years. When the pilot died in 1831 he was seventy and surrounded by the family he had led to safe harbor. Theresa Sagory's relationship with Silva may well have been "incited more by money than any attachment," but she hardly fits the profile of a cold-blooded seductress.[58]

Whether illustrated by a case such as Theresa Sagory's, with her stable relationship with a white man, or by accounts of women scrambling to support children born to temporary lovers, the immediate reproductive success of the refugees was striking and would have been cause for alarm among those in New Orleans who feared the growth of the city's free black population. There were already 3,000 free people of color in the city when the refugees arrived, but between 1810 and 1812 these free people of color were not nearly as fertile as the same number of free black refugees. Dominguan free women of color baptized 308 infants to free black Orleanians' 266. Another phenomenon may have confirmed ideas about the predatory nature of the Dominguan *mûlatresse*'s sexuality. While nearly two-thirds of the fathers of children born to New Orleans free women of color were Louisiana born, many of them free men of color, white, foreign-born fathers featured much more prominently among Dominguan births. Frenchmen represented between one-fifth and one-fourth of fathers identified in the baptisms of refugee women's children between 1810 and 1819, while French fathers never made up more than 10 percent in the baptisms of children born to Orleanian women. Baby booms and boomlets often follow the kind of collective trauma experienced by the 1809 refugees, an affirmative expression of renewal.[59] Whether the children born to refugee women originated in hope, exigency, or exploitation was immaterial, however, to anxious white Orleanians who watched the free black birthrate rise.

Americans in 1809, whatever their ethnic, linguistic, or racial heritage, were conditioned by the existing discourse about the Dominguan *mûlatresse* to expect a limited range of behaviors as hundreds of free women of color debarked the ships in New Orleans in the spring and summer of 1809. They imagined them either as the pampered concubines of French men or as unattached women on the make in search of economically advantageous relationships with white men that ran the gamut from long-term cohabitation to prostitution. What the anxious observers in continental America were not prepared to anticipate was the more complex reality of Dominguan free people of color. Such observers were unaware, for example, that among many free black Dominguans marriage was increasingly the preferred family strategy and was a growing phenomenon. And few, if any, North Americans were familiar with the role of the *ménagère*, a free woman of color who managed a white bachelor's household and frequently became his life partner. The refugee influx of 1809 included many, perhaps a majority, whose lives on Saint-Domingue had been defined by one of these two family formations, and the refugees brought these arrangements to New Orleans with them. The difficulties they encountered as refugees, however, often posed insurmountable obstacles to sustaining their families in these accustomed ways.

"I am the legitimate son and grandson of European property owners of Saint-Domingue," Julien Raimond proclaimed in his fiery 1791 contribution to the Parisian pamphlet war over the rights of free people of color.

Raimond was born in 1744 in Saint-Domingue's rural southern peninsula to Frenchman Pierre Raimond and Marie Begasse, the legitimately born daughter of a French planter and free woman of color. Marie Begasse brought a dowry of 15,000 livres to her marriage, an impressive amount by any standard. And she was literate. In 1771 Julien Raimond married a cousin, Marie Marthe Vincent, who brought a stunning dowry of 60,000 livres. Raimond, a third-generation planter and slave owner, was born into a family that epitomized the bourgeois economic and family values of France. The women of his family bore no resemblance to Moreau de Saint-Méry's footloose seductresses.[60]

Julien Raimond is the most famous of the elite free colored planters of Saint-Domingue, but there were many others of his racial ancestry who shared his values. Hilliard d'Auberteuil counted 300 white men married to women of African descent in 1777. More recently, a French historical demographer found that 17 percent of the marriages in the southern district of Saint-Domingue were between white men and African-descended women.[61] In 1778, such marriages were outlawed, and though some continued to take place, intermarriage among free people of color became the norm and gained momentum in the last quarter of the eighteenth century.[62] One historian has found that half of the free people of color who were born free were born legitimately of married parents and comments that "marrying put the seal on a claim to traditional bourgeois morality that was important for those free coloreds aspiring to community leadership." Wealthy free families of color who were planters and slave owners "valued marriage and legitimacy to such an extent that one rarely finds illegitimate children in their ranks beyond the first generation." In a study of the rural southern peninsula, Raimond's home ground, another scholar found the same phenomenon was especially pronounced.[63]

Some of these families were among those who arrived in New Orleans in 1809, and some of their children sustained the matrimonial tradition. For example, Benjamin Bosse and Marguarita Dió of Cap Français and Basille Mignon and Theresa Maurin of Port de Pas were among the free colored refugees who arrived in New Orleans as married couples with children. In 1813 the four of them saw their children, Francisco Bosse and Rose Mignon marry in St. Louis Cathedral in a festive celebration before a "great multitude."[64] The married couples Charles Durouleau and Maria Charitte and Pierre and Isabel Antoine similarly saw their own children, Pierre Durouleau and Marie Françoise Antoine, marry at the cathedral in 1816.[65] There may even have been a relative of Julien Raimond among the grooms at St. Louis Cathedral. Michel Raymond of the southern peninsular port of Les Cayes married Marie Magdaleine Savournée early in 1814.[66]

Some couples embraced the legal and economic pragmatism of marriage after their departure from Saint-Domingue. Adrian Jessé and Hortense Noleau, who had been wealthy planters from the Artibonite region east of St. Marc, were unmarried when they arrived in New Orleans with their four children. Adrian had himself been born of a legitimate marriage, and when he fell gravely ill in the spring of 1810, he and Hortense hastily exchanged vows and legitimated their offspring. The marriage contract they had drawn up on the day of their wedding reveals that they were representatives of the free colored planter elite that Julien Raimond claimed were the bulwark of bourgeois values in Saint-Domingue. They stated that they brought to the marriage seven coffee plantations in the St. Marc district, together with 300 slaves, as well as a cotton and indigo plantation worked by 25 slaves in the mountains of Artibonite that had been given to the bride by her father. When they married in 1810, Jessé and Noleau had obviously not abandoned hopes of returning to Artibonite to reclaim their enormous wealth. But in 1822 they were still in New Orleans, where they presided over the marriage of their daughter Marie Joseph to Jean Louis Denis, legitimately born to married parents in Govaives, just to the north of the Jessés' native St. Marc. A year later, their daughter Antoinette married, this time to a native of St. Marc.[67]

Such marriages were, however, not as frequent as refugee parents might have hoped. Only 35 of the 141 weddings of free people of color that took place in New Orleans between 1810 and 1819 involved Dominguans. Half of these represented intermarriage between refugees.[68] Some marriages, such as that between Jean Bartholomy of St. Marc and Isabel François of Port-au-Prince in 1812, united people who lived in neighboring areas and may have known each other or had common acquaintances before they became refugees. Other marriages seem to have been born of economic considerations. Joaquin Vitry, a few years shy of thirty, wed the fifteen-year-old Marie Joseph Chais in 1811. Chais brought a dowry worth $1,600, comprising three slaves and personal goods, including silver tableware. Her assets certainly did not represent a fortune by any measure, but it was substantial when compared with what most refugees claimed in marriage contracts from the same period. Cecile Emmanuel, for example, brought only $200 in household effects and clothes when she married in 1816.[69]

If the tradition of marriage was to be sustained among the Dominguans in New Orleans, they would need eventually to venture beyond the refugee community for mates. This proved difficult, especially for women. Adult males had been prohibited entry in 1809, and though many slipped through the net, refugee and refugee-descended women remained at a demographic disadvantage. Joseph Savary, a veteran of the Haitian Revolution who commanded over 200 Haitian-descended free black militiamen at the Battle of New Orleans in 1815, subsequently led two filibustering expeditions of free black men to the western Gulf Coast. Savary returned to New Orleans, but some of his men may have remained in Mexico and Texas, depleting the ranks of prospective Haitian-descended grooms left in Louisiana. At the end of the 1820s, there were 2.2 free women of color for every free man of color in New Orleans.[70]

Only six Dominguan women found marriage partners among New Orleans–born free men of color in the decade after 1809, while eight Dominguan men took Orleanian brides. Marriage contracts between Dominguan men and New Orleans women reveal the dynamic that may have enticed refugee men to favor local brides. Port-au-Prince native François Courreur declared assets of $350 in his marriage contract in 1817, while his seventeen-year-old bride, New Orleans–born Rose Aldoin claimed $1,500. When New Orleans native Zacharine Rouzan married refugee Louis Charles Ferant a year later, she brought $1,500 in earnings from her work as a couturier. Ferant brought nothing. Much the same transpired when New Orleans native Marie Laveau, who would later gain fame as the city's leading voodoo priestess, married refugee Jacques Paris. Marie's father, a married free man of color himself, gave his daughter a half-interest in a piece of property, which supplemented the two slaves and $500 worth of personal goods she brought to the marriage.[71]

All refugees were economically disadvantaged by their circumstances to one degree or another. The Jessé marriage contract speaks to the wealth that was lost, and the modest assets declared by the fifty-eight Dominguans who signed marriage contracts in the 1810s and 1820s confirm the difficulty refugees encountered as they sought an economic footing in New Orleans. It would have been difficult for a Dominguan woman to compete with the inheritances that many New Orleans women could bring to marriages, and the connections and social capital their well-established local families could provide. The combination of economic and demographic factors made it extremely difficult for Dominguan women and their daughters to compete for marriage partners in New Orleans. Many women born to married free people of color would find themselves unable to replicate their parents' family formation in New Orleans. And many women born into families that were moving toward the respectability of marriage in prerevolutionary Saint-Domingue saw their opportunities foreclosed by the trauma and dislocation they experienced in flight.

Refugees made up half of the city's population of free people of color when they arrived in 1809. In the three years following their arrival, their numbers grew through natural increase at a rate that outstripped native Orleanians of color. Some 54 percent of the free infants of color baptized at St. Louis Cathedral between 1810 and 1813 were born to refugee parents, compared to 44 percent born to Orleanians.[72] Not a single one of the 155 daughters born to Dominguan parents married as the cohort came of age in the 1820s, while 10 of the 132 Orleanian girls baptized during the same years wed that decade.[73] Between 1810 and 1819, more than two-thirds (68 percent) of the brides at St. Louis Cathedral were New Orleans born. Brides born in Saint-Domingue or in one of the refugee colonies in Cuba represented only a fifth (21 percent) of the free colored young women who went to the altar during the first decade following the 1809 influx. Marriage prospects improved a bit for Dominguan women in the 1820s, when they made up slightly more than a quarter of brides (27 percent), but New Orleans–born women still vastly outnumbered the refugees, accounting for more than half (60 percent) of the city's brides of color during the decade. Three Dominguan-descended girls baptized before 1813 did marry in the first half of the 1830s, but they were outnumbered nearly three to one by girls from old New Orleans families.[74]

It is impossible to know whether the high rate of marriage that historians of colonial Saint-Domingue have found among free people of color would have survived had the colony not been torn by revolution. What is clear is that the trajectory toward this bourgeois institution faltered and fell back dramatically among the refugees in New Orleans. The high proportion of "single" mothers among the refugees along with the low rate of marriage among them and their daughters reveal that any resumption of the trend toward marriage was stopped in its tracks in New Orleans. Most Dominguan women did not arrive in the city embodying the seductive *mûlatresse*, but exigency nudged many of them toward survival strategies that recapitulated the stereotype's features, reinforced its mythology, and transferred the primary site of the figure of the seductive *mûlatresse* from Saint-Domingue to New Orleans.

One of the mainstays of *mûlatresse* identity in Saint-Domingue was the role of *ménagère*, or housekeeper. Contemporaries invariably described the *ménagère* as a combination housekeeper and sexual partner, though Girod de Chantrans added bodyguard to her repertoire in his prerevolutionary descriptions. "Imagine an unmarried man, the only white in his house in the country," he invites his readers, "surrounded by a troop of black men and women who are his domestics, his slaves, and consequently his enemies." Amid this precarious situation, "a *mûlatresse* conducts his household; in her rests all of his trust." The *ménagère* was "no less useful to him for his safety than for his pleasure."[75]

Moreau de Saint-Méry insisted that serving as what might be termed a *ménagère* with benefits was a nearly universal occupation among Saint-Domingue's free women of color. "Most of them [*mûlatresses*] live with a white man, where, under the modest name of '*ménagère*' they have all the functions of a wife, without being much disposed to execute the responsibilities of that title." The reality of their situation was hardly masked by the title of housekeeper. "It is thus actually to the state of a courtesan that *mûlatresses* are generally condemned."[76] Baron de Wimpffen was slightly more charitable in his assessment. "It is from these women that the *ménagères* are usually taken; that is to say, the acknowledged mistresses of the greatest part of the unmarried whites," he explained. "They have some skill in the management of a family, sufficient honesty to attach themselves invariably to one man, and great goodness of heart."[77]

Historians probing beyond the sensationalizing discourse of the late eighteenth century provide a more nuanced picture of the Dominguan *ménagère*.[78] The most detailed study of the role admits that many *ménagères* became the lovers of their white employers and often bore them children. However, it also draws attention to the more mundane, nonsexual nature of many of these arrangements. *Ménagères* executed formal contracts with their employers that detailed what services would be rendered by the *ménagère* and what salary and other emoluments would be provided by her employer. For example, in 1778, François Siriery, a shipping merchant, engaged Hélène Piquery to be his *ménagère* for two years. She was to "carry out the direction of the household with all the economy and vigilance of which she is capable." Hélène's duties included administering the budget necessary to keep the household running smoothly, managing the shopping, overseeing the preparation of meals, and supervising cleaning and laundry.[79] The 1779 *ménagère* contract of Marie-Louise à Traitté of Port-au-Prince stipulated, among other things, that in addition to a salary of 2,400 livres she would receive lodging, meals, laundry service, and medical care should she fall ill—hardly the baubles and other luxuries *mûlatresses* were said to have demanded of their lovers.[80]

Ménagères, like their counterparts in France, often received their compensation at the end of their terms of employment, and it was most often here that their employer's concern for their support beyond the terms of their formal contract was demonstrated. For example, Marie Dubreuil acquired a piece of property worth 20,000 livres in 1789 from her employer of seven years, the postmaster of Port-au-Prince. In the act of sale, she tendered only 3,000 livres, the remainder of 17,000 livres was declared to be equivalent to "seven years of service at 1,000 livres per year, the sum decided when she began her service."[81] There is no hint in this transaction that Dubreuil was the sexual partner of her employer, but wills sometimes singled out *ménagères* and their children for bequests that suggest such attachments. "In return for her good and essential services these past thirty-five years, with so much zeal and devotion," Thomas Piganau of Croix-des-Bouquets gave his *ménagère* Marie-Françoise Julie Dahay 30,000 livres, as well as a buggy and three horses, twelve silver place settings, table linens, glassware, and furniture. He also left 30,000 livres to each of the six sons of the *ménagère*, and 50,000 livres to her daughter. Piganau did not recognize the *ménagère*'s children as his own, but the relationship is clear in his explanation for the bequests. "Having so far done nothing for them, although they constantly aided me in the various work that I undertook to build my fortune."[82]

Moreau de Saint-Méry's portrait of the *ménagère* stipulated a *mûlatresse* who served a white Frenchman or Creole, but not all *ménagères* served the households of white Frenchmen, nor were all *ménagères* of mixed race. Marie Louise à Traitté was the *ménagère* for the free colored planter Paul Bonneau. Jean-François Leveille, who would later become one of Toussaint Louverture's black generals, employed a free *négresse* as his *ménagère* on his plantation in the north district.[83] His decision to hire a *négresse* rather than a *mûlatresse* may have been influenced by his own racial ancestry, but the same cannot be said of the white Monsieur Delisle of Port-au-Prince and of Paul Bonneau, a free colored planter in Borgne, both of whom opted to hire women described as *négresse*. These women of unmixed African descent may well have been African-born.[84]

Ménagères may, according to their most authoritative historian, perhaps best be compared to young girls in France who took up the duties of housekeeper or governess "in large rural farms or bourgeois townhouses in order to save money for a dowry or simply to survive."[85] Women in such situations might find themselves sexually pursued by the master of the house, but that role was not universally part of their portfolio. *Ména-*

gères were enterprising single women who entered into service on terms they could influence, if not dictate. They were a well-established part of the social landscape in Saint-Domingue, but their position and livelihood were obviously threatened by the disruptions of the Haitian Revolution. Although fragile, the institution seems to have survived long enough to resurface with the refugees of 1809 in New Orleans. But there it died, transformed into a concept more palatable to American tastes and politics.

Marie Louise Tonnelier, a Haitian refugee, brought suit in New Orleans in 1812 to recover property to which she believed she was entitled by virtue of her position as *ménagère* to a white man, Jean Baptiste Maurin. The court record states that Tonnelier had lived with Maurin "as his menagere. She had with her in his family, several grown daughters of hers. It was in evidence that he hired out some of the plaintiff's slaves, and received their wages. They had lived together in this manner for several years, in Hispaniola, St. Yago de Cuba, and New Orleans."[86] Superficially, the cohabitation of this Dominguan *ménagère* with her white employer resembles the standard description of *plaçage*, a term commentators began applying in the twentieth century to liaisons between white men and free women of color in antebellum New Orleans. As we shall see, the free black women in *plaçage* were imagined as romantically tragic kept women. A woman in *plaçage*—a *placée*—was dependent and defenseless against the exploitation of her affections by a fickle white lover. Marie Louise Tonnelier was a *ménagère* who believed herself entitled to the contractual rights that structured arrangements such as the one she had with Maurin in Saint-Domingue. She was not a dependent without resources when she arrived with Maurin in New Orleans, but part of a team, her slaves serving as a source of income for the household. But severed from the society that had recognized the place of the *ménagère* and without friends or protectors, her bid for agency failed and she lost her lawsuit. Marie Louise Tonnelier came to New Orleans a *ménagère*, but like so many other unmarried refugee women and their descendants, she is remembered as a *placée*.

Among the things that marked a New Orleans *placée* in popular discourse was the origination of her situation in a particular setting, the quadroon ball. These were understood to be affairs from which free men of color were excluded in order to allow white men exclusive access to beautiful women of color and an entrée to more intimate encounters than the dance floor could accommodate. Visitors reporting on these entertainments as early as the 1820s presented them as one of the city's most notable traditions. But the dances were not a deeply rooted New Orleans practice at all. When Auguste Tessier, whom we met at the beginning of this chapter, advertised in 1805 that free women of color and white men would be welcome at his dance and free men of color barred from it, he was not upholding New Orleans custom but introducing a Haitian import.

During the pre-Lenten carnival season of 1776, a French promoter named Pamelart opened a dancehall known as the Vauxhall on the northern outskirts of Cap Français, near the battery and docks of the city. The festivities at Pamelart's facility were apparently wildly popular, especially the Sunday dances organized for free people of color but open to whites as well. Ash Wednesday came and went without closing down the merry-making, but in 1777 officials stepped in and threw a wet blanket on Pamelart's parties when they issued a prohibition against whites attending the Sunday balls. The move "particularly disgusted the free women of color," according to Moreau de Saint-Méry, presumably because it robbed them of opportunities to meet the unattached white men that Moreau de Saint-Méry was convinced *mûlatresses* stalked at these events. In any case, this new rule served as a death knell for Pamelart's dancehall. He tried to bring people back with every trick he could think of, including fireworks, but to no avail. Within a year, Pamelart's ballroom had disappeared.[87]

Occasions where white men could enjoy the spectacle of free women of color dancing did not die, however, with the demise of Pamelart's establishment. Indeed, they survived and remained a popular attraction for visitors. Baron de Wimpffen describes the scene at dances for free people of color in Jacmel, in the western part of the colony, in the late spring of 1789. Just after sunset the revelers gathered and took to the floor, where "the females more especially, discover such justness of ear, such precision of movement, and such volubility of reins [hips], that the quickest eye can with difficulty seize a few shades of the rapid and fugitive development of their lascivious graces." There was one dance that completely captivated the baron. When the women of color danced the Chica, he enthused, "never did voluptuousness in motion spread a more seducing snare for the eager and insupportable love of pleasure: — Hence, *to dance the chicca*, is considered as the supreme good." In a candid aside, Wimpffen confides to his readers, "I confess, with no little confusion, that the austerity of my principles never prevailed so far as to interdict me from the enjoyment of this singular spectacle, as often as it was in my power."[88]

Notwithstanding his general disapproval of the *mûlatresse*, Moreau de Saint-Méry was equally enthusiastic about the magic of the Chica, a dance to which he ascribed African origins. "It is a kind of lute where all the tricks of love and all its means of triumphing are put into action," he explains. "Fear, hope, disdain, tenderness, caprice, pleasure, rejection, delirium and finally drunkenness, annihilation," all are enacted in a language of movement familiar to "the inhabitants of Paphos," birthplace of Aphrodite. "The art for the female dancer," who either held the sides of her skirt or a handkerchief in each hand "consists mainly of shaking the lower part of her hips, while she keeps the rest of her body in a kind of immobility." When a man wanted to "enliven," the female dancer, "he approaches her and darts suddenly toward her, nearly touching her, then he withdraws and then darts towards her again," becoming the charmer instead of the charmed. "Finally, when the Chica appears in its most expressive form, there is in the gestures and the movements of the two dancers a unity that is easier to conceive of than to condemn." This amorous dance, which showed "every aspect of lasciviousness and voluptuousness" imaginable, had once been danced in the Antilles by "young beauties whose naïve graces embellished it and made it perhaps more appealing. They danced it alone, it is true, or with one of their friends who took the role of the male dancer, without however thereby limiting the vivaciousness of the dance." But in the closing decades of the eighteenth century, Moreau de Saint-Méry lamented, "our morals are not pure enough that such a test can be attempted; the Chica is no longer allowed at the balls for white women, except at some fortuitous gatherings where the small number of people and the choice of spectators reassures the dancer."[89]

Auguste Tessier, one of the hundreds of refugees who arrived in New Orleans before 1809, created a space there where the Chica might have been danced again for white men who would never have a chance to duplicate Wimpffen's guilty indulgences in Saint-Domingue.[90] A native of Paris, Tessier and his life partner, Francisca Besinon, a free woman of color and native of Port-au-Prince, found their way to Louisiana from Saint-Domingue early in the nineteenth century. In 1805, Tessier took over from New Orleans native Bernard Coquet the management of a popular ballroom on St. Philip Street. Since the late 1790s, Coquet had hosted dances in the space where a rabble of slave and free, black, white, and "saffron color," made merry in what Berquin-Duvallon disapprovingly dubbed "tricolor balls."[91] Tessier, rechristening the dancehall the Salle Chinoise, introduced an innovation to the proceedings. He proposed "to give a ball two evenings each week for free women of color to which free men of color will not be admitted."[92] While such a restriction had never applied to dances in New Orleans before, it had been common in Saint-Domingue.

"There are balls where the free women of color dance only with white men," Moreau de Saint-Méry testified in his 1796 essay on dance. "They want there not to admit men of the same color as themselves."[93] Prior to Tessier's intervention, there had been no attempt to keep free men of color from vying for the attentions of mixed-race women on the dance floor, but white men now had unchallenged access to them two nights a week at the Salle Chinoise.[94] Coquet, who had moved on to a new space that he called the Tivoli, copied Tessier and added similarly restricted balls to his usual "tricolor" offerings within the year. A third dance hall, the Union on Ursulines Street, joined the fray just before Christmas in 1808.[95]

Tessier was himself the father of two mixed-race daughters born in New Orleans to a refugee woman, Rosa (1808) and Maria (1811).[96] As was typical for girls born to émigré parents during this critical moment, there is no record of either of the daughters marrying when they were in their early twenties. Rose Tessier would have been eighteen when Karl Bernhard, the Duke of Saxe-Weimar, visited New Orleans in 1826 and was "hastened away to the quadroon ball, so called." The duke began his evening in the company of several "gentleman" acquaintances at a masked ball for whites. It was staid, with many women sitting sedately in alcoves, rendered wallflowers by the scarcity of sufficient male dance partners. Most of the men had put in a quick appearance at the masked ball before moving on to the "quadroon ball . . . where they amused themselves more, and were more at their ease." Unimpressed by the white ball, the duke was quick to accept the offer of his local hosts to take him to a quadroon ball so that he could experience the difference for himself.[97]

Eyewitness the duke may have been, but his description of the quadroon ball and of the young women he encountered there present an amalgam of much of what had already been said by those who preceded him in chronicling the charms and living habits of mixed-race women in the Antilles and Circum-Caribbean.[98] Because his description was so widely circulated and has become such a common source for historians, however, the implicit link that he made between the ball and the arrangement of liaisons for the young women is important. So is the color terminology he chose to use. The beauty who captivates white lovers is no longer a *mûlatresse* but a quadroon, and she lends her name to a kind of entertainment that became a byword for the illicit pleasures of white men in nineteenth-century America, the quadroon ball.

"The quadroons are almost entirely white," the duke observed. "Still, however, the strongest prejudice reigns against them on account of their black blood." Marriage between people of unmixed European descent and those of African ancestry was proscribed by United States law, and "as the quadroons on their part regard the negroes and mulattoes with contempt, and will not mix with them, so nothing remains for them but to be the friends, as it is termed, of the white men." Such an arrangement was viewed by the quadroon, according to the duke, as a matrimonial contract, "though it went no farther than a formal contract by which the 'friend' engaged to pay the father or mother of the quadroon a specified sum."[99] The duke transformed the black or *mûlatresse ménagère* who negotiated her own contract to act as housekeeper to a white man into a passive beauty whose parents undertook the dirty work of striking the bargain that consigned their daughter to concubinage.

The enterprising *ménagère* had become the compromised *placée*. The metamorphosis accomplished by the duke's description rendered the mixed-race temptress several degrees less dangerous. She was now fully mastered by the white men whose patriotism and security she had once threatened. Symbolically, the danger of Haiti was mastered. The trick by which the threat of the Haitian *mûlatresse* was neutralized, built on sensationalized descriptions of quadroon balls and concubinage such as Karl Bernhard's, masks the tragic reality of the young refugee women and the extraordinary nature of the strategies they deployed. Writers such as Bernhard and those who followed him with romanticized and sensationalized descriptions of New Orleans quadroons and quadroon balls have successfully obscured not just the tragic situation of Haitian-descended refugees but the history of the city's other free women of color. Theirs is the story to which we next turn.

CHAPTER THREE

Con Otros Muchos
Marriage

On 29 July 1822 after performing the usual diligences and reading
the three bans . . . I joined in marriage Baltasar Noel Carriere free
man of color and native of this city, legitimate son of Noel Carriere
and of Maria Ana Thomas and Maria Scipion Sarpy free person of
color and native of this city, legitimate daughter of Scipion Sarpy and
of Melisse Aubry . . . witnesses Don Joseph Vidal, Don Francisco
Pizzaro, Don Juan Rodon, Vicente Cupidon, Pedro Laviolette and
Noel Carriere, brother of the groom with many other persons . . .

—Fr. Antonio Sedella, St. Louis Cathedral, 1822[1]

On the first day of March 1829, Noel Carriere made his way to
St. Louis Cathedral to play his part in a tradition that his family had sustained in New Orleans for more than half a century. Carriere joined two
other men at the altar to witness the marriage of Marie Celeste Claver,
whose late father had fought with Carriere's father against the British in
the American Revolution. Comrades in arms for three decades, the elder
Carriere and Claver had also been partners in encouraging the growth of
marriage among free people of African descent in Spanish colonial New
Orleans. By 1829, when Marie Celeste Claver pronounced her vows, the
legacy of their matrimonial campaign was impressive. New Orleans free
women of color were believed by contemporary commentators to engage
universally in illicit liaisons with white men, a proclivity that forever excluded them from a claim to the ideal of chaste womanhood embodied
by antebellum white women. But Marie Celeste and women of color who
shared her ancestral roots in New Orleans participated in a culture of sacramental marriage and family formation that made them exemplars of
the very paradigm of which they were supposed to be the antithesis. The
marriage acts of free black Orleanians in the 1820s, like the one that opens
this chapter, often closed with the words *con otros muchos*—with many
others. The priest meant to record that many people joined the couple in
the sanctuary to witness and celebrate the wedding, but the phrase unwit-

tingly gestures as well to the many others among the free black population who had embarked on matrimony since the city's colonial era.

This chapter traces the growth of marriage among people of African descent in New Orleans from its earliest manifestation during the French colonial era to the mid-1830s, when the discourse of the universal quadroon concubine established itself in the American imagination. The origins of the marital tradition were multiple and followed various developmental paths that only fully converged in the 1820s. The earliest appearance of European marriage among enslaved Africans in French colonial Louisiana was largely driven by religious imperatives, but a hiatus in the slave trade of several decades' duration fostered a pronatal strategy among slave owners that expanded sacramental marriage beyond the circle of the pious. During the Spanish colonial period, people of African descent took initiative for promoting marriage under the influence of the members of the free black militia, who adopted the European family formation for purposes of advancement and community building. At the beginning of the nineteenth century free people of color beyond the ambit of the militia embraced matrimony, perhaps because of changes in Louisiana law that disadvantaged children born of nonmarital unions. Children born of life partnerships between women of color and white men were notable participants in this trend. The 1809 Haitian refugee influx seems to have inclined yet more Orleanians toward matrimony, perhaps in order to distinguish themselves from the newcomers both socially and politically. Additional changes in inheritance law triggered a rash of marriages among cohabitants with children in the mid-1820s. With the glaring exception of second-generation refugee women, the practice of sacramental marriage had become common among all branches of the city's free colored population by 1830.

The elder Noel Carriere, the Revolutionary War hero who led the free black community in its adoption of sacramental marriage, was born to an African father in the mid-1740s. His family history exemplifies one of the main evolutionary arcs among the captive Africans brought to Louisiana during the French colonial period (1699–1767) and the children born to them. His father, Joseph Leveillé, was born in Africa in the early 1720s and almost certainly arrived in Louisiana as a small child. Leveillé spent most, if not all, of his enslaved life in Louisiana laboring for the community of Ursuline nuns who had established a convent in New Orleans in 1727.[2] There, his life was shaped by the sisters' insistence on baptism and sacramental marriage for their bondpeople. Leveillé's would become one of nine nuclear families grounded in Christian matrimony formed under the watchful eyes of the sisters. His experience was not unique among the enslaved in and around New Orleans. The Capuchin friars charged with the settlement's pastoral care predictably shared the nuns' stance and oversaw the emergence of a similar cluster of families among their bound servants. Together the two religious communities were among the largest slaveholders in the New Orleans area, and their example doubtless registered on the consciousness of local planters. Secular owners saw some 359 enslaved children born between 1744 and 1769 to sacramentally married parents, reflecting 11 percent of the total number of marriages during this period.[3]

Deference to the pious example set by the Ursulines and Capuchins may have played a part in the appearance of sacramental marriage among other proprietors, but another, more powerful factor made enjoining marriage on one's laborers a rational choice. Only one ship bearing captive Africans arrived in French colonial Louisiana after 1731. Encouraging reproduction was essential for Louisiana planters who wanted to maintain, let alone increase, their workforce during this thirty-year drought in Louisiana's slave trade. The surest way to promote planters' interests was not only to encourage family formation among the enslaved, but to engineer it within their own slaveholdings by marrying their slaves to each other. All of the enslaved children born to married parents between 1744 and 1769, including those born to Ursuline and Capuchin bondpeople, were born to parents who belonged to the same master. Marriage records for the French colonial period are spotty, but the sixty-five weddings between enslaved people that took place between 1759 and 1770 all united couples who belonged to the same master or mistress. That there were thirty-seven different owners of these couples indicates how widespread the practice had become. And although the married couples represented a small minority in the enslaved population of the New Orleans region, their weddings represented about a fifth of all those celebrated at the parish church during the French colonial period. When Spain assumed authority over Louisiana's colonial regime in the late 1760s, European sacramental marriage was well established among the enslaved, its unattractive coercive underpinnings notwithstanding.[4]

The Ursulines seem to have been among the few slave owners reconciled to their lack of absolute control over their bondpeoples' mating. If attraction leapt the confines of the convent and its plantations, the nuns often took steps to unite the couple under a single owner to pave the way to fidelity as they understood it. Such was the case with Noel Carriere's father, Joseph Leveillé. He formed an attachment to Marie Victoire, who belonged to a single white woman living in New Orleans. Marie Victoire bore Leveillé a son named Louis in 1753. Five years later, when Marie Victoire's owner asked to be admitted to the convent as a permanent boarder, the nuns accepted her on condition that ownership of Leveillé's wife and child be transferred to the sisters as part of the arrangement. In 1758 Leveillé and Marie Victoire, already sacramentally bound to one another, were presented with a conjugal bed under the aegis of the Ursulines. The nuns doubtless took comfort in having brought the couple together, but Leveillé may have thought himself ensnared. As the sisters reallocated space within the servants' quarters to accommodate Marie Victoire and little Louis, Leveillé was almost certainly consumed with the logistical problem presented by his new situation. Elsewhere in the city he had formed another family with bondwoman Marie Therese Carriere. The first of their five children, Noel Carriere, was born in 1746, seven years before the birth of his half-brother, Louis.[5]

Noel Carriere's family offers a rare glimpse of what the transition from African family forms to the European model may have looked like in Louisiana. Leveillé is identified in his marriage record as a native of "Guinea," an imprecise eighteenth-century geographic term that comprised west and west-central Africa from the Senegambia region south to the Kingdom of Kongo. Polygamy was practiced throughout this area, and was observed by the French missionary Jean-Baptiste Labat in the regions of West Africa from which captive Africans were most frequently brought to Louisiana in the early eighteenth century.[6] Leveillé evidently maintained two wives simultaneously in New Orleans, practicing a family formation that was common in his homeland but anathema to the nuns who owned him. Yet it would be a mistake to assume that his polygyny indicated ignorance of the rules of sacramental marriage or that he did not respect the tenets of Christianity that the Ursulines enjoined upon him. Leveillé was not only baptized but was a frequent godparent in the Ursuline slave community. In later life he offered a more explicit indication of the quality of his piety when he asked the nuns in 1785 to manumit his six-year-old granddaughter, Julie, but to keep her with them at their house "so that she will continue to be instructed in religion and good conduct."[7]

Noel Carriere, Joseph Leveillé's first-born son by Marie Therese Carriere, demonstrated a much less ambiguous commitment to Christian monogamy, one that was almost certainly shaped by his participation in a free black military tradition that was already well established by the time he was born in the mid-1740s. The French had employed men of African descent in a military capacity in Louisiana at least as early as their 1736 and 1739 expeditions against the Chickasaw. An account published in 1753 tells of Simon, captain of the company of free blacks, who "distinguished himself by an act of singular boldness" in the 1736 campaign, pushing through a hail of Chickasaw musket fire on foot in order to capture a horse and bring it back into the French camp.[8] This was almost certainly Simon Calpha, who was still at the head of the free black militia in 1769 when the Spanish extracted an oath of loyalty from the thirty-four free black men bearing arms who presented themselves for service to their new sovereign.[9] Simon Calpha, sacramentally married to free woman of color Marthe Anne and the father of four children, modeled for Noel Carriere the combination of valor and subscription to European social norms that would become a hallmark of Louisiana's free black militia.[10]

Noel Carriere was an extraordinary man by many measures, the ideal person to transform Simon Calpha's singular example into a sustainable and powerful social norm in his own generation. Carriere demonstrated both his status as a leader and his commitment to Catholicism while still a slave. Over a ten-year period between 1757 and 1767, he stood as a godfather at more than a dozen baptisms, three of them as the sponsor of an adult. Such frequency was extraordinary, especially for a man in his teens and twenties, but there was even more that set Carriere apart. Between 1764 and 1771, he seems to have lived as a *libre de fait*, a man who had never been legally manumitted but who lived as free. Many *libres de fait* in other French colonies continued to live with their masters and might even be referred to occasionally as slaves.[11] Noel Carriere, a skilled tanner and cooper, apparently continued to live in the household of his owner, Marguerite Trepagnier Carriere, and was inventoried as part of her estate in 1769.[12] Yet, in 1770 Carriere was listed in one of several lists of free men of color that Spanish governor Alexander O'Reilly commissioned.

It is quite clear from other sources that Noel Carriere was understood not only to be a free man, but a man of property with authority over others. Technically, enslaved people could not themselves own others, but Carriere was identified as the owner of two slaves before his own legal manumission in 1771. Baptiste, the godfather of an enslaved child baptized in the summer of 1764, and Marie, who sponsored an enslaved girl for baptism later that year, were both identified as the slaves of Noel Carriere. The officially enslaved Noel Carriere had somehow managed to acquire two servants widely recognized to be *his* slaves while still in his teens. This improbable feat was an indication of the energetic personality that would preside over the remaking of a large swath of free black society in late colonial New Orleans.[13]

Carriere achieved his official freedom in 1771, paying 500 piastres for his self-purchase. Seven years later he followed in the footsteps of Simon Calpha and pronounced his wedding vows before the altar at St. Louis Church. His choice of a free black woman named Mariana Thomas as his bride may have been dictated by love alone, but it cemented his place in Louisiana's black military establishment. Mariana's father was Pierre Thomas, one of the thirty-four men who pledged their arms to Spain under Simon Calpha in 1769. "Pierre son of Thomas," like his captain, was married. Mariana was proclaimed in her marriage record to be "legitimate daughter of Pierre Thomas and of Marie Jeanne, her parents," a mark of pride that may have stung the ambitious Noel Carriere. When he celebrated his nuptials late in 1777, he was identified as "natural son of Joseph free negro and Marie Therese free negress," marking him as the progeny of unmarried parents.[14]

The spring after Carriere's wedding, Spain entered the American Revolution on the side of the Thirteen Colonies and Carriere began to build what would become a distinguished military career. Bearing the rank of second lieutenant in Captain Simon Calpha's free black militia, the young man first saw action in a campaign led by Spanish colonial governor Bernardo de Galvez in August 1778 at Baton Rouge. Galvez submitted Carriere's name for a commendation, and in 1780 Carriere received a silver medal of honor for his role in the battle. He distinguished himself again in expeditions that Galvez led against the British at Mobile early in 1780 and at Pensacola in February 1781. He received another medal of honor and a bonus of 300 pesos. Peace did not bring an end to his service. Now commissioned as a captain, Carriere and his father-in-law Pierre Thomas led special expeditions to capture runaway slaves in 1782 and 1784, signaling in yet another way their identification with the European colonial establishment.[15]

Noel Carriere has already drawn attention from historians for bearing arms in the name of a European sovereign and acquiring slaves, but his unheralded role in promoting marriage among his fellow militiamen and their families was arguably his most notable achievement.[16] He began close to home. In the spring of 1786, Joseph Leveillé finally married Noel's mother in a Catholic ceremony, almost certainly with the strong encouragement of Captain Carriere. It was a quiet affair, with only two employees of the church as witnesses, but the celebrant carefully noted that Noel and his siblings Louis, Joseph, Marianne, and Suzanne were legitimated by the nuptials.[17] With the marriage of his father to his mother, the filial order implied by blood was confirmed in law, and Noel Carriere's personal manifestation of it perfected.

This milestone was not of superficial concern to Carriere. He was a commissioned officer in the service of His Most Catholic Majesty, Charles III of Spain, a monarch who had promulgated new standards for the preservation of social and political order through marriage in his *Real Pragmática* (Royal Pragmatic on Marriage) of 1776.[18] The *Real Pragmática* was essentially crafted to reinforce the ideology of absolutism embraced by European monarchs by buttressing the authority of patriarchy, absolutism's mirror and philosophical foundation. It was extended to Spain's American colonies in 1778, the year of Carriere's own marriage. In light of Carriere's subsequent behavior, the timing of his nuptials does not seem to be simple coincidence. Carriere was not technically a free man when Simon Calpha and thirty-three other free men of color signed an oath of allegiance to Carlos III in 1769, and he had fought for his monarch only once when he and Marianne Thomas were united at the altar in 1777. Entering into matrimony not only linked Carriere with the nascent tradition of married free black soldiers such as Simon Calpha and his father-in-law, Pierre Thomas, it sealed his allegiance to the new regime of filial and political order prescribed by his monarch.[19]

The *Real Pragmática* of 1776 required children under the age of twenty-five to obtain their parents' permission to marry, and those above that age were required to ask for parental consent. Parents had the right to stop the marriage of minor children and to disinherit those of age if the match was unequal. If the prospective bride or groom was an orphan, the rights conferred by the *Real Pragmática* passed to the grandparents or eldest brother. The execution of the law obviously rested on legitimate marriage as the means by which a father claimed legal authority to regulate his children's marriage. In the Americas, where nonmarital partnerships between Iberian men and women of Indian, African, and mixed descent were common, the enactment of the *Real Pragmática* faced a significant practical problem. The Council of the Indies believed that "Mulattos, Blacks, Coyotes and individuals publicly reputed to be of similar castes and races" often did not even know the identities of their fathers and saw this as a barrier to their marriage, and thus an obstacle to the necessary realization of absolutism in all of Spain's dominions. The council's solution was to exempt colonial inhabitants of mixed ancestry from the letter, but not the spirit, of the law. Such persons were to be advised of their "natural obligation to honor and veneer their Fathers and superiors," but would not be legally bound to do so.[20] Noel Carriere was over thirty when he married, and exempt under any circumstances from seeking paternal blessings. Given his subsequent championship of matrimony, however, it is easy to imagine him solemnly announcing his marital intentions to his father and taking it upon himself to ask Pierre Thomas formally for the hand of his twenty-year-old daughter.[21]

Marriage may have been newly yoked to the project of absolutism, but it had long performed a crucial function in the performance of honor in Spanish colonial culture. According to the classic rubric of Iberian honor, men attained honor through bearing arms and protecting the virtue of female family members. Feminine honor could be achieved only through chastity except within the institution of sacramental marriage. Status, reputation, and careers depended upon the possession of honor. Legitimacy, by extension, became a prerequisite for status in Spain and its colonies and among the most precious legacies a parent could confer upon a child.[22] Honor was obviously unattainable for the enslaved woman, whose chastity was not hers to preserve, and for the enslaved man, who could neither protect the honor of his womenfolk nor bear arms. The Council of the Indies decision that people of mixed descent should be exempted from the requirements of the *Real Pragmática* reiterated the presumptive incapacity of such persons with respect to honor even as it delineated yet another way they fell short of fully meeting what was asked of other subjects of the king. The marriage acts recorded in the New Orleans parish registry in the wake of the *Real Pragmática*'s promulgation in the Americas testify to Carriere's determination to show that the Council of the Indies had misjudged the capacity of people of African and mixed descent to uphold its standards of honor and absolutism.

Carriere acted within the realm of his own family in the 1770s and 1780s to claim honor and demonstrate his allegiance to the ideology embodied in the *Real Pragmática*, and seven other members of the militia did the same when they took brides at St. Louis Cathedral. Their weddings were generally small, private affairs, with church staff serving as the only witnesses on all but two occasions. Late in 1789, Carriere's sister, Marianne, married militia member Antoine Canoay in such a ceremony. Within a year, almost as though prodded into action by his sister's virtually invisible wedding, Noel Carriere launched his career as a ceremonial sentinel at the weddings of the city's free people of color. During the 1790s, he served as a witness at eighteen weddings, and though militia members were the grooms on three of these occasions, what is striking is how frequently Carriere lent the luster of his uniform and decorations—and perhaps his approbation—to the weddings of those beyond the militia's ranks. He would certainly have been particularly pleased as he stood witness at the 1796 wedding of his own brother, Joseph, to the enslaved woman Augustine, but he could celebrate a more public triumph in the spread of marriage among free people of color through his presence at some thirty nuptials between 1790 and his death in 1804. Carriere officially witnessed roughly half of the weddings of free people of color during this period, including the marriages of nearly half of the militia members who wed. Other militia officers followed Carriere's lead, standing as witnesses at the weddings of fellow militia members and other free people of color. Pierre Claver witnessed eighteen, standing beside Carriere at four of them. Half of all weddings of free people of color in the 1790s involved militia members as grooms, witnesses, or both, and many different militiamen participated in this way, though no witness approached Carriere's virtuosity. Only François Dorville, captain of the *pardo* regiment of the free black militia, even came close, with twenty wedding appearances under his belt (see Figure 7).[23]

Noel Carriere's personal standard regarding marriage survived his death through his children and grandchildren. Marianne bore him five sons and five daughters over nearly a quarter of a century, beginning with namesake Noel in 1780 and ending with François, born in 1804, months before Carriere's death at the age of fifty-eight. Seven of these children married before 1830, and since the first of the weddings occurred two years after his death, his offspring's actions indicate either respect for their father's example or posthumous obedience to his precept.[24] Carriere's material success provided an estate sufficient to provide each of his daughters and granddaughters with a dowry of about $350 each, a factor that would have improved their chances in the limited marriage market among free people of color. His bequest helped situate daughter Marie Arthemise in a comfortable marriage in 1822 with Pierre Laviolette, son of a militia member and owner of a sizable livestock holding in Attakapas. Granddaughter Maria Deseada Carriere made an even better match the same year. She brought her $350 share of Captain Noel Carriere's succession as her dowry

Miliciano Moreno de Puerto-Rico.

Los Sarg.ᵒˢ de esta Milicia llevan el mismo distintivo q͠ los del Exer.ᵗᵒ y su Vestuarios son de gen.ᵒ mas finos. Los Cabos prim.ˢ de la misma restingui= guen con dos cintas angostas de hilo en la Divisa. Los Cabos segund.ᵒˢ con una sola; y los Tamb.ᵉˢ y Pfanos por medio d͠ galon de franja angosta en la Chaq.

FIGURE 7. Free black militiaman. Noel Carriere and his fellow militiamen probably donned uniforms such as this one, worn by a member of the free black militia of Puerto Rico, when they stood as witnesses at the marriages of free black Orleanians. José Campeche, *Diseño de Uniforme de miliciano moreno de Puerto Rico*, c. 1785. AGI MP-Uniformes 113. Courtesy of España, Ministerio de Educación, Cultura y Deporte, Archivo General de Indias, Seville.

to a groom who declared $3,000 in horses and movables. Another grand-daughter, Anne Hermione Daquin, also brought a dowry supplied by Carriere's succession to her marriage in 1824.[25]

The prominence of the Carriere clan among the ranks of the married is unsurprising, but their behavior was not exceptional among the progeny of militia members. Thirteen sons and daughters of militia members celebrated their nuptials in the first decade of the nineteenth century, and more than a third of the free people of color who married between 1810 and 1820 were either militia members or their children. The children of siblings Maurice and Vincent Populus, like those of Carriere, were especially consistent in observing sacramental marriage. Maurice himself married in 1804 and lived to preside over the weddings of daughters Margarita in 1821 and Maria in 1827. Four of Vincent's children also married, Françoise in 1808, Maria Martine in 1815, Dorothée in 1815, and Carlos in 1819. Dorothée was widowed and married for a second time in 1826. Both brothers were frequent wedding witnesses in the two decades after Noel Carriere's death. Maurice appeared at a dozen weddings and his brother Vincent at ten between 1800 and 1827. Curiously, Vincent, who was a captain in the *pardo* militia, never married his life partner, Marianne Navarre. The commander of the *pardo* regiment, François Dorville, likewise remained technically a bachelor. When Commander Dorville's daughter married in 1801, she was identified with her mother's surname and designated "natural daughter of François [D]Orville, captain of the pardo companies of this place and of Isabel Boisdore."[26] It was the dark-skinned captain of unmixed African descent, Noel Carriere, who set a personal example for the troops, not his racially privileged counterparts.[27]

Carriere was captain of the *moreno* regiment of the militia, the corps to which were assigned men who, like him, were of unmixed African descent. The *pardo* regiment over which François Dorville had command was reserved for men of mixed African and European ancestry, men who were designated in official records with the color term mulatto or quadroon. Eighteenth-century contemporaries such as Moreau de Saint-Méry observed that people of mixed descent in the French Antilles held themselves to be superior to those of pure African ancestry and even adopted mating strategies to lighten the skin color of their children. The eighteenth-century Spanish *casta* paintings depicting the moral implications of various admixtures of African, Indian, and European blood likewise suggest a hierarchy of color in the colonial consciousness. Carriere's leadership as a marriage proponent, as well as the nature of some of the unions formed among New Orleans free people of color, suggest that hierarchies of race and phenotype preoccupied Europeans more than they did the men and women upon whom they were inscribed.

The effective onset of the Spanish regime in Louisiana in 1769 introduced a new level of attention to color terms and racial distinctions in the administration of the colony. French sacramental registers often assigned a phenotype to individuals of mixed descent, but the baptisms, marriages, and funerals of people of unmixed European, African, Indian, and mixed descent were all recorded in a single register. The Spanish instituted separate registers for those of unmixed European descent considered to be "white" and those of African, Indian, and mixed ancestry. Color terms that had been inconsistently deployed during the French period were diligently noted in official records, including sacramental registers. Spanish civil and clerical officials applied the term *moreno* to anyone whose ancestry was less than half white, *pardo* to those who could claim half or more. A *negro* was a person of unmixed African descent, a *mulato* a person of half unmixed European descent and half unmixed African ancestry. *Grifo* referred to a person born to a *pardo* and a *morena*, and a *cuarterón* was the offspring of a white and a *parda*. One of the most commonly used phenotype labels in Mexico, *mestizo*, child of a European and an Indian, was rarely used in late colonial Louisiana.[28]

The use of phenotype labels in sacramental records had no direct bearing on the daily experience of New Orleans free people of color, but the application of Spanish colonial racial hierarchy to the organization of its free black militia had the potential to instill an effective color consciousness among them. Most members of the free black militia belonged to one of the four companies of the *pardo* regiment commanded by Captain François Dorville, which totaled 362 men at arms in 1801. Noel Carriere commanded the *moreno* regiment of 134 men in two companies.[29] These figures may well indicate that it was easier for men of mixed European and African descent to attain freedom in Spanish colonial New Orleans, but they do not predict the way status operated within the city's free black community. Noel Carriere was the featured witness at the weddings of twelve *pardo* men who were categorized as his racial superiors by colonial officials. Two of them, Henri Bricou and Stephan Saulet were members of the *pardo* militia commanded by Dorville, yet Noel Carriere was the ranking officer at their weddings.[30]

Even more telling are the marriages that occurred between women identified with a color label superior to that of their grooms. The common wisdom among Europeans was that women of African descent sought to "whiten" their children by mating with Europeans or men whose ascribed phenotype indicated a racial rank superior to their own. There were certainly marriages among the free colored population of New Orleans that fit this pattern, but there were fourteen marriages between 1790 and 1815, when color labels were abandoned, that invert it. In eight of them, the women who married down in phenotypic terms married militia members. Celeste Hugon, the *grifa* daughter of the *mulato* militia captain Baptiste Hugon, married *negro* militia member Pierre Claver in 1794. The *mulato* Maurice Populus, an officer in the *pardo* militia, married the *cuarterona* Artemise Celestin. Just before the transfer of Louisiana from Spain to the United States in 1803, the *cuarterona* Maria Francisca married *mulato* militia member Pierre Aubri. The *grifa* Luisa Gonzales married Noel Carriere II, *negro* lieutenant of the *moreno* militia and son of Captain Noel Carriere, in 1806.[31] Service in the militia, especially as an officer, trumped race as a marker of status in such matches.

Noel Carriere's influence certainly played a part in the prominence of militiamen among the grooms and witnesses in the 1790s and early 1800s. It may also help explain the marriage of thirteen free African-born men. The two weddings of free African men that took place before Carriere's death both involved him directly, that of his father Joseph Leveillé and that of Santiago Apolon, at which he and fellow militia member Pierre Laviolette served as witnesses.[32] Subsequent weddings of African-born men often included other militiamen as witnesses. Pedro Sarpy, identified as a Bambara, married the Senegal-born Catherine, legitimating their four children, in the presence of three militiamen in 1804. Militiaman Pierre Claver witnessed the nuptials of Carlos, of Congo. And Honoré Destrehan, whose father was a member of the *pardo* militia in 1801, witnessed the 1823 wedding of Africans Antoine Castor and Cecile Palus. Many of these African-born brides and grooms embraced marriage late in life or when they were ill and on the point of death. Antoine Castor was fifty-five and Cecile Palus sixty-five when they married, for example, and Jean Casimire and Felicité Abat aged forty-eight and thirty, respectively. Marie Jeanne of Congo was gravely ill when she married Charles, a native of her homeland, in 1806. Other Africans married only after cohabiting for a long period of time and having several children together. When Pierre Lange and Marie François Lucile married in 1811, they legitimated five children ranging in age from sixteen to three. The timing of these African marriages suggests lives influenced gradually by a new set of values introduced by leaders in the free black community like Noel Carriere.[33]

There was only one wedding between free people of color in 1804, the year that Noel Carriere died. His disappearance from the matrimonial theater of New Orleans may help explain a shift in the ceremonial performance of the marriage rite in the city a few years later. Carriere had presided over the emergence of a community performance of marriage at which members of the militia stood in for the blood relatives that were missing in many free families of color. The notation "unknown father" was typical in the baptismal records of free people of color of Carriere's generation, particularly for those of mixed race whose white fathers usually did not officially acknowledge their paternity. Africans were obviously separated by time and space from their kin. Parents of first-generation freed people, whether of unmixed or mixed descent, often remained enslaved, creating a different kind of absence in the nuptial mise-en-scène. The militia sentinels supplied a fictive family to witness the wedding and incorporate the couple into a new web of relations. Before the militia sentinels took the stage at weddings in the 1790s, marriages of free people of color were private, impersonal affairs, usually witnessed only by church staff. During Carriere's life, free black men replaced the white male choirmasters and sacristans, creating a space within the ceremony for the constitution of lineage, connection, and community through the substitution of the black militia for absent family. As the children of Carriere and his generation began to marry in the nineteenth century, the exigencies that had produced this adaptation faded. The blood kin of brides and grooms joined the militia to produce a nuptial tableau that announced free blacks' achievement of the filial ideal that Europeans had presumed to be beyond their reach.

Occasional appearances by fathers or mothers at weddings at the turn of the nineteenth century paved the way for the new family-centered wedding celebration. Father of the bride Joseph Dupart, accompanied by fellow militia members, attended the wedding of his daughter, Maria, to Juan Bautista Pedro in 1803. Margarita Ricardo, who attended the wedding of Julian Vienville and Maria Ricardo, has the distinction of being the first mother of the bride whose presence was recorded. This preamble introduced a sudden, marked transition in 1807, when nearly every wedding began to include family members and *otros muchos* (many others). The nuptials of Charles Vivant and Iris Lugar on October 4, 1810, combined both the old and new traditions. Militia officers Charles Brulé and Joseph Cabaret stood as traditional sentinels but were joined by the mother of the bride and many other guests. The 1815 wedding of Manuel St. Martin and Dorothée Populus was a very grand family occasion. The father and uncle of the bride, along with "many other relatives," turned out to witness this union of a woman described as a *mulata* with a man described as a *negro*.[34]

The male-dominated weddings of the eighteenth century emphasized the responsibility of free black men to uphold the honor of their women and their sovereign. By the second decade of the nineteenth century, the old Spanish priest who usually registered the weddings of free people of color often noted the attendance of "otras muchas personas de ambos sexos"—many other people of both sexes. Now women drawn from beyond the immediate family of the bride and groom joined their men in the public spectacle of the wedding, proclaiming by their visibility at these affairs black women's attainment of the nineteenth-century version of female honor: respectability. When "many persons of both sexes" donned their finest clothes and made their way through the streets of New Orleans to attend the wedding of Firman Christobal Haydel and Maria Francisca Mayeux at St. Louis Cathedral at the end of November in 1816, they invited observers to register the celebration of free black feminine respectability in their midst. Inside the cathedral, a young *mûlatresse*, the legitimate child of free black parents, defied the trope of the universal free black concubine. She and the women who strolled to the cathedral on the arms of their husbands undercut Thomas Ashe's 1808 proclamation that the free women of color of New Orleans were "extremely numerous, and are mistresses to the married and unmarried, and nearly to all the strangers who resort to the town." The permanency of marriage was unknown to such women, according to Ashe. "They are no sooner disengaged from one attachment than they are at liberty to form another," he had assured his readers. But Maria Francisca Mayeux and the women who joined her to celebrate her wedding challenged Ashe's most famous observation about New Orleans even as they confirmed another usually overlooked. "Custom has made the church the theatre for the creation, discovery, and progress of first loves," Ashe observed. A visitor to New Orleans in 1816 setting out to have their own look at this incubator of romance might have stumbled across a merry party of people of color assembled to celebrate the declaration of love that concluded in its public sacramental sealing.[35]

The tempo of marriages among free people of color in New Orleans gathered speed in the second decade of the nineteenth century, nearly doubling in frequency between 1810 and 1819 and again between 1820 and 1829. The twofold increase in the free black population after the refugee influx of 1809 might seem the most obvious explanation for the upswing. After all, most of the refugees were women and children, and by the late 1820s the girls born to refugee mothers in New Orleans would have been coming of age. But as we saw in the last chapter, none of the 155 girls born to Dominguan mothers between 1810 and 1812 married in New Orleans in the 1820s. Yet the Dominguan influx almost certainly did play a part in the rash of Orleanian weddings in the 1810s and 1820s, for it exacerbated the increasingly precarious position of free black Orleanians as Louisiana made its bid for political and cultural inclusion in the young American republic.

"We are Natives of this Province and our dearest Interests are connected with its welfare," read a petition that members of the free black militia submitted to territorial governor William C. C. Claiborne within weeks of the transfer of Louisiana to the United States. "We are duly sensible that our personal and political freedom is thereby assured to us for ever, and we are also impressed with the fullest confidence in the Justice and Liberality of the Government towards every Class of Citizens which they have here taken under their Protection." Unrepresented at the official exchange of documents that transferred Louisiana, which took place behind closed doors in the New Orleans Cabildo, Maurice Populus and other free black militiamen made an early attempt to claim citizenship and offer their loyalty to the United States. It was a preemptive act. Haitian independence had been declared less than a year before and the free black militia of Francophone Louisiana and the large free colored community of which they were a part seemed to apprehensive whites to have all the makings of a dangerous fifth column. Free people of color were already generally cast as the villains of the Haitian Revolution for having made common cause with the enslaved. Secretary of State James Madison had believed that fomenting rebellion among Louisiana's blacks was one of the strategies considered by Leclerc during his campaign to reclaim Saint-Domingue, which made the black troops of Louisiana especially suspect.[36]

Populus and his fellow militiamen must have hoped to nip such suspicions in the bud when they quickly offered their military services "to the government as a Corps of Volunteers agreeable to any arrangement which may be thought expedient." Claiming to be "free Citizens of Louisiana," they proclaimed their "Sentiments of respect & Esteem and sincere attachment to the Government of the United States," before that government had a chance to call them in and strip them of the leadership they claimed and the arms they had traditionally borne. Claiborne was uneasy about the potential threat posed by the militia, but on balance believed that recognizing it could have a palliative effect on the territory's free blacks, while suppressing it could well stir them to precisely the hostility the U.S. government feared. Territorial legislators, however, did not share his view, and the free black troops were not included in the militia acts of 1804–5, 1806, and 1807. The men continued to act as a corps as they organized themselves to witness marriages, but they probably donned mufti for their walk to the cathedral, perhaps quietly pinning on their medals once the doors to the sanctuary were safely closed.[37]

The territorial legislature dealt other blows to Louisiana's free black population in 1806 and 1808 with the adoption of new laws that shrank their freedoms and limited their horizons. The Black Code of 1806 stipulated that only enslaved people above the age of thirty could be freed, and ordered the newly manumitted expelled from the territory. These provisions obviously aimed to forestall the growth of a newly freed population that might be inclined to rebellion and young enough to carry it off, but the effect was to cripple the manumission by free people of color of children and other young relatives born into slavery. This was a practice that had played a crucial role in reconstituting families beyond the bounds of slavery among New Orleans free blacks for generations and its suppression would have been keenly felt.[38] Other articles of the new code reinforced the distinction between slave and free, underlining the legal gulf the state opened between free people of color and family members still in bondage. And one provision struck a particularly humiliating blow at militia members. "As slaves may say they are free," section twenty-one of the code begins, "free people of color who carry arms shall have with them a certificate attesting their freedom, or they shall be liable to lose their arms."[39]

The comprehensive civil code of law adopted for territorial Louisiana in 1808 constrained and challenged free black families in still other ways. On the first day of December 1805, a free African-born woman named Ignes married Francisco, an enslaved Bambara man, with Captain François Dorville serving as witness. Theirs was the last of the eleven marriages between enslaved and free people that took place before the Civil Code of 1808 proclaimed that "Free persons and slaves are incapable of contracting marriage together; the celebration of such marriages is forbidden, and the marriage is void; it is the same with respect to the marriages contracted by free white persons with free people of color." The new civil code also provided for the forced heirship of legitimate children and complicated inheritance by natural children. Natural children were defined as "illegitimate children who have been acknowledged by their father"who were not "children born from an incestuous or adulterous connection." Children born to an unmarried white father and a free woman of color could be recognized as natural children, but they could never be legitimated. Their capacity to inherit was always vulnerable to the claims of more-distant white relatives. The children of free men and women of color who cohabited without benefit of marriage were at less risk, but were still exposed.[40]

The 1808 code did offer a remedy that prompted free black couples long bound together by children and household to make the trip to the altar. "Children born out of marriage, except those who are born from incestuous or adulterous connection, may be legitimated by the subsequent marriage of their father and mother." Once the implications of the 1808 law registered among the city's free blacks, a rash of weddings legitimating well-established families ensued. Joseph Beaulieu and Josepha Jalió were one of thirty free black couples that legitimated children at weddings celebrated between 1811 and 1824. They began their family together in 1790 with the birth of daughter Luisa. Two other children followed in the next four years, but it was perhaps the surprise appearance of little Urbano in 1808 that prompted them to marry in the spring of 1811, legitimating all four. Juan Castelan and Juana Nivet legitimated ten children ranging from twenty-five-year-old Juan to two-year-old Melicen later that same year. Lieutenant Jean Doliole stood witness at ten weddings between 1812 and 1818 before tying the knot himself in 1818 with Hortanza Dussuau, who had borne him three children over the previous nine years.[41]

When free black Orleanians like Beaulieu, Castelan, and Doliole legitimated their children through marriage, financial practicalities probably weighed most heavily in their decision to wed. At the same time, they and the rest of the 160 other ancestral Orleanians who exchanged nuptial vows between 1810 and 1819 were perhaps also motivated by a desire to project themselves as culturally and politically distinct from the newly arrived Haitian refugees. The Haitian *mûlatresse* arrived in New Orleans with a reputation for licentiousness, and the circumstances of refugee status produced evidence to confirm it in the form of "fatherless" children. More than half of the free infants of color baptized in New Orleans between 1810 and 1812 were born to refugee mothers, who also bore two-thirds of the free colored children for whom no father could be named in the baptismal register. By contrast, fathers were unlisted in only a fifth of the births to Orleanian free women of color during these years. The details of these numbers would have been beyond the awareness of the people living in New Orleans, but the baby boom among unattached colored refugee women likely registered in some way on their consciousness. Among white people, it would have exacerbated the general alarm raised by the refugee influx.[42]

Marriage was a way for free black Orleanians to distinguish themselves from the Dominguan refugees, reassert their attachment to European cultural norms, and implicitly reject the interracial family formation that produced the trope of the politically treacherous *gens de couleur* of the Haitian Revolution. The uptick in apparently fatherless mixed-race babies was not the only refugee-related phenomenon that put Orleanians of color on the defensive in this respect. Free black Dominguan women were three times as likely as Orleanians to name French-born men as the fathers of their children between 1810 and 1819.[43] The stereotype of the free black woman who attached herself to a European man in preference to men of her own race became manifest in New Orleans after 1809. The march of Orleanians of color to the altar had its roots in the eighteenth century, but the surge in the second decade of the nineteenth century suggests a conscious campaign to establish a counterexample to the refugees.

Free Orleanians of color began to whittle away at pejorative presumptions of their immorality and political sympathies with their resolute march into matrimony. They did so without the visible participation of the free black militia that had traditionally supported the institution. Left to languish without the dignity of a commission, hundreds of militiamen mothballed their uniforms and their pride for seven years after the Louisiana Purchase. Paradoxically, a massive slave uprising north of the city in January 1811, commonly known as the Deslondes Rebellion, was what finally gave the militia an opportunity to reconstitute itself. Dormant militiamen presented themselves to the regular federal troops and local white militia who set off to quash what was the largest slave revolt in U.S. history. Although the rebellion's leader, Charles Deslondes, was a Louisiana-born mulatto, contemporary whites believed that Haiti provided inspiration for the uprising. The participation of armed free black men in the expedition against the rebels announced in dramatic terms Orleanians' intention to distance themselves from association with the Haitian menace. Four years later, when the city prepared for the Battle of New Orleans, which ended the War of 1812, four regiments of free black militia totaling more than 700 men were mustered without any of the hesitation that had marked the American administration a decade earlier.[44]

After the Battle of New Orleans in 1815, free black militiamen could openly don their uniforms and decorations as they performed their sentry duty at the weddings of their friends and kin. The festive tableau that combined military ceremonial display and massed family and friends resumed at the cathedral under a new generation of militiamen. The nuptials of Maria Populus, daughter of the First Battalion's second-highest-ranking officer, Major Vincent Populus, brought out the organization's top brass the summer after the battle. As she exchanged vows with Hipolito Lafargue, first lieutenant and uncle Maurice Populus, Quartermaster Joseph Cabaret, and Sergeant Joseph Camps stood prominently among the crowd of well-wishers who attended the ceremony. The Populus brothers, Vincent and Maurice, witnessed twelve weddings between 1815 and 1830, either individually or together, and Sergeant Joseph Camps, nine. Noel Carriere II, who served as a first lieutenant at the Battle of New Orleans, was a leader in the revival during the 1820s, beginning with the weddings of his sister Maria Deseada and brother Baltasar in the summer of 1822. Frequently joined by fellow militiaman and brother-in-law Pierre Laviolette, Carriere served at seven more weddings before the end of the decade. The proud wedding traditions of the city's free blacks may have gone unnoticed by white Orleanians and visitors to the city in the 1820s, but the cathedral's rector, Aloysius Moni, revealed his awareness of its history when he registered the wedding of Marie Celeste Claver and Leandre Bijout in 1829. Moni dignified lead witness Noel Carriere II, continuing the role his father had pioneered, with the title "Sieur,"—Sir—when he entered his name into the act.[45]

The members of Saint-Domingue's free black militia were also proponents of marriage, according to historian Stuart King, but this aspect of their history and culture did not survive the rupture of revolution and its aftermath. A regiment of nearly 300 men of Dominguan descent was mustered into the second battalion of the free black militia for the Battle of New Orleans, but they did not figure prominently as witnesses or as grooms after 1815. The few Dominguan veterans of the battle who appear as grooms do highlight, however, how much more likely it was for refugee men to find a way into the close-knit free black Orleanian community than it was for their sisters. Hipolito Lafargue, who fought in the Haitian second battalion in the Battle of New Orleans, was one of twenty-six men of Dominguan descent to marry into a New Orleans family. When he wed Maria Martina Populus in 1815, he joined one of the most prominent and oldest of the city's free black families. Perhaps his service in the battle won him acceptance into the Populus clan, but the dynamics of family economies were more likely responsible.

Maria Martina's father, Vincent Populus, was a partner in a thriving shoemaking business with his brother, Maurice. Their shops occupied prominent locations in the center of the city, on Bourbon Street, in the 1810s and 1820s. In 1816 Maurice purchased an enslaved skilled cobbler, an indication both of his prosperity and the need for additional workers in the business. Welcoming a refugee groom into this family would have brought an extra pair of hands to the enterprise at a significantly lower cost than the purchase of yet another skilled hand. During the 1820s, when the city's population nearly doubled and brought even more demand for their products, the Populus family acquired another refugee son-in-law when Maurice's daughter married Agustin Alexandre of Port-au-Prince. Orleanians showed a strong preference for marrying one another throughout the 1810s and 1820s, when more than 80 percent of them married other Orleanians. There were only forty-five adult free men of color in the city for every one hundred free women, so competition for grooms was stiff. The twenty Dominguan men who found brides among Orleanians in the 1820s broke into the city's free colored establishment thanks to a booming economy and the demand for free black husbands.[46]

The demography that helped Dominguan men seriously disadvantaged female refugees and refugee-descended women in the New Orleans marriage market. New Orleans brides had to fight the same odds, but they could offer both native and foreign grooms the advantages of their connections to local economic and social networks. Statistics tell a chilling story about refugee women's chances to emulate their Orleanian counterparts in the trip to the altar. There were 3,682 adult free women of color in New Orleans in 1830. It is fair to assume that at least half of them were of Dominguan ancestry, but they made up less than a fourth of brides of color between 1820 and 1829, while Orleanians supplied nearly 60 percent. A free woman of Dominguan origins had about one chance in a hundred of marrying at the end of the 1820s. A wedding took place in 1828 and 1829 for every twenty adult white women in the population, and for every forty-three free women of color of Orleanian ancestry, but for only one in every ninety-seven free women of color of Dominguan ancestry. The dismal marriage prospects of Dominguan women are masked by the overall picture for these years. Of the 272 weddings that took place in 1828 and 1829, nearly a third were among people of African descent, a proportion equal to their representation in the total free population of New Orleans. Yet, the free women of color who did marry overcame daunting demographic odds. While white women, outnumbered more than two-to-one by white men, presumably had no trouble marrying, free women of color suffered the inverse of that ratio. That weddings between free people of color continued apace in New Orleans—about twice a month in 1825 and roughly once a week in 1829—suggests no small degree of resolve among them. But the registers reveal the divergent paths of Orleanians and Dominguans. More than two-thirds of the weddings in the 1820s involved people of New Orleans ancestry, and Orleanian brides outnumbered Dominguan brides more than two-to-one.[47]

Karl Bernhard, the Duke of Saxe-Weimar, visited New Orleans in 1826, a year when some twenty-three free women of color took free black husbands at the altar of St. Louis Cathedral. He nonetheless pronounced that "the quadroons on their part regard the negroes and mulattoes with contempt, and will not mix with them." Shunning marriage with men of their own race, "nothing remains for them but to be the friends, as it is termed, of the white men." Bernhard's account, like Thomas Ashe's twenty years before, assures readers that the free women of color of New Orleans typically bypassed matrimony in favor of concubinage. Both men may indeed have seen unmarried free women of color whose partners were white men. But the free women of color that Ashe saw in 1806 and those that Bernhard saw in 1826 were separated by more than years. Partnerships between Orleanian women of color and white men were not uncommon in New Orleans in 1806, though as the next chapter shows, these unions were not the prurient dalliances that they were presumed to be. This practice, however, began to die out among Orleanians as the colonial era drew to a close. By the 1820s, when Bernhard offered his observations, daughters born to white fathers and Orleanian free women of color increasingly chose marriage to men of their own race. The free women of color in New Orleans who did not marry were more likely than not those who could not marry, the women whose Dominguan origins handicapped their chances in the city's crowded free black marriage market.

Marguerite Henriette Toutant was among the many daughters of African-descended mothers and European fathers who did not replicate their mothers' mode of family formation. She was the first in her mother's line of descent to wed. Her mother was absent from her 1793 nuptials, and there was no mention of her white father in the marriage act, which, like so many others in the 1790s was presided over by the ubiquitous Noel Carriere. At first glance, her ancestry seems to reflect perfectly the paradigm so often assumed to apply to couplings between African-descended women and white men during the colonial period. White men, with the deficit of European women in colonial Louisiana, were supposed to have formed liaisons with women of color, often when the women were still enslaved. At some point, the white partner might free his children and, less frequently, their mother. Had Marguerite been produced of such circumstances, the absence of her unmarried mother and the wedding act's silence on her paternity would appear unremarkable. Yet Marguerite's family history is, if not remarkable, at least instructive of the ways that free black lives unfolded in patterns that confound simple generalization.

Marguerite Toutant was not freed by her white lover, nor was she the beneficiary of a European father's largesse. She was not one of the industrious enslaved women who exploited the provision for self-purchase that came with the promulgation of Spanish slave law in Louisiana in 1769, nor was she rescued from slavery by a generous family member who paid her freedom price. None of these routes to freedom, each common to one degree or another during the Spanish regime, maps Marguerite's path. Marguerite Toutant was born free to a free black mother. The roots of her liberty reach back to 1738, when her grandmother's family was one of two freed by the will of a white settler named Joseph Meunier. Leveillé and his partner, Manon, were freed along with their children Jean Baptiste, Marie Jeanne, Françoise, and Marguerite Toutant's grandmother, a seven-year-old named Marianne. Marianne gave birth to a daughter eleven years later in 1749 and named her Marguerite. At a time when other slaveholders were promoting the formation of nuclear families welded together by sacramental marriage to guarantee a growing workforce for themselves and their descendants, Meunier adopted a contrary course. Leveillé, Manon, and their children were all identified as black, so Meunier's gesture was not born of blood ties. The spare language of his will offers no clues about his motives. For reasons that fit none of the typical manumission narratives of colonial Louisiana, Marguerite Toutant's mother was born free, descended from one of the nuclear families that set a precocious precedent for those that only became common generations later.[48]

Marguerite Toutant's grandmother, known as Marianne Pantalon, did not marry. The official number of free men of color in 1769, twenty years after Marguerite's birth, stood at less than forty. Marianne Pantalon would have had difficulty finding a free black man to marry, even had she wished to emulate her parents' example. She bore her first child, a son identified as a mulatto, in 1746. But Marianne Pantalon did not form a lasting partnership with the white father of her firstborn. Three years later she bore Marguerite, identified in her baptismal record as a *negritte* and elsewhere as a *négresse*, suggesting a father of unmixed African descent. When Marguerite came of childbearing age in the mid-1770s, her odds of finding a free man of color to marry were not significantly better than her mother's had been, but unlike her mother, she did form a life partnership with a white man. Martin Barthelemy Toutant Beauregard was a bachelor merchant of forty-six from a small village on the outskirts of La Rochelle in France when Marguerite bore his first child in 1773, a daughter who was named for her mother. Three more daughters were born to the couple over the next seven years, Françoise, Louise, and Emelite. All of them, like their mother, took the surname Toutant.[49]

Marguerite Toutant was the only one of the four sisters to marry and recapitulate the example of her great-grandparents, Leveillé and Manon, but Françoise and Louise both formed life partnerships with free men of color. Esteban Dorville, son of *pardo* militia captain François Dorville was the father of Louise's children, while Philippe Populus, another man with ties to the militia, shared a life with Françoise. Sacramental marriage took root among the children of the next generation. Louise's daughter, Victoria Dorville, married Honoré Rillieux in 1819, and her sister, Adelaide, wed Cyril Arnoult in 1823. Honoré Toutant Beauregard, Emelite's son, took Maria Kernion as his bride early in 1823.[50] Marguerite Pantalon Toutant formed a relationship with a white man and bore him children, but she neither replicated a long family tradition of such arrangements nor instigated their continuation among her children and grandchildren. She did not live long enough to defend herself against Harriet Martineau's observation that "quadroon girls of New Orleans are brought up by their mothers to be what they have been; the mistresses of white gentlemen."[51] How her granddaughters Victoria and Adelaide and their husbands might have reacted to her assault on their respectability can only be imagined.

The Toutant women were not alone in their trajectory. Marianne Brion was the daughter of a French father and his African-born slave. Sold away to another owner, she and her four children were freed in 1772 *graciosa*—without charge. A decade later a free man of color left her considerable property, an act that suggests that he was probably the father of at least some of her children. Brion's daughter, Marianne Piquery, diverged from her mother's path and around 1790 formed a partnership with a French-man, Michel Meffre-Rouzan. Over the next three decades they had seven children together, all of whom Meffre-Rouzan acknowledged in baptismal and other records. Like many other such men, Meffre-Rouzan never married and remained involved in the lives and financial affairs of his partner, her mother, and his children and grandchildren for the rest of his life. Notwithstanding the apparent stability of the biracial family that Piquery and Meffre-Rouzan formed, their own children did not adopt this family formation. Their daughter, Jaqueline Meffre-Rouzan, married a Port-au-Prince native in 1818 when she was nineteen. She brought $1,500 earned from her career as a couturier while her refugee groom brought only his social capital as an eligible free man of color. Jaqueline's white father witnessed the marriage contract. When daughter Maria married in 1826, her mother accompanied her to the notary's office to witness her daughter's declaration that she brought $2,500 of her own earnings to the marriage. Groom Jean Fleming declared nothing of value. Economic advantage clearly did not dictate these young women's choice of mate, nor did a desire to lighten their progeny through alliances with white men. Both chose marriage to men of their own racial ancestry rather than the presumably more financially and racially advantageous sponsorship of a white lover. When Michel and Marianne's son Jacques Meffre-Rouzan married his dying partner, free woman of color Catherine Andre Cavelier, in 1825, he legitimated their two children and fell into line with his family's new matrimonial tradition.[52]

The daughters of many other biracial partnerships followed suit. Julie Tio, the daughter of free woman of color Victoria Wiltz and her life partner, Spaniard Marcos Tio, married Louis Coussey in 1824. Her cousin Victoire Tio, daughter of Marcos's brother Francisco and Josephine Macarty, married three years later. Carlos Decoudreaux was born to a free woman of color named Fanchonette and a white man who served as a captain in the Spanish regiment in New Orleans. Decoudreaux's father could not marry Fanchonette but remained faithful to her and provided generously for the family they made together. His son mapped out a different future for himself and his own daughters. He married a Havana-born free woman of color in 1789, and in 1824 his daughter Josephine married free man of color Francisco Trevino. Isabel Cazelar, the daughter of a white father and a free woman of color named Charlotte Wiltz, married a free man of color from Attakapas in 1806, and her brother married the mixed-race daughter of a former Spanish colonial officer in 1823. The children of the white Samuel P. Moore and free woman of color Dorothée Lassize likewise celebrated sacramental marriages, all in the 1820s. Marie Antoinette Moore married in November of 1825, with the parents of bride and groom looking on. Samuel Moore II married Marie Françoise Lowell in December of 1826. Euranie Eulalie Moore married Noel Dalcour on the first day of December 1828, and Charlotte Eugenie Moore married Eloy Valmont Mathieu, a free black refugee of the Haitian Revolution, in September 1829.[53]

Marriage, not concubinage, was the tradition New Orleans free people of color established and perpetuated. The historical invisibility of the sacramentally and legally bound families they created is a disquieting reflection of the power of expectation, past and present. Women of African descent were supposed to be hypersexual Jezebels, beings whose libidinous essence inexorably roused white male lust. The exploitation of black women by white men turned on this convenient trope. So, too, did the rubric of true—white—womanhood. The assemblage of qualities that constituted the perfect antebellum lady, domesticity, piety, modesty, and above all, contained sexuality, could be imagined to be the sole preserve of white women only if they were categorically denied their black sisters. Free or enslaved, black women's incapacity to be wives and mothers who domesticated the passions of their husbands was an essential fiction in antebellum America. In the slave South, it obviously guaranteed the sexual privilege of white men, but it served a powerful function in northern abolitionist circles too. As we shall see, the figure of the sexually exploited woman of color was a central element in antislavery discourse.[54]

Most African-descended women in antebellum America were vulnerable to rape and sexual exploitation by white men, but universalizing their plight hides from view black women and men who contested the awful paradigm by their example. Contemporaries conveniently ignored the weddings that Noel Carriere witnessed, the celebrations that announced the capacity of black women and men to match the moral and social standards claimed exclusively by the whites around them. History, as a consequence, has been left with the quadroon *placée* to represent New Orleans free black womanhood, paradoxically confirming the mythology that served antebellum white men's fantasies so well, and tragically erasing the black models of true womanhood who insisted on a less convenient truth.

CHAPTER FOUR

Bachelor Patriarchs

Life Partnerships across the Color Line

The connexion now and then lasts for life: usually for several years.
In the latter case, when the time comes for the gentleman to take
a white wife, the dreadful news reaches his Quadroon partner. . . .
Many commit suicide: more die brokenhearted. Some men continue
the connexion after marriage. Every Quadroon woman believes that
her partner will prove an exception to the rule of desertion. Every
white lady believes that her husband has been an exception to the
rule of seduction.

—Harriet Martineau, 1837[1]

More than a little heartbreak touched the life of Agnes Mathieu, a free woman of color born into slavery in Louisiana in 1759. The
1837 passage by Harriet Martineau that opens this chapter proclaims that
emotional suffering was the inescapable fate of mixed-race women who
became the companions of white men because their white lovers would
almost always abandon them for a legitimate white wife. Agnes Mathieu
never knew that particular grief. Instead, it was her French-born lover,
Mathieu Devaux, who lost her to matrimony nearly a quarter of a century
after he had gone to court to gain her freedom. Their story stands out for
its inversion of the abandonment trope, but in other ways it is typical of
the partnerships between African-descended women and white men in
late colonial New Orleans. Permanent bachelorhood marked most of the
men, yet their attentiveness to the large families they created with their
free black partners paralleled what was expected of contemporary married white patriarchs. Fidelity to a doomed love that could be legitimated
by neither church nor state was supposed to be a hallmark of the New
Orleans free women of color, but it was just as often a defining feature of
the men who made their lives with them. Before the refugee influx of 1809,
and alongside the development of marriage between free people of color,
many free women of color did cohabit with white men. The contours of
these relationships, however, were almost as poor a fit for the "quadroon

connexions" immortalized by Harriet Martineau as were the marriages of families such as the Carrieres.

Agnes Mathieu grew to adulthood just upriver from New Orleans in a region known as Côte des Allemands. Settled by immigrants from German-speaking parts of France and Switzerland, the area was characterized by small plantations and tightly knit extended families. Agnes was born about 1759, and when her original owner died in 1771 a neighbor bought her, along with two brothers and her mother. The young woman came of age at a fortuitous moment in Louisiana's history, just as Spanish slave laws came into effect and put liberty within reach. An owner could free a slave by means of a simple notarial act under Spanish law, which also provided for *coartación*, or self-purchase. Any enslaved person had the right to purchase their own freedom for a fair price established by a team of two appraisers, one representing the slave, the other representing the owner. A third party, a family member or a friend, could initiate *coartación* on behalf of an enslaved person, triggering the appraisal process. Nearly 200 people gained their freedom through self-purchase between 1771 and 1779, most of them quite easily. Agnes, however, traveled a rocky road to the liberty that was finally granted her in the last month of 1779.

Agnes was not a likely candidate for self-purchase. Enslaved women could earn money from marketing, mending, and laundering for cash on Sundays and after the official workday was done. But Agnes lived in the country, where such opportunities were much more limited than they were in the bustling town center of New Orleans, and she was only nineteen, hardly old enough to have accrued enough money for her freedom price. Her *coartación* would have to come at the hands of a generous third party, and it did. Forty-year-old Mathieu Devaux appeared at the office of the city treasurer on December 15, 1778, to deposit the 425 piastres that appraisers agreed was a fair price for the young woman's freedom. Declaring that he was not married, had no relatives with claims on him, and was in possession of some 1,500 or 1,600 piastres, he demonstrated that there were no legal or financial obstacles to his purchase of Agnes's freedom. A court deputy set out for the Côte des Allemands to hand deliver the tribunal's order to Agnes's owner, Barbara Herterlin Harang, instructing her to grant the young woman her liberty.

Deputy Pedro Cowley returned to New Orleans from the Côte des Allemands empty-handed, reporting that Madame Harang "did not wish to give the said negro slave her freedom, contested the court order, and refused to comply." Mathieu Devaux petitioned the court to reassert its order more forcefully, and another hapless official messenger was dispatched from New Orleans to the plantation upriver, this time with a three-day deadline for compliance. Madame Harang refused again. Months dragged by and the American Revolution intervened. Devaux was among the artillery corps that Governor Bernardo de Galvez deployed against the British at Baton Rouge in the early autumn of 1779. Once the battle was won in late September, Devaux renewed his efforts to free Agnes, taking his cause to the tribunal presided over by the man who had recently commanded him in combat. Governor Galvez ordered Agnes freed. The governor's authority was irrefutable. Madame Harang handed Agnes over to Mathieu Devaux as the year 1779 drew to a close.[2]

Agnes was now free. Or was she? Mathieu Devaux's 1810 will suggests that she merely traded a mistress for a master. Declaring himself to be seventy-two years old and a bachelor, Devaux stipulated that his estate was to be divided among his six living natural children and the five children of his deceased daughter, Marguerite. All seven of his children, he noted, were the children of "my former slave, Agnes."[3] With this passing reference, Devaux complicates speculation about the circumstances that produced freedom for the mother of his children. The widow Harang's objection to parting with Agnes may not have originated in bull-headed opposition to Spanish law's infringement on the privileges she had enjoyed as a slaveholder under French rule. Perhaps she believed that Devaux dangled the promise of freedom before Agnes in order to gain unobstructed sexual access to her. That Devaux identified Agnes as his former slave in his will suggests at the very least that she came to his household indebted to him in some way. Hers may have been an obligation Agnes willingly undertook to gain her liberty and Devaux's purchase of her freedom born of genuine affection for her, but the circumscribed nature of her agency is clear.

Mutual affection may well have developed between Agnes and Devaux as one child after another was born to them, but Agnes did not remain true to her emancipator. In 1803 she bore a child to a free man of color named Joseph Mathieu and three years later she married him.[4] When he drew up his will some years later, Mathieu Devaux left nothing to Agnes, and although it was not unusual for white fathers to bypass free black mothers and leave all to their mixed-race children, her omission from his bequests registers more as the act of a spurned lover than that of a callous rake. Evidence of Agnes's economic success at the outset of the nineteenth century suggests that she gained enough material and emotional independence to free herself from her connection with Devaux. In 1806 she owned an enslaved woman who was described as being good at all types of plantation work, and especially good at selling milk and vegetables, implying that Agnes was proprietress of a successful dairy and vegetable farm. A couple of years later she bought an African woman and a mulatto boy, purchases that amounted to nearly a thousand dollars.[5] When Agnes married free man of color Joseph Mathieu, she did so on her own terms.

The lives of Agnes and Mathieu Devaux expose the ambiguous nature of relationships between free women of color and white men that developed in the first decades after the introduction of Spanish slave law.[6] At the same time, they exemplify two opposing but typical scenarios. On the one hand, Agnes followed in the footsteps of other free women of color, who increasingly chose marriage to men who shared their racial ancestry after the turn of the nineteenth century. Her early life, however, draws back the curtain on the figure of the white bachelor patriarch. Such men were numerous in late colonial New Orleans, and much more visible in the historical record than the carefree cads that commentators such as Harriet Martineau condemned in the 1830s.

The contours and chronology of partnerships between white men and free women of color in late colonial New Orleans have repeatedly been elided with those that typified other places and other times. Those who visited the city in the 1820s and 1830s observed the improvisational response of the refugee generation and presumed it a tradition of long standing among the city's free women of color. Decades earlier, late colonial observers assumed that the relationships between white men and free women of color in New Orleans duplicated the role of the *ménagère* in Saint-Domingue and the established conventions of concubinage practiced throughout the French Antilles.[7] The sexual exploitation of women of African descent, rooted in the absolute power of enslaver over the enslaved, was universal in the Atlantic world. The ways that white men and black women negotiated their relations when freedom entered the equation shared that origin and never shed the imbalance of power inherent in it. Otherwise, the forms taken by such relationships were as various as the times and places that produced them. French colonial Saint-Domingue spawned the *ménagère*, Spanish colonial New Orleans the bachelor patriarch.

Demography and law came together to generate circumstances that favored life partnerships between white men and free women of color in late colonial New Orleans. There were nearly two white men for every white woman there in 1777, and two free women of color for every free man of color. The sex ratio remained skewed in 1791, when there were only 912 white women for 1,474 white men. It was statistically impossible for every New Orleanian to marry within the racial category to which he or she was assigned until well after 1800.[8] The liberalization of Spanish slave law produced a large free black population that represented a fourth of the free population of New Orleans by 1791. More than a third of the free women in New Orleans in 1791 were of African descent. Partnership with a free woman of color was the obvious option for white men who desired a settled conjugal life but could not or did not wish to contract a marriage with a woman of unmixed European descent.[9] While there was no law specifically prohibiting marriage between white men and women of color under Spanish law, in 1778 Louisiana planters had drafted for royal approval a new slave code that proscribed marriage and concubinage between whites and people of African descent. Although the Spanish Crown never enacted this legislation, known as the *Loi Municipal*, its provisions supply a telling reflection of elite attitudes toward interracial unions and the hostile environment for them. The introduction of Spanish law in Louisiana made it technically legal for a white man to marry a free woman of color, but the planters' proposal of the *Loi Municipal* made it a risky action that could be outlawed if the Crown decided to promulgate the legislation. Few male New Orleanians bet on the planters' failure. There is evidence of only three interracial marriages taking place in Spanish colonial New Orleans.[10]

Rejecting a bald choice between marriage and illicit sexual promiscuity, many white men in Spanish colonial New Orleans formed long-term and life partnerships with free women of color. The heyday of such relationships lasted from the late 1770s until the end of the eighteenth century, when sex ratios among white Orleanians evened out and marriage among free people of color became prevalent.[11] In addition to a timeframe that spanned roughly a quarter of a century at the end of the colonial period, these partnerships were usually marked by several other distinguishing characteristics. The fathers, for example, typically acknowledged their paternity both officially and within their extended European families. The clergy routinely employed the convention of entering "father unknown" in the baptismal records of children born to unmarried interracial couples, a practice that has generally been taken as an indication of white fathers' desire to mask their identities and their relationships. The archives are filled, however, with paternal acknowledgements, tacit and overt. Many fathers rejected the clergy's offer of a cloak of anonymity and had themselves clearly identified in their children's baptismal and marriage records.

Another feature common to these interracial families was the incorporation of the unofficial families into the European kin, social, and economic networks of the father. White family members were often enlisted as godparents and guardians of the children, and many white fathers entrusted their children's affairs to socially prominent friends and business associates. The church, state, and social elites all opposed sexual partnerships across the color line—the church for moral reasons, the state to establish economic and political order, and the elites to buttress the racial hierarchy that protected their interests as plantation masters. This united front of disapproval and obstruction undoubtedly played a part in the rising popularity of marriage among free people of color, but it did not consign the couples whose stories unfold in this chapter to a veiled social netherworld in New Orleans.

The men who formed families with free women of color in late colonial New Orleans shared a constellation of behaviors and practices but were otherwise a diverse lot. Many of them were newcomers, outsiders, and economically challenged in some way, making them unpromising competitors for the scarce supply of European women in the city and its environs. But a number of them were wealthy scions of prosperous families, and more than a few shared the surnames of illustrious figures in American history. Although Catholics of Mediterranean ancestry were presumed by Anglophone Protestant observers to be culturally predisposed to the kind of immorality exemplified by interracial sex, the life partnerships between free women of color and white men in New Orleans observed neither a confessional nor a linguistic divide.

The permanent bachelorhood of the men who formed relationships with free women of color in late colonial New Orleans together with the pains many of the men took to create families that reassembled the markers of conventional contemporary families are particularly striking features of these partnerships. Shared households, notions of paternal duty, recognition of filial obligations fulfilled, and attention to extended families swelled by grandchildren characterized many of these men's lives. They did not abandon their free black partners to make a legitimate marriage with white women, but instead found ways to constitute the ideals of patriarchal responsibility and fidelity in a family form that was otherwise fundamentally illicit. Some of these bachelor fathers succeeded brilliantly in eluding laws designed to prohibit the formation of families like theirs in ways that mocked legal constructions that yoked patriarchy to the racial hierarchy on which slavery rested.

Historians have explored the interracial relationships of colonial New Orleans with increasing sensitivity and penetrating analysis over the past two decades. Hidden in plain sight in New Orleans sacramental and notarial records for centuries, the stories of dozens of such partnerships have now been recovered and described so extensively as to leave no doubt that they were widespread and well known among contemporaries.[12] The form and chronology of interracial relationships that involved a "bachelor patriarch" has not yet been explicitly singled out for investigation, though they seem to have been the majority of interracial partnerships for which there is evidence. When considered together with the marriages between free black partners discussed in the previous chapter, they suggest that the typical experience of a woman of color born free in colonial New Orleans was that of a long-term relationship with a single partner.

The partner of Martin Barthelemy Toutant Beauregard, whom we met in the last chapter, was one such woman. Martin Barthelemy came to New Orleans in the 1750s from a village near La Rochelle on the west coast of France with his older brother, Jacques, who brought his bride with him. Martin Barthelemy, in his twenties, was unmarried and remained a bachelor for the rest of his life. As middling merchants, the brothers were economically comfortable, but there was nothing in Martin Barthelemy's lineage or modest success in Louisiana to make him a particularly attractive marriage partner. When he reached his forties, he began a relationship that lasted for the rest of his life with free woman of color Marguerite, freeborn daughter of Marianne Pantalon. About 1773 she bore Martin Barthelemy's first child, a daughter named Marguerite after her mother. As we saw in the previous chapter, he provided generously in his 1792 will for this child, her sisters Françoise, Louise, and Emelite, and their mother, Marguerite, by making them his universal heirs. Implicitly he did more than simply leave them material wealth. Declaring that his brother's widow owed him several thousand piastres for having managed her business, he demanded that she settle her debt with his estate. The widow Beauregard was thus forced to acknowledge the existence of her brother-in-law's mixed-race family and their primacy in his affections.

The mixed-race Toutant Beauregards were rendered visible in New Orleans for generations to come by their adoption of the family name. Marguerite was identified in documents produced after Martin Barthelemy's death as the widow Toutant and her daughters claimed the Toutant name as well. Until the 1820s, the branch of the Toutant Beauregard family descended from Martin Barthelemy and Marguerite was distinguished from the descendants of Martin Barthelemy's only brother, Jacques, by the use of the abbreviated version of the family surname, Toutant. But when Emilite Toutant's son Honoré married a free woman of color in 1823 at St. Louis Cathedral, he claimed Beauregard as part of his name. Honoré also saw to it that the four children born to him and his wife over the next eight years were inscribed in the sacramental records as Beauregards. Five years before Honoré's marriage, his second cousin, the white grandson of his great-uncle, Jacques Toutant Beauregard, was baptized. This child, Honoré's white cousin, Pierre Gustave Toutant Beauregard, grew up to attend and teach at the U.S. Military Academy at West Point. On April 12, 1861, he dramatically turned his expertise to the secessionist cause, ordering provisional Confederate forces to fire on U.S. troops garrisoned at Fort Sumter in Charleston, South Carolina. As a brigadier general in the Confederate army, P. G. T. Beauregard, as he was known, was victorious at the First Battle of Bull Run at Manassas, Virginia, later that year. Beauregard's fame as a Confederate warrior, commemorated with an imposing equestrian monument prominently placed at the entry to a large public park in New Orleans, has diverted attention from the racially entangled history of his family.[13] The relatively small world of Orleanians who could trace their ancestry to the colonial era made it unlikely, however, that General Beauregard was ignorant of the African-descended second cousins who shared his name when he went to war to defend slavery.

The three Hazeur brothers, Louis, François, and Antoine, came from a more socially prominent French colonial family than Martin Barthelemy Toutant Beauregard. When their sister, Marie Jean Constance, married Pierre François Dreux in 1767, more than a half dozen representatives of the region's planter and military elite witnessed the ceremony.[14] The brothers, meanwhile, inherited from their Quebec-born military father a huge plantation on the outskirts of New Orleans that stretched from the Metairie ridge to Lake Pontchartrain. The three men, born between 1746 and 1754, came of age too late to follow their father into French service in Louisiana, so they left the colony to serve with France's troops stationed in Guadeloupe. They returned to Louisiana as middle-aged bachelors in the 1780s and 1790s. Antoine, who came home after 1790, formed a partnership in Guadeloupe with Jeanette Favre, a free woman of color. Jeanette and the son she had borne Antoine traveled back with him to Louisiana. Brothers Louis and François entered relationships with free women of color in Louisiana and settled with Antoine and Jeanette into a sprawling complex of buildings on the family plantation.

Pierre Clement de Laussat, the French prefect who oversaw the transfer of Louisiana to American sovereignty in 1803, visited the Hazeur brothers and produced a famous account of their enviably well-managed plantation, marred, in his judgment, only by the presence of the brothers' numerous "offspring whose color betrayed their origin." Indeed, by the time Laussat paid his visit to the Hazeurs, fourteen young children were growing up under the watchful eyes of their fathers and mothers. Antoine's children, Louis, Antonia, Maria, Charles Homere, Thomas Hiacinthe, and Jean Baptiste; Louis's daughters, Helena, Antonita, and Luisa; and François's Paul, François Prospere, Susanne, Marie, and Eulalie, were doubtless kept by their mothers from disturbing the conversation of the brothers and their distinguished visitor. Echoing the French metropolitan critique of interracial relationships that had emerged in Saint-Domingue after the Seven Years' War, Laussat pronounced the Hazeurs' decision to forgo marriage in favor of partnerships with free women of color "their shameful side, their colonial weakness." Otherwise, "no others were better company, had a greater sense of honor or more loyalty, nor were more faithful Frenchmen."[15]

Laussat might have added that not many were more faithful fathers than the Hazeur brothers. None of the brothers ever married and all provided in various ways for their life partners and children. Antoine and Jeanette's union was the most fruitful, producing ten children by 1811. Perhaps because his family had grown so large, Antoine sold his brothers his share in the family plantation and bought another of his own nearby in 1816. In 1828, to get around legal prohibitions against his children's unfettered inheritance from him, he "sold" his sons this plantation. On another occasion he donated slaves to them. Antoine was not among the white fathers who made a point of acknowledging their paternity in their children's baptismal records, but both of his brothers were. Louis's partner Felicité was the slave of his widowed sister, Marie Jeanne Constance Dreux, when he began his relationship with her. His firstborn, Helena, was technically born a slave, but Louis signed her baptismal record in a bold hand. Mother and daughter were freed soon after. Louis maintained his practice of acknowledging paternity at his children's baptisms, signing the records of the four other children that Felicité bore him. Both Louis and Antoine involved their white relatives in the lives of their children. Two of Marie Jeanne Constance Dreux's children served as godparents to Louis's second-born, who was named Antonita after the white aunt who stood at the font with the family. Another daughter of Marie Jeanne Constance

Dreux, Pelagie, served as godmother to one of Antoine's daughters.[16] The Hazeurs' sister, the respectable widow of a member of a well-established colonial family, seems to have had no qualms about exposing her young daughters to the unconventional households of her brothers. Nor did the young white women's reputations seem to suffer from their relations with their mixed-race kin. Both Antonita and Pelagie married well.[17]

Like others born into such families, many of the children of Antoine, Louis, and François Hazeur married. Antoine and Jeanette's daughters Antonia and Matilde both married in the late 1820s.[18] Three of Louis and Felicité's daughters also married— Louisa in 1822, Susana in 1825, and Antoinette in 1831. Louisa and Susana married men born to married free people of color.[19] Sons of the Hazeur brothers also married. François Hazeur's son Prospero married a legitimately born free woman of color in 1812.[20] Antoine's firstborn, Louis, was one of the few Orleanian free men of color to take a refugee wife. His bride's $3,000 dowry made her a more attractive marriage prospect than most of her peers.[21]

When twenty-two-year-old Jean Pierre Cazelar formed a life partnership with a free woman of color named Charlotte Wiltz in the mid-1780s, he saw all around him older white men like Mathieu Devaux and Martin Barthelemy Toutant Beauregard who had made similar choices and were able to provide for their mixed-race families through bequests in their wills. There was no reason for him to think that his path would be different, yet he took special pains to make certain that his children's paternity was established at multiple sites. The baptismal records of all five of Cazelar's children by Charlotte Wiltz bear some indication that he was their father. The entries for his first three children, Adelaide's in 1787, Marie Felice's in 1789, and Isabel's in 1791, all bear his signature and various emendations to indicate his paternity. He was not the first white father to sign the baptismal records of his mixed-race children, but he was among the earliest and was the first to verify textual corrections made to the record with his signature. To Cazelar also belongs the distinction of being the

FIGURE 8. (opposite) Claiming paternity. Jean Pierre Cazelar acknowledged paternity of his five children by his free colored partner, Charlotte Wiltz, in these entries made in the sacramental registers of St. Louis Cathedral, New Orleans: Adelaide, September 15, 1787, SLC B12; Maria Feliciana, March 23, 1789, SLC B12, 97; Ysabel Pompona, May 5, 1791; Maria Luisa Marta, April 2, 1793; and Juan Pedro, April 18, 1800. Courtesy of the Office of Archives and Records, Archdiocese of New Orleans.

782

Adelayda Cacelar
quarterona
Libre

Murió a 13
Abril 1839.

En la Ygª Parrocquiª de Sᵊⁿ Luis de la Nueba Orleans en quinze de septiembre de ochenta y siete Yo el Sacristan mayor Bautice solemnem.ᵗᵉ y puse los santos oleos seg.ⁿ año de N.S. la Sta Ygª a una Nª n[ac]ida [...] mulato que nacio el veinte y siete de este mes del año que puse por nombre Adelayda hija de [...] mulata libre [...] fueron sus Padrinos Dⁿ Thomas Lopez, y Dª Margarita Lopez, y p.ᵃ q.ᵉ conste lo firme en dho dia, mes y año ut supra. Fr. Antonio de la Madrid — P.ᵉ Cuelar

---

645. 1

Maria Feliciana Guerbo Cacelar quarterona libre

En la Yglesia Parroq.ᵃᵈᵉ Sⁿ Luis de la Nueba Orleans en veinte y tres de Marzo de mil sete.ᶜⁱᵉⁿᵗᵒˢ ochenta y nueve Yo el infras.ᵗᵒ P.ᵉ [...] la Santa Ygª bautice solemnem.ᵗᵉ y puse los s.ᵗᵒˢ oleos seg.ⁿ a una niña quarterona, q.ᵉ nacio el dia diez y seis de N.º del año prox.ᵒ pasado, a q.ᵉ puse por nombre Maria Feliciana, hija de Carlota [...] libre [...] fueron P.ⁿᵒˢ Dⁿ Juan 3.ᵉ Cabatut, y Dª Mª Feliciana [...] espi.ˡ y p.ᵃ q.ᵉ conste lo firme dho dia, mes, y año, ut supra. Fr. Ubaldo Delgado — P.ᵉ Cuelar

---

1223

Ysabel Pompa
ria [...]
Cacelar
quarterona libre

En cinco de Mayo de mil setecientos noventa y uno Yo el infrascrito teniente de Cura de la Yglesia Parroquial de S. Luis de la nueva orleans, Provincia de la Luisiana bautice solemnemente a Ysabel Pompeana nacida el veinte y tres de enero ultimo hija natural de Carlota Delt. Malata Libre, fueron sus Padrinos Alberto Ventura, (Blanco) y Carlota Dorneville mulata libre, y para que conste lo firme en el mismo dia, mes, y año [...] bautizada. P.ᵉ Cuelar — Fr. Luis de Quintanilla

---

156

Maria Luisa Gonzalez Morta quarterona libre

En dos de Abril de mil setecientos noventa y tres, yo el infrascrito teniente de Cura de la Yglesia parroquial de S. Luis de la nueva orleans bautice solemnemente a Maria Luisa Morta nacida en treinta de enero ultimo, hija de Carlota mulata libre, y de Pedro Careton, que se dice su padre, bien que no legitimo: fueron padrinos Dⁿ Pedro Lacoste, Cadete de este Re-gimiento fixo de la Luisiana, y Dª Maria Luisa Morta Deblanc, quienes quedaron enterados del parentesco espiritual, y obligaciones: y para que conste, lo firme en dicho dia, mes, y año. Fr. Luis de Quintanilla.

82

Juan Pedro
Cacelar, mu
lato libre

Dia diez y ocho de Abril de este año, de mil y ochocientos: Yo Fr. Antonio de Sedella, Religioso Capuchino, Cura del Saggario de la Santa Yglesia Cathedral de la Ciudad del Nuevo Orleans, bautize, y puse los santos oleos, a un niño, mulato libre, que nacio el dia veinte y seis de Marzo proximo pasado, hijo natural de Dⁿ Pedro Cacelar, y de Carlota [...] matura, y vecinos de esta feligresia: se ignoran los nombres de los abuelos paternos y maternos: en el qual niño exercí las Sacras ceremonias y preces, y le puse por nombre, Juan Pedro; fueron sus Padrinos, Dⁿ Juan Francisco Idechs, y Dª Clara Victoria Jourdan; y para que conste, lo hizo con el mencionado Padrino, y con Dⁿ Nicolas Deliste en el mis-mo dia, mes, y año ut supra. Fr. Antonio de Sedella — P.ᵉ Cacelar

8.21

Nicolas — Fr. Juan [...] — R. Deliste — Cacelar

first to have himself identified in the body of the record. The 1793 entry for the baptism of his daughter, Marie Louise Marthe, declares that she was the child of "Charlotte Wiltz, free mulatress and of Pierre Cazelar, who says that he is her non-legitimate father." By the time of his only son's baptism in 1800, the clergy of St. Louis Cathedral must have been well aware of how Cazelar wished his children's baptisms recorded. Father Antonio Sedella penned a clear entry that proclaimed the baby "the natural son of Don Pedro Cazelar and Carlota Wiltz," (see Figure 8).[22]

Jean Pierre Cazelar made the first of his three wills in 1797, three years before the birth of his son. In it he declared that he had never been married, recognized his four daughters by Charlotte Wiltz, and left them slaves, houses, and usufruct of the rest of his estate, including a plantation and two dozen additional slaves. The will established Cazelar as the father of his daughters but not of his as-yet-unborn son, which may explain why he visited notary Philippe Pedesclaux in 1822 and had him draw up and execute a formal declaration of paternity for all five of his children. He turned his mind toward his will again in 1829, when he was in his midsixties. Charlotte Wiltz had long since died, so this will attended only to his five living children. Cazelar wrote out his testament himself, producing what was known as a holographic will, a document that was technically as legally effective as one drawn up by a notary. The new will named the five children borne him by Charlotte Wiltz, "whom I have always recognized as my natural children." After making several specific bequests, including an impressive donation of $2,500 to indigent families, he named his five children his universal heirs, each to receive an equal share of his estate. The will reveals that in later life his eldest daughter, Adelaide, had become Cazelar's housekeeper, intellectual companion, and business confident. He singled Adelaide out for special bequests, stipulating that she receive all of his furniture, his silver collection, and his library, "in compensation for all the pains and care which she has always taken, as much for me personally as for my interests."[23]

Cazelar raised his mixed-race family in a fine house on his sugar plantation downriver from New Orleans. As with the Hazeurs, his situation was well known, and he made no attempt to hide it from those who were his racial and social peers. Nearly all of his children's godparents were white men and women. Thomas Porée and his wife, Louise Marguerite Foucher, who served as eldest daughter Adelaide's godparents, have been described as "belonging to two of the first families of the city."[24] The white overseer of a nearby plantation reported to his absentee employer in France shortly before Cazelar's death that the old planter's enormous wealth would all go to his "numerous colored progeny."[25] An unusual group of visitors would have had a chance to make the acquaintance of the Cazelar family in the winter of 1814–15. In the weeks leading up to the Battle of New Orleans on January 8, 1815, U.S. troops built fortifications on the Cazelar plantation and engaged the enemy nearby. Though the Cazelars likely sought safety within the city limits, the military planners doubtless knew something about the wealthy man whose plantation they turned into a battlefield.[26]

Jean Pierre Cazelar lost his partner, Charlotte Wiltz, before his children were grown, perhaps at the birth of his son in 1800. He endured the trauma of war and experienced the tragedy of losing his fine plantation house to fire. But there were achievements to celebrate and joys to reflect upon, too, and he approached his death in 1836 as any nineteenth-century southern patriarch would have wished. Over a lifespan of seventy years, he had presided over a large plantation on the banks of the Mississippi River a few miles below New Orleans that prospered thanks to the labor of sixty enslaved workers. With a material fortune that was the envy of less-successful planters, he was rich by other measures of southern manhood, too. The only child of his French-born parents to survive and have children of his own, this father of five ensured that Cazelar would not be among the French colonial family names that withered and died. As his health failed, he sought the comfort of the family he had made, leaving his plantation to stay with the family of his daughter, Marie Louise. There, in the company of five young grandchildren and their parents, Cazelar dictated his last will and testament to notary Felix de Armas. In this, his final will, made literally in the bosom of his interracial family, he left everything . . . to a white man named Emile Sainet.[27]

The inconsistency between this final act and the text of Cazelar's life is jarring. The documentary trail that he took such great care to create, the affection evident in his bequest to daughter Adelaide, his decision to die surrounded by his grandchildren, all seem bizarrely at odds with the will that Cazelar signed on his deathbed. But they are not. Emile Sainet was not a random choice. He was the life partner of Cazelar's daughter Marie Louise, and the house that he shared with her and their five children was the place that Cazelar came to write his will and die. With the complicity of the man who would be Cazelar's son-in-law had the law allowed it, notary Felix de Armas drew up a document that ironically obscured the true geography of Cazelar's family in order to preserve its patrimony. When Cazelar died, Sainet duly inherited his considerable estate, including the plantation and sixty-one slaves, all together valued at nearly $150,000—nearly $3 million in today's dollars. In the months that followed, Sainet systematically set about transferring Cazelar's wealth to his children. He set up two auctions about a year after Cazelar's death, one selling parcels of Cazelar's main plantation, the other his slaves. Most of the slaves and much of the land passed through these sales into the hands of Cazelar's children, in some cases through agents, suggesting that the auctions were rigged and the sales a sham. The deception ensured that Cazelar's children would enjoy the wealthy futures he planned for them. When the Civil War broke out in 1860, Pierre Cazelar III, the grandson of bachelor patriarch Jean Pierre Cazelar, was a wealthy Louisiana planter whose ancestry defied the racial hierarchy that was supposed to define the planter class.[28]

Jean Pierre Cazelar's deceptive scheme was the only way he could pass all of his wealth on to his children. When he made his children his universal heirs in his 1829 holographic will, he was apparently unaware that the civil code adopted for Louisiana in 1808 and revised in 1825 made it impossible for them to inherit his full estate. The code defined children like Cazelar's as "natural children." Natural children were those "born from two persons, who at the moment when said children were conceived, might have been duly married," who were also legally acknowledged by their father. Natural children could inherit from their fathers, but there were limits. The 1808 version of the civil code stipulated that if the father left any legitimate children, he could leave natural children nothing "beyond what is strictly necessary to procure them sustenance, or an occupation or profession which may maintain them." Even if there were no legitimate children, a natural father was restricted. If he had living ascendants—parents or grandparents—he could leave his natural children no more than a third of his property. If he had any living brothers and sisters, he could bequeath his children no more than half his estate. Even if all he left behind were collateral relatives such as cousins, he could bequeath his children no more than three-fourths. The 1825 revision of the code tightened the restrictions. If there were any legitimate relatives at all, no matter how remote, natural children could inherit no more than one-third of their father's estate.[29]

The new rules that applied to testamentary bequests, or *mortis causa* donations, also applied to gifts made by natural fathers to their children during their lifetimes, known as *inter vivos* donations. To leave no doubt about the intent of these provisions, the civil code also stipulated that those "who have lived together in open concubinage, are respectively incapable to make to each other any universal donation . . . whether between *inter vivos* or *mortis causa*."[30] Charlotte Wiltz was dead by the time Cazelar contemplated his own demise, but even had she survived him, he could not have provided for his children by turning over his wealth to her. Cazelar resorted to a tactic known as interposition in order to bequeath his fortune to his children. He made Sainet his legal universal heir, trusting in him to convey the inheritance to his children. The plan worked, but the jurists who constructed and upheld the provisions of the civil code designed to thwart the formation and survival of families like Cazelar's became more and more vigilant in the years to come. Cazelar was able to arrange matters so that his son and grandson succeeded him as wealthy planters, but the mixed-race descendants of another bachelor father, Augustin Macarty, found themselves caught in the legal web Louisiana's slave society had spun to separate black and white.

Like Jean Pierre Cazelar, Augustin Macarty was a scion of an old French Creole family who formed a life partnership with a free woman of color in the 1790s. At the end of his life, like Cazelar, he tried to provide for his mixed-race children and grandchildren by the legal subterfuge of interposition. His ploy failed, however, undermined by the way he negotiated the briar patch of interracial partnership in early national New Orleans. Cazelar's example stands as a model of how to successfully elude and ultimately subvert the social and legal apparatus of a slave society. Macarty's life, by contrast, offers a step-by-step illustration of how not to travel the twisted terrain that presented itself to white men who made families with black women.

As a young man of seventeen in 1791, freshly commissioned as an ensign in the Spanish colonial military, Macarty lived in the unconventional household of his uncle, Eugene Macarty. Eugene, himself only five years older than his nephew, already shared his home with free woman of color Eulalie Mandeville. Eugene and Eulalie did not baptize their first child until 1794, but the precocious Augustin bedded Victoire Wiltz, who bore him a daughter identified as a quadroon in the record of her baptism early in 1792. Augustin's brother Jean Macarty served as the child's godfather and the girl was given the Macarty surname in the baptismal register, but Augustin did not sign the record, never lived with Wiltz, and moved on to another free woman on whom he fathered a daughter named after his cousin, Brigitte.[31] Augustin Macarty finally settled down in 1798, setting up a household with yet another free woman of color, Céleste Perrault. Their son, Patrice, was born the following year, and Macarty's uncle Louis and his cousin, Marie Delphine, served as godparents. Macarty remained with Perrault until his death in 1844.[32]

Macarty clearly did not keep the existence of his natural children a secret from his blood relations. It was a family tradition to enlist uncles and cousins as godparents to Macarty infants, and Augustin did not break with that precedent. Unlike Cazelar, however, he never signed the baptismal records of his natural children and allowed the conventional "father unknown" to stand uncorrected. Elected mayor of New Orleans in 1815, Macarty drew a curtain between his public persona and his private family life. One of the former mayor's "most intimate friends and his habitual companion," averred "that he never heard him acknowledge the children of his mistresses, and that he always denied having any." On one occasion when the friend was with Macarty, a man approached them and told Macarty in his presence that he was his son-in-law, to which Macarty replied, "'You my son-in-law: I have no children.'"[33]

Macarty's was an implausible deniability, as events after his death revealed, and his insistence on asserting it destroyed his posthumous attempt to provide for his family. Two years before his death in 1844, Macarty drafted a holographic will. After declaring that he had no forced heirs under Louisiana law, which was to say no legitimate children, he named Spanish-born Francisco Tio his universal legatee and testamentary executor. Tio was to inherit everything after executing several smaller bequests. Macarty directed that three of his slaves be freed. Since all were minors, he appointed Céleste Perrault their tutrix and stipulated that they were to serve her until they came of age. He bequeathed to Patrice Macarty his clothing and the furniture in his bedroom and declared that all other furniture and movable property in his house belonged to Céleste Perrault. To Perrault he gave the use of the residence until six months after his death.[34] The considerable residual of Macarty's $58,000 estate, comprising other slaves and property, went to Francisco Tio as universal heir.[35]

Augustin Macarty wrote a series of letters to his relatives living outside of Louisiana at roughly the same time he prepared his will. The missives reveal that he was "completely estranged from them, and disclose a strong desire on his part to convince them that he was poor and that they had nothing to expect from him."[36] When these out-of-state collateral heirs learned of Macarty's death and of his enormous bequest to Francisco Tio, they filed suit against the Spaniard. The distant relatives claimed that Macarty's will was null since he had interposed Tio as universal legatee in order to transfer his estate through him to individuals incapable of lawful inheritance. The relatives knew, and the court proceedings confirmed, that although Augustin Macarty went to his grave denying that he had any children, Francisco Tio was the life partner of Josephine Macarty, Augustin's daughter by Victoire Wiltz.[37]

The suit brought by Macarty's collateral heirs in 1847 against Francisco Tio was ultimately decided by Louisiana's Supreme Court in 1851 and the concurring and dissenting opinions written by the three justices who heard the case unspool in a surreal display of double consciousness. The plaintiffs, Macarty's collateral heirs, requested that the court nullify the will that made Tio the universal legatee citing the article of the Louisiana civil code that stipulated that "every disposition in favor of a person incapable of receiving, shall be null, whether it be disguised under the form of an onerous contract, or be made under the name of persons interposed. The father and mother, the children and descendants, and the husband and wife of the incapable person shall be reputed persons interposed."[38] Tio, the plaintiffs claimed, was interposed by Macarty as a sham heir so that the daughter he never acknowledged, together with her children, could inherit his wealth.

The same civil code that gave the plaintiffs a way to claim Macarty's inheritance with one hand took it away with another. In order to prove that Tio was interposed, the plaintiffs had to provide acceptable evidence that the ultimate recipients of his largesse were incapable of inheriting from Macarty. The only people incapable of inheritance under Louisiana law were a man's known concubine and the unacknowledged natural children of a white man and a woman of color. Macarty could leave his money to whomever he liked—Francisco Tio, Josephine Macarty, or a stranger in the street—so long as none of these individuals was his unacknowledged natural child by a black woman or his own colored life partner. In order to prove that Francisco Tio had been interposed so that Josephine Macarty could inherit, all the collateral heirs had to do was prove that she was indeed Macarty's daughter. But, since the civil code held that only "an authentic act in favor of colored children" by the natural father that acknowledged paternity constituted acceptable proof, the plaintiffs were left without a legal way to prove that Tio was interposed. If there were technically no natural children, there were technically no individuals incapable of inheriting, and so Tio could not possibly have been knowingly interposed by Macarty![39]

In order to find a way to keep Macarty's legacy out of the hands of his mixed-race progeny, the Supreme Court had to resolve the conundrum created by the civil code: they could only rule that Tio was interposed if it could be legally proven that Josephine Macarty was Augustin Macarty's natural child. Since paternity could only be verified by a father's personal declaration, and Augustin had never made one, the court's hands seemed to be tied. Two of the justices simply cut through this Gordian knot and declared Tio's actions fraudulent, nullifying Macarty's will on that basis. The dissenting judge, Isaac Trimble Preston, ruled with his colleagues in favor of the plaintiffs, but the expedient of pronouncing Tio's actions fraudulent offended his legal sensibility and stirred his moral outrage. In response, Preston stepped through the looking glass and crafted as convoluted a piece of jurisprudence as any produced in the name of racial order. Preston attempted in his dissenting opinion to reconcile the legal Catch-22 that would logically lead to a ruling in favor of Tio and, by extension, Josephine Macarty.

In Louisiana, Preston noted, "marriage between the two races is forbidden by law; the honor of marriage shall not be debased by the connection," and "the inestimable advantages of marriage to society, shall not be disregarded by encouraging illicit and debasing concubinage with the colored race." For these reasons, he continued, the civil code made it impossible for natural mixed-race children to inherit unless their fathers explicitly and publically acknowledged paternity. "If colored children might make proof of their paternal descent from a white father," in the absence of such acknowledgment, "they might receive by testamentary dispositions, portions of the father's estate, and without a will, claim alimony from his legal heirs." That, Justice Preston pointed out, would give "direct encouragement to the degrading evils" which the exclusion "of anything but the father's acknowledgement" had effectively curbed. Under the law, only men "so lost to shame as to make an authentic act of his degradation" were able to leave wealth to their natural children. If the children themselves were allowed to establish their ancestry, white fathers would not have to face this shame, and mixed-race children would be able to "diminish the father's estate to the prejudice of his white and lawful heirs." The law was designed to deter white men from interracial procreation, but its intention was also to obstruct the improper posthumous consequences of their actions. "Shall concubinage with an illegitimate colored woman, so degrading to society, be rewarded by all the beneficence to her which a parent could bestow on his lawful issue," Preston demands, "while the white natural child who enters into the honored bonds of matrimony with one of his own race, under a similar bequest, could receive nothing from the wealth of the author of his existence." Justice Preston enlisted "the rough language of Lord Coke," the venerated seventeenth-century English magistrate beloved of the American Revolution to pronounce that "this would be the cursed interpretation that corrodes the text."[40]

Preston's conclusion demanded that the court take upon itself the onus of establishing paternity in order to see that the spirit of the law was properly executed. And so he carefully laid out not only proofs of Augustin Macarty's paternity of Josephine, but a detailed reconstruction of the life and affections the dead man had so assiduously concealed. To that end, Preston recapitulated the testimony of various free women of color who testified to Augustin Macarty's paternity of Josephine. Witness Sanite Rivere swore that Josephine Macarty was Augustin's child, an assertion to be trusted since Rivere "knew *Macarty* well, because she lived with, and had a child by him herself." Brigitte Macarty attested that Josephine "is her eldest sister, and the daughter of the testator; that he always treated her as his child, called her so, and she called him father, and that her children were received at his house as grand-children, and called his grand-children, and that they called him grand-father." With the testimony of these two women of color, Preston wrote, "enough has been detailed to establish fully that *Josephine Macarty* is the natural daughter of the testator."[41] Preston proceeded to describe Josephine Macarty's life with Francisco Tio to establish why Macarty believed that Tio would act to pass his inheritance on to Josephine Macarty and her children.

Josephine Macarty, Preston wrote, "has lived with the defendant since 1807." Tio acknowledged their cohabitation, as well as his paternity of their six children.[42] There was sufficient evidence, Preston continued, to believe that the two "have lived and still live together as a family; that the children have been reared Tio and educated as such." And although the Louisiana civil code proscribed marriage between them, "a priest has performed the religious ceremony of marriage between him and Josephine: so that every relation growing out of marriage, in point of fact, existed between them."[43] The justice admitted that "Francisco Tio and Josephine Macarty are not husband and wife in law; and, therefore, the law creating a legal presumption of interposition does not in terms apply to them." But, he insisted, "every consideration and motive for the adoption of the principle of law exists equally as to them, with the lawful husband and wife," on the basis of a series of marital qualities that the judge tenderly enumerated. Francisco Tio and Josephine Macarty shared "the same physical connection; the same affection growing out of mutual dependence and daily reciprocity of domestic services; the same objects of intense interest for all their mental and physical exertions." These conjugal ties were strengthened by their mutual bond to "a numerous family of children, as dear to them, no doubt, and as constantly the objects of their joint solicitude, hopes and prayers, as if they were their lawful offspring."[44] Based on the intimate family portrait that Preston had conjured out of his own imagination, he delivered his considered legal opinion that there was "great reason to believe that [Macarty] intended to confer the benefits on his descendants, by making *Tio* the real owner of the property." Not only would Tio, "an industrious, economical and prudent man," be a good steward of the inheritance, he would discharge his duties as a respectable white patriarch would, because he was "attached to his concubine and children, as much as if married to the one and the lawful father of the others, he would be likely to employ the property more to their real advantage than they would themselves."[45]

In every way but their transgression of the color line, Justice Preston found Francisco Tio and Josephine Macarty to be a model couple dedicated as parents should be to the loving upbringing of their children; and so, in his own way, was Augustin Macarty a good father. "Macarty, by his youthful imprudence, had brought into existence an illegitimate daughter, and she had become the mother of numerous offspring in the same situation." But Macarty tried to put things right. "When age and infirmity indicated to him the approaching termination of his life, he deemed it his duty to repair, as far as possible, the misfortune he had brought upon his innocent offspring, and bequeathed them the greater part of his estate." The former mayor's "immorality consisted in being the author of the existence of his offspring, not in the dispositions of his will. These were dictated by nature and the deepest affections of the heart—which all acknowledge and cherish—the love of a father for his offspring, however unfortunate."[46]

Augustin Macarty's paternal affection and sense of duty were beyond reproach, in Preston's opinion, but in view of the compromised origins of his children, he could still be faulted for a failure in judgment that could not be explained away as a youthful indiscretion. Preston observed that Macarty's "folly consisted, like that of most misers, in not doing the good he intended in death during his life, by removing his offspring and fortune to other countries, where they might enjoy it, without the stigma he had imprinted upon them." The court should not "denounce the intentions of Macarty," but instead regret his failure to ameliorate his foible by the socially acceptable expedient of transferring them and his wealth to a foreign country. Macarty had not "committed an offence or quasi-offence, or fraud, in making his will and not dying intestate," Preston opined, but rather, "disposed of his fortune as his heart and judgment dictated."[47]

Justice Preston has provided posterity with a remarkably detailed and compassionately imaginative portrait of the extended Macarty family, but the law he served dictated strict limits to his sympathy. "It is the spirit rather than the letter" of the civil code that Preston was bound to uphold, and this, he wrote, "requires that the universal legacy in favor of *Tio* should be annulled" and the entire estate turned over to the collateral heirs.[48] Bachelor patriarchs Augustin Macarty and Francisco Tio were stripped of their ability to fulfill their paternal duty to preserve their wealth for the benefit and security of their progeny. Patriarchy could be allowed to serve only one master in the slave South.

Tragically, Augustin Macarty actually could have left up to a third of his estate to Josephine and her children had he openly acknowledged his paternity in any one of a number of ways. He might, for example, have made a point of signing Josephine's baptismal record. Or he could have filed a simple declaration of paternity before a notary public or mentioned Josephine in his will. Any of these modes of acknowledgement, all of which Macarty's contemporary Jean Pierre Cazelar had employed, would have sufficed under Louisiana's civil code. The justices speculated in their 1851 decision that Macarty purposely did not acknowledge his natural children precisely so that he could devise a way to leave them more than the limited amount of his estate prescribed by law. But this could not have influenced his decision not to sign the baptismal records since all of his natural children were born well before the civil code of 1808 was enacted with its restrictions on the inheritance of natural children. Many of Augustin Macarty's contemporaries who formed unions with women of color and baptized children in the 1790s acted as Jean Pierre Cazelar had and made a point of signing the register, often squeezing their signatures into cramped spaces and forcing the sacramental scribes to correct the entries to reflect their paternity. Despite Justice Preston's evocation of Macarty's paternal tenderness, it seems likely that the former mayor really was unwilling to acknowledge himself the father of mixed-race children. The two justices who wrote the majority opinion may have been right in their assumption that "he never could bring himself to speak or to write that humiliating truth."[49]

The man who stopped Augustin Macarty in the street declaring that he was his son-in-law may very well have been Francisco Tio, and his actions with respect to his partner and children indicate that Justice Preston hit closer to the mark in his sketch of this father's affections and motives. Indeed, Francisco and his uncle Marcos Tio were among many contemporaries who behaved in ways that suggest that the example of Cazelar was the norm and that of Augustin Macarty the outlier.

Marcos Tio was one of a number of Catalonians who emigrated from Spain to late colonial New Orleans to establish small businesses and trading operations. In 1787 he operated a corner tavern on the east side of the city's central square, the Place d'Armes. Within a few years, Tio formed a relationship with the spurned Victoire Wiltz, taking her and her infant daughter, Josephine Macarty, into his household. Victoire bore Tio the first of eleven children in 1794. The family gained another member about 1804, when Marcos's nephew, Francisco Tio, moved to New Orleans and joined his uncle in his growing business enterprises. The twenty-six-year-old Francisco formed an attachment to his uncle's young stepdaughter, Josephine, and she bore him the first of seven children in 1808.[50]

On the face of it, Josephine Macarty appears to be flesh-and-blood confirmation of Harriet Martineau's pronouncement that the "Quadroon girls of New Orleans are brought up by their mothers to be what they have been; the mistresses of white gentlemen." She grew up under the wing of a mother who was herself the illicit partner of a white man. As a girl of twelve, her mother stood by as Josephine's future lover joined their household. The circumstances look incriminating. Yet there are pieces of evidence that disturb the presumption that Josephine was trained up by her mother to be the luxuriously kept woman of a "white gentleman." Josephine was not paraded on the levee in her finery to attract the attentions of white men on the prowl, or conveyed to Auguste Tessier's ballroom to be displayed to potential suitors. Her future partner met her in a house filled with children, where the prospect dangled before his eyes was not a life of sexual adventure and ease but the quotidian chaos, lack of privacy, and endless responsibility of family life. Nor was Francisco the refined gentleman for whom quadroon women like Josephine presumably set their caps. Catalonians like Francisco and his uncle Marcos were hardscrabble characters who arrived in New Orleans "from their poor country with very little" and worked their way to prosperity through industriousness and frugality as grocers and bar owners. Despite their honesty and work ethic, the Catalan immigrants in early nineteenth-century New Orleans were "held in low esteem," and essentially equated by other Europeans in the city to be "on the same level as blacks."[51]

An impression of intertwined lives shaped by domesticity and strong family bonds pokes through in the glimpses we catch of the extended Tio family in the historical record. Francisco Tio joined his uncle's business, which had expanded to include a successful wholesaling enterprise. In 1808, mother Victoire and daughter Josephine both became pregnant, and although Josephine had moved in with Francisco in 1807, mother and daughter would certainly have shared their common condition with special intimacy. On the February day they baptized their first child, Francisco and Josephine walked through the winter streets to St. Louis Cathedral with Marcos Tio and Victoire Wiltz, who were carrying their sixth child to the baptismal font that day. Victoire gave birth to her child in September, but she and Marcos waited to arrange the baptism of the new baby until daughter Josephine bore her daughter, three months to the day after Victoire delivered. Father Antonio Sedella baptized Josephine and Francisco's baby first, and grandparents Marcos and Victoire served as the godparents for the little girl, who was named for her grandmother. It is virtually impossible to imagine that the four parents did not go back to the house on St. Phillip Street that had been bought in Victoire Wiltz's name to celebrate with the best wines and foods stocked by the family's business.[52] The baptism of their children may not have been the only sacrament the Tio family celebrated together on that February day. We know from the court case that stripped her of her natural father's intended bequest that Josephine and Francisco were married in a religious ceremony. The decision to baptize the babies of mother and daughter on the same day may have been made to facilitate another ceremony, one that Father Sedella could not record in the register.[53]

Like Jean Pierre Cazelar, both Tio men took care to acknowledge paternity of their natural children from the beginning, consistently signing the baptismal registers, sometimes clearly asking for corrections in entries that did not originally name them as the fathers.[54] Marcos Tio acknowledged his children again in his 1823 will. Despite all these pains, the men and their free black partners must have been keenly aware of the legal disadvantages of their family arrangements. It comes as little surprise that the next generation of Tios opted for marriages recognized by the law, which allowed them to pass on their wealth to their progeny without the heartbreaking restrictions that scarred Josephine's life. In some instances the guiding hand of the parents can be detected in the timing and arrangements of the marriages. Josephine and Francisco's firstborn, Victoire, married Dominguan Jean Baptiste Chon in 1827. Though most refugee grooms brought few or no assets to their marriages to Orleanian women, Chon declared a net worth of $1,500 in his marriage contract. Francisco and Josephine accompanied Victoire to notary Joseph Arnaud's office, where they attested that their daughter brought a dowry of an equal amount consisting of an enslaved girl of nine worth $400 given Victoire by her father, $600 in cash, and $500 in furniture and other movables.[55] The aunt who had shared Victoire's baptism day, Julie Tio, married another well-heeled Dominguan less than two months later. Groom Louis Coussey brought $2,000 to the marriage, the bride an equal amount, including a half-lot near the French Quarter, a trousseau worth $600, and her share in the succession of her father, Marcos Tio, which amounted to $900.[56] Luis Marcos Tio, Julie's older brother, also married in 1827.[57] By 1831, all three of these Tios lived with their spouses and children on the same block of St. Claude Street on the southern edge of the Faubourg Treme.[58]

Establishing families blessed by the church and recognized by the state was ultimately not enough to protect the Tios from the aggressive racism that permeated the antebellum South. In the decade before the outbreak of the Civil War proslavery rhetoric stoked fears of racial "amalgamation" to fever pitch. Interracial sex no longer represented a simple moral lapse. It was an evil that imperiled the natural order because its result was the obliteration of racial distinctions and the disappearance of the white race. The very numerousness of New Orleans free people of color rendered them a threat to those who feared the erasure of the white race through amalgamation. Two sensational trials in 1850s New Orleans contesting the race of women who looked white must have seemed to white supremacists to confirm that the racial Armageddon they feared was at their doorstep. Free people of color were judged dangerous on another, more immediate count. The free black, one New Orleans newspaper opined in 1859, "gets drunk, debauches our slaves, and preaches insubordination to them," while another paper approved talk of expelling free people of color from Louisiana to protect the citizenry from their attempts to "tamper with slaves and thereby make them discontented." The threat of black rebellion aided and abetted by free people of color seemed as imminent on the eve of the Civil War as it had been in the era of the Haitian Revolution. In response, the Louisiana legislature entertained a bill that proposed the enslavement of all people of African descent who did not leave the state by a specified deadline. Though this and other legislative assaults on the rights of Louisiana's free blacks failed, the poisonousness of the environment was unbearable to some who joined colonization projects in Mexico and Haiti.

Several members of the Tio family left their homes in New Orleans behind in the summer of 1859 to participate in the formation of the Eureka Colony in the Mexican state of Vera Cruz, imposing upon themselves the exile that Justice Preston thought the best solution for Augustin Macarty's descendants.[59]

Pierre Clement de Laussat condemned the Hazeur brothers for their "colonial weakness," joining a chorus of late colonial social critics who viewed interracial sex as a vice restricted to the Circum-Caribbean. A further presumption with respect to New Orleans emerged in the nineteenth century as Anglophones from the American territories to the east and the north filed their reports on the prize acquisition of the Louisiana Purchase. Sex across the color line in New Orleans was portrayed as the particular foible of men of French or Spanish descent, a corollary to their morally permissive Catholicism and the Continental appetite for pleasure. Anglophone Protestants who took up residence in the city were accounted too industrious to fall into the bad habits of the city's natives and Continental immigrants. The enterprising Anglophones, Thomas Ashe observed in 1808, "since their arrival here, have been so occupied by politics and legislation, that their minds have never been sufficiently unbent to form a course of pleasures for themselves." The city's Frenchmen, by contrast, "do things with ladies, including concerts, dancing, promenade."[60] Anglophone Protestant visitors to New Orleans were always quick to point out the Catholic city's pleasure-seeking ways. "It is well known that the Catholic religion does not forbid amusements on the Sabbath," Presbyterian missionary Timothy Flint intoned in his 1826 memoir of life in the Lower Mississippi Valley. "They fortify themselves in defending the custom of going to balls and the theatre on the Sabbath, by arguing that religion ought to inspire cheerfulness."[61]

Frolicking on the Sabbath and cultivating the company of women led to an easy association of the city's non-Anglophone men with the depravity of interracial sex. A sensational article published in Cincinnati's Methodist-affiliated *Western Christian Advocate* illustrates a trope well established by the late 1830s. "A young Spaniard, named Pedro Garces, stabbed a beautiful quadroon girl named Petronolla, with whom he cohabited" in New Orleans, the paper reported. "The cause was jealousy; and the writer says it was jealousy of the same girl which caused the recent death of the Count de Montezuma, by his own hand."[62] Protestant men who spoke English and carried names such as Smith and Jones were spared the tragic and violent ends that came to hot-blooded men named Garces and Montezuma caught in imbroglios with the legendary quadroons of New Orleans.

Among the late colonial bachelor patriarchs of New Orleans was a man who shared all the typical features of his type, except the religious and ethnic origins that were supposed to predispose him to his transgressive lifestyle. Samuel Moore began his life partnership with free woman of color Dorothée Lassize just after the Louisiana Purchase. This moment in the city's history has long been viewed as a watershed, marking the ascendancy of the "Americans" and their entrepreneurial bustle, while the carefree *ancienne population* danced and gambled their way into a dissipated twilight. Samuel Moore's story unsettles this old formula and its assertion of unbridgeable cultural and social divides between Anglophones and Francophones in early national New Orleans. At the same time, a tangential piece of Moore's family history suggests that newly arrived Anglophones played a critical role in changing the terms under which the city's interracial partnerships had long been conducted.[63]

Territorial and early national Orleanians would have called Samuel Philip Moore an American, the term they applied to Anglophone Protestants from elsewhere in North America. Samuel was the son of Alexander Moore, an Irish Protestant who immigrated to the backcountry of Virginia in the mid-eighteenth century. After the end of the Seven Years' War, Alexander pulled up stakes again and moved to British West Florida. There he quickly rose to prominence in Pensacola, gaining a place in the inaugural colonial assembly in 1766 and rising to become a member of the colonial council two years later.[64] Shortly after Samuel was baptized at the Anglican Church in Pensacola, Alexander Moore uprooted his family to take advantage of a new land policy designed to encourage settlement at the western edge of British territory. A 1770 grant of 1,000 acres just north of the settlement at Natchez on the Mississippi River placed the Moores among the leaders in what was effectively a British colonization effort on the eve of the American Revolution.[65] Samuel Moore's native tongue was English, his baptismal faith Protestant, and his family among those who aimed to sow the Franco-Iberian Gulf Coast with the seeds of British culture and political institutions. For all intents and purposes, he was what historians have commonly identified as an American, an identity presumably distinct from the native-born Catholics among whom he lived in late colonial New Orleans.

The Moores remained in the Natchez district after 1783 when it came under Spanish sovereignty, and they prospered there. In addition to his enormous land-holdings, Alexander Moore established himself as a general merchant in Natchez in time to profit from the quickening of trade down the Mississippi from the trans-Appalachian U.S. territories. Alexander Moore's business tied him to New Orleans, where he died in 1795, abjuring his Protestantism on his deathbed. Twenty-five-year-old Samuel and his brother, James, took over the family business.[66] James took charge in Natchez while Samuel quickly expanded commercial activities in New Orleans, where he brokered the sale of large amounts of timber from upriver and emerged as a small but steady slave trader, buying and selling nearly thirty men, women, and children between 1795 and 1811. Moore's main business, however, seems to have been buying and developing land in New Orleans during its rapid expansion between 1790 and 1820.[67]

Sometime before 1803, the young entrepreneur met Dorothée Lassize, the free woman of color who became his life partner. Dorothée and Samuel appear together in the public record for the first time in 1804, when the baptism of their daughter, Sara, was recorded in the sacramental register of St. Louis Cathedral reserved for slaves and free people of color. Sara's baptismal record stands out for its unaffected clarity. There are no lines scratched out, no corrections made in the margin. When Father Antonio Sedella penned the entry, all the elements of the child's identity and lineage were unambiguously recorded. "Don Samuel Moore" is identified as the father of the infant and "Dorothée Lassize, free mulatress" as her mother. Moore linked his daughter to his family by naming her for his sister, Sara Virginia Moore, and making certain that the names of her paternal grandparents were included in the record. At the bottom of the entry, Moore signed with a flourish.[68] Seven more children were born to Dorothée and Samuel. Their baptismal records tell the story of a growing family and an enduring partnership, but they also hint at the challenges couples like Samuel and Dorothée encountered in early national New Orleans.[69]

Samuel and Dorothée began their family together just as Louisiana was passing under the sovereignty of the United States, and they were among the first generation of Orleanians who would raise their children under the new civil code adopted in 1808 by the territorial government. As we saw in the previous chapter, one of the effects of the adoption of the civil code was to encourage free black couples to formalize their unions with sacramental marriage, an action that would automatically legitimate their children and qualify them as legal heirs. Over the thirteen-year period spanning 1811 to 1824, thirty couples legitimated children—many of them fully grown adults—at their marriage ceremonies at St. Louis Cathedral.[70]

Couples like Samuel and Dorothée did not have that option. Though Spanish law threw up obstacles to "unequal marriages," it did not categorically prohibit interracial marriage, and a handful did take place in New Orleans. The 1808 civil code shut this route down completely.[71] From this single prohibition followed all the others that compromised the financial futures of Moore's children. Jean Pierre Cazelar and Augustin Macarty responded to the inheritance obstacles thrown up by the civil code with legal subterfuge. The sacramental registers hint that Moore and Lassize toyed with a different strategy.

Sara Virginia Moore's baptismal entry was made before the civil code of 1808 imposed legal disadvantages on children like her. It is unambiguous and open, and even conveys a sense of pride and joyfulness. The baptismal entries of the brothers and sisters born after her are evasive, crabbed, and hemmed in. Samuel Moore senior did not bring his son Samuel Jr. and daughter Eurania to the baptismal font as infants in arms, as he had Sara Virginia. His son was six years old, his daughter two, when he conveyed them together to the cathedral to be baptized in 1812. Their records recorded the names of their paternal grandparents, Alexander Moore and Jane Scott, but the name of their mother was omitted. And unlike Sara Virginia's baptism, which was recorded in the register reserved for people of African descent, the acts for Samuel Jr. and Eurania were recorded in the register reserved for whites. The names of white fathers were routinely omitted in the baptismal records of mixed-race children, but the omission of a mother's name under any circumstances was extremely rare. The oddities in the 1812 Moore baptisms suggest that Samuel and Dorothée were making an attempt to establish white identities for their children in the wake of the civil code's discriminatory measures.[72] If these baptismal records represent a plan of racial subterfuge, however, it was a strategy Moore and Lassize deployed inconsistently. Their daughter Marie Camille, baptized in 1817, was registered in the book used for slaves and free people of color.[73] Their sons, Alexander James and Antoine Robert, baptized in 1821, both some years after their births, were registered in the volume designated for whites, but with their mother's name listed.[74] Sara Virginia died less than two months after her baptism, and Samuel could presumably at this point have easily ended his connection with Dorothée.[75] But he did not. Almost exactly nine months after the death of Sara,

Dorothée bore Samuel the son who was his namesake. Samuel Moore remained faithful to his partner and his children, but the baptismal entries reveal that theirs was a compromised future.

Samuel Moore retained his official residence at his business, which was on Bienville Street. There he presumably occupied bachelor quarters with only two enslaved men for company. Dorothée owned several properties nearby, however, and it seems likely that Samuel spent most of his time in the company of her and their children. Certainly, their finances and family affairs were closely interwoven. Dorothée's mother was a prosperous free woman of color named Amaranthe Lassize, whose considerable estate at her death in 1815 included several slaves. Amaranthe made Samuel Moore her testamentary executor, and he and Dorothée conspired to distribute her estate without paying the fees charged for official registration for property transferred from a succession to the heirs. Their attempt at what amounted to tax evasion must have been detected, because they subsequently executed two complicated affidavits to put the matter to rights. In a transaction equally revealing of shared financial planning and family management, Dorothée and Samuel arranged to sell a young slave girl to a Baton Rouge inhabitant named Valerian Allain, sharing the proceeds between them. In the same notarial act, Allain donated the slave girl that he had just purchased to Eulalie Allain, his natural daughter. Dorothée Lassize was identified in the act as the natural tutrix of Eulalie. In fact, Dorothée was Eulalie Allain's mother, a relationship revealed in the baptismal act of Sara Virginia Moore. Eulalie served as godmother and was identified as Sara's sister. The sale and donation of the slave girl was obviously organized by Dorothée and Samuel to secure a form of child support from Eulalie's natural father, who lived outside of New Orleans.

Samuel and Dorothée's finances could not be legally merged via the instrument of marriage, but the couple found ingenious ways to act economically as a family.[76] They also seem to have shared an adventurous entrepreneurial streak that left them prone to dramatic financial vicissitudes. Samuel bought and sold timber, slaves, and properties around New Orleans at a restless pace, occasionally taking in windfall profits, more frequently hounded by debtors.[77] Dorothée carried out an unconventional moneymaking scheme in 1825 when she successfully petitioned the state legislature for authorization to sell two properties on Dauphine Street in the French Quarter by lottery. After turning over 1 percent of the proceeds to the state, Dorothée had enough left to move into a grand new townhouse she had built on St. Louis Street.[78]

Samuel and Dorothée had to work hard to make their partnership succeed within the constraints of a legal system designed to subvert it at every turn. As their children came of age, one after the other married. It is possible that each independently chose to avoid their parents' difficult path, but it is equally likely that Samuel and Dorothée exerted influence over their children's futures. The daughter that Dorothée brought to her union with Samuel, Eulalie Allain, married a free man of color in 1813 as her mother looked on. Samuel and Dorothée's three eldest daughters were all married in their teens, daughter Marie Antoinette in 1825 at the age of seventeen, her sister Eurania in 1828 at eighteen, and Charlotte Eugenie in 1829 at sixteen. Son Samuel Jr. married at twenty-two in 1826.[79] Dorothée, raised by a single free woman of color in the 1790s, fits Harriet Martineau's 1830s model of New Orleans quadroons "brought up by their mothers to be what they have been," but not one of her daughters does. The crippling civil code would certainly have been one reason that Dorothée would have been reluctant to see her daughters choose white partners. The origins of the man her daughter Marie Antoinette married points to other developments that made such relationships less attractive in her children's generation than they had been in hers.

The wedding of Marie Antoinette Moore and John Clay was a quiet one, attended only by the bride's brother and brother-in-law and the parents of the bride, Dorothée Lassize and Samuel Moore, and those of the groom, free woman of color Adelaide Raguet and John Clay Sr., a white man.[80] On the face it, the record seems to present us with a marriage between parallel families. In fact they were very different. Adelaide Raguet and Dorothée Lassize were both natives of New Orleans who bore children to Anglophone Protestant men whom they could not legally marry, and both women bore children to two different men. One of the fathers of Dorothée's children formed a life partnership with her and died a bachelor. Adelaide and her children found no such security. John Clay ended his relationship with her two years after the birth of his namesake to marry a white woman. Adelaide moved on to a relationship with another Anglophone Protestant, who apparently left her soon after the birth of their daughter in 1812. Dorothée's partnership with Samuel was a permanent one, Adelaide's relationships with the white fathers of her children transient.

The reasons for the divergent trajectories of these two New Orleans women of color and their Anglophone Protestant lovers can never be fully known, of course. The Anglo-American origins of Adelaide Raguet's lovers may have had nothing to do with their behavior. There were, in fact, Francophone white men who were inconstant paramours. Some, like Augustin Macarty, enjoyed serial partnerships in their youth. Others fathered children with free women of color and went on to marry white women. André Jung, for example, fathered three mixed-race children on three different women of color before marrying a white woman, by whom he had no children. And there were men such as Joseph Dusuau de La Croix who had mixed-race children during and after their marriages to white women. La Croix fathered two children by different women of color while he was married and then formed a partnership with a *mûlatresse* named Maria with whom he had four children.[81] Yet examples of white men who made lifelong, exclusive commitments to a single free woman of color in late colonial New Orleans are far more numerous, numbering well into the dozens.[82] The equation begins to shift only after the Louisiana Purchase.

It is tempting to blame the waning of life partnerships across the color line on what many historians have identified as the Americanization of New Orleans. But Dorothée's life partner and the fathers of Adelaide's children shared the English language and Protestant legacy that were supposed to define the cultural and political unity that drove Americanization. The difference between the two Anglophone men was subtle but important. Samuel Moore grew up in the colonial Lower Mississippi Valley, where interracial partnerships were an established practice. The fathers of Adelaide Raguet's children were both new to New Orleans and its unwritten codes of conduct. As the other relationships described in this chapter reveal, by the 1790s certain expectations seem to have developed about the course and conduct of these associations. Children took their white fathers' names and paternity was usually acknowledged in baptismal records, wills, and other legal documents. The white families and friends of such fathers were not only aware of these interracial households but often involved themselves intimately in their affairs, frequently acting as godparents to the children. Perhaps most important of all, many of these families were permanent, headed by men who went to their graves legal bachelors. The Louisiana Supreme Court, ruling in 1848 on the disputed succession of none other than Eugene Macarty, Augustin's uncle, confirms the widespread recognition of the formal, if extra-legal, nature of such families. It noted of Eugene's life partner, Eulalie Mandeville, that the "state in which she lived was the nearest approach to marriage which the law recognized," and that in 1796, when "their union commenced it imposed serious moral obligations."[83] Eugene Macarty and Samuel Moore were well aware of the traditional terms of the partnerships they entered into with Eulalie Mandeville and Dorothée Lassize. Adelaide Raguet's lovers may have heard about the seductive free women of color described by Moreau de Saint-Méry and relocated by Berquin-Duvallon to New Orleans, but were almost certainly ignorant of the local codes that actually governed relations with women like Lassize and Raguet.[84]

John Clay came to New Orleans at the turn of the nineteenth century on the heels of business reversals in his native Kentucky. When Adelaide Raguet bore him a daughter nearly a year before Louisiana was officially transferred to the United States, he did not sign the baptismal register, and the celebrant at first mistakenly entered his name as "Blay," with no given name. These omissions and mistakes set the record apart from those of the Cazelars, Tios, and Moores. Clay was more visible in the 1806 baptism of his namesake son, John, identifying the child's paternal grandparents in the register entry and signing at the bottom of it. These signs of willingness to be associated with his interracial family did not develop into a lasting commitment to them, however. Shortly after the baptism of his son, Clay ended his relationship with Adelaide and married Louisiana native Julie Duralde, the sister of territorial governor William C. C. Claiborne's wife. Adelaide almost immediately formed a liaison with another Anglophone Protestant, Boston native William Lowell, to whom she bore a son and a daughter. But Lowell, too, disappeared from her life. William Lowell's relationship to the prominent Lowells of Massachusetts is elusive, but John Clay's family ties are clear. He was the elder brother of Henry Clay, Kentucky statesman and 1844 Whig presidential candidate.[85]

The ephemeral nature of Adelaide's relationships with Clay and Lowell may have had nothing to do with their newcomer status. Or much. Unmarried Anglophone Protestant men poured into early national New Orleans. Gender balance had almost been achieved in the city's white population by 1805, when there were 115 adult white men for every 100 white women, but by 1810 it was becoming skewed again, with 130 men for every 100 women. Ten years later, in 1820, the gap between white adult men and women was worse than it had ever been in late colonial New Orleans. With 3,421 men and 1,866 women aged between eighteen and forty-five, the sex ratio for the white population of marriageable age stood at 183, or nearly two men for each woman. The sex ratio among free people of color had also slid back toward colonial-era levels, with more than two free women of color for every free man of color. The unbalanced demography that created an environment that encouraged relationships between free women of color and white men in the late colonial era developed again in the 1820s, but the constituencies that created the disequilibrium were very different. People of Haitian origin or ancestry doubled the New Orleans population of free people of color after 1809, swelling its female ranks disproportionately. And masses of unmarried Anglophone Protestant men, from Yankee merchants to rough hewn "Kaintuck" flatboat men, made their way to the boomtown at the mouth of the Mississippi after the Louisiana Purchase.[86] The pieces were in place for a reconfiguration of relationships across the color line that replaced the figure of the native bachelor patriarch with the untethered parvenu.

Despite the general presumption of Yankee immunity from the temptations of New Orleans free women of color, the same commentators who laid the foundations for quadroon mythology and those who later sustained it unwittingly reveal the centrality of Anglophone Americans to the practice of interracial relationships in the city. The lengthy description of New Orleans quadroons and quadroon balls in 1826 written by Karl Bernhard, the Duke of Saxe-Weimar, is almost universally cited as an authoritative source for the phenomena. Quadroons, Bernhard explained, were the children of "a mestizo mother and a white father," who, despite great beauty, education, and wealth, were "unhappy and oppressed beings" because they could never legally marry the white men with whom they carried on amorous liaisons. Echoing Ashe and Berquin-Duvallon, he explained that New Orleans quadroons were steered by their parents into these relationships, which were contractually arranged.[87]

Bernhard's introduction to these fascinating and tragic figures was not made by Gallic Romeos on the prowl, but rather occurred in the company of his Anglophone travel companions and their friends in New Orleans. His chief tour guide in the city seems to have been John Randolph Grymes, a Virginia-born lawyer with close ties to the administration of Andrew Jackson. Grymes saw to it that Bernhard attended the theater and several balls in New Orleans, including a ball featuring the city's free women of color. "As a stranger in my situation should see every thing, to acquire a knowledge of the habits, customs, opinions and prejudices of the people he is among," Bernhard confided to his readers, "I accepted the offer of some gentlemen who proposed to carry me to [a] quadroon ball." Anglophones introduced Bernhard to the spectacle of the quadroon ball and were undoubtedly his source for his explanation of their habits. In fact, Bernhard's visit took place almost exclusively among Anglophones, who entertained him with lavish parties and a military review, in addition to excursions to the ballroom and the theater. Apart from Grymes and his Anglophone orbit, which included fellow Virginian Governor Henry S. Johnson, Bernhard met only three Francophones, one of them a wealthy white Haitian-born refugee, and the bishop of Louisiana, Louis Dubourg. His only exposure to native Louisianans was a fleeting encounter at the military review with a man who had served in the Spanish colonial forces and an excursion to the rural plantation of Jacques Philippe Villere, the sixty-five-year-old former governor of Louisiana.[88] It is unlikely that impressions gathered from these three outweighed those of the men who took charge of acquainting the visitor with the city and its customs. Bernhard's influential observations on the free women of color of New Orleans and the balls they attended were refracted by an Anglo-American lens.

Most of Harriet Martineau's informants in the early 1830s were likely Anglo-Americans as well, and at least some of them were not even inhabitants of Louisiana. She relays a tragic story about the fate of some free women of color in Louisiana that had "found its way into the northern States (as few such stories do) from the circumstance that a New Hampshire family are concerned in it." Martineau likely picked up the story from the abolitionist circle of Maria Weston Chapman, with whom she spent time during her American tour.[89]

Frederick Law Olmsted's report on New Orleans in the early 1850s provides the most direct account of the role of Anglo-Americans in describing and defining interracial partnerships in antebellum New Orleans. The arrangements that he details bear little resemblance to the households and families of men like Jean Pierre Cazelar and Samuel Moore. Olmsted observed that setting up housekeeping with a free woman of color was a "way of living to be frequently adopted by unmarried men, who come to New Orleans to carry on business," because it was "much cheaper than living at hotels and boarding-houses." A man who had adopted this strategy gave Olmsted a detailed description of his arrangements. "He hired, at a low rent, two apartments in the older part of the town," and the free woman of color who lived with him "did the marketing, and performed all the ordinary duties of housekeeping herself; she took care of his clothes, and in every way was economical and saving in her habits." It was in her interest, Olmsted's informant explained, "to make him as much comfort and as little expense as possible, that he might be the more strongly attached to her, and have the less occasion to leave her." The bachelor businessman concluded, "by assuring me that whatever might be said against it, it certainly was better than the way in which most young men lived who depended on salaries in New York."[90]

Men like Olmsted's informer arrived in New Orleans in the 1850s expecting to find free women of color ready to set up housekeeping with them for a reasonable price and no guarantee of permanency. The prototype of this obliging figure likely lies in the free colored women of Dominguan origin and ancestry who could not find black husbands in New Orleans in the 1820s and 1830s. They were edged out of the marriage market as white Louisiana-born fathers and their free colored partners steered their daughters toward marriage, having seen the prospects for their mixed-race children's security evaporate under the terms of the new civil code of 1808. With their options limited in the 1820s and 1830s, the Haitian refugees and their descendants were the most likely free women of color to seek partnerships with unmarried white men. During those decades, the majority of such men were newcomers to New Orleans who negotiated their relationships outside of the framework that had developed in late colonial Louisiana.

The "quadroon connexions" that Karl Bernhard and Harriet Martineau described between 1826 and 1836 were not a long-established New Orleans tradition, but an adaptation shaped by new exigencies. The 1840s and 1850s saw the transformation of this new prototype into an elaborate literary and commercial trope that served a complex array of cultural and political purposes. Though her roots in New Orleans were shallow, the notorious quadroon who took shape during these decades in the pages of antislavery novels, poetry, and plays and in the lurid hawking of traders selling light-skinned "fancy maids" was yoked in the American imagination to the Crescent City as if she had always been there and always would be.

CHAPTER FIVE
Making Up the Quadroon

The apartment into which she entered was well fitted to receive so fair a mistress. It was a small boudoir, characterized throughout by the most exquisite taste. The floor was inlaid with mosaic in flowers and figures, as finished as a painting in fresco, and shining with the lustre of polished marble. Over its mirrorlike surface were strewn gorgeous mats of dyed Angola hair; the walls were hung with figured tapestry, and around them were ottomans and divans of the most luxurious description.

—Joseph Holt Ingraham, *The Quadroone* (1841)[1]

Joseph Holt Ingraham creates an unmistakably oriental tableau in his portrait of New Orleans and its free women of color in his novel, *The Quadroone; or, St. Michael's Day*, published in 1841. In a city with "the massive look of a Morisco town," the home of his heroine, Azèlie, transports readers to an enchanted garden a world away from the hard edges of American cities. A "partly-opened Venetian door" led onto a luxuriant walled courtyard "filled with flowers, which imbued the air with fragrance, and a white column or two, just visible through the foliage of lemon and orange trees dropping with their golden fruit," while "from an invisible fountain came the sound of water, falling on stone, refreshingly to the ear." The luxurious furnishings with "rich Damascene hangings," mosaic floors, velvet cushions, and cashmere carpets of Azèlie's chamber and the lush hidden courtyard signaled an ambiance that would have been recognizable to the cultured readers of 1841 who picked up Ingraham's popular book. Azèlie's surroundings were those of the harem.[2]

The sultry beauty of the Dominguan quadroon was not new, but Ingraham's evocation of the seraglio heralds a new and powerful episode in the history of the American quadroon. The compelling foreign beauty of Moreau de Saint-Méry's eighteenth-century quadroon undermined patriotic duty and threatened Saint-Domingue's place in the French Republic. The orientalized New Orleans quadroon could be tamed and mastered to serve American interests. Once in America, the figure shed her manipulative agency and assumed a position subordinated to white male interests. Her seduction by white men symbolically emasculated black men. The quadroon was an antidote to the contagion of slave rebellion borne on the currents of masculine violence that Americans so feared.

By the 1830s, the figure of the quadroon had acquired yet another purpose. Antislavery activists showcased her suffering at the hands of white male desire in a powerful indictment against slavery. Kept by her race from claiming the respectability of marriage, the quadroon's dilemma pointed to the central immorality of slavery. Ingraham and the novelists and playwrights who followed him in the depiction of the New Orleans quadroon as an exoticism strengthened her didactic power in the antislavery debate. Like the concubine in an oriental harem, the quadroon was the victim of a corrupt culture foreign to American values in the nonslave states. Through the trope of the quadroon, orientalism, which served as a rationale for nineteenth-century European colonialism, was yoked in America to the politics of abolition. After the Civil War, the quadroon became a vehicle for the exploration of race and the legacies of racism, and the association of New Orleans and its free women of color with the seraglio served a new function as the American imagination grappled with the city's place in a postemancipation nation. This chapter leaves behind the reconstruction of the historical experience of New Orleans free women of color to trace the nineteenth-century literary construction of the quadroon and its role in shaping the history and lives of African-descended women who followed in its wake.

THE FICTIONALIZED FIGURE of the New Orleans quadroon has long been subsumed in the field of literary criticism by the figure of the "tragic mulatto." First identified and defined by Sterling Brown in the 1930s as one of seven literary stereotypes of African-descended people employed by white authors, the tragic mulatto debuted in antebellum antislavery fiction in the 1840s. The character, which could be either male or female and was actually more often identified as a quadroon or an octoroon than a mulatto, invariably came to a catastrophic end. For example, a young mixed-race man might murder his abusive master only to discover that he has unwittingly killed his father. A beautiful young woman might discover on the eve of her wedding that she is of mixed race and thus legally prohibited from marrying her beloved white suitor, a plot that was sometimes complicated by the revelation that the suitor is the girl's half-brother. The most typical situation was that of the beautiful mixed-race girl who has lived free but is actually a slave who must be sold to settle debts. Faced with some horrible twist of fate upon these lines, the tragic mulatto usually commits suicide, perishes of heartbreak, or dies some other dramatic death.[3]

The tragic mulatto illustrated the horrors of slavery at the same time that it exposed the impossible position of mixed-race people in a society defined by a racial binary. The trope was deployed before and during the Civil War by antislavery authors, including Harriet Beecher Stowe, to arouse sympathy for the enslaved and rally support for abolition. After emancipation, the figure became a vehicle for the exploration of racism and race. Both periods spawned a prodigious literary output by American and European authors. Among more than three dozen novels, poems, and plays written between 1834 and 1865 were Lydia Maria Child's "The Quadroons," (1842) Henry Wordsworth Longfellow's "The Quadroon Girl" (1842), Hans Christian Andersen's *Mulatten: originalt romantisk Drama i Fem Akter* (1840), Victor Séjour's "Moeurs coloniales: le Mulâtre" (1837), Harriet Beecher Stowe's *Uncle Tom's Cabin*, (1852), and Dion Boucicault's *The Octoroon* (1859). After the Civil War, the tragic mulatto's popularity grew, inspiring an even more prolific literary output, ranging from Lydia Maria Child's *A Romance of the Republic* (1862) to Edna Ferber's *Show Boat*, William Faulkner's *Absalom, Absalom!* (1936), Langston Hughes's *Mulatto* (1936), and most recently, Isabelle Allende's *Island Beneath the Sea* (2010).[4]

Many of the works featuring the tragic mulatto were set in New Orleans or employed characters that originated in the Crescent City or had ties to it. Literary critics have generally not focused on this aspect of the trope, fixing instead on the thematic continuities of race and slavery. Historians of New Orleans, on the other hand, have typically isolated fictional representations of the city's quadroons from the larger body of literature and analyzed them as representative of a type peculiar to New Orleans. Neither approach produces an entirely satisfactory delineation of the currents of history and culture that met to produce the powerful stereotype of the New Orleans quadroon that has marked the Crescent City as an alienated American site. The figure of the tragic mulatto served to condemn the universals of slavery and racism with morality tales set in multiple sites: the Caribbean, Virginia, and even New York and Massachusetts. The trope of the New Orleans quadroon, on the other hand, singled out one place as the unique locus of an alien cultural artifact that invites colonization of the city by the country of which it is a part.

The best way to untangle the intertwined literary histories of the tragic mulatto and the New Orleans quadroon is to embark on a tour of the writing that produced them. Werner Sollors, who has written extensively on mixed-race figures in literature, suggests that the tragic mulatto is a distinct type whose tragedy rests not on his or her slave status but on the impossible position of the mixed-race person in a society shaped by racial slavery. This archetypal figure, Sollors suggests, appeared first in Lydia Maria Child's 1842 short story "The Quadroons." In Child's tale, the beautiful young quadroon Rosalie and the "handsome and wealthy young, Georgian" Edward fall in love with one another. Though she "well knew that a union with her proscribed race was unrecognised by law," Rosalie agrees to live with Edward as his wife after the two undergo a religious wedding ceremony. They set up housekeeping in a romantic little cottage in a town near Columbus, Georgia. There, Rosalie bears Edward a daughter, Xarifa, and the family lives together happily for ten years. The idyll comes to a crashing halt when Edward sets his sights on a political career that can be most readily advanced by his marriage to Charlotte, the daughter of an influential white man. Edward attempts to have his cake and eat it too, proposing to Rosalie that she remain his "real wife" even after he has legally married Charlotte. Rosalie refuses and sends Edward to his white bride. About a year after Edward's marriage to Charlotte, Rosalie dies of a broken heart. Edward provides for Xarifa's education as a gentlewoman, but he dies a dissolute drunk and so is unable to intercede when it is revealed that Rosalie had never been legally freed. Xarifa is claimed by the descendants of Rosalie's owners and auctioned for an exorbitant sum to serve her new master as a sex slave. She soon loses her mind and dies.[5]

The crux of Rosalie's tragedy is indeed her race, which prevents Edward from marrying her and leads to her abandonment by him, but the greater catastrophe befalls Xarifa, triggered by her status as a slave. An earlier short story, Joseph Holt Ingraham's 1839 "The Quadroon of Orleans," actually comes closer to meeting the classic criterion Sollors delineated and has a better claim on being the seminal text for the stereotype of the tragic mulatto. Set in 1793, the story tells of a young aristocratic refugee of the French Revolution, Baron Championet, who falls in love with a beautiful devotee he sees at prayer in St. Louis Cathedral in New Orleans. The baron is so smitten with her that he pursues her even after he learns that she is not white like himself, but a quadroon named Emilie. He immediately sets out to capture her heart and "one month afterwards the gay Baron Championet boasted the finest establishment and the loveliest mistress in New-Orleans." As soon as the Revolution settles down, however, Championet returns to France, "settling upon Emilie a noble income" and promising her that he will send for her. Predictably, he soon forgets the distant quadroon and weds a wealthy French aristocrat. Within a few months of Championet's departure, Emilie gives birth to his daughter, Louise. Having vowed to the Virgin Mary "that her daughter should never know her mother's degradation nor the race from which she herself had sprung," Emilie leaves New Orleans with Louise when the child is five years old and settles in Paris, where she presents herself as Madame D'Avigny, the widow of a wealthy Caribbean planter.

Louise, whose African descent is, like her mother's, undetectable to the eye, becomes the most admired of the Paris season's debutantes. Leaving the cathedral in Paris with her mother, Louise catches the eye of young Baron Caronde, who very soon proposes marriage to her. The day of the nuptials arrives, and the lovers exchange vows surrounded by their friends in Paris's great cathedral. As soon as the wedding ceremony concludes, Baron Caronde's father, who has been away at war, enters the sanctuary. He is none other than Baron Championet and he and Emilie realize the incestuous tragedy that has just occurred. Emilie falls to the floor and dies; Louise is sent to a convent; and Championet and his son die in battle soon afterwards.[6] Race, not slavery, is at the root of the tragedy. Ingraham's tale, not Child's, is the first to fill Sollors's prescription for the classic tragic mulatto narrative.

Ingraham's fancy had its roots in experience. He was an Episcopal clergyman from Maine who visited New Orleans in the early 1830s before settling into a teaching job in Washington, Mississippi. In a nonfiction account of his travels, *The South-West, by a Yankee*, published in 1833, he offered a cursory, bland description of New Orleans free women of color. "Many fine women, with brunette complexions, are to be seen walking the streets with the air of donnas," he observed. Drawing attention to details that he would later embroider to dramatic effect, he noted that these women wore "no bonnets, but as a substitute, fasten a veil to the head; which, as they move, floats gracefully around them. These are termed 'quadroons,' one quarter of their blood being tinged with African." Ingraham proceeded with more noncommittal comments. "I have heard it remarked, that some of the finest looking women in New-Orleans are 'quadroons.' I know not how true this maybe, but they certainly have large fine eyes, good features, magnificent forms, and elegantly shaped feet."[7]

Just a few years later, in his short story "The Quadroon of Orleans," Ingraham spins these details into a confection of exotic beauty indebted to the Dominguan *mûlatresses* and early nonfiction descriptions of New Orleans free women of color, but moving beyond them to create a new type. Emilie and her daughter Louise are like nothing that has preceded them in American letters. As Baron Championet looked about the cathedral in New Orleans, he "stopped with his eyes resting on the most faultless female figure he thought he had ever beheld." This was the quadroon Emilie, who possessed "a strikingly elegant figure, a lofty carriage, a superb neck and bust, and surpassing symmetry of arm and foot." She diverged from European ideals of beauty only in ways that made her more irresistible. "The soft olive of her complexion was just tinged with the rich blood beneath. Her profile was accurately Grecian, her lips a little too full, perhaps, but her finely shaped mouth lost nothing of its beauty by their richness." As she noticed Championet staring at her, Emilie's sensuous lips "parted in her surprise, and displayed small white teeth; not that glaring ivory white, which is so much admired by those who have not seen such as here described, but of the liquid lustre of pearls." The "large fine eyes" of the quadroons described in *South-West* become intoxicatingly exquisite in Ingraham's portrait of Emilie. "Large-orbed, jet-black eyes, that seemed to float in lakes of liquid languor" loomed out of her face. "They were exceedingly fine. Human eyes could not be finer."[8]

These details of the quadroon's physical charms—blushing cheek, pearly teeth, small hands and feet, extraordinary dark eyes—gestured toward the exotic and were to appear time and again in subsequent descriptions of the female tragic mulatto. But it is an item of Emilie's attire that places Ingraham's heroine firmly in the orientalist tradition: the veil. Casually mentioned in Ingraham's first description of quadroons in *South-West*, in "The Quadroon of Orleans," the veil serves as a powerful signifier. Emilie "wore no bonnet, but instead, a black veil, that fell from a gold comb set with precious stones, down to her feet." This is no evocation of the habit of the Catholic nuns of France and Spain. Kneeling on the cathedral floor, her head bowed to the floor in prayer, Emilie's veiled form mirrors Muslim devotional prostration, and her veil functioned as it would for a woman of the harem, shielding her from the prurient glances of would-be admirers even as it magnified her desirability. Baron Championet is enticed by the veil that "fell in thick folds and hid her face, which, if in harmony with the exquisite symmetry of her figure could not be less than beautiful." When Emilie "lifted her head from the stone floor, the veil fell back from her face, and the eyes of the two met." With the revelation of the face he had imagined, "the young man uttered an exclamation of admiration at her strange and extraordinary beauty." Emilie sustains her performance of the subtle art of oriental seduction as she takes her leave of the cathedral: "Hastily wrapping her veil about her head, she passed him with a stately, undulating motion, and by a side door, hitherto concealed by a curtain, left the Cathedral, though not without glancing over her shoulder ere she disappeared."[9]

The veil is what confirms Emilie's identity as a quadroon when Baron Championet describes to his New Orleans host the mysterious beauty he has spied at the cathedral:

> A veil only you are sure?
>
> A black lace veil, that dropped to her feet. A becoming mode, and one I wish to see take the place of the unsightly bonnet with which the European women choose to disfigure their heads.
>
> You have fallen in love with a *quadroon*, Championet.
>
> If "quadroon" be American for *angel*, by the mass! you say truly!
>
> Ha, ha, ha! Pardon me, my dear baron! I see I must initiate you, or you will be getting into more of these Cathedral adventures with dark-eyed devotees veiled to the feet. First let us fill a bumper to your olive-browned divinity.
>
> Yes. Her veil marks her, if nothing more.—Quadroons alone wear veils.[10]

Ingraham followed his quadroon short story with a full-length novel in 1841, *The Quadroone; or, St. Michael's Day.* Set in the late 1760s, when the Spanish took control of New Orleans from the French, the work is saturated in orientalism. The villain of the piece, the Spanish Count Osma, comes to New Orleans to take possession of the city for Spain. One of the cavaliers he sends as his advance guard, Don Henrique, is wounded and brought unconscious to the home that the beautiful quadroon woman Azèlie shares with her quadroon brother, Renault. As Henrique awakens, "His glance at the instant rested on a hand and arm like moulded pearl, laid upon the head of the ottoman. His heart leaped to his mouth" as he gazed at the figure before him. "Half in the moonlight, half in the shade, supported by her arm, with her face hidden in the abundance of her jetty hair that fell over it, reposed the most graceful form his imagination could pencil." Henrique, thinking he must have died from his wounds, exclaims, "Surely this is Paradise; and this is an Houri!"[11] Henrique, the Catholic Castilian, awakes not to an angel welcoming him to a Christian heaven, but to a houri, "a nymph of the Muslim Paradise," a being of incomparable beauty and sensuality that some believed welcomed virtuous Muslim men to the afterlife.[12]

Azèlie is dressed for the part of a Muslim beauty, in attire that would be very much at home in a famous North African scene conjured by the French orientalist Eugene Delacroix in 1834 and recapitulated in similar images created on both sides of the Atlantic (see Figures 9 and 10).[13] Dressed in a vest "of the finest lawn, with large and loose sleeves, open at the neck and breast, embroidered with gold, and ornamented with little diamond buttons," Azèlie's costume mimics exotic sartorial habits, with "drawers of the finest linen, deeply bordered with lace, and around her waist . . . a broad sash of silk and gold folded together, the ends of which, entwined with precious stones, hung long from behind." To complete her incarnation as an oriental enchantress, Azèlie replicates the signature conventions of the seraglio right down to her toes. "Her slipper of golden tissue, curiously embroidered, had fallen off too, and a naked little foot, all warmth and beauty, and like a child's in its minute and soft proportions, caught the moonlight and finished the picture."[14]

Not only is Azèlie taken for a houri and dressed appropriately for a North African harem, but the dramatic conclusion of the novel reveals that she is not a quadroon at all, but a Moroccan princess. In his youth, Count Osma was held captive by the "Emperor of Morocco" for several years. While there, the emperor's daughter, Zillah, fell in love with him, and they were married in a Muslim ceremony. Osma, however, abandoned his Moroccan wife and returned to Spain, where he took a Christian wife. Zillah followed him to Spain and died giving birth to their daughter, rejected and abandoned by all but her faithful servant woman, who traveled the world with the infant seeking to avenge her mistress. On the trail of the evil Osma, the servant and her noble charge come to New Orleans, where both are sold into slavery. The servant escapes, and the Moroccan princess becomes the property of a conniving free woman of color who intends to sell her adoptive enslaved daughter into concubinage to the highest bidder. Years later, the servant woman returns to New Orleans in the guise of a Muslim sorceress and devises the revelation of Azèlie's true identity.

Ingraham's extraordinary depiction of Azèlie resonates startlingly with what was probably the best-known orientalist female portrait in literature at the time, Sir Walter Scott's depiction in *Ivanhoe* of the Jewess Rebecca. Like Azèlie's, Rebecca's "form was exquisitely symmetrical, and was shown

FIGURE 9. *Une Mulatresse.* By the 1830s, free women of color were imagined as orientalized odalisques. Compare this depiction of a mixed-race woman from the French colony of Martinique with the odalisque painted by Frenchman Jean-Auguste-Dominique Ingres (Figure 10). From Alcide Dessalines d'Orbigny, *Voyage pittoresque dans les deux Amériques* (1836), facing p. 19, fig. 2. Courtesy of the John Carter Brown Library, Brown University.

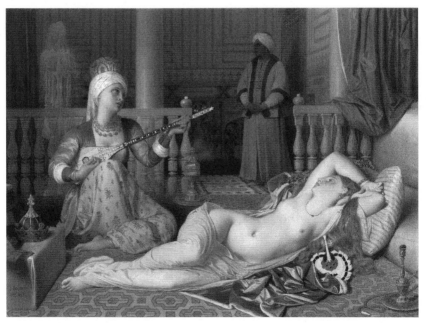

FIGURE 10. Jean-Auguste-Dominique Ingres, *Odalisque with Slave*, 1839. Courtesy of the Morgan Library and Museum, New York.

to advantage by a sort of Eastern dress, which she wore according to the fashion of the females of her nation." Rebecca's mode of dress offers multiple parallels to Azèlie's in its Eastern references and casual display of opulence. "It is true, that of the golden and pearl-studded clasps, which closed her vest from the throat to the waist, the three uppermost were left unfastened on account of the heat," Scott writes of Rebecca, foreshadowing Azèlie's elegant vest, "open at the neck and breast, embroidered with gold, and ornamented with little diamond buttons."[15]

Ingraham's descriptions of his quadroon heroines' physical features mirror those of Scott's Rebecca, as well. The "profusion of [Rebecca's] sable tresses, which, each arranged in its own little spiral of twisted curls, fell down upon as much of a lovely neck and bosom as a simarre [vest] of the richest Persian silk," are a model for those described by Azèlie's admirer. "What can compare with the glossy softness of those tresses, or the blackness of their hue! They concealed all her face and bosom like a veil." Ingraham's earlier quadroon incarnation, Emilie, was possessed of a similar crowning glory. "Her raven hair was gathered behind, and fell in rich tresses about her finely shaped head." Ingraham might have lifted his descriptions of his quadroon's teeth nearly verbatim from Scott. Compare Rebecca's "teeth as white as pearl" to Emilie's "small white teeth; not that glaring ivory white, which is so much admired by those who have not seen such as here described, but of the liquid lustre of pearls."[16]

Eyes were perhaps the most common diagnostic feature of Jewish and Muslim descent in orientalist literature in the nineteenth century.[17] A character in Ingraham's "Quadroon of Orleans" claims that he knows "some beautiful quadroons in the fifth descent, who, save a certain indescribable expression in the centre of the pupils of their fine eyes, have the appearance of lovely Italian women." And in his preface to *The Quadroone*, Ingraham explains that people "who retain even a tenth part of the African blood, and, to all appearance, are as fair as Europeans, and undistinguished from them save by the remarkable and undefinable expression of the eyes, which always betrays their remote Ethiopian descent, come also under the general designation of Quadroon."[18] Scott provides Ingraham with a perfect model for the eyes of his New Orleans quadroons. His introduction of Rebecca draws attention to the "brilliancy of her eyes, the superb arch of her eyebrows," while in Ingraham's Emilie, "silken eye-brows were penciled in perfect arches" over her languorous black eyes.[19]

Ingraham's explicit orientalism may have been informed by earlier works that evoked the brilliant eyes, pearly teeth, and gold-spangled costume that gestured more subtly to women of the seraglio. Joanna, the *mû-latresse* paramour of John Gabriel Stedman described in his account of the five years he spent in Surinam in the 1770s, foreshadows Azèlie and Emilie in numerous particulars. "Her Eyes as black as Ebony were large and full of expression," her hair formed "a beauteous Globe of small ringlets, ornamented with flowers and Gold Spangles," and a "Shaul of finest indian Muslin the end of which was negligently thrown over her polished Shoulder gracefully covered part of her lovely bosom." And, of course, when she spoke and her lips parted they disclosed "two regular rows of pearls." Stedman's narrative, originally published in English in 1796, was popular enough to warrant reprints in 1806 and 1813, but Ingraham is more likely to have encountered these details of Joanna's appearance in Lydia Maria Child's edited presentation of Stedman's dalliance published in the antislavery journal *The Oasis* in 1834.[20]

Stedman's account of his encounter with Joanna is not the primary focus of his wandering narrative, but in it Child obviously saw a morality tale that could be extracted and used to advantage in the campaign against slavery.[21] Conveyed in interspersed short episodes and allusions, the romance between the Anglo-Dutch soldier Stedman and the teenaged slave Joanna develops obliquely over more than 800 pages in the original 1796 publication. From these narrative fragments, readers learn that Stedman was instantly captivated by the fifteen-year-old Joanna's beauty and gentle nature and that she reciprocated his affection with steadfast loyalty. Although the impecunious soldier was unable to marshal the funds necessary to liberate her, he "married" Joanna in a religious ceremony and fathered a child with her. He was sent back to England before securing his family's freedom, and Joanna died. Child did not embroider or fictionalize Stedman's narrative in *The Oasis*, but instead reproduced large portions of it verbatim, interleaving it with antislavery observations to supply it with a new, coherent moral thrust. In Child's hands, the story of Joanna served as an example of the inevitable tragedy that befell enslaved women and their children when they crossed paths with a white lover.[22]

The cad's abandonment of a virtuous woman, especially a foreign or exotic woman, was not a new narrative device. Indeed, this storyline reaches back to Biblical and Classical literature. The eighteenth century saw a marked surge in its appearance, however, as Europe's first round of colonization projects in the Americas, Africa, and Asia matured. Now, New World women began to assume the role of abandoned heroine for the first time. The fictional prototype for the abandoned foreign woman in the

Atlantic setting was Yarico, an Indian woman who saves the Englishman Thomas Inkle during his expedition to America in 1647. The two fall in love and enjoy a sensuous idyll before Yarico flags down a European ship that conveys the two to Barbados. There, short of funds, the reprehensible Inkle sells Yarico into slavery. Stedman's later account transfers the role of the tragic outsider to an enslaved woman of African descent, Joanna, and Child's treatment of Stedman implied its relevance for the slavery question in the United States.

In her 1837 *Society in America*, English sociologist Harriet Martineau supplied a final piece in this literary construct to connect the tragic mixed-race woman with New Orleans, putting into place all of the elements that Ingraham drew together to create his prototypical quadroon.[23] Martineau was publicly committed to the cause of antislavery before she set out for a sojourn in the United States between 1834 and 1836 but traveled extensively throughout both North and South to see and hear for herself slavery's defenders and opponents.[24] Since she granted her informants the courtesy of anonymity, it is impossible to know how she came by an account that had "found its way into the northern States (as few such stories do)," the tragic story of a New Hampshire man and his quadroon daughters.[25] Martineau spent considerable time in Boston, where she attended a ladies' meeting of an unnamed antislavery society and developed what would become a close friendship with abolitionist Maria Weston Chapman. Chapman and Lydia Maria Child were members of the same activist circle, and it seems more than a little likely that Martineau heard the story from someone in their circle. It is impossible to know if the story was grounded in fact or was merely apocryphal, but its veracity is less important than the relocation of the figure of the quadroon it effects. The tale of the New Hampshire man and his tragic family reconfigures and complicates the essential elements of Joanna's narrative and sites them in Louisiana. Since it provides such a critical link in the literary genealogy of the New Orleans quadroon, it is worth reproducing most of it here.

Martineau notes that the story "has excited due horror wherever it is known; and it is to be hoped that it will lead to the exposure of more facts of the same kind, since it is but too certain that they are common." She proceeds to relate how a "New Hampshire gentleman went down into Louisiana, many years ago, to take a plantation." There he "pursued the usual method; borrowing money largely to begin with, paying high interest, and clearing off his debt, year by year, as his crops were sold." The Yankee planter also "followed another custom there; taking a Quadroon wife: a mistress, in the eye of the law," Martineau clarifies, "since there can be no legal marriage between whites and persons of any degree of colour: but, in nature and in reason, the woman he took home was his wife." The quadroon "was a well-principled, amiable, well-educated woman" who "had only the slightest possible tinge of colour."

The planter from New Hampshire and the Louisiana quadroon "lived happily together for twenty years." But she was not completely at ease. "Knowing the law that the children of slaves are to follow the fortunes of the mother, she warned her husband that she was not free, an ancestress having been a slave, and the legal act of manumission having never been performed. The husband promised to look to it: but neglected it. At the end of twenty years, one died, and the other shortly followed, leaving daughters; whether two or three, I have not been able to ascertain with positive certainty; but I have reason to believe three, of the ages of fifteen, seventeen, and eighteen: beautiful girls, with no perceptible mulatto tinge."

The orphaned girls' uncle came to Louisiana from New Hampshire to settle his dead brother's affairs. "He was pleased with his nieces, and promised to carry them back with him into New Hampshire, and (as they were to all appearance perfectly white) to introduce them into the society which by education they were fitted for." There was just one obstacle: their father "had died insolvent." In order to settle things with his brother's creditors, the uncle made an inventory of his brother's effects and presented it to the creditors.

"Some of the creditors called on him, and complained that he had not delivered a faithful inventory. He declared he had. No: the number of slaves was not accurately set down: he had omitted the daughters. The executor was overwhelmed with horror, and asked time for thought. He went round among the creditors, appealing to their mercy: but they answered that these young ladies were 'a first-rate article,' too valuable to be relinquished." The uncle, a father of six with little money of his own, offered "all he had for the redemption of his nieces; alleging that it was more than they would bring in the market for house or field labour. This was refused with scorn. It was said that there were other purposes for which the girls would bring more than for field or house labour. The uncle was in despair, and felt strongly tempted to wish their death rather than their surrender to such a fate as was before them."

Despondent, the uncle tells his nieces the awful truth, that they are slaves and must be sold to the highest bidders. The nieces become despondent, tearing at their uncle's heart. "He declares that he never before beheld human grief; never before heard the voice of anguish. They never ate, nor slept, nor separated from each other, till the day when they were taken into the New Orleans slave-market." Martineau does not turn away from the inevitable conclusion of the daughters' story. "There they were sold, separately, at high prices, for the vilest of purposes: and where each is gone, no one knows. They are, for the present, lost. But they will arise to the light in the day of retribution."[26]

Ingraham was the first to draw together from the succession of nonfiction sources and traditions exemplified by Stedman, Bernhard, and Martineau the complex of elements that scholars have subsequently identified as central to the figure of the tragic mulatto. And his association of the figure with New Orleans, though not copied by Child in "The Quadroons," was to become a key characteristic of the stereotype in subsequent fiction. Ingraham was conservative. He turned Azèlie into a Moroccan princess to avoid the consummation of the interracial romance at the center of his narrative. His reticence has placed him at the margins of critical studies of the tragic mulatto, but his New Orleans–based pastiche was arguably more influential than Child's in shaping this literature. It certainly cemented the Crescent City's reputation as the site where the quadroon was most reliably to be found.

Ingraham was the first to fully orientalize the quadroon, and no other author matched his saturation of exotic detail. But once introduced, the comparison of the position of the quadroon to the harem recurred regularly. Three years later, Lydia Maria Child herself followed Ingraham's lead. Although she offered a minimalist portrait of her heroine, Rosalie, who was simply "graceful as an antelope, and beautiful as the evening star," with no veil or exotic jewels to gesture toward the East, the name of Rosalie's doomed daughter pointed explicitly in that direction. Xarifa was named for the Moorish heroine in a popular song of the era, "The Bridal of Andalla." In the ballad, onlookers enjoin Xarifa to look down from her screened balcony in the Muslim city of Grenada to see the gallant Andalla ride through the streets to meet his bride, Zara. Xarifa, her tears falling onto the golden cushion she is embroidering, finally reveals the reason she will not join the wedding spectators. "The dark-eyed youth pledged me his truth with tears, and was my lover," she explains. "I will not rise, with weary eyes, nor lay my cushion down, To gaze on false Andalla with all the gazing town!"[27] Americans understood, by this simple device, the parallel that Child wished to draw between the quadroon and the compromised women of the Muslim world.[28]

SUPERFICIALLY, IT APPEARS that orientalism faded from the fictional evocations of the quadroon that followed Child's short story. There are no more heroines with Muslim names, veils, glittering vests, or ottomans. The tropical verdure, foreign tongues, languid bayous, and mysterious Catholicism of New Orleans and its nearby plantations, however, indexed the same exoticism and became the stock setting for the tales of quadroons of the 1840s, 1850s, and 1860s. The crew of the "Slaver in the broad lagoon," of Henry Wadsworth Longfellow's "The Quadroon Girl," watched "the gray alligator slide/Into the still bayou," taking in "Odors of orange-flowers, and spice," while they waited for a greedy planter to hand his quadroon daughter over to the slave trader, "To be his slave and paramour/In a strange and distant land!"[29] Cassy, the quadroon slave in *Uncle Tom's Cabin*, describes her New Orleans upbringing with similar telling details. "There was a garden opening from the saloon windows; and there I used to play hide-and-go-seek, under the orange-trees, with my brothers and sisters. I went to a convent, and there I learned music, French and embroidery."[30] The hero of Mayne Reid's *The Quadroon; or, a Lover's Adventures in Louisiana* awakens after a steamboat accident in a plantation guesthouse suffused with the fragrance of tropical flowers, "the rare camellia—azaleas, and jessamines—the sweet-scented China-tree—and farther off a little I could distinguish the waxen leaves and huge lily-like blossoms of the great American laurel—the *Magnolia grandiflora*."[31]

By the 1850s the foreign qualities that designated New Orleans the natural habitat of the American quadroon were understood without the botanical and sartorial signifiers that accompanied the figure in its earlier appearances. The distinguishing physical markers of the orientalized quadroon herself, however, assumed a canonical quality. The "masses of glossy black hair, waving along the brows and falling over the shoulders in curling clusters," of Mayne Reid's 1856 quadroon heroine, Aurore, could have belonged to Ingraham's Azèlie. And Reid's depiction of Aurore's eyes upheld the convention that made them the centerpiece of a quadroon's distinction. "The eye I fancied, or remembered well—better than aught else," Reid's white lover relates. "It was large, rounded, and of dark brown colour; but its peculiarity consisted in a certain expression, strange but lovely. Its brilliance was extreme, but it neither flashed nor sparkled. It was more like a gorgeous gem viewed by the spectator while at rest. Its light did not blaze—it seemed rather to *burn*."[32] Marie St. Vallé, the quadroon mother in James Peacocke's *Creole Orphans*, conformed to the model set by Ingraham's Azèlie. "Her form was of that voluptuous, flowing mould, whose every action is grace," and her eyes, of course, "were large and dazzling, as ebon as her hair." And Marie shared one other signature trait of her literary forebears. "As she entered the room, a smile illuminated her beautiful face and showed her pearly teeth."[33]

Mayne Reid's Aurore served as the prototype for the most famous tragic mulatto of them all, Zoe, in Dion Boucicault's melodrama, "The Octoroon; or Life in Louisiana." The play opened in New York in 1859 to immediate notoriety North and South and has been frequently revived, including an Off-Broadway spinoff staged in 2010.[34] Zoe is the daughter of a quadroon slave and a white father who has freed her. She and a young white man, George Peyton, are in love with one another, and the wealthy belle of a neighboring plantation, Dora Sunnyside, is in love with George. The evil overseer, Jacob M'Closky, desires Zoe for himself and uncovers an obscure obligation of her father's that not only renders her a slave but requires that she be auctioned to settle the debt. Zoe is taken to the New Orleans slave market, where M'Closky bids for her against Dora, who has nobly sold her own plantation so that George's beloved will not be sold into sexual slavery. After Zoe is sold to M'Closky for the outrageous sum of $25,000, she commits suicide with poison. The scene of the apparently white Zoe on the auction block was the dramatic highpoint of the play, and with each restaging of the play New Orleans grew more powerfully linked to the figure of the tragic mulatto.[35]

Through the medium of the fictional quadroon, New Orleans was imaginatively construed as a place apart in the American polity, the only place in the nation where the strange fruit bred of slavery and white desire grew and met its inevitable, tragic destiny. Tragic mulattos did occasionally turn up in other locales. Richard Hildreth's novel *The Slave* (1840) and Emily Preston's *Cousin Franck's Household* (1853) were set in Virginia, and John Townsend's *Neighbor Jackwood* in Vermont.[36] The majority, however, were situated in New Orleans, giving the impression, to the antislavery reading public at least, that this was the place within the United States that was most, if not exclusively, tainted by the most odious features of slavery. In New Orleans, fathers sold their daughters into slavery, saw them auctioned off to settle debts, or died before they could free their children, condemning them to lives of misery in the fields or worse. New Orleans, with its population of beautiful quadroons, became the place to buy and sell women who, except for the "remarkable and undefinable expression of the eyes, which always betrays their remote Ethiopian descent," appeared to be white. New Orleans was the only place in the United States where a man could purchase the makings of his own harem.[37]

Fictional quadroon heroines were all either enslaved or faced the threat of being sold into slavery. Even Ingraham's Moroccan princess Azèlie, though born free and noble, grew up believing that she was not free, dreading being peddled by her mother to the highest bidder for sex.[38] The living quadroons described by journalists and visitors to New Orleans, however, were understood to be free women of color who chose to ally themselves with white men in an arrangement that Ingraham described as "a system of concubinage that has been without a parallel even in Oriental countries."[39] The New Orleans quadroons could not be bought as slaves against their will, but they agreed to exchange their favors on specified terms. This system came to be known in the twentieth century as *plaçage*. Since it is impossible to find good evidence for the use of the term *plaçage* by antebellum New Orleanians, the assemblage of features that defined it for twentieth-century authors is referred to here as the *plaçage* complex. The *plaçage* complex played a role as important as that of the tragic mulatto in distinguishing New Orleans and its mixed-race women. Abolitionists, fed on the fictional fare of the tragic mulatto, expected New Orleans to be filled with "white" slaves catering to the sexual appetites of immoral men. Other visitors to the city, informed by sensationalized travelers' accounts, hoped for a glimpse of one of its renowned kept women of color, and perhaps contemplated engaging one for themselves. The literature that generated this prurient anticipation was nearly as prolific as the fictional evocations of the tragic mulatto designed to snuff it out.

The *plaçage* complex was delineated in nonfiction with a repertoire of standard elements. Foremost among them was a belief that New Orleans free women of color did not marry but instead formed relationships with white men on a contractual or quasi-contractual basis. The women were presumed to have chosen this way of life because law forbade their marriage to white men and they held themselves above men of their own racial background. Such a partnership was generally described as having been brokered by a woman's parents, with terms including a house and provision for any children born of the relationship. Once the terms of the arrangements were settled, the woman was known as a *placée*, and it was understood that she would restrict her sexual favors to the man who supported her. The term of the engagement might be for months or years, but the common assumption was that it lasted until the white lover married a woman of his own race. New Orleans *placées* were often portrayed as wealthy heiresses to the fortunes of their white fathers, well educated and accomplished. Demure and proper in public, they were renowned for the pleasure they brought their lovers in private.

The origins of the *plaçage* complex have their roots in the figurative and literal immigration of the Dominguan *mûlatresse* to New Orleans, as we have seen.[40] Subsequent accounts of it in English echo one another so consistently that it is difficult to credit any of them as original.[41] All the same, these are the sources that not only informed travelers who visited antebellum New Orleans but have served as the basis of historical examinations of the city's free women of color. And as we shall see in the next chapter, this literature created a circular feedback phenomenon that fed the invention and proliferation of activities in New Orleans designed to satisfy the market for encounters with quadroons aroused by the earliest accounts. The discursive construction of the quadroon and the *plaçage* complex in nineteenth-century travel literature may be nearly as fanciful as the tragic mulatto's, but it was equally constitutive of the image of New Orleans free women of color that took up residence in the antebellum American mind and remained rooted there in the twentieth century.[42]

Thomas Ashe's description of New Orleans women of color in his 1808 *Travels in America* is the first to delineate many of the stock attributes of the *plaçage* complex. According to the Englishman, free women of color "who are but one remove from the African cast [*sic*], are subordinate to those who are from two to three, or more, and are interdicted, by custom, from intermarrying with the whites; but they are allowed, by the same authority, to become mistresses of the whites." Ashe thus seems to suggest that only *mûlatresses* participated in the arrangement he goes on to describe. These women, he reported, "are esteemed honorable and virtuous while faithful to one man," and "the instances of their infidelity are very rare, though they are extremely numerous, and are mistresses to the married and unmarried, and nearly to all the strangers who resort to the town." There was, Ashe explained, a protocol for those who wished to form an attachment with one of these women. "The introduction of strangers to them is attended with some ceremony, and must always be through the means of the mother, or female adopted to supply her place. The inhabitants of the town never break down their regulations, or treat them abruptly, and strangers are instructed by their acquaintance how to proceed. The Levée at sunset, is the principal market for all this traffic *de coeur*."

Ashe was wonderfully explicit about how matches were sealed. "The mothers always regulate the terms and make the bargain. The terms allowed the parents are generally fifty dollars a month; during which time the lover has the exclusive right to the house, where fruit, coffee, and refreshments may at any time be had, or where he may entirely live with the utmost safety and tranquility."[43]

The "Levée at sunset," not the ballroom, was where men went to meet prospective mistresses by Ashe's account, though he does mention entertainments that would later come to be known as quadroon balls. "Notwithstanding the beauty and wealth of these women, they are not admitted, as I before remarked, to the white assemblies. They have therefore a ballroom of their own, which is well attended, and where as beautiful persons and as graceful dancing is witnessed, as in any other assemblies of the sort whatever."[44]

New Yorker Christian Schultz was so outraged by the inaccuracies in Ashe's long-winded travel narrative that he published his own as a corrective in 1810.[45] Schultz may have supplied more-reliable descriptions of topography than Ashe, but his portrait of the free women of color in New Orleans essentially recapitulates Ashe. He makes observations on "that unfortunate class of females, the mulattoes, who from their infancy are trained in the arts of love." The rest of his discussion virtually repeats whole sections of Ashe's. The rationale for the women's behavior is unchanged. "Since custom has planted an insurmountable barrier to their ever forming an honourable connexion with white men, necessity has compelled them to resort to the practice of forming temporary engagements with those whom they may fancy." Schultz reiterates Ashe's comments on the women's sexual loyalty. "During any engagement of this kind, it is in vain to solicit improper favours: they are generally as strictly continent as the marriage ceremony could possibly make them. When the term is expired, or the lover gone, they accept of the next best offer that may be made to them."[46]

"The season for balls is already past," Schultz admitted, explaining to his readers that, "of course I shall have no opportunity of saying any thing respecting them, except from information." Nevertheless, he did not hesitate to offer a report on quadroon balls that echoes Ashe and adds new details that remain part of the canonical description of these events. "The coloured people have likewise their separate ball-room, from which all are excluded who have not some white blood in their veins. The white gentlemen of course are freely admitted, who generally prefer this assembly to their own, which it at all times surpasses both in the elegance of its decorations, and the splendour of the dress of the company."[47]

Ashe and Schultz were almost certainly the sources that Amos Stoddard drew on for his 1812 account of New Orleans free women of color. He was the U.S. commandant of Upper Louisiana for a brief period after 1804 and acknowledged basing his *Sketches, Historical and Descriptive, of Louisiana* on manuscripts and printed sources rather than personal observation.[48] Stoddard's version, however, may have carried more authority by virtue of his official position and may have been standard reading for government functionaries and serious-minded immigrants to Louisiana from other parts of the country. "The *Quaterons* or free people of color, in New-Orleans, are not the least interesting in point of beauty and dress," Stoddard wrote, continuing to explain that they "enjoy much more consideration in that country than is usual in any other. They never associate with blacks; and as there is a strong barrier between them and the whites with respect to marriage, they may be said to form a distinct class. The females possess the most beautiful forms and features. If they are accustomed to bestow their favors on the higher orders of society, it is always for stipulated periods, and no depravation of manners is observable among them. Gentlemen of distinction resort to their ball-rooms, and other places of amusement, where decency and decorum maintain their empire."[49]

An anonymous observer writing from Mobile recapitulated these early accounts of New Orleans free women of color in a letter that was published in Providence, Rhode Island, in 1820. Like many who followed, the author relied on what he was told, not what he saw. "I was in New-Orleans but a very short time, I saw but little, but heard sufficient to convince me that gambling and sensual pleasures were practised to such a degree as nearly to destroy domestic happiness and tranquility," the correspondent reported, before launching into his disquisition on the city's free women of color and their dances. His is the earliest use of the term famously associated with these entertainments. "Every Saturday night is ushered in with splendid quadroon balls; at these balls none but the quadroon ladies (that is, women of mixed blood) and white gentlemen are allowed to attend," he wrote, before admitting that his experience of these events was secondhand. "I had a polite invitation to attend, but as my dancing days have passed by, I declined the honour." He had to rely on his traveling companions to describe the ball and the women they encountered there. All of the standard elements of the *plaçage* complex were already in place. The quadroons "were highly accomplished in their manners, were handsome, well behaved and well dressed." Since they were "prohibited by law, or a custom which has become a law, to marry a white man, and they are too proud and high minded to marry one of their own colour," the women "become openly, without any degradation, kept mistresses, and will, it is said while engaged, if it be for a week, month or year, be true to their employers." He continued to explain that it was "said to be the common practice of the mothers of such daughters to educate them for the purpose of pleasure, and barter them away during their minority to the best bidder."[50]

By the time Karl Bernhard, the Duke of Saxe-Weimar, visited New Orleans in 1826, these earlier descriptions had established a set of well-defined expectations about the behavior of the city's free women of color, labeled them all under the term "quadroon," and virtually invited male visitors to have a look for themselves by attending one of their balls. Bernhard did just that, adding his commentary to the canon. In the company of his Anglophone hosts, the duke set off for a night of dancing. He and his companions went first to a masked ball restricted to whites, a dull affair where "unmasked ladies belonging to good society, sat in the recesses of the windows, which were higher than the saloon, and furnished with galleries," apparently unwilling to descend to the dance floor where any man who paid a dollar could claim a waltz. His party soon departed for the "quadroon ball" being held on the same night.

The duke plainly cast his forays into the ballrooms of New Orleans as tourist excursions, stops that were widely appreciated as part of any curious traveler's itinerary. "As a stranger in my situation should see every thing, to acquire a knowledge of the habits, customs, opinions and prejudices of the people he is among, therefore I accepted the offer of some gentlemen who proposed to carry me to this quadroon ball," he explains, before proceeding to praise the experience in comparison to the white ball he had just left. "I must avow I found it much more decent than the masked ball. The coloured ladies were under the eyes of their mothers, they were well and gracefully dressed, and conducted themselves with much propriety and modesty. Cotillions and waltzes were danced, and several of the ladies performed elegantly."[51]

It was perhaps from the men who brought him to the quadroon ball that Bernhard learned an additional detail about the city's free women of color that he could incorporate into his version of their habits. "The quadroons," he notes, "assume the name of their friends." Otherwise, he simply reiterates features introduced by earlier commentators. "I am assured," he writes, revealing the hearsay nature of much of his information, "[that they] preserve this engagement with as much fidelity as ladies espoused at the altar." He confirms earlier accounts that spoke of the women's wealth and gentility, noting that "several of these girls have inherited property from their fathers or friends, and possess handsome fortunes," and that some "have enjoyed the benefits of as careful an education as most of the whites; they conduct themselves ordinarily with more propriety and decorum."[52]

Bernhard closed his remarks by speaking to the exclusive nature of the event at which the city's free women of color can be seen, hinting that visits to these balls are not for the rabble and are, rather, a gentleman's entertainment. "At the quadroon ball, only coloured ladies are admitted, the men of that caste, be it understood, are shut out by the white gentlemen. To take away all semblance of vulgarity, the price of admission is fixed at two dollars, so that only persons of the better class can appear there."[53]

The English sociologist Harriet Martineau was the first to set down in print the apocryphal story of the three quadroon girls who found themselves sold into sexual slavery upon their white father's death, but she followed Bernhard's models and some of his methods in her own reporting on New Orleans free women of color. Like Bernhard, she relied on what she had been told by others. "The Quadroon connexions in New Orleans are all but universal, as I was assured on the spot by ladies who cannot be mistaken," she explains. Like earlier commentators, she affirmed the role of mothers in perpetuating the *plaçage* complex, noting that "Quadroon girls of New Orleans are brought up by their mothers to be what they have been; the mistresses of white gentlemen." According to her sources, quadroon women rejected marriage with men who shared their racial ancestry, dismissing the prospect with a condemnatory, "ils sont si degoutants!" (They are so disgusting!). She repeats earlier reports of the quadroons' assets: "The girls are highly educated, externally, and are, probably, as beautiful and accomplished a set of women as can be found." And, like Bernhard before her, she introduces a new detail to be added to the catalogue of the *plaçage* complex. "Every young man early selects one, and establishes her in one of those pretty and peculiar houses, whole rows of which may be seen in the Remparts."[54]

Martineau also offered more information about the duration of such arrangements, and the tragedy and willing suspension of disbelief that accompanied them. "The connexion now and then lasts for life: usually for several years," she informs her readers. The ends of such affairs were tragic, for "when the time comes for the gentleman to take a white wife, the dreadful news reaches his Quadroon partner, either by a letter entitling her to call the house and furniture her own, or by the newspaper which announces his marriage." The marriage of their lovers marked the end of the women's lives, figuratively and sometimes literally. "The Quadroon ladies are rarely or never known to form a second connexion. Many commit suicide: more die broken-hearted." The inevitability of this course of events was suppressed by all concerned. "Every Quadroon woman believes that her partner will prove an exception to the rule of desertion. Every white lady believes that her husband has been an exception to the rule of seduction."[55]

Bernhard and Martineau are the two most commonly referenced non-fiction sources on New Orleans quadroons. Despite their dependence on earlier accounts and hearsay, these descriptions of the city's free women of color, the *plaçage* complex, and quadroon balls have often been accepted as authoritative by modern scholars of these phenomena.[56] British traveler James Stuart observed in 1833 after a visit to New Orleans that, "The tales which have been told of the assemblage of beauties on the levee at sunset, where the mother or female relation makes the best bargain she can for her daughter or her ward, are, I am quite satisfied, merely traveller's stories." Stuart admitted that because "the prejudices which exist on the American continent prevent a regular marriage from being entered into," that "connections are formed by the quadroon or coloured ladies with the whites." But, he insisted, "the attachment of the quadroons is so constant, and their conduct so free from stain, that the connection is considered in the light of a left-handed marriage. It very generally lasts for life, almost always where it is not the fault of the husband."[57] Stuart, alone of the observers who preceded and followed him, seems to have become acquainted with the life partnerships formed by the bachelor patriarchs we met in the last chapter.

What, then, did Karl Bernhard really see when he attended the quadroon ball on a January night in 1826? If we separate his rehashing of Ashe and Schultz from his account of the ball and consider it in light of the situation of Haitian-descended women in New Orleans in the 1820s, it makes plausible the proposition advanced earlier. What Bernhard encountered in New Orleans in the 1820s, and the *plaçage* complex that he described, were likely manifestations of an adaptation made by refugee and refugee-descended women to their circumstances. New Orleans–born and -descended free women of color met husbands and made partnerships with white men by means of long-established networks of sociability and kinship. Refugee and refugee-descended women had to find a different way, especially since there were few potential husbands among the refugee community. The revival in New Orleans by Auguste Tessier in 1805 of the Dominguan tradition of balls frequented by free women of color and white men gave refugee and refugee-descended women a chance to meet men who might provide them with some measure of financial and social security.

The possibility that the quadroon balls and the liaisons they facilitated were especially, if not entirely, linked to the plight of Dominguan women is strengthened by the poetry and short stories authored by free men of color of Haitian descent in the 1840s. In Armand Lanusse's 1843 short story "Un Marriage du Conscience" (A Marriage of Conscience), a young free woman of color is persuaded by her mother to rise from her prie-dieu to attend one of the carnival balls of the season. There she meets the gentleman Gustave, and after several nights of waltzing, she explains to her sympathetic interlocutor, "The depths of my heart reverberated with a love that I thought Gustave also shared—the love that he so often professed to me." Her mother pressures her to submit to a secret marriage ceremony with Gustave, who "could not legally wed me because his social situation was superior to ours."

After the secret "marriage of conscience," however, the young woman finds, "My happiness was short lived." At the balls she and her lover both continue to attend, she watches "Gustave shower his affections on other women." Ashamed, she hides her pain. After months of such suffering she "greeted with joy the moment that I became a mother, and thought that this sacred status that I had just earned would win back all of the love and affection of my husband." But Gustave soon reveals that he is going to marry another woman. That wedding, unlike the secret ceremony that had united her to Gustave, is public and "celebrated with great ceremony." At the end of the story the abandoned woman confronts Gustave as he rides past her in an elegant coach, his white wife at his side. The horses pulling the carriage trample Lanusse's protagonist to death, and before the sympathetic bystander to whom she has told her story can reveal to the young wife the relationship between the dead woman and her husband, Gustave orders, "Whip the horses!" heartlessly putting his past dalliance behind him once and for all.[58]

Lanusse never directly identifies the wronged woman in his story as a quadroon, but the racial identity of his heroine was well understood by his readers. Lanusse was a leading member of the circle of well-known free black literary figures in antebellum New Orleans, and "Un Marriage du

Conscience" was not his only attack against mothers who encouraged their daughters to form transient relationships with white men. His 1845 poem "Épigramme" succinctly summarizes the evil of the practice:

> Vous ne voulez donc pas renoncer à Satan,
> Disait un bon pasteur à certaine bigote
> Qui d'assez gros péchés, à chaque nouvel an,
> Venait lui présenter l'interminable note.
> Je veux y renoncer, dit-elle, pour jamais;
> Mais avant que la grâce en mon âme scintille,
> Pour m'ôter tout motif de pécher désormais,
> Que ne puis-je, pasteur—Quoi donc?—*plaçer* ma fille . . .

> ["So you do not wish to renounce Satan?"
> Said a good pastor to a certain bigot
> Who, with a substantial list of weighty sins, came once a year
> To relate to him the endless account.
> "I want to repent," she said, "forevermore,
> But before the first glimmer of grace
> Purges my soul of all sinful desires,
> Can I only, pastor . . ." Well what? . . . "place my daughter?"][59]

Lanusse's poem is the only time the root word of *plaçage* appears in a contemporary source, and his use of *placer* in "Épigramme" may well be the earliest published use of the term in New Orleans. This is significant in its own right, but more important to the popular history of the quadroon is that Lanusse's literary condemnation has generally been read as reflecting a widespread practice among the city's free people of color. As such, it marks an important—and unique—congruence between the accounts of visitors and the observations of antebellum New Orleanians themselves. Lanusse, however, must be read and interpreted with care. He was born in New Orleans in 1812 to Haitian refugee parents.[60] His was the generation that experienced the constraints on marriage for free black women of Haitian descent. The *femmes de couleur libres* unable to find free black marriage partners were his contemporaries among the refugee social circles in New Orleans. The daughters of his parents' friends and perhaps his own relatives were among those left with few options but to develop a new version of the *ménagère* in New Orleans. Theirs were the stories he knew best, not the happier marriage narratives of the Carriere and Populus children with their deep New Orleans roots.[61]

Lanusse's poems appeared in *Les Cenelles* (The Hollyberries), a volume of poetry written by New Orleans free men of color, compiled by Lanusse and published in 1845.[62] The collection's most prominent contributors were all of Haitian descent, including Lanusse and his brother, Numa Lanusse, Camille Thierry, and Victor Séjour.[63] The group's identification with Haiti and its struggles was strong. Numa Lanusse organized a collection in 1832 from nearly 200 free black Orleanians to relieve the suffering of hurricane victims in Les Cayes and Jérémie in southern Haiti.[64] The poetry of most of the contributors was in the French Romantic style, with the same meditations on love, sorrow, and death that were typical of that tradition. Armand Lanusse's critiques of alternatives to marriage among free women of color are different, clear in their allusions to the local predicament. In "La Jeune Fille au Bal" (Young Woman at the Ball), the poet implores a young woman to retreat from the ball, where she is being drawn, like a moth to the flame, to her doom. Lanusse introduces the poem with a line from Victor Hugo's "Fantomes," which communicates the social critique embedded in his poem. "She loved the ball too much, and that is what killed her."[65] Lanusse's poetic lament links the ballroom to the melancholy fate of young free women of color with the power and passion of someone intimately touched by the phenomenon.

Lanusse, through the prism of his experience as the son of refugees, was the first New Orleanian to use his literary gifts to shine a spotlight on the plight of the quadroon. His powerful indictment magnifies and confirms contemporary external critiques of illicit relationships across the color line, but it also obscures the alternate narratives that unfolded in the lives of many, if not most, of the city's free women of color. The married mothers who inherited the matrimonial legacy of Noel Carriere's generation and the women whose long-settled life partnerships were decades old when Lanusse lifted his pen are as invisible in his work as they were to foreign voyeurs like Karl Bernhard. Lanusse surely knew some of these families. One of the poems in *Les Cenelles* was dedicated to a man named Populus, a member of one of the New Orleans families most prominent in the free black matrimonial tradition.[66] That these were not the life histories that insisted he raise his poetic voice has left the impression among those who read him that his critique was directed at a universal phenomenon.

One of Lanusse's fellow Haitian-descended contributors to *Les Cenelles*,

Victor Séjour, presented a tragic narrative set not in New Orleans, but in Haiti. His 1837 short story "Le Mulâtre" tells the story of Georges, born to an enslaved woman after her rape by a white man. Years later, his evil master, Alfred, attempts to force himself on Georges's wife, Zélie, who resists, injuring her attacker in the process. Zélie is condemned to death and executed for this crime against the *Code Noir*. In despair, Georges flees and joins a band of slave rebels. Georges returns years later to kill Alfred, learning as he does so that Alfred is his father.[67] Séjour engaged literary themes that transcended the situation of Haitian émigrés in New Orleans. His contribution to *Les Cenelles*, "Le Retour de Napoleon" (The Return of Napoleon), was a romantic homage to the glory of Napoleon.[68] "Le Mulâtre," with its emphasis on the unnatural plight of the enslaved child of rape and its connection to slave rebellion is in the tradition of the tragic mulatto narratives and their attack on slavery. Séjour was born to a Haitian refugee father and an Orleanian mother who married when Séjour was seven years old, legitimating him and his older brother.[69] When he was nineteen, Séjour left New Orleans and lived most of the rest of his life in Paris.[70] That Séjour's literary gaze was directed beyond the issues that preoccupied Armand Lanusse is not surprising. Séjour belonged to a radical circle of free men of color in Paris who engaged global issues of rights, equality, and republicanism. Lanusse remained in New Orleans and witnessed the transformation of the survival strategy of Haitian-descended women of his generation into a lasting phenomenon that compromised the reputations and dignity of the free men and women of color who stayed behind.

Armand Lanusse's work confirms the relationship between the Haitian refugee influx and the emergence of the *plaçage* complex in travelers' accounts in the 1820s and 1830s. It also marks the phenomenon of the quadroon ball as a particular concern of the Haitian-descended free people of color in New Orleans. Other evidence points to the relationship between women of Haitian ancestry and the discursive emergence of the *plaçage* complex. New Orleans historian Charles Gayarré's 1883 manuscript essay on antebellum New Orleans quadroons adds little to what had already been developed by the outbreak of the Civil War, but the personal circumstances that gave shape to his pronouncements are worth noting. At the age of twenty, Gayarré was himself the father of a mixed-race child born to a free woman of color of Haitian descent. Carlos Hartur Nicolas Gayarré was born in 1825 to Charles Gayarré and Delphina Le Maitre and baptized the following year. A marginal note placed in the St. Louis Cathedral register for white baptisms is quite blunt about the racial ancestry of the child. "By error this Baptismal record of Carlos Harthur [*sic*] Nicolas Gayarré y Les Maitres [*sic*] was placed in this register; not being supposed to be here but in that reserved for people of color, such being the mother of the said child." Le Maitre's Haitian roots are confirmed by other sacramental records that identify hers as a refugee family.[71] Perhaps the refugee from Saint-Domingue who was light-skinned enough to pass for white at her child's baptism tricked Gayarré into thinking she was of his own race, though it seems more likely that she enchanted the guileless Gayarré when the nineteen-year-old treated himself to the experience of a quadroon ball. His youthful indulgence marked him. When Gayarré finally took a wife, at the age of fifty-one, she was a sedate widow.[72]

The Haitian link probably also explains how the term *plaçage* came to be used to describe liaisons between free women of color and white men in New Orleans. E. Franklin Frazier was the first to use the word in this context in his 1939 study, *The Negro Family*. Relying on secondary sources written between 1856 and 1928, Frazier describes the "extramoral associations" between free women of color and white men in New Orleans. This "recognized system of concubinage or *plaçage*," he writes, "existed alongside of the moral and juridic family."[73] None of his sources uses the term *plaçage*. Instead, Frazier almost certainly appropriated it from Melville Herskovits, who explains the term and its use in twentieth-century Haiti in his 1937 book, *Life in a Haitian Valley*. Families in Haiti were formed in two ways, Herskovits notes, by conventional sacramental marriage and "by means of the institution known as *plaçage*, wherein a man and a woman who desire to live together fulfill certain obligations."[74]

Herskovits's aim as an anthropologist was to describe Haitian *plaçage* and its operation within the communities he studied. He was nonetheless attentive to history, too, using the account of Spenser St. John to show the longevity of the practice. St. John, who served as British consul to Haiti for ten years between 1863 and 1874, was often wildly sensational in his account of the black republic, but his description of family life there rings true in light of what Herskovits later found. "Few of the lower orders go through any civil or religious marriage ceremony," St. John observed, "in fact, it was at one time the custom of all classes to be '*placé*,' and only since the priests have regained some of their ancient influence have those who are considered respectable consented to go to church." Such relationships, St. John noted, were not fleeting or casual; instead, "the agreement to live together, as in our old common law, was considered equivalent to marriage."[75] In nineteenth-century Haiti, *plaçage* referred to long-term relationships between men and women of the same racial ancestry, and to be placé(e) was to be a partner, male or female, in such an arrangement.[76]

The Haitian refugee community would have been familiar with the term, either through oral tradition in their families or by means of the friendships and correspondence between Haitians and Haitian-descended Orleanians such as Numa Lanusse. Adrian Jessé and Hortense Noleau, members of the free colored planter elite in Saint-Domingue, might have understood themselves as *placé* and *placée* before these parents of four children legally married each other 1810. Armand Lanusse almost certainly meant to convey that the conniving mother in "Épigramme" intended that her daughter be the *placée* of a white man. If so, his use of the word signals a shift in its meaning for Orleanians of Haitian descent. Men and women of the same race could be *placé* and *placée* to one another in Haiti. In New Orleans the mutuality of the arrangement and the bi-gendered language that described it had fallen away by the 1840s. When Olmsted penned his description of the free colored women with whom white Anglophone bachelors contracted for housekeeping and sex and applied the label *placée* to them in 1856, he unwittingly confirmed the transformation of the Haitian term in New Orleans, oblivious to the currents of history that had produced it.[77]

Accounts of the quadroons of New Orleans and their balls continued to appear until the Civil War, rarely adding anything new to the formula that was in place by the late 1820s. George Featherstonhaugh's 1844 description merely recapitulates what had gone before. He trots out the usual explanation of the origin of the women and their peculiar ways: "Quadroons, who are the daughters of white men by half-blooded mothers, whatever be their private worth or personal charms, are forbidden by the laws to contract marriage with white men." He affirms the quadroon's rejection of men of her own race and the fate to which it consigns her: "Such a woman being over-educated for the males of her own caste, is therefore destined from her birth to be a mistress, and great pains are lavished upon her education, not to enable her to aspire to be a wife, but to give her those attractions which a keeper requires." He maintains the ballroom as the site of courtship: "The Quadroon balls are places to which these young creatures are taken as soon as they have reached womanhood, and there they show their accomplishments in dancing and conversation to the white men, who alone frequent these places." And he upholds the implication of mothers in the transaction: "When one of them attracts the attention of an admirer, and he is desirous of forming a liaison with her, he makes a bargain with the mother, agrees to pay her a sum of money, perhaps 2,000 dollars, or some sum in proportion to her merits, as a fund upon which she may retire when the liaison terminates."[78] Matilda Charlotte Houstoun's 1850 contribution to the literature, as well as Olmsted's in 1856, reproduce these same details quite faithfully, attesting to how firmly fixed the stereotype had become in the antebellum American mind.[79]

The discursive creation of the New Orleans quadroon, in both fiction and nonfiction, has had the effect of defining the city as a foreign space within the United States. Abolitionist authors constructed it as the epicenter of the most offensive aspects of slavery. Less-politicized writers construed it as exotic, a site of oriental excess. To complicate the city's position in American consciousness, the heyday of the literary quadroon coincided with more than one critical moment in American history. Heavy immigration in the 1840s and 1850s throughout the United States sparked debates about the nature of American identity, giving birth to vitriolic nativist politics. Nativists and the Know-Nothing party of the 1850s favored exclusion and the limitation of rights for those not born in America.[80] New Orleans had been part of the United States since 1803, but the lurid mythology of its quadroons begged the question as to whether it properly belonged.

Alongside these political implications, the production of the literary quadroon exercised a powerful effect on the living women of color, free and enslaved, not only in New Orleans but beyond. Visitors came to New Orleans expecting to find beautiful quadroons to dance with and bed. Slave traders scoured the city and markets outside it to find light-skinned enslaved women who could be sold as "fancy girls" to satisfy the fantasies launched by the literary world. Some slaveholders found a new vocation as pimps in the underworld of prostitution. Once the figure of the quadroon had been produced, the market for her grew, and eddies of enterprise sprang up to sell her.

CHAPTER SIX
Selling the Quadroon

Colonel Pointdexter: Gentlemen, I believe none of us have two feelings about the conduct of that man; but he has the law on his side—we may regret, but we must respect it. Mr. M'Closky has bid twenty-five thousand dollars for the Octoroon. Is there any other bid? For the first time, twenty-five thousand—last time! (*Brings hammer down.*) To Jacob M'Closky, the Octoroon girl Zoe, twenty-five thousand dollars.

—Dion Boucicault, "The Octoroon" (1859)

When the beautiful girl Zoe steps onto the block in the New Orleans slave market near the end of Dion Boucicault's play, "The Octoroon," the auctioneer exhorts the assembled crowd to act nobly. "Gentlemen," he cries, "we are all acquainted with the circumstances of this girl's position, and I feel sure that no one here will oppose the family who desires to redeem the child of our esteemed and noble friend, the late Judge Payton." The room answers with cheers of "Hear! bravo! hear!" But noble sentiments have no place in the slave market. The bidding begins at a modest one thousand dollars, but the coarse and conniving overseer, Jacob M'Closky, drives the price for the octoroon Zoe ever higher. A friend of the young woman's white father warns him, "Jacob M'Closky, you sha'n't have that girl. Now, take care what you do. Twelve thousand." M'Closky shoots back, "Shan't I? Fifteen thousand. Beat that any of ye." Dora Sunnyside, who has sold her plantation to save the octoroon girl from sexual slavery to M'Closky suddenly enters the room calling out, "Twenty thousand." But the crowd's cheers quickly turn to groans as M'Closky snarls, "Twenty-five thousand." To the dismay of the people who have assembled to save her, the reluctant auctioneer accedes to the rule of law, and turns Zoe over to M'Closky (see Figure 11).[1]

Twenty-five thousand dollars was an inconceivable price for a slave, even for a beautiful light-skinned octoroon raised to be a lady and sold to be a concubine. Boucicault's hyperbole reflected a reality, however. Young enslaved women did bring extraordinarily high prices in New Orleans,

FIGURE 11. *The Octoroon, or Life in Louisiana*, c. 1861. Lithograph. Courtesy of
Collections, Templeman Library, University of Kent, Canterbury, United Kingdom.

sometimes three times as much as the median slave purchase price.[2] The "fancy trade" in attractive young women sold for sexual companionship and service was among the most notorious features of the New Orleans slave market. But the fantasies aroused by the literary figure of the New Orleans quadroon could also be satisfied in ways that fell short of the absolute mastery of ownership. The alluring free woman of color in search of a white lover in the ballroom evoked by Karl Bernhard or the tragic slave conjured in the abolitionist fiction of Lydia Maria Child created expectations of a specific experience in New Orleans that entrepreneurial women and men tried to supply in a variety of ways. From her earliest appearances at the turn of the nineteenth century, the New Orleans quadroon was a woman whose favors could be bought. And like all good commodities, her charms were priced along a spectrum to fit any pocketbook.

Outright ownership of a light-skinned "fancy maid," a real-life version of Boucicault's ill-fated Zoe, was the ultimate realization of white male mastery fantasies. As one historian has noted, "the bodies of light-skinned women and little girls embodied sexual desire and the luxury of being able to pay for its fulfillment—they were projections of slaveholders' own imagined identities as white men and slave masters."[3] Such "near-white enslaved women symbolized the luxury of being able to pay for service, often sexual, that had no material utility," another scholar has observed.[4] Canny slave traders made New Orleans the premier market for the fancy trade that supplied this market, exploiting the city's reputation as the home of the mythic quadroon. The Crescent City was where men seeking girls like the fourteen-year-old Mary Ellen Brooks, a "very pretty girl, a bright mulatto with long curly hair and fine features," went shopping. The comely, teenaged Brooks was not a pedigreed product of New Orleans, however. Hope H. Slatter of Baltimore assembled groups of light-skinned teenage girls and transported them to New Orleans for private sales brokered by salaried local representatives. Brooks was a member of one of these consignments, a light-skinned girl from the upper South sold down the river to satisfy a market swollen by fantasy.[5]

The going price for a "fancy maid" ranged from $1,500 to $5,233 in antebellum New Orleans, well above the cost of a female field hand or a domestic undistinguished by light skin.[6] By the late 1840s, however, men could purchase a light-skinned girl for well under $1,000. Mary Ellen Brooks sold for $600 in 1847; and James White bought Alexina Morrison, a fifteen-year-old with a "light sallow complexion, blue eyes, and flaxen hair," from an Arkansas man for $750 in 1857. Morrison was fair enough to pass for white and sued for her freedom on that basis. Mary Ellen Brooks was so sick when she arrived in New Orleans that she died shortly after she was sold.[7] Such cases suggest the fancy trade was not an exclusive, high-end business in late antebellum New Orleans and that slave traders resorted to a variety of shady expedients to supply the market.[8]

More reasonably priced, temporary access to the charms of light-skinned women of color was available as early as 1804, when visiting Philadelphian John Watson noted in his journal that "there are beautiful yellow women here" willing to become paid sexual companions at an annual rate more affordable than the purchase price of a slave. "They are content to live at an expense of about four hundred dollars a year," Watson observed, adding that the women were also willing to make shirts at a cheaper price than was charged by tailors.[9] Watson's observations on New Orleans were not published until the 1840s, but Thomas Ashe provided instructions to men who wanted to know how to purchase their own fleeting encounter with a New Orleans quadroon in his 1808 *Travels in America*. First, as we saw earlier, he advises them that the showroom is on the riverfront, where women available for such purposes promenaded back and forth for the benefit of potential suitors. Ashe next reveals the etiquette of encounter. "A stranger passes and repasses, before he can assume sufficiently to tell the one he admires the most *qu'elle est belle comme une ange*, and so forth," he instructs. Then, anticipating the demand among Anglophone visitors to New Orleans for a dalliance with one of these women, he offers them special counsel. "To an Englishman, this timid, bashful silent demeanour" of the quadroons strolling the riverfront "opposes the difficulties which require his utmost resolution to surmount, and he walks the Levée many a pensive evening before the sense of virtue is sufficiently consumed by the new passion of his breast, to permit him to speak."[10]

It was Ashe, whose actual familiarity with New Orleans was questionable, who established the parents of the women, especially the mothers, as the agents of their daughters' amorous engagements with fumbling visitors to the levee.[11] More crucially, he exposes the interplay of buyer and seller in establishing a new culture of sexual encounter in New Orleans. "Some mothers now, on becoming acquainted with the English timidity," Ashe reports, "begin to alter their line of conduct, and suffer their daughters to remove their veil *en passant un Anglois*, or flirt their fan, or drop a handkerchief, which they receive with such gracious accents of gratitude, that a conversation may easily succeed." Once the English-speaking stranger has been comfortably enticed to pursue a tryst, the "mothers always regulate the terms and make the bargain." For men wondering how much they should budget for the service rendered them under such an arrangement, Ashe helpfully supplied concrete details. "The terms allowed the parents are generally fifty dollars a month; during which time the lover has the exclusive right to the house, where fruit, coffee, and refreshments may at any time be had, or where he may entirely live with the utmost safety and tranquility." The monthly rate was not out of line with the general cost of living in New Orleans. In 1805 a traveler paid a monthly sum of forty-five dollars for accommodation that did not include the personal companionship of a quadroon woman.[12]

Ashe's guide to securing the services of a New Orleans quadroon imply that the ladies who strolled the levee were free women of color peddled by their own mothers. As we have seen, however, the trend in the early nineteenth century among Orleanian free women of color who bore daughters to white men was to nudge their progeny toward marriage. What Ashe describes is more suggestive of the relationship between prostitute and madam than mother and daughter, despite the delicate window dressing that he supplies. Catering to the tourist trade would hardly be the strategy of an Orleanian mother, even if she thought a white partner preferable to a free colored husband, nor would it appeal to a Dominguan woman hoping to replicate the position of *ménagère*. Moreover, a going monthly rate points to an expectation of transitory relationships, not permanent and secure arrangements. To be sure, the young ladies of the levee seem not to have been available for a few hours' entertainment, but they do appear to have functioned as a cross between a courtesan and a temporary wife for visitors and bachelor businessmen who could afford the fees that Ashe helpfully advertised for them.

It is not beyond the realm of possibility that some mothers paraded their daughters before the shy Anglophones who haunted the levee in search of sexual adventure, but it is more likely that the "mothers" were businesswomen who ran a placement agency for women of color. Some may have provided living space to the young women between or during engagements. While it is all but impossible to find traces of the kinds of temporary partnerships that Ashe describes, a tantalizing bit of evidence from a later period suggests how such an operation might have worked and the circumstances that called it into existence. The 1830 census for New Orleans shows that a woman named Marie Louise Labretonniere lived on Rampart Street in a household comprising five free women of color, three of them in their late teens and early twenties. Sacramental registers show a son but no daughters born to Labretonniere in New Orleans. And they offer a clue about the exigency that may have shaped the nature of her household. Labretonniere was a native of Jacmel, a Haitian refugee. She and her housemates may be representative of emigrant women for whom sex work was the most viable route to financial security, embodiments of the transformation from *ménagère* to *placée*.[13]

Writing on the heels of Ashe, Christian Schultz confirmed the essentially commercial nature of the liaisons between free women of color and white men in New Orleans. "Since custom planted an insurmountable barrier to their ever forming an honourable connexion with white men," Schultz explained in 1810, free women of color were compelled "to resort to the practice of forming temporary engagements with those whom they may fancy. Engagements of this kind are every day formed, for a month or a year, or as much longer as the parties may be pleased with each other." Although the women were expected to be faithful to the man who had engaged their services, "when the term is expired, or the lover gone, they accept of the next best offer that may be made to them." Business, not love, dictated the object of their attentions, yet the women of color were, Schultz observed, "far from being considered in the same humiliating light with those white ladies to whom they are nearly allied in profession."[14]

The line separating these free women of color from prostitutes was perhaps less clear than commentators such as Ashe and Schultz suggested, and by 1810, a year after the refugee influx, the ready availability of alternatives to formal courtship and marriage was clear. A reader who signed the pseudonym "Lucinda Sparkle" complained in an open letter to the mayor and city council of New Orleans that it was impossible for respectable white women to meet and enjoy the company of young men except during the Carnival season. She contended that "the depravity which exists among the unmarried gentlemen of this city" could only be remediated if "the best female society" had a public walk dedicated to their recreation to counteract the enticements of the ladies of the levee.[15] The implication is all too clear: any woman promenading the levee would be taken for a harlot. A visitor from Rhode Island writing a few months later commented on the impermanence and commercialization of the levee dalliances, railing against mothers of quadroons who "barter them away during their minority to the best bidder." He reflected that even in New Orleans there must be some "'who have not bowed the knee to Baal,' nor offered incense to the *god of sensuality*," and who "instead of selecting a miss for a month, would select a wife for life."[16]

Perhaps it was critiques such as these that shaped a new framework for the business side of liaisons between New Orleans quadroons and white men—at least rhetorically. The putative negotiations for a quadroon's favors moved from the levee to the notary's office in the 1820s, and the length of the engagement was extended to a more respectable term. "In New Orleans, when a white man is desirous of living with a coloured female," Englishman Isaac Holmes wrote in 1823, "it is common to get a notary to draw up something like articles of copartnership; these in general are for a certain number of years."[17] James Stuart, as we have seen, confirmed in 1833 that the riverfront was no longer the venue for arranging assignations with quadroon women. Instead, the quadroons formed a partnership with white men that was "considered in the light of a left-handed marriage," one that "very generally lasts for life."[18] Karl Bernhard did not repeat the detail of notarial participation in his account of the more settled nature of the quadroons' living arrangements, but he noted that the "female quadroon looks upon such an engagement as a matrimonial contract," one that is affirmed with "a formal contract by which the 'friend' engages to pay the father or mother of the quadroon a specified sum."[19]

These reverse dowries are nowhere to be found in the notarial archives of New Orleans. There are numerous instances of *inter vivos* donations of property by white men to women who had borne them children, as well as what appear to be sham sales designed to convey to them more property than the law allowed, but these transactions obviously occurred after, not before, the relationships commenced.[20] Perhaps Holmes's lone reference to a notarial contract is indebted to a garbled bit of hearsay about Dominguan *ménagère* contracts that he stumbled across in New Orleans. Such notarized agreements did, indeed, exist in prerevolutionary Saint-Domingue, and the provisions of some that were established there apparently survived migration to New Orleans.[21] Or maybe the notion of a formal contract executed before the white lover claimed the exclusive affections of his quadroon mistress was a polite fiction fabricated to elevate the tone of the arrangement above the level of base procurement. The appearance in the 1820s of references to the equivalent of prenuptial contracts did confer an air of respectability on the liaisons, and their debut in that decade may not be mere coincidence. Dominguan-descended free women of color faced the greatest challenge to their marriage prospects in the 1820s. Talk of contracts, if not their execution, perhaps reflects part of a strategy by refugee mothers to manage their daughters' futures.

Whatever the origin of the notion that liaisons with quadroons were

governed by a formal agreement and entailed substantial financial investment, the idea was one that transported the experience beyond the reach
of the majority of men who visited or resided in New Orleans. Few, if any,
visitors were in a position to essay the legendary negotiations and test the
veracity of their reputation. The fantasy slipped such binding realities in
subsequent decades as fabulists such as Joseph Holt Ingraham roused the
popular American imagination. The New Orleans host of Baron Championet in "The Quadroon of Orleans" gives a good imitation of Schehe-
razade as he initiates Championet into the mysteries of the city's quadroon
culture without masking the commercial nature of the enterprise. At the
age of "sixteen or seventeen years, when their daughters are in market, (I
speak plainly)," the interlocutor begins, "the mother, who has kept her till
now in great seclusion, begins to cast about for a protector for her." Like
any good *vendeuse*, the mother tempts buyers without spoiling the allure
of her merchandise. "She allows her with this object in view, to attend
balls and masquerades, frequent public walks, and go to mass, but always
attended by a confidential slave, or herself in person; while her eye is ever
watchful, and the reins of maternal vigilance are drawn with careful hand,
lest the daughter, from feeling, should form an unprofitable *liaison*."

Ingraham underlined the theme of commodification by drawing a parallel between New Orleans quadroon culture and another well-known
tradition of human trafficking: "It will not be long before she attracts
several admirers, and proposals are made in due form to the quadroon
mother—for the system, as you will discover, is as regularly organised and
understood here, as that for the buying and selling Circassian girls." The
Circassian girl was a famous index to a titillating imaginary. According
to Voltaire, "Circassians are poor, and their daughters are beautiful, and
indeed it is in them they chiefly trade"; and Mark Twain reported that
Circassian women were still being sold privately in Istanbul in the 1860s.[22]
The trade in the Ottoman Empire of Circassian maidens, who were
thought to embody the epitome of Caucasian feminine beauty, fascinated
Europeans and Americans. By linking New Orleans quadroons to Circassian women, Ingraham at once established their extraordinary beauty and
their position as a sexual commodity.

Once the match was made, Ingraham's expert explained, it was time
for the formalities of the bargain. First "come the preliminary settlements,
previously agreed upon, between buyer and seller," which are set down in
a written agreement. Mother and suitor "are closeted together with pen,
ink and paper. The mother, who has the conditions drawn upon a piece of

paper she holds in her hand, insists on a house containing a certain number of rooms, richly furnished, particularizes each article of their furniture, demands a certain number of servants; bargains for a specific sum to be paid quarterly to her daughter for pin-money, and insists that she shall be indulged in all the expensive luxuries of her class." The scheming mother "does not neglect her own interests" as the deal is drawn up, "but bargains for a present in hand for her own part, such as an expensive shawl, a costly veil, a set of jewels, or something of that sort." The expense of the transaction is such that financing has to be arranged. The white lover "pays a certain sum down, often so high as two thousand dollars, and seldom less than one thousand, and receives his unmarried but virgin bride."[23]

The lore about the price and particulars of free quadroon women sold for the exclusive sexual pleasure of a single white man continued to circulate into the 1850s. Edward Sullivan, a British tourist who visited New Orleans at the beginning of the decade, averred that a "handsome quadroon could not be bought for less than one thousand or fifteen hundred dollars! though the market is well supplied at that price."[24] Sullivan's observation begs the question of which market was supplied. The price that he and others quote is commensurate with the price paid for enslaved "fancy maids" earlier in the century. In the face of the absence of evidence for the formal transactions for quadroon favors so elaborately detailed by Holmes, Bernhard, and Ingraham, the possibility presents itself that such reports conflated concrete information about the market in enslaved women with the dimly perceived practices of the city's population of free women of color. Ingraham hints at the existence of such confusion about the status of quadroon women in his short story "The Quadroon of Orleans," where his resident expert on such matters tells a visitor that, "Indeed, many quadroons are really slaves, whose maternal ancestors have been for generations in the same family."[25]

The luxuriously kept quadroon woman sold by her mother to the highest bidder was probably the projection of male fantasy leavened with just enough gossip and sightings at the ballroom and the theater to make the legend as plausible to the men whose writing disseminated it as it was to the reading public titillated by it. The imaginary figure fed more than fantasies, however. Its reputation also put food into the mouths of women who supplied less fantastic realizations of elements of the quadroon myth as housekeeper companions and commercial dance partners. In antebellum New Orleans, entrepreneurial antebellum men and women laid the foundations of the city's famous postbellum sexual-tourism industry when they exploited the potential of the hyperbolic legend and transformed unattainable fantasy into affordable pleasure.

Frederick Law Olmsted, writing in the 1850s, sustained the legend of the expensive kept woman at the same time that he offered a glimpse of the much more mundane arrangement that may actually have existed. After confirming the canonical elements of the myth, including a mother who "inquires, like a Countess of Kew, into the circumstances of the suitor," he admits, "I have described this custom as it was described to me." Olmsted follows his hearsay recapitulation of the standard description with a more credible account supplied by a northern businessman living in New Orleans who had engaged a free woman of color as his housekeeper and companion. Olmsted's informant, as we saw earlier in Chapter 4, presented his way of life as an economic adaptation rather than a sensual indulgence. Men who came to New Orleans on business did not want to resort to matrimony to supply their domestic needs because it took a fortune to set up a wife in the style that was expected. Hotels and boardinghouses were likewise too expensive for a long-term business resident. It made sense, instead, simply to rent a set of modest rooms in a part of the city where the rents were low and engage a free woman of color to keep house. Olmsted's source made much of the thriftiness of the women who provided such services, but made no reference to their beauty or sexual charms.[26]

Businessmen temporarily located in New Orleans to advance their fortunes might, it seems, have provided a secure living to free women of color of limited resources.[27] The arrangement that Olmsted describes resembles the Dominguan *ménagère* much more than it does the pampered mistress sketched by the pens of Bernhard and Ingraham. Some free women of color may well have aimed at the life of luxury and quasi-respectability of the mythic quadroon, but many more probably settled for more prosaic and modest arrangements. New Orleanian Charles Gayarré describes the domination by free women of color of the city's domestic and hospitality services. These women "may be truly said to have monopolized the renting at high prices of furnished rooms to the whites of the male sex." Gayarré, who came of age in the mid-1820s, was full of praise for the women of this profession. "These furnished rooms were models of Dutch cleanliness—large beds with immaculate mattresses, sheets and mosquito bars as white as snow—no dust visible any where, everything for comfort and the toilette at its precise place and in the best order," he enthused. "In the morning the nicest cup of hot coffee; in the evening at the foot of the bed, for ablution, the never failing tub of fresh water, over which was spread a sweet smelling towel." All of this was provided by charming women who "were always affable, a cross one would have been a phenomenon; intent on guessing at your wants or wishes, and showing their pearly teeth through smiling lips." Gayarré speaks elsewhere in the same source about the ensnaring charms of quadroon women, but this passage confirms their ubiquity in a less glamorous niche in the New Orleans hospitality industry. It remarks, too, on the origin of at least some of them. "Many of them," in addition to being excellent landladies, were also skilled in nursing their white tenants through yellow fever, "particularly those who had come from St. Domingo."[28]

Between them, Olmsted and Gayarré provide an alternative narrative for New Orleans quadroons. Free women of color were, in effect, selling their services as substitutes for wives, but not in the way newcomers to the city might expect from their advance press. The fantasies of tender seductresses whose beauty rivaled that of Circassian beauties were not to be found in the rooms hired at a low rent in the run-down part of the city, nor in the boardinghouses that were "models of Dutch cleanliness." These New Orleans women of color succeeded in living more as *ménagères* than *placées*. There was, however, one place in New Orleans where a piece of the mythic *plaçage* complex was for sale, and at a bargain price at that. In the city's ballrooms men could take in the spectacle of quadroon women, flirt with them, and perhaps purchase their company for an evening or two. Nineteenth-century visitors to the city presented quadroon balls as an indigenous entertainment that was expressive of a deeply rooted social culture. In fact, they were a Haitian import adapted to exploit the boom-town, male-dominated market of New Orleans, perhaps promoted in the 1820s to advance the material prospects of refugee-descended women. By the 1830s, however, they had become commercialized tourist attractions that sold a taste of New Orleans naughtiness to all comers.

John Watson's journal gives a glimpse of the New Orleans ballroom before it became a legendary attraction and reveals the role of visitors and newcomers in its transformation. "The dashing Americans coming in daily, are affecting to raise extravagance among the simple & frugal, in-habitants," he admitted to his journal in 1805. It was easy and affordable to have fun in New Orleans thanks to the joie de vivre of the natives, who "are fond of gaiety & especially of dancing; but it is cheap. The admittance to a ball is but 1/2 Dollr." The helter-skelter dancing democracy where "La-dies of the finest families" rode to the dances in an ox cart and a tinsmith could waltz with the daughter of the former Spanish governor were a refreshing alternative to the straitlaced habits of his compatriots, who were "great sticklers" on matters of rank.[29] Watson worried that Anglophones' appetite for conspicuous consumption and social distinction would spoil this rough-and-ready dancing culture. He may have been right. Toward the end of his stay in New Orleans he lamented that "proud, vain glorious, ostentatious" Americans like him had "begun to aim at Select balls & to raise the price of admission."[30]

More changes followed. When Watson visited New Orleans dancehalls in 1805, there was gaiety but little spectacle. "The ladies dresses are muslin & sometimes silk of gay colours, but never costly & always very neatly & modestly made." At the start of the ball season two decades later, dry-goods merchants Petellat, Gillet & Co. advertised an astonishing inventory of sartorial splendors imported from France and New York. There was silk gauze in four different colors, taffeta, and plaids that could be made up by seamstresses into unique creations for the dance floor, as well as "Mandarine Crape" dresses and "Elegant Ball Dresses and Ornaments" for those who preferred a ready-made gown. Outfits could be enhanced with silk and taffeta ribbons, gilt hair combs, ostrich feathers, and mock pearls. And, to complete the ensemble, ladies could purchase a pair of elbow-length kid gloves.[31]

There was no masking at New Orleans balls, quadroon or otherwise, when Watson visited, and there had not been any since the 1790s.[32] Auguste Tessier's introduction in 1805 of the first dance exclusively for free women of color and white men triggered an attempt to reinstate the masking tradition in 1806. The territorial government, perhaps fearing the practice would exacerbate the louche tone of the city's dances, quickly stepped in to stop it. Even without the added titillation of masking, Tessier's "quadroon balls" grew in success so quickly that in 1810 the proprietor of a rival ballroom catering to an unmixed white clientele upbraided the reading public for their lopsided patronage of Tessier's dances. By 1823, masking had crept back into all New Orleans ballrooms, adding piquant allure to the quadroon dances. The pointed, self-righteous opposition to masquerade hints that its reintroduction may have been linked to the maturation of the generation of Dominguan-descended women in need of financial sponsorship. Masking would have added mystery and glamour to the balls at precisely the time this cohort of free women of color were most in need of expanded opportunities. Whether it was a savvy marketing intervention or not, masking's return incited controversy among members of the city council in 1827. The revival of masquerade invited "indecencies" that the city should be at pains to suppress, some argued. Commerce and laissez-faire, however, won the day. As one councilman bluntly observed of masked balls, "one doesn't go there to take lessons in morality . . . it is for those who fear unconventionalities not to go there."[33] The city council agreed and authorized masked balls between January 1 and Mardi Gras beginning with the 1828 Carnival season.[34]

The controversy over masking has been read as evidence of an Anglophone-Creole divide in the city, but it seems more likely that the debate was really about whether or not to cater more openly and imaginatively to the fantasies of forbidden sex and exoticism already on offer at the quadroon balls. The price structure of the affairs that Bernhard attended in 1826 suggests that men who attended the quadroon balls understood themselves to be paying for more than a typical night of dancing. The white masked ball cost a dollar to enter, the quadroon ball twice as much.[35] Bernhard's experience in the mid-1820s reveals the quadroon balls as events invested with both cachet and an appeal to sexual adventure. Such an equipoise was especially well suited to the delicate situation of free women of color of Dominguan descent, the most obvious candidates for the alternatives to marriage that might be facilitated by this venue. The ballroom that Bernhard visited in 1826 carefully preserved the illusion of gentility. The young women were chaperoned, "well and gracefully dressed, and conducted themselves with much propriety and modesty. Cotillions and waltzes were danced, and several of the ladies performed elegantly." There is no hint that the dancers left the party with the white men who came to view their charms at the ball, but the possibility that bargains might have been struck between the parties outside the showroom of the dancehall is implicit.[36]

The 1830s saw the development of a more vulgar variation of the quadroon ball. As Bernhard's popular account spread through the country, the market for firsthand experience of this novel entertainment grew and percolated below the ranks of gentleman travelers into a less well-heeled population.[37] Early in the winter season of 1834–35, John Latrobe of Baltimore joined a group of male friends in an expedition to a masked quadroon ball at the Washington Ballroom on St. Phillip Street in the French Quarter. The price of entry was only a dollar, and the evening was decidedly down-market from the expedition Bernhard had made a decade before. The pretense of respectability had effectively vanished. In a brightly lit hall hung with mirrors "were about forty women present of all shades, from the dark mulatto to the light quadroon" who "pass their life in prostitution." Beauty was not in abundance. "Some of the women, but not many, had fine forms." The young girls in attendance, "as yet destitute of a keeper," were obviously on the market, unmasked to "show their faces as a merchant shows samples of his wares to entice purchasers." The spectacle was tawdry, but Latrobe quit the ballroom only when another of his senses was offended. "Towards the close of the ball the room became very warm, and the smell of the heated quadroons and mulattoes was disagreeable to me who was not accustomed to it. I could not stand it and I went away."[38]

A year later another tourist found himself equally uncharmed by the scene at the Washington Ballroom. Virginian James Davidson confided to his diary that the dancehall, glittering with gilt mirrors and crystal chandeliers, did not deliver the elegance the decor suggested would be in the offing. Among the masked throng were "all sorts of characters except virtuous women." Most of the revelers of both sexes were masked and costumed, but two of the dancers hinted at how the evening might have been expected to end. "There were two females promenading in their night garments," Davidson drily observed, concluding his report by noting that the outing "sated my curiosity, and left me without relish for another."[39]

Male visitors like Davidson were not the only people who made their way to the Washington Ballroom to satisfy their curiosity about the notorious quadroon balls. White women were apparently donning masquerade and infiltrating the quadroon balls at the beginning of the 1837–38 dancing season. The officials of the First Municipal District, where the Washington Ballroom, among others, was located, responded to the invasion by making it "a penal offence to give a masked ball, and admit 'white and colored women together.'" The newspaper reporting the new ordinance observed that "it would require more ingenuity than any Aldermen of the First Municipality possesses, to discover the *color* of some who attend; they go so habited that there is no discovering whether they are black or white."[40]

What the white women who spied on the salacious doings at the Washington Ballroom thought about the proceedings is lost to history, but the judgment of at least part of the city's free black community is clear. They rejected the commercially oriented affairs that subjected their daughters to the prurient stares of white men and organized an alternative entertainment. As Latrobe noted, the spectacle at the Washington "by no means exhibited the handsomest and gentlest of the quadroons." Not only was it the unfashionable opening ball of the season, it was "more promiscuous than those balls which they have, and where a ticket is not a matter of purchase, but a favor." These more exclusive dances, Latrobe explained, "are called society balls, and the best quadroon society is to be found at them." He did not add, and may never have known, that neither he nor any other white man would ever be granted the favor of an invitation to one of these affairs. Called by some "Bals du Cordon Bleu," these private dances were reserved for free people of color only, male and female. Their purpose is clearly implied by the histories of two young women known to have frequented them, Fortunée and Desirée Ste. Gême. These mixed-race daughters of a white Haitian refugee remained in New Orleans when their father returned to France, growing up under the watchful eye of their father's business manager, Jean Boze. The girls, Boze reported to their father, coveted the kind of expensive, flashy wardrobe that would have made a splash at the Washington Ballroom. It was just as well, Boze mused, that when they went into society during the 1830 season they attended only the segregated dances "consisting of respectable members of their class belonging to families of the same social circle."[41] At the private balls their social standing, not their fashionable ostentation and reputation for sexual virtuosity, was what counted. The exclusive alternative served its function well. Fortunée settled into a marriage with a free man of color in 1833.[42]

Armand Lanusse's poem about the young free woman of color who was fatally attracted to the ball like a moth to the flame suggests controversy within the free colored community in the 1840s over the choices available to their daughters in New Orleans. The life partnerships and *ménagère* arrangements of earlier generations were not founded on equality, to be sure, but they implied more than a transitory dalliance that could be bought by anyone who had the price of admission to the dancehall. The crass commerciality of the quadroon ball reduced free black women to sexual commodities destined for the consumption of white men, essentially replicating the position of enslaved women. Black men were emasculated in the process. The effective difference between slavery and freedom for those who participated in this transaction, whether white or black, barely registered. This capitulation to the reestablishment of white male mastery over black womanhood would have been particularly bitter to those who, like Lanusse, claimed ancestral roots in the black republic that had abolished slavery.

Some free black women must have chosen the prospect of an indulgent, rich white sugar daddy over the respectability of marriage to a free black husband in the 1830s and 1840s, but public quadroon balls did not remain

FIGURE 12. The Globe Ballroom (left). Located on the edge of the city on the Basin, convenient to sailors and dockworkers, the Globe was the site of quadroon balls in the 1840s and 1850s and perhaps later. Courtesy of the Historic New Orleans Collection.

a promising entrée into such arrangements. The dances devolved into cheap, rowdy gatherings that catered directly to the tourist trade and transient boatmen, sailors, and military men. The Washington Ballroom, with its gilt mirrors and chandeliers in the heart of the French Quarter, was supplanted by the cavernous Globe Ballroom at the city's edge, a stone's throw from a shantytown of cheap brothels. Abutting the docks of a busy internal harbor called the Basin, the Globe was convenient for sailors and dockworkers on the prowl once their work was done (see Figure 12). A stop at a quadroon ball became part of a well-oiled tourism machine that supplied a ready-made itinerary of dissipation to other male visitors in the 1840s and 1850s. Albert Pickett described a thousand "cabs and coaches moving in all directions, with lights attached," that rattled through the streets and "never stop, but go the whole night; for the gay and dissipated, surfeited with one amusement, seek another." After taking in a performance at the theater, visitors "are escorted by the eager cabmen proposing to convey them to the Quarteroon Ball, the St. Louis Masquerade, and many other places."[43]

The price of admission to the balls continued to drop, making them accessible to all but the most destitute of the city's visitors. Englishman Edward Sullivan paid only fifty cents in 1852 to attend a quadroon ball where a woman danced something "resembling the Spanish fandango," an observation that suggests the staged nature of the spectacles by this date.[44] The women on the dance floor of the Globe Ballroom were not just performers, they were now almost certainly more likely to be professionals than amateurs in the amorous arts, and skilled in other techniques that effectively parted tipsy carousers from their money.[45] While women reporting on New Orleans as late as the 1850s continued to sustain the mythic gentility of the quadroon ball, male visitors who actually attended them in the 1840s and 1850s related hair-raising stories that leave no doubt that all vestiges of romance and respectability had vanished.[46]

The actor Louis Tasistro attested to the national notoriety of quadroon balls in the early 1840s, acknowledging in his travel account that "all my readers have no doubt heard of the famous 'Bal Masques' so much in vogue in the 'Crescent City.'" The events had become so popular that they were not restricted to the winter Carnival season but were held year round, even during yellow fever epidemics, the better to supply visitors with a chance to experience the revelry no matter when they came to town. "Few strangers, I believe, ever visit New-Orleans without attending, at least for once, these nocturnal haunts of libertinism," Tasistro observed. There were usually three balls every night during Tasistro's stay, "the 'White Ball,' the 'Quadroon Society Ball,' and the 'Coloured Ball.' With the exception of the Quadroon Ball, which is really a respectable affair, the others are of a very low character, being, in fact, mere places of rendezvous for all the gay females of the town." White tourists were effectively consigned to the sleaziest of the options, since they presumably continued to be barred from the Bal du Cordon Bleu.[47]

Security precautions at the entry to the ballroom signaled the kind of atmosphere visitors could expect inside. As a patron made his way toward the hall, Tasistro advises, "You are somewhat unceremoniously accosted by a dare-devil-looking sort of individual, who, after feeling you all over, to ascertain that you have no concealed weapons about your person, politely insists upon seeing the interior of your hat, and, if satisfied on that point, condescendingly permits you to pass." The pat-down was not foolproof, however. "Scarcely a night passes without exhibiting some scenes of violence, frequently ending in bloodshed," inflicted by "Arkansas toothpicks (as the Bowie-knife is facetiously designated,)" that passed through undetected by the doorman.[48] The clientele at the ballrooms was hardly select. "Every clerk or scrivener who can muster up a few dollars, hurries to these unhallowed sanctuaries, and launches unreservedly into every species of sensual indulgence." More unsavory still, "every flat-boatman or cattle-dealer, as soon as he has disposed of his merchandise, finds his way to these abodes of enchantment, and seldom thinks of returning home until he has paid a dear tribute to the Paphian shrine."[49]

A rough-hewn visitor to New Orleans at about the same time revealed in a retrospective account of his adventures how predatory the sexual-tourism industry in New Orleans had become. Passing through New Orleans on his way from Texas to Virginia to attend to some family business, William "Big-Foot" Wallace, "Indian fighter, hunter, and ranger," found himself unprepared for the city's flaunting females. Sitting on the front porch of his hotel, his feet propped up on the railing, "as comfortable as an old sow in a mud-hole on a hot day," he was beckoned by a young woman on the other side of the street. She insisted that he treat her to a brandy. "'There,' said I, and I threw her a slick quarter; 'that'll buy you one;' and I turned on my heel and made tracks for the tavern as fast as I could." Furious, the spurned streetwalker let loose a spectacular stream of profanity. "I thought I had heard the rangers on the frontiers of Texas make use of pretty hard language, but they couldn't hold a candle to that young woman."[50]

The Texan bolted himself in his room after this fracas, but his appetite for adventure revived later that evening. "After supper, I fixed up a little, slicked down my hair with about a pint of bear's grease (some of my own killing), and went off to a 'Quadroon Ball' in the French part of the city, for I was determined to see a little of everything going," Big-Foot reported. Like Tasistro, he was searched for weapons at the door to the hall and relieved of "a pair of Derringers and 'Old Butch,'" his well-worn scalping knife. The doorman advised the ranger that he had better check any cash at the door, too, if he wanted to be able "to put your hand on it when you want it." Undeterred by the warning, Wallace proceeded into the dancehall, where he was tricked into buying expensive rum and pineapple cocktails at the bar and had his coat pocket slashed and robbed of its contents. A dainty masked woman approached him, "holding out a little paw about the size of a possum's, with a flesh-colored glove on it," and offered to tell his fortune in exchange for money. Big-Foot had his fortune told and bought the woman cocktails at the bar, where the two stood "laughing and talking, and sipping our liquor, until we got on the best of terms, and at length I ventured to take her hand in mine and give it a gentle squeeze." The Texan pressed her to unmask as the evening drew to a close. "So she took off her mask, and—what do you think? If she wasn't a full-blooded 'mulatto' I wish I may never lift the hair from another Indian! I was so astonished I couldn't say a word." Before Big-Foot could regain his composure, a spectacular brawl broke out that sent women screaming from the hall and chairs flying across the room.[51]

The brazen women and mayhem that shocked Big-Foot Wallace in the 1850s were a far cry from what Karl Bernhard encountered in the 1820s, when the "coloured ladies were under the eyes of their mothers, . . . were well and gracefully dressed, and conducted themselves with much propriety and modesty."[52] Contemporary observers and historians alike have treated quadroon balls and the *plaçage* complex as relatively static, fixed phenomena. Scholars recognize the commodification of sexual fantasy and white mastery embedded in them but have missed the narrative circularity that continuously reinvented the quadroon and repurposed her, both for new markets and for shifting political objectives. Wallace's is among the last of the antebellum personal memoirs of a New Orleans quadroon ball, and it is no coincidence that he was an altogether different kind of tourist from the titled Europeans and gentlemen travelers of an earlier era. The police blotter and newspaper reports of the 1840s and 1850s reveal the balls' degeneration into bawdy, popular male entertainments pervaded with criminality. No longer an acceptable destination for curious middle-class visitors and residents in search of the occasional risqué night on the town, quadroon balls became portholes to a demimonde of vice, a forerunner of the city's famous postbellum red-light district, Storyville.

In antebellum America, the quadroon was used to sell sex and mastery in the South and to arouse abolitionist sentiment in the North. After the Civil War, only a vestigial version of the tragic quadroon survived, functioning as a reminder of past southern sins in the literary discourse of unification.[53] But the quadroon fancy maid survived the passage to freedom to become the hyperlibidinous star of the sex industry in postbellum New Orleans. The rape fantasy that had fueled the fancy-maid trade before the war was eclipsed by a wild magnification of black women's sexual desire. Sexual insatiability was projected onto black women now that slavery no longer compelled them to capitulate to the sexual mastery of white men. And because, in the eyes of white men, quadroon women were the most desirable among women of African descent, they were deemed to be the most libidinous of all. New Orleans, constructed as the homeland of the American quadroon, naturally became the place most associated with postbellum commercial sex across the color line.

The quadroon sex slave became the quadroon prostitute in postbellum New Orleans, marketed to locals and visitors alike as descendants of the beautiful, exotic women described by Karl Bernhard and Frederick Law Olmsted. As one historian of New Orleans's postbellum sex industry observes, "While the city has always had a reputation for difference and decadence, between 1865 and 1920 New Orleans began to exploit that reputation in order to profit from it and draw people to the city."[54] Scholarly focus has illuminated the business of prostitution and the emergence in 1897 of the legalized red-light district known as Storyville, but quadroon balls played a part in the sex industry boom, too. The entertainments were revived as staged recreations to tempt carpetbaggers into sampling the city's forbidden fruits and to palliate former Confederates yearning to relive their mastery. But indulgence came at a high price, complicating the volatile politics of Reconstruction.

The Louisiana gubernatorial election of 1876 between Republican Stephen B. Packard and Democrat Francis T. Nicholls was a dirty business. White supremacist Democrats lined up behind Confederate veteran Nicholls and, with a combination of intimidation and violence, suppressed the black vote in an attempt to prevent the election of the Republican. President Ulysses S. Grant anticipated a close election and feared that both sides would attempt to tamper with the results. "Either party can afford to be disappointed in the result but the Country cannot afford to have the result tainted by the suspicion of illegal or false returns," he confided to General William T. Sherman. Three days after the election, Grant enlisted Sherman and other Republican luminaries to go to New Orleans to oversee the processing of the election returns and indirectly blessed the parallel participation of Democrats. "It is to be hoped that representative and fair men of both parties will go" to New Orleans, he told Sherman.[55] Grant got his wish, but his bipartisan embassy of electoral overseers fouled the integrity of their mission when they decided to investigate more than the vote count.

Rumors circulated that some of the official observers had gone "to the black women's hop" in New Orleans. When pressed in early February of 1877 about the veracity of such reports at a meeting of the Committee on the Powers and Privileges of the House, C. Irving Ditty, one of the Republicans deputized by President Grant to oversee the election returns in Louisiana, confessed that he and several other official observers had gone to a "dance given by some very light-colored people." The committee chair, a Democrat, seized his opportunity. "So, then this was the way the Republican statesmen amused themselves? They were away from their families, and took the opportunity to go to balls given by colored women?" In an attempt to dig himself out, Ditty blurted out, "I told my wife all about it."

Mr. Ditty's peccadillo had ramifications beyond the Louisiana gubernatorial election. The presidential contest between Republican Rutherford B. Hayes and Democrat Samuel J. Tilden was in dispute, and the polling in Louisiana was critical to its resolution. Louisiana was one of three southern states that returned a majority of ballots for Tilden, but the three state election committees, dominated by Republicans, disallowed large numbers of them as fraudulent. The result was that the twenty electoral votes of Louisiana, Florida, and South Carolina were awarded to Hayes, giving him a majority of one in the Electoral College. Democrats predictably made accusations of fraud, and a full-blown political crisis erupted. To resolve the election Congress created a fifteen-member Electoral Commission, which began its deliberations on the last day of January 1877. When Mr. Ditty was called before the Committee on the Powers and Privileges of the House and admitted that he had attended a quadroon ball, Washington erupted into an uproar. The salacious, racially freighted scandal could be effective ammunition in the partisan battle that threatened the fragile union. President Grant's attempt to head off crisis in Louisiana by sending observers to New Orleans was worse than futile.[56]

Ditty and the Republicans were not the only casualties, however. Under friendlier questioning from a Republican member of the committee, Ditty revealed that two Democratic observers from Illinois, Lyman Trumbull and former governor John Palmer, also attended the ball, "and both of them danced with the girls." The hearing room was stunned. "For a moment there was an almost painful silence in the committee-room, and then, as the spectators recalled old Mr. Trumbull's white hair, and lank, withered form, and imagined him dancing with a blooming New-Orleans quadroon, they broke into a shout of laughter which could not be controlled or suppressed."[57]

Trumbull's age was not the only thing that made him an unlikely dance partner on this occasion. A stalwart Republican and chair of the powerful Senate Judiciary Committee during the Civil War, he introduced the resolution that became the Thirteenth Amendment on the Senate floor.[58] A year later, he introduced the Freedmen's Bureau and Civil Rights Bills. He parted ways with the Radical Reconstructionists in his party over the impeachment of President Andrew Johnson and became an unlikely Democrat in the 1872 presidential election. Catching the man who had advocated for the abolition of slavery and freedmen's rights on the floor of the Senate in the compromising arms of a New Orleans quadroon was a timely godsend for the Republicans as the work of the Electoral Commission got underway early in 1877. Trumbull was counsel for the Tilden side in the hearings on the Louisiana election. When he rose to begin his two-hour indictment of the long list of the irregularities perpetrated by the Republican-dominated returning board and testified that "all the decisions of the returning board were made in secret session," he must have known that the credibility of his report was undermined by his lapse of judgment in New Orleans.[59]

Republicans and Democrats were equally exposed by the episode that made a fool of Lyman Trumbull, however. Irving Ditty had revealed the bipartisan participation in the excursion to the quadroon ball, and newspapers across the country delighted in the scandal. The *San Francisco Bulletin* reported bluntly that electoral observers in New Orleans went "to a quadroon ball at a house of prostitution the night before they left" the city.[60] More than a dozen similar stories appeared, most of them gleeful at the prospect of unmasking the hypocrisy and immorality of the commissioners. An attempt by the *Philadelphia Inquirer* to reduce the damage to Trumbull was risible. The former Republican senator went to the ball "as an artist to study a peculiar phase of Southern society; his gravity all through was the most amusing thing witness ever saw; he couldn't have been more solemn if he had been bishop of the diocese." In April of 1877, a ditty published in the *Georgia Weekly Telegraph* revealed how quickly and irretrievably those associated with electoral oversight in Louisiana had become objects of popular disdain (see Figure 13).[61]

As the Congressional Electoral Commission contemplated a way forward in the resolution of the intertwined gubernatorial and presidential elections, they had to step carefully and craft a compromise for many reasons. Peace, the Union, and civil rights hung in the balance, and powerful lobbies pressed for outcomes favorable to their interests. The compromise that emerged settled the matter but satisfied no one. The Electoral Commission awarded the election to Hayes, and President Grant recognized Francis T. Nicholls as governor of Louisiana and ordered the withdrawal of federal troops from the South. The presidency would remain in the hands of the Republicans, but Reconstruction was effectively ended. Among the many astute analyses of the compromise of 1877, sometimes known as the

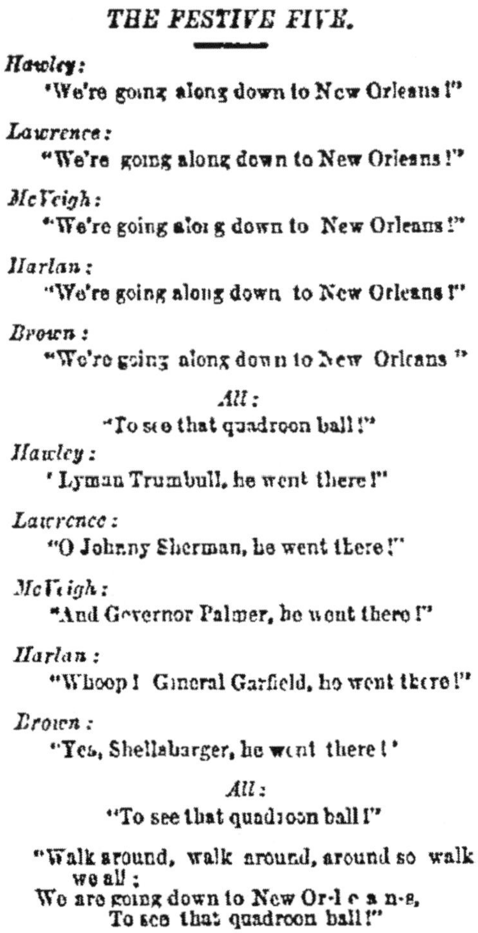

THE FESTIVE FIVE.

Hawley:
  "We're going along down to New Orleans!"

Lawrence:
  "We're going along down to New Orleans!"

McVeigh:
  "We're going along down to New Orleans!"

Harlan:
  "We're going along down to New Orleans!"

Brown:
  "We're going along down to New Orleans"

  All:
    "To see that quadroon ball!"

Hawley:
  ' Lyman Trumbull, he went there!"

Lawrence:
  "O Johnny Sherman, he went there!"

McVeigh:
  "And Governor Palmer, he went there!"

Harlan:
  "Whoop! General Garfield, he went there!"

Brown:
  "Yes, Shellabarger, he went there!'

  All:
    "To see that quadroon ball!"

  "Walk around, walk around, around so walk
      we all;
  We are going down to New Or-l e a n-s,
      To see that quadroon ball!"

FIGURE 13.
"The Festive Five," *Georgia Weekly Telegraph* (Macon), April 10, 1877, 6. Courtesy of the Digital Library of Georgia.

second Corrupt Bargain, none has contemplated the mythic quadroons of New Orleans. Still for sale a decade after the passage of the Thirteenth Amendment, the quadroon was a disruptive presence who could derail Republicans and Democrats equally effectively.[62]

The New Orleans quadroon fantasy survived the crisis of 1877 and provided one of the most lucrative commodities on offer in the city's infamous Storyville from its birth in 1897 to its demise in 1917. The Crescent City's pervasive postbellum vice industry had extended its tentacles into virtually every neighborhood. In an attempt to tame it, Alderman Sidney Story introduced a city ordinance restricting prostitution to a geographically prescribed area bounded by North Robertson, North Basin, Customhouse, and St. Louis Streets, a neighborhood just across the Basin from the Globe Ballroom. Women of mixed race, now identified with the color term "octoroon," were among the specialties advertised in an 1898 guidebook published to promote Storyville's attractions. The madam Lulu White claimed the largest concentration of light-skinned women of color, advertising "Miss White's Octoroon Club" of ten women at her establishment at 235 Basin Street, Mahogany Hall.[63]

Lulu White's marketing of the quadroon myth was artful. She tapped into the rhetoric that had established the antebellum figure to recreate an aura of exoticism that had irresistible appeal. White advertised herself as a "West Indian octoroon" and declared of her prostitutes, "all are born and bred Louisiana girls," preserving the illusion of the quadroon's tropical provenance (see Figure 14).[64] One can almost imagine her cribbing from Karl Bernhard or Joseph Holt Ingraham as she catalogued in herself and her employees the stock attributes of the perfect quadroon. She claimed to have "made a lifelong study of music and literature," like the legendary antebellum quadroons. White and her girls were presented as models of Circassian beauty. The madam herself claimed "an elegant form" and "beautiful black hair and blue eyes," and touted her employee Georgie Wilson as "fair, blue eyes, a typical blonde." Only the "finest Wines and Liquors" were served to visitors, including Roederer and Mums French champagne. The setting for all this indulgence was appropriately luxurious, "the most elaborately furnished house in the city of New Orleans," built "specially for Miss Lulu White at a cost of $40,000." Four stories tall and faced with expensive marble, the house boasted five parlors and fifteen bedrooms decorated with chandeliers and velvet hangings. And to ensure the comfort and privacy of Mahogany Hall's guests, each room had "a bath with hot and cold water and extension closets." The stage for the fantasy was perfectly set.[65]

Lulu White's evocation of the antebellum quadroon was a roaring success. "Nowhere in this country will you find a more popular personage than Madam White, who is noted as being the handsomest octoroon in America," the 1905 guide to Storyville observed. White literally wore her wealth. "She has the distinction of possessing the largest collection of diamonds, pearls, and other rare gems in this part of the country," the guidebook noted. "To see her at night, is like witnessing the late electrical display on the Cascade, at the late St. Louis Exposition."[66] In 1906 she advertised the availability of seventeen octoroons, making hers the largest of the Storyville brothels.[67]

Historians have argued that Storyville, especially as exemplified by Lulu

MISS LULA WHITE.

This famous West Indian octoroon first saw the light of day thirty-one years ago. Arriving in this country at a rather tender age, and having been fortunately gifted with a good education it did not take long for her to find out what the other sex were in search of.

In describing Miss Lulu, as she is most familiarly called, it would not be amiss to say that besides possessing an elegant form she has beautiful black hair and blue eyes, which have justly gained for her the title of the "Queen of the Demi-monde."

Her establishment, which is situated in the central part of the city, is unquestionably the most elaborately furnished house in the city of New Orleans, and without a doubt one of the most elegant places in this or any other country.

She has made a feature of boarding none but the fairest of girls—those gifted with nature's best charms, and would, under no circumstances have any but that class in her house.

As an entertainer Miss Lulu stands foremost, having made a life-long study of music and literature. She is well read and one that can interest anybody and make a visit to her place a continued round of pleasure.

And when adding that she would be pleased to see all her old friends and make new ones. What more could be added?

FIGURE 14. Miss Lula White. From the souvenir guide for New Mahogany Hall, c. 1900. Courtesy of the Historic New Orleans Collection.

White's enterprise, provided a way for white men of all classes to buy for themselves the experience of sexual mastery enjoyed only by elite planters before the Civil War.[68] The implication is that Lulu White and Storyville helped democratize white supremacy after the Civil War, cultivating in men who were too poor ever to have enjoyed the privilege and prerogative of slave ownership the taste for mastery that upheld race-based subordination. But there was nothing new in selling the quadroon to the white male rabble. The figure was as important to forging a brotherhood of white solidarity before the Civil War as she was after it.

EPILOGUE

Reimagining the Quadroon

How does one write a history of the impossible?

—Michel-Rolph Trouillot[1]

Thanks to Martin Scorsese's eponymous film, sensationalist urban historian Herbert Asbury is most famous for his 1928 exposé, *The Gangs of New York*, but it is his hefty tome detailing the lurid underbelly of old New Orleans that sells more copies these days.[2] Entitled simply *The French Quarter*, Asbury's tour of Crescent City debauchery dedicated ten pages to the city's mythic quadroons. Apart from the trademark wink in his prose, his description of the women and their ways did not stray from the nineteenth-century rubric he mined for his material. Details about the "amorous excitement aroused by the beautiful quadroons" and the balls to which "the mothers of the quadroon girls brought their daughters, dressed in their finery," were cribbed shamelessly from the likes of George Featherstonhaugh and Maltida Charlotte Houstoun. Channeling Harriet Martineau, Asbury assured his early twentieth-century readers that "rare indeed was the young Creole gentleman who didn't have a quadroon sweetheart cozily installed in one of the little houses 'near the ramparts,' where he supported her in a style commensurate with his wealth." The most recent edition of *The French Quarter* came out in 2008, ensuring that twenty-first-century readers will not be without an introduction to the lore of New Orleans quadroons faithful to nineteenth-century orthodoxy.[3]

Asbury has had plenty of company spilling ink to keep the quadroon alive in America's consciousness. Some of his fellow authors, by dint of their popularity or genius, have been so critical to preserving and fixing the essential outlines of the figure that they and their work have become part of the canon. George Washington Cable, a New Orleans native writing during Reconstruction, provided Asbury and others with a critical bridge between the antebellum tradition and the figure's postbellum career. The free black female heroines of his popular fiction remain a favored subject of critical studies that engage the figure of the tragic mulatto.[4] And his vivid prose, wide readership, and status as a native son have led some readers, past and present, to invest his characters with more than literary meaning.

Cable wrapped the salient features of the women described by Martineau and Bernhard in artfully plotted moral fiction that reached an enormous popular audience through serialization in *Scribner's Monthly*. When Cable began his career at *Scribner's* in 1874, circulation stood at 40,000. By the time the magazine finished publishing his ambitious serialized novel *The Grandissimes* in 1880, circulation had risen to more than 100,000.[5] Cable's retrospective depiction of the quadroon and her plight in New Orleans, vivid, romantic, and charged with a racial sensibility honed by the violence of the closing years of Reconstruction in Louisiana, made a powerful imaginative impact beyond the middle-class subscribers to *Scribner's*. Historian Charles Gayarré's 1883 rebuttal of Cable's depiction of the situation of New Orleans quadroons suggests that many readers accepted Cable's work as historically accurate. Gayarré's intervention was never published, and subsequent generations have been susceptible to accepting Cable as a reliable source on the free women of color who inhabited the Crescent City before the Civil War. Even historians have occasionally evoked Cable to illuminate the past in which he set his fiction.[6]

Cable's own historical sources for his quadroon portraits insured that he would preserve intact the familiar trope, as would, in turn, any historians who embraced him.[7] His short story "'Tite Poulette" (1874) and his novel, *Madame Delphine* (1881), are clearly indebted to the observations of Karl Bernhard and others.[8] Cable's quadroons were "sprung, upon the one hand, from the merry gallants of a French colonial military service which had grown gross by affiliation with Spanish-American frontier life, and, upon the other hand, from comely Ethiopians culled out of the less negroidal types of African live goods." The progeny of these first encounters "afforded a mere hint of the splendor that was to result from a survival of the fairest through seventy-five years devoted to the elimination of the black pigment and the cultivation of hyperian excellence and nymphean grace and beauty."[9] The teenaged 'Tite Poulette was hailed by Creole boys of New Orleans as "so beautiful, beautiful, beautiful! White?—white like a water-lily! White—like a magnolia!" Both 'Tite Poulette and Olive, the quadroon girl at the center of *Madame Delphine*, were in love with white men whom they could not marry. Instead of allowing 'Tite Poulette and Olive to suffer the traditional tragic fate of quadroons, however, Cable transferred the burden to their mothers. Madame Delphine and Olive's mother, Madame John, both renounced their maternity so that their daughters could pass for white and marry white lovers.[10] Sympathetic as he was to women of African descent, Cable could not imagine them desiring and marrying black men. The heart of the familiar tragic mulatto plot remained intact.

New Orleans historian Grace King was decidedly unsympathetic to New Orleans quadroons, but the limits of her imagination with respect to black female desire and respectability were similarly drawn. "Unscrupulous and pitiless, by nature or circumstance, as one chooses to view it, and secretly still claiming the racial license of Africa, they were, in regard to family purity, domestic peace, and household dignity, the most insidious and the deadliest foes a community ever possessed." Quadroon women, according to King, had "an aversion on their part to marrying men of their own colour," which led to "their relaxation and deviation from, if not their complete denial of, the code of morality accepted by white women, and their consequent adoption of a separate standard of morals for themselves." The objective that provoked such licentiousness, to the fury of white supremacist King, was to claim a white person's birthright. "The great ambition of the unmarried quadroon mothers," she railed, "was to have their children pass for whites, and so get access to the privileged class. To reach this end, there was nothing they would not attempt, no sacrifice they would not make."[11]

Subsequent authors—too many to name—rang the changes on the two poles of interpretation that had been established by antebellum authors. The quadroon was either tragic or a sexual predator. Her fate was either to pass for white or remain ensnared in the *plaçage* complex.[12] The literature that reproduces these formulae is not marginal, nor has interest in the figure of the quadroon waned with the years. William Faulkner gives Thomas Sutpen, the protagonist of *Absalom, Absalom!* (1936), a quadroon lover from Haiti. She and the son she has borne Sutpen come to New Orleans where the young man, ignorant of his race, falls in love with Sutpen's daughter by his white wife. Faulkner's is no ordinary quadroon tale in the telling, but its plot barely strays from the pattern set by Joseph Holt Ingraham's 1839 incestuous tragedy, "The Quadroon of Orleans."[13]

Isabelle Allende grants the quadroon heroines of her 2010 novel *Island Beneath the Sea* more agency than Ingraham or Faulkner, and the women inhabit an admirably rendered revolutionary Atlantic. Otherwise, however, her characters and plot are all too familiar. The beautiful Haitian refugee Violette Boisier carefully plans New Orleans's first quadroon ball to attract only the elite young men of the city. The event would be elegant and extravagant, "a ball as selective as those held by white debutantes" where "only young whites with a fortune, and those seriously interested in *plaçage*, would attend." Violette's hope that such a ball would result in her daughter finding a wealthy white man to take her as his *placée* goes awry in what would be an entirely predictable way to readers of Ingraham and Faulkner. The man into whose arms Violette's daughter falls at the ball is her white half-brother, with whom she defiantly elopes.[14]

Popular fiction can hardly be held to account for the recirculation of dubious details from nineteenth-century sources in the service of artistic creation. Literature is undoubtedly the richer for the endeavors of the likes of Faulkner and Allende. There is less excuse for popular films that trade on the familiar stereotype (see Figure 15). But art, good and bad, has unwittingly impoverished history along the way. What has made for dynamic fiction has reinforced a stillborn narrative of the past. The figure of the quadroon continues to be invested with fresh poetic power, but its outlines remain fixed. Fiction gives license to create alternative pasts, but literature has locked the quadroon into a powerfully established storyline from which deviation is virtually unimaginable, even for historians.

This is especially true for historians who depend on the same nineteenth-century sources that have inspired the fiction. Alice Dunbar-Nelson's pioneering 1916 article "People of Color in Louisiana" relied on a long footnote quoting Harriet Martineau to substantiate her observation that in antebellum New Orleans, "the tendency seemed to be not to check promiscuous miscegenation but to debase the offspring resulting therefrom."[15] E. Franklin Frazier's *The Negro Family in the United States* (1939) borrowed from Grace King and Frederick Law Olmsted for its characterization of New Orleans quadroons and to assign culpability for their immorality. The "daughters of these quadroon women," Frazier informs his readers, "followed in some cases the pattern set by their mothers."[16] Joseph G. Tregle Jr. proclaimed in 1952 that "a large if undetermined number" of New Orleans free women of color "monopolized the task of accommodating the licentiousness of the male part of New Orleans."[17] Henry Sterkx wrote in his 1972 book on free blacks in antebellum Louisiana that "it was at free Negro balls where women of color concluded agreements to become mistresses of White men."[18] In an essay published in 2000, Joan M. Martin explains that once a young woman of color had met a suitable white protector at a quadroon ball, "she sent him to her mother or guardian," who concluded negotiations. "Once agreement was reached,

FIGURE 15. Poster for the movie *Quadroon* (1972), which economically captures all the major elements of the antebellum quadroon stereotype.

the girl was spoken of as *placée*. . . . Custom dictated that the man buy a small house on or near *rue de Rampart* and present it to her." Martin based her rendition of *plaçage* on a fanciful account produced by Boston travel writer Eleanor Early in 1947, which was loosely based—without attribution—on Harriet Martineau.[19] At the beginning of the twenty-first century, the history of the American quadroon was still anchored in the same handful of nineteenth-century sources it began with.

This may not seem a grave problem on the face of it, but complacency about sources is a comfort few historians allow themselves these days. As the late British philosopher Bernard Williams has said, "Facts have to be discovered, and the interests that shape the narrative also shape the inquiry that discovers them."[20] When American scholars began investigating the quadroon, the historical exceptionalism of New Orleans was unquestioned. It made sense for this strange figure to have been produced in a place that had always been so different from the rest of America. The historical facts conveyed in the familiar nineteenth-century sources filled the bill. There was no reason for historians to go in search of others. That changed when Hurricane Katrina blew through New Orleans in 2005.

In the first few days after the catastrophic storm made landfall and floodwaters poured through faulty levees, a woman at the New Orleans Convention Center, desperate for food, water, and rescue cried out: "We are American!" Reflecting on this scene, a well-known public intellectual observed that, "having been abandoned, the people in the convention center were reduced to reminding their fellow citizens, through the medium of television, that they were not refugees in a foreign country."[21] Brian Williams, of NBC, the only national news anchor in the city during and immediately after Katrina, recalled at the time his first visit to the city years before. As his plane rolled to a stop on the runway, the pilot came over the public address system "and welcomed his passengers to New Orleans by noting that they'd just left the United States."[22] The national response to Katrina and memories like Williams's reveal a widespread belief that the people of New Orleans *do* occupy a foreign country, thanks to a long-lived, historically constructed definition of New Orleans as "other," an island of exotic, erotic creole something-or-other that is essentially foreign to what is "American." The quadroon has played a central role in sustaining the city's reputation as an alien place improbably situated within American borders.[23]

Tourism is the lifeblood of the New Orleans economy, a lamentable reality not only because it locks thousands of New Orleanians into minimum-wage jobs as cleaners and waiters, but because it sells an image of the city that damns it to eternal exclusion from the American mainstream. History—or what passes for it—is the tourism industry's trusty handmaiden in this enterprise. If you were among the 3,000 hospital administrators who attended an annual professional meeting in New Orleans in 2007, you were tempted to the city by a colorful brochure dominated by the figure of a contemporary Louis Armstrong look-alike blowing his trumpet in front of a building with the iron grillwork and mansard roof that let you know you were not in Kansas anymore. And to keep family members occupied while conferees attended sessions on "Pandemic Preparedness" and "Operating Room HVAC Design," a series of tours were available to show off the city's "special mystique" and acquaint visitors with its "inordinately colorful history," its "ghosts, voodoo priestesses, and haunted mansions" and "wonderful tales of Creole courtyard soirees, quadroon balls, and midnight duels."[24] Fifty years ago, if you were an indulgent father or mother feeling guilty about leaving your daughter at home while you ate, drank, and made merry in New Orleans, you might have picked up one of the ubiquitous Mammy dolls that lined the shelves of French Quarter shops. These days, the offensive Mammy dolls having mostly disappeared, you might be tempted instead to bring home a quadroon doll. The prototype advertised is named Gabrielle, and her dishabille, bare feet, and bedroom eyes suggest just how she is "getting ready for the New Orleans Quadroon Ball."[25] Like jazz and voodoo, the quadroon has been pressed into service by those whose job it is to sell New Orleans.

Jazz *was* born in New Orleans, and Louis Armstrong was its greatest genius and ambassador. But as we have seen, the quadroon and the quadroon ball—epitomizing the linked sins of slavery and interracial sex—were born someplace else—in many other places, actually, many of them detached from geographies beyond those of the imagination. These imaginary progeny have become an enduring part of the fabric of an illusory version of New Orleans, a postlapsarian city that secures the prelapsarian pretensions of other American sites. If Boston and Philadelphia can be imagined as the cradles of American identity and culture, it is partly because New Orleans has relieved them of the burden of embracing pasts as deeply entangled as its own in the Atlantic world dynamics of slavery, sex across the color line, and black revolution. New Orleans and its quadroons allow Puritanism and the Declaration of Independence to represent the American past by shouldering the full symbolic burden of a more complicated, diverse, and contested history.

The Haitian intellectual Michel-Rolph Trouillot offers insight into the operation of such selective historical memory. "When reality does not co-incide with deeply held beliefs," he argues, "human beings tend to phrase interpretations that force reality within the scope of these beliefs. They devise formulas to repress the unthinkable and to bring it back within the realm of accepted discourse."[26] The repression of the unthinkable can occur even in the face of personal experience of it and despite good inten-tions, Trouillot points out. The enslaved men who rose in rebellion on the sugar plantations of the French colony of Saint-Domingue in 1791 were chiefly African-born veterans of military campaigns in Congo. Trouillot exposes the incredulity of European observers who attributed their up-rising to outside agitators and their military success to mixed-race lead-ers. They could not imagine the truth: African-born men understood the brutality of slavery and put their fighting skills to work to end it. Trouil-lot famously proposed that the real past that unfolded in the course of the Haitian Revolution was "an unthinkable history" to those who took it upon themselves to write about it.[27]

Blindness to an unthinkable past neither targets the bigot nor spares the sympathizer. The "apologists and detractors alike, abolitionists and avowed racists, liberal intellectuals, economists, and slave owners used the events of Saint-Domingue to make their case, without regard to Haitian history as such," Trouillot observes. "Haiti mattered to all of them, but only as pretext to talk about something else."[28] The same might be said of the quadroon, and her connection to the unthinkable Haitian Revolution may be relevant.

The New Orleans quadroon matters to American historians, if current scholarship is any indication, but whether New Orleans matters enough to change the shape of the inquiry that discovers the facts of the city's his-tory is another question. Even the most sensitive and sophisticated recent scholarship on New Orleans quadroons and the *plaçage* complex elides discourse and history. George Washington Cable is evoked to illuminate the position of antebellum free women of color, and Harriet Martineau and Fredrick Law Olmsted, their confessions to hearsay notwithstanding, remain foundational texts.[29] The titles of books about colonial and ante-bellum New Orleans relentlessly draw attention to the city's exceptional-ism in terms that evoke sex, race, and sin. In the first decade of the twenty-first century, the city appeared on scholarly book covers as a "Southern Babylon," the "Devil's Empire," and the scene of "Spectacular Wicked-ness."[30] Even though most of the books between these covers approach

FIGURE 16. Edouard Marquis, *Creole Women of Color Out Taking the Air,*
1867. Watercolor. These women of color, modestly dressed for a walk through
New Orleans, were sketched from life shortly after the Civil War and offer
an alternative to more familiar sensationalized antebellum literary portraits.
Courtesy of the Collections of the Louisiana State Museum, New Orleans.

the city's complicated past with respect and impeccable scholarly scruples, by bearing titles that evoke sex and race they reinforce habits of thought about New Orleans as exotic, lascivious, black, and essentially different from the rest of America. And they make it possible for Americans to continue to believe that their nation's messy Atlantic legacies were sequestered in a kind of virtual colonial space at the mouth of the Mississippi.

The purification of the rest of the country at the expense of New Orleans was not accomplished overnight. The quadroon has not always been a synecdoche for the Crescent City. She once ranged broadly across New World terrain and was quarantined at the mouth of the Mississippi only by degrees and over many years. She was the villainess who precipitated the downfall of colonial Saint-Domingue, the spurious issue who unsettled Philadelphia politics, and the indulged temptress who mitigated the threat of black rebellion as white America shuddered in the wake of the Haitian Revolution. She was, as well, a wife and mother who watched her husband's militia unit march off to the Battle of New Orleans and stood in the sanctuary to see her daughter marry the boy from around the corner (see Figure 16).

What is strange about the history of the American quadroon is what is strange about all history: the story of how and why some things are observed and others ignored, some things remembered, others forgotten. When we are able to recover how and why "that which is said to have happened" sometimes diverged from what did happen, we not only make the past more knowable, we make a more just and humane future imaginable.[31]

Notes

ABBREVIATIONS

1808 Civil Code   *A Digest of the Civil Laws Now in Force in the Territory of Orleans*, electronic version, http://www.law.lsu.edu/index. cfm?geaux=digestof1808.home (accessed November 10, 2011)

AANO   Archives of the Archdiocese of New Orleans

AGI PC   Archivo General de Indias, Papeles Procedentes de la Isla de Cuba

HNOC   Historic New Orleans Collection

NONA   New Orleans Notarial Archives

RSCL   Records of the Superior Council of Louisiana, Louisiana State Historical Center, New Orleans

SLC B1   St. Louis Cathedral Baptisms, 1731–1733

SLC B2   St. Louis Cathedral Baptisms, 1744–1753

SLC B3   St. Louis Cathedral Baptisms, 1753–1759

SLC B4   St. Louis Cathedral Baptisms and Marriages, 1759–1762

SLC B5   St. Louis Cathedral Baptisms and Marriages, 1763–1766

SLC B6   St. Louis Cathedral Baptisms, 1767–1771

SLC B7   St. Louis Cathedral Baptisms, 1772–1776

SLC B8   Libro donde se asientan las partidas de baptismos de negros esclavos y mulatos que se han celebr[a]do en esta Iglesia parroquial de Sr. San Luis de la ciudad de la Nueva Orleans desde el dia l de enero de 1777 que empezo hasta el ano de 1781 que es el corrente

SLC B9   St. Louis Cathedral Baptisms, 1777–1786

SLC B10   Libro donde se asientan las partidas de bautismos de negros y mulatos libres o esclavos el que dio principio en 17 de junio de 1783 para el Isso. de esta parroquial de San Luis de Nueva Orleans en la provincia de la Luisiana

SLC B11   St. Louis Cathedral Baptisms, 1786–1796

SLC B12   Libro de bautizados de negros y mulatos, [1786–1792]

SLC B13   Libro quinto de bautizados negros y mulatos de la parroquia de San Luis de esta ciudad de la Nueva Orleans: contiene doscientos trienta y sieta folios utiles, y da principia en primero de octubre de mil seteceintos noventa y dos, y acaba [en 1789]

SLC B14   St. Louis Cathedral Baptisms, 1796–1802
SLC B15   Baptisms of Slaves and Free Persons of Color, 1798–1801
SLC B16   St. Louis Cathedral Baptisms of Slaves and Free Persons of
               Color, 1801–1804
SLC B17   St. Louis Cathedral Baptisms, 1802–1806
SLC B18   St. Louis Cathedral Baptisms of Slaves and Free Persons of
               Color, 1804–1805
SLC B19   St. Louis Cathedral Baptisms of Slaves and Free Persons of
               Color, 1805–1807
SLC B20   St. Louis Cathedral Baptisms, 1806–1809
SLC B21   St. Louis Cathedral Baptisms of Slaves and Free Persons of
               Color, 1807–1809
SLC B22   St. Louis Cathedral Baptisms, 1809–1811
SLC B23   St. Louis Cathedral Baptisms of Slaves and Free Persons of
               Color, 1809–1811
SLC B24   St. Louis Cathedral Baptisms of Slaves and Free Persons of
               Color, 1811–1812
SLC B25   St. Louis Cathedral Baptisms, 1811–1815
SLC B26   St. Louis Cathedral Baptisms of Slaves and Free Persons of
               Color, 1812–1814
SLC B27   St. Louis Cathedral Baptisms of Slaves and Free Persons of
               Color, 1814–1816
SLC B28   St. Louis Cathedral Baptisms, 1815–1818
SLC B29   St. Louis Cathedral Baptisms of Slaves and Free Persons of
               Color, 1816–1818
SLC B30   St. Louis Cathedral registro o libro 16 de bautismos de gente de
               color, 1818–1820
SLC B31   St. Louis Cathedral Baptisms, 1818–1822
SLC B32   St. Louis Cathedral libro decimo septimo de bautismos de sola
               gente de color, 1820–1823
SLC B33   St. Louis Cathedral Baptisms, 1822–1825
SLC B34   St. Louis Cathedral Baptisms of Slaves and Free Persons of
               Color, 1823–1825
SLC B35   St. Louis Cathedral Baptisms of Slaves and Free Persons of
               Color, 1825–1826
SLC B36   St. Louis Cathedral Baptisms, 1825–1827
SLC B37   St. Louis Cathedral Baptisms of Slaves and Free Persons of
               Color, 1826–1827
SLC B38   St. Louis Cathedral Baptisms, 1827–1828
SLC B39   St. Louis Cathedral Baptisms of Slaves and Free Persons of
               Color, 1827–1829
SLC B40   St. Louis Cathedral Baptisms, 1828–1832

SLC B41	St. Louis Cathedral Baptisms of Slaves and Free Persons of Color, 1829–1831
SLC B42	St. Louis Cathedral Baptisms of Slaves and Free Persons of Color, 1831–1834
SLC M1	St. Louis Cathedral Marriages, 1720–1730
SLC M2	St. Louis Cathedral Marriages, 1764–1774
SLC M3	Libro primero de Matrimonios de Negros y Mulatos en la Parroquia de Sn. Luis de la Nueva-orleans; en 137 folios da principio en 20 de enero de 1777 y acaba en 1830
SLC M4	St. Louis Cathedral Marriages, 1777–1784
SLC M5	Libro de matrimonios celebrados en esta Inglesia parroq.l de San Luis de Nueva Orleans, provincia de la Luisiana, el que da principio en el mes de abril del año de mil setecientos ochenta y quatro en adelante
SLC M6	St. Louis Cathedral Marriages, 1806–1821
SLC M7	St. Louis Cathedral Marriages, 1821–1830
SLC M8	St. Louis Cathedral Marriages, 1830–1834
SLC M9	St. Louis Cathedral Second registre des Actes de celebrations de Mariages [couleurs libres]. Il commence en août 1830. Et Finit en octobre 1835, conenant 245 actes
SLC M10	St. Louis Cathedral Marriages, 1831–1833
SLC F1	St. Louis Cathedral Funerals, 1772–1790
SLC F2	Continuación de las partidas de blancos, muertos en esta parroquia de San Luis de la Nueva Orleans, desde el primero de 8.bre de año de 1784, hasta concluirse este libro [1793]
SLC F3	Libro de diffunctos. D[e negros y] mu[latos . . .]
SLC F4	"Libro quarto de difuntos blancs de esta parroquia de San Luis de la Nueva Orleans, en 284 folios, da principio al primero folio, partida primera en treze de septiembre de mil setecientos noventa y tres; y acaba [1803]
SLC F5	Funerals of Free Persons of Color and Slaves, 1797–1806
SLC F6	St. Louis Cathedral Funerals, 1803–1807
SLC F7	St. Louis Cathedral Funerals, 1803–1815
SLC F8	St. Louis Cathedral Funerals of Slaves and Free Persons of Color, 1806–1810
SLC F9	St. Louis Cathedral Funerals of Slaves and Free Persons of Color, 1810–1815
SLC F10	St. Louis Cathedral Funerals of Slaves and Free Persons of Color, 1815–1819
SLC F11	St. Louis Cathedral Funerals, 1815–1820
SLC F12	St. Louis Cathedral Funerals of Slaves and Free Persons of Color, 1819–1825

SLC F13	St. Louis Cathedral Funerals, 1820–1824
SLC F14	St. Louis Cathedral Funerals, 1824–1828
SLC F15	St. Louis Cathedral Funerals, 1829–1831
SLC F16	St. Louis Cathedral Funerals of Slaves and Free Persons of Color, 1829–1832
SMNO B1	St. Marie Baptisms, 1805–1838.
UCANO	Ursuline Convent Archives, New Orleans

NOTE ON NAMES

Variations in given and family names in eighteenth- and nineteenth-century manuscript records from New Orleans are common. Some scribes recorded French versions, some Spanish, some English. Even within each language tradition, there could be multiple, sometimes curious variations, such as "Santyague" for "Santiago," the Spanish version of "Jacques." When a name appears in multiple sources in different versions, it has been standardized to the most common or best-known variation.

PROLOGUE

1. Thomas Jefferson to Francis Gray, March 4, 1815, Library of Congress, American Memory.

2. Sullivan, *Rambles and Scrambles*, 223.

3. Martineau, *Society in America*, 2:326.

4. Olmsted, *Journey in the Seaboard Slave States*, 694.

5. Edward Hepple Hall, *Appletons' Hand-book of American travel*.

6. "New Orleans Sights: Quadroon Ballroom."

7. See, for example, Morris, *Southern Slavery and the Law*, 26, 28, for legal cases in southern states that referred to quadroons. Pascoe, *What Comes Naturally*, illustrates the widespread reaction to racial mixing throughout America after the Civil War.

8. Gordon-Reed, *Thomas Jefferson and Sally Hemings* and *The Hemingses of Monticello* are the definitive works on the relationship between Thomas Jefferson and Sally Hemings. See also Stanton, *Free Some Day*, 103–4; and Thomas Jefferson Foundation, "Research Committee Report on Thomas Jefferson and Sally Hemings."

9. Sollors, *Neither Black Nor White Yet Both*, 112–41.

10. Jefferson, *Notes on the State of Virginia*. The passage, which forms part of Jefferson's section entitled "Laws," is as follows:

Whether the black of the negro resides in the reticular membrane between the skin and scarf-skin, or in the scarf-skin itself; whether it proceeds from the colour of the blood, the colour of the bile, or from that of some other secretion, the difference is fixed in nature, and is as real as if its seat and cause were better known to us. And is this difference of no importance? Is it not the foundation of a greater or less share of beauty in the two races? Are not the fine mixtures of red and white, the expressions of every passion by greater or less suffusions of colour in the one, preferable to that eternal monotony, which reigns in the countenances, that immoveable veil of black which covers all the emotions of the other race? Add to these, flowing hair, a more elegant symmetry of form, their own judgment in favour of the whites, declared by their preference of them, as uniformly as is the preference of the Oranootan for the black women over those of his own species. The circumstance of superior beauty, is thought worthy attention in the propagation of our horses, dogs, and other domestic animals; why not in that of man? Besides those of colour, figure, and hair, there are other physical distinctions proving a difference of race. They have less hair on the face and body. They secrete less by the kidnies, and more by the glands of the skin, which gives them a very strong and disagreeable odour. This greater degree of transpiration renders them more tolerant of heat, and less so of cold, than the whites. Perhaps too a difference of structure in the pulmonary apparatus, which a late ingenious experimentalist has discovered to be the principal regulator of animal heat, may have disabled them from extricating, in the act of inspiration, so much of that fluid from the outer air, or obliged them in expiration, to part with more of it. They seem to require less sleep. A black, after hard labour through the day, will be induced by the slightest amusements to sit up till midnight, or later, though knowing he must be out with the first dawn of the morning. They are at least as brave, and more adventuresome. But this may perhaps proceed from a want of forethought, which prevents their seeing a danger till it be present. When present, they do not go through it with more coolness or steadiness than the whites. They are more ardent after their female: but love seems with them to be more an eager desire, than a tender delicate mixture of sentiment and sensation. Their griefs are transient. Those numberless afflictions, which render it doubtful whether heaven has given life to us in mercy or in wrath, are less felt, and sooner forgotten with them. In general, their existence appears to participate more of sensation than reflection. To this must be ascribed their disposition to sleep when abstracted from their diversions, and unemployed in labour. An animal whose body is at rest, and who does not reflect, must be disposed to sleep of course. Comparing them by their faculties of memory, reason, and imagination, it appears to me, that in memory they are equal to the whites; in reason much inferior, as I think one could scarcely be found capable of tracing and comprehending the investigations of Euclid; and that in imagination they are dull, tasteless, and anomalous.

11. Thomas Jefferson to Martha Jefferson Randolph, March 24, 1791, *The Papers of Thomas Jefferson Digital Edition*, http://rotunda.upress.virginia.edu/founders/TSJN-01-19-02-0165 (accessed July 10, 2012); Thomas Jefferson to Martha Jefferson

Randolph, November 13, 1791, ibid., http://rotunda.upress.virginia.edu/founders/
TSJN-01-22-02-0270 (accessed July 10, 2012); Thomas Jefferson to William
Moultrie, December 23, 1793, ibid., http://rotunda.upress.virginia.edu/founders/
TSJN-01-27-02-0544, (accessed July 10, 2012); Thomas Jefferson to James Monroe,
July 14, 1793, ibid., http://rotunda.upress.virginia.edu/founders/TSJN-01-26-02-0445
(accessed July 10, 2012).

12. The quadroon appears in the history in British colonial America primarily as
a descriptive phenotype inhabiting the Caribbean. The earliest use in English seems
to have been in Hans Sloane's 1707 account of his voyage to the Caribbean, in which
he describes the inhabitants of Jamaica as "for the most part Europeans . . . who are
the Masters, and Indians, Negros, Mulatos, Alcatrazes, mestises, Quarterons, &C.
who are the Slaves." Sloan's spelling of the word, "quateron," follows the Spanish,
"cuarteron," suggesting that he and other Anglophone contemporaries adopted the
term directly from the Spanish, who previously held Jamaica. *Cuarteron* was one
of the *castas*, or mixed-race categories, constructed in Spanish colonial America.
Although *casta* taxonomy was not codified until the middle of the eighteenth
century, Spanish colonial America began in the late sixteenth century to label
people believed to have three European and one African among their grandparents
cuarteron—meaning a quarter or one-fourth. The term *cuarteron* was probably used
informally by the middle of the seventeenth century in both Mexico and the Spanish
Caribbean, including Jamaica, where it passed into English usage. By the eighteenth
century, *cuarteron* was formally utilized in sacramental and legal records to identify
individuals deemed by appearance or testimony to be three-quarters European and
one-quarter African. The Spanish term was also adopted in the French colonies,
where its use was not restricted to the islands: A baptismal entry from 1751 in French
colonial Louisiana identifies the infant as a *quarteron*, with precisely the same spelling used by Sloane. Bennett, *Africans in Colonial Mexico*, 198; Sloane, *A Voyage to the
Islands*, 1:xlvi; Stedman, *Narrative, of a Five Years' Expedition*, 1:vi:126, 296.

13. Katzew, *Casta Painting*.

14. Moreau de Saint-Méry, *Description Topographique*, 71–74.

15. For a full discussion of this aspect of Moreau's work, see Chapter 2.

16. Stedman, *Narrative, of a Five Years' Expedition*, 1:vi:126, 296.

17. Summers, "What Happened to Sex Scandals?" 487.

18. Stoler, *Haunted by Empire*, esp. Stoler, "Tense and Tender Ties," 23–67.

19. Doris Garraway, *Libertine Colony*, focused on the French Antilles, is a similar
attempt to expose the dynamic interplay of the discourse on sexuality and race and
the historical process and illustrates the usefulness of such an approach. As a work
of literary analysis, however, it relies on secondary sources for the construction of
historical context. This study brings new archival material into conversation with
literary sources to add yet another layer to the analysis of the discourse and its role
in shaping historical events.

1. "Quadroons," *Spirit of the Press* (Philadelphia), November 1, 1807, 1. *The Spirit of the Press* was irregularly published by Richard Folwell, a hunchbacked dwarf known for the application of nicknames to the objects of his colorful critique and invective, according to Scharf and Westcott, *History of Philadelphia*, 3:1982.

2. Egerton, *Death or Liberty*.

3. Egerton, *Gabriel's Rebellion*.

4. Shankman, "Democracy in Pennsylvania," esp. chapter 9; and Shankman, "Malcontents and Tertium Quids," 43–72.

5. The best discussion is Dun, "Dangerous Intelligence."

6. Ibid., 29.

7. Ibid., 28–34.

8. Richard E. Powell, "Coachmaking in Philadelphia," 247–77.

9. Dun, "'What Avenues of Commerce,'" 484.

10. "Philadelphia, Nov. 15," *Carlisle Gazette*, November 23, 1791, 3.

11. Dubois, *Avengers of the New World*; Fick, *The Making of Haiti*, 22; James, *The Black Jacobins*.

12. Dun, "Dangerous Intelligence," 28–32.

13. Popkin, *You Are All Free*, 85–120.

14. Nash, *Forging Freedom*, 9–10.

15. Vermont was the first state to pass abolition legislation, in its 1777 state constitution, though the effects of its legislation are debated. "[Vermont] Constitution of 1777"; Melish, *Disowning Slavery*, 64.

16. Dun "Dangerous Intelligence," 244–66.

17. Popkin, *You Are All Free*, 137–45; "Extract of a letter, dated, Cape Francois, Jan. 11th, 1793," *General Advertiser* (Philadelphia), February 14, 1793, 3; "For the General Advertiser," ibid., February 19, 1793, 3.

18. Popkin, *You Are All Free*, quote is on 147.

19. Ibid., 187–245.

20. Ibid., 250; 256; Dubois, *Avengers of the New World*, 166, 176–80.

21. Madison Smartt Bell, *Toussaint Louverture*, 18.

22. Proclamation of Sonthonax, August 29, 1793, in Debien, "Aux origines de l'abolition de l'esclavage," 348–56.

23. Loi du 16 Pluviôse an II, in Mavidal and Laurent, *Archives parlementaires*, 84:285–87.

24. The earliest account of the events at Cap Français published in Philadelphia appeared on July 8. Published in a Federalist newspaper, it blamed the disaster on Sonthonax and Polverel, who "insulted the most respectable merchants that came to them with complaints against the mullattoes, this encouraged the latter to the greatest degree of insolence, and they began to fire the town on the 20th." "Shipping

News," *Dunlap's American Daily Advertiser* (Philadelphia), July 8, 1793, 3. An account more favorable to the commissioners was published the following day in Benjamin Franklin Bache's Democratic Republican paper. "Conflagration of Cape-Francois," *General Advertiser* (Philadelphia), July 9, 1793, 3. For the political loyalties of these newspapers, see Scharf and Westcott, *History of Philadelphia*, 3:1977. For yet another account of the Cap Français disaster, see, "At a meeting of the Democratic Society," *Pennsylvania Gazette* (Philadelphia), July 17, 1793.

25. "St. Domingo Sufferers," *Federal Gazette* (Philadelphia), August 5, 1793, 3.

26. *National Gazette* (Philadelphia), II:85:337, August 21, 1793.

27. "Philadelphia, July 17, At a meeting of the Democratic Society," *Pennsylvania Gazette* (Philadelphia), July 17, 1793.

28. "Extract of a Letter from Baltimore, Aug. 30," *National Gazette* (Philadelphia), II:91:363, September 11, 1793.

29. "New-York, Nov. 9," *Federal Gazette* (Philadelphia), November 22, 1793, 2.

30. "Important Communications," *Federal Gazette* (Philadelphia), November 29, 1793, 3.

31. "From a Correspondent," *Gazette of the United States* (Philadelphia), December 28, 1793, 3; "From the General Advertiser," ibid., December 30, 1793, 2.

32. "Island of St. Domingo," *Dunlap's American Daily Advertiser* (Philadelphia), June 3, 1793, 3.

33. Ibid.

34. Childs, *French Refugee Life in the United States*, 65–6, reports the number of Haitian refugees in Philadelphia in the winter of 1794; "Official Account of the Cannonade of Port-Au-Prince, on the 12th of April," *National Gazette*, II:62, June 1, 248.

35. "St. Domingo, July 17," *National Gazette*, II:104, 410, October 26, 1793. The *National Gazette*, published by Philip Freneau, was a Democratic Republican paper. Burns, *Infamous Scribblers*, 281.

36. [French Society of the Friends of Liberty and Equality], *General Advertiser*, July 12, 1793, 3.

37. "St. Domingo Sufferers: A Hint from a Correspondent," *General Advertiser*, July 31, 1793, 2. The Stanwix Treaty of 1784 was made between the U.S. government and the Iroquois, who ceded land that other tribes contended was not theirs to cede.

38. Childs, *French Refugee Life in the United States*, 67–72.

39. Contemporary newspaper articles about the epidemic include "Letter," *Independent Gazetteer*, August 31, 1793, 2; "For the American Daily Advertiser," *Dunlap's American Daily Advertiser* (Philadelphia), September 2, 1793, 2; *Federal Gazette* (Philadelphia), September 13, 1793, 3; "Baltimore, Sept. 14," *National Gazette* (Philadelphia), September 25, 1793, 2:95, 380. The most widely read contemporary chronicle of the epidemic was Carey, *A Short Account of the Plague or Malignant Fever*. See also, A. J. and R. A., *A Narrative of the Proceedings of the Black People During the Late Awful Calamity in Philadelphia*. Scholarship on the epidemic includes John Harvey Powell, *Bring Out Your Dead*; and Pernick, "Politics, Parties, and Pestilence," 559–86.

40. Dalmas, *Histoire de la Révolution de Saint-Domingue*, 184, translated and quoted in Popkin, *You Are All Free*, 182.

41. Popkin, *You Are All Free*, 174, 177, 182–83; 186.

42. Moreau de Saint-Méry, *Moreau de Saint-Méry's American Journey*, 309; Lyons, *Sex among the Rabble*, 193–96.

43. Murdock, "The Triumphs of Love," line 199–219.

44. Dun, "Dangerous Intelligence," 280–93

45. "United States, Philadelphia District," *Dunlap's American Daily Advertiser* (Philadelphia), December 27, 1793, 4.

46. "For Sale or Charter," *Federal Gazette* (Philadelphia), December 27, 1793, 1.

47. "Extract of a Letter from St. Domingo," *Pennsylvania Gazette* (Philadelphia), April 1, 1795.

48. Philadelphia merchants usually sympathetic to the Federalist administration of President Washington opposed Jay's Treaty in view of the particularly negative effect it would have on their Saint-Domingue trading interests. Samuel Bayard, the brother of merchant Andrew Bayard and an official in the Washington administration, surprised his fellow Federalists by his public opposition to Jay's Treaty. Sterling, "A Federalist Opposes the Jay Treaty," 408–13.

49. Ronald Angelo Johnson, "A Revolutionary Dinner," 141–68.

50. John Adams to Timothy Pickering, April 17, 1799, in Adams, *The Works of John Adams*, 129.

51. Oberholtzer, *Robert Morris*, 214–61.

52. Ferguson, *Golden Rule*, 53–54.

53. Ronald Angelo Johnson, "A Revolutionary Dinner," 139; Elkins and McKitrick, *The Age of Federalism*, 657.

54. Richard Yates to Timothy Pickering, April 30, 1798, quoted in Ronald Angelo Johnson, "A Revolutionary Dinner," 128.

55. Louverture and Stevens, "Letters of Toussaint Louverture and of Edward Stevens, 1798–1800," 72.

56. Ibid., 80, 101–2.

57. Elkins and McKitrick, *The Age of Federalism*, 520–22

58. "Jefferson's Draft of a Constitution for Virginia," [May-June 1783], in Jefferson, *The Papers of Thomas Jefferson*, 6:298. The ban on slavery in Jefferson's draft of the report on a plan of government for the western territories is in ibid., 607–8. For further discussion and scholarship on Jefferson's thinking on slavery and Saint-Domingue, Haiti, see Matthewson, "Jefferson and Haiti," 209–48.

59. Egerton, *Gabriel's Rebellion*; Matthewson, "Jefferson and Haiti"; Sidbury, *Ploughshares into Swords*.

60. Matthewson, "Jefferson and Haiti."

61. Tench Coxe to Madison, [ca. November 28, 1801], in Madison, *The Papers of James Madison*, 2:281–83. Jefferson to St. George Tucker, August 28, quoted in Mathewson, "Jefferson and Haiti," 222.

62. Matthewson, "Jefferson and Haiti," 232.

63. James A. Bayard spoke negatively of the Jefferson administration's embargo of Haiti in a letter to his brother, merchant Andrew Bayard, in 1806. James A. Bayard to Andrew Bayard, Washington, February 25, 1806, in Bayard, *Papers of James A. Bayard, 1796–1815*, 2:167.

64. Nash, *Forging Freedom*, 174–75.

65. *New York Evening Post*, July 10 and 12, 1804, copied from *Philadelphia Freeman's Journal*, quoted in Nash, *Forging Freedom*, 176.

66. Ibid., 177.

67. On the growth of racism among Philadelphia's laboring class in this period, see Nash, *Forging Freedom*, 172–211.

68. *Aurora* (Philadelphia), January 15, 1805.

69. Ibid.; Shankman, "Malcontents and Tertium Quids," 49.

70. Shankman, "Malcontents and Tertium Quids," 45.

71. For a full discussion of the rise of factionalism within the Pennsylvania Democratic Republicans, see Shankman, "Democracy in Pennsylvania."

72. Meigs, "Pennsylvania Politics," 462.

73. Peeling, "Governor McKean and the Pennsylvania Jacobins (1799–1808)," 320–54, quote 321.

74. *Pennsylvania Gazette* (Philadelphia), December 14, 1791, contains the marriage announcement of Elizabeth McKean and Andrew Pettit; Andrew Bayard is identified as the brother-in-law of Thomas McKean in Shankman, "Malcontents and Tertium Quids," 53; Dun, "Dangerous Intelligence, 31; *Pennsylvania Gazette* (Philadelphia), July 17, 1793.

75. Meigs, "Pennsylvania Politics," 466.

76. Peeling, "Governor McKean and the Pennsylvania Jacobins," 335–38; Wright, "Artisans, Banks, Credit, and the Election of 1800," 221; Lloyd, "The Courts from the Revolution to the Revision of the Civil Code," 106–9, quote 107.

77. Peeling, "Governor McKean and the Pennsylvania Jacobins," 335–38.

78. On the Passmore case as a turning point in Democratic Republican politics in Philadelphia, see Meigs, "Pennsylvania Politics," 469–70; Shankman, "Malcontents and Tertium Quids," 52–53; and Peeling, "Governor McKean and the Pennsylvania Jacobins," 335–38.

79. Dun, "Dangerous Intelligence," 31.

80. Ibid., 66.

81. Wright, "Artisans, Credit, and the Election of 1800," 221; Scoville, *The Old Merchants of New York City*, 5:256; "Discovering Lewis & Clark: Outfitting the Corps," http://lewis-clark.org/content/content-article.asp?ArticleID=2977 (accessed March 29, 2011); Lloyd, "The Courts from the Revolution to the Revision of the Civil Code," 106.

82. Ferguson, *Golden Rule*, 53–54, fn. 65, 97.

83. Girard, "Trading Races," 364; 351–76; Greg H. Williams, *The French Assault on American Shipping*.

84. Girard, "Trading Races," 364, quoting *Aurora* (Philadelphia), March 22, 1802.

85. Ibid., 374.

86. *The Quid Mirror*, 10.

87. Jefferson, *Notes on the State of Virginia*.

88. See, for example, *Democratic Press* (Philadelphia), September 3, 1807, 3; *Aurora General Advertiser* (Philadelphia), September 18, 1807, 2; "Robert Grant," *Democratic Press* (Philadelphia), September 16, 1807, 3; "The Fourth Coalition, or Feds, Quids, and Quadroons," *Aurora General Advertiser* (Philadelphia), September 25, 1807, 2; "To the Editor of the Aurora," *Aurora General Advertiser* (Philadelphia), September 28, 1807, 2; "A Defence of Mr. Leib," *Democratic Press* (Philadelphia), October 2, 1807, 3; "To the Republicans of the City and County of Germantown, October 10, 1807," *Democratic Press* (Philadelphia), October 19, 1807, 3; *American Citizen* (New York), October 30, 1807, 2.

89. Egerton, *He Shall Go Out Free*.

90. "Pennsylvania," *American Citizen* (New York), September 5, 1807, 2.

91. "Mr. Scratch'em," *Tickler* (Philadelphia), September 5, 1810, 3.

92. *Tickler* (Philadelphia), December 30, 1807, 3.

93. "Ran-away on Tuesday the 5th," *Pennsylvania Packet and Daily Advertiser* (Philadelphia), August 29, 1788, 4; "State of Maryland, Allegany county, as," *Aurora General Advertiser* (Philadelphia), September 19, 1807, 2.

94. "For the Democratic Press," *Democratic Press* (Philadelphia), September 11, 1807, 3.

95. For example, the *Portland Gazette* noted, "The Philadelphia City Elections take place about this time, and we have no doubt they will be democratic, for on these occasions the Foreigners emerge from all the dark alleys and purlieus and appear in such force that they completely outflank the natives. These Aliens, Half breeds, and Quadroons, are great Spirits of '76 . . .," October 18, 1813, 2.

CHAPTER TWO

1. Although Tessier was born in France, he immigrated to Saint-Domingue and was among the first wave of refugees who reached New Orleans between 1791 and 1808. Burial of August Tessier, October 13, 1817, SLC F7, 83, AANO, gives his birthplace as Paris. For his status as a Saint-Domingue refugee, see Debien, "Saint-Domingue Refugees in Cuba," 63.

2. Chevalier, "Un colon de Saint-Domingue pendant la Révolution: Pierre Collet, planteur de Jean-Rabel," *Revue d'histoire et de géographie d'Haïti, XXXIX* (January, 1940-January, 1941), quoted in Debien, "Saint-Domingue Refugees in Cuba," 85.

3. *Moniteur* (New Orleans), November 23, 1805; Couch, "The Public Masked

Balls of Antebellum New Orleans," 406; Kmen, "Singing and Dancing in New Orleans," 70–74; Morazan, "'Quadroon' Balls in the Spanish Period," 310–15.

4. Popkin, *You Are All Free*, 187–245; Childs, *French Refugee Life*, 65–66.

5. Ashli White, *Encountering Revolution*, esp. 124–202.

6. Refugees arrived in Louisiana in two stages, with a trickle beginning in 1792 and continuing sporadically until Haitian independence in 1804, followed by a massive influx in 1809. Estimates for the number of refugees in the first wave vary, but most historians agree that they numbered only a few hundred before 1803, with some arriving directly from the Caribbean but most from other American ports. These early migrants tended to come as family groups and were most frequently white, though some of them brought enslaved servants with them. A sizable group, numbering as many as a thousand, arrived directly from Saint-Domingue after the evacuation of French troops in 1803. For many, Louisiana was the last in a succession of temporary refuges. Those who fled the destruction of Cap Français in the summer of 1793 began their American sojourns in Norfolk and Baltimore, sometimes moving on to Philadelphia or New York before settling in New Orleans. Some Dominguans, again mostly whites, fled with the British forces when they withdrew from Saint-Domingue in 1798 and spent time in Jamaica before making their way to Louisiana. Debien and Le Gardeur, "Saint-Domingue Refugees in Louisiana," 113–243; Lachance, "The 1809 Immigration of Saint-Domingue Refugees to New Orleans," 23–25.

7. Debien, "Saint-Domingue Refugees in Cuba," 248–49. Scott and Hébrard, *Freedom Papers*, 49–63, provide a sensitive overview of the experience of the refugees in Cuba.

8. Debien, "Saint-Domingue Refugees in Cuba," quoting Chevalier, "Un colon de Saint-Domingue," 85.

9. Debien, "Saint-Domingue Refugees in Cuba," 33.

10. Rebecca Scott, "Paper Thin," 1061–71, offers an excellent overview of the western and southern Dominguans and the people they claimed as slaves after the general abolition of 1794.

11. Debien, "Saint-Domingue Refugees in Cuba," citing Chevalier, "Un colon de Saint-Domingue," 33; Rebecca Scott, "Paper Thin," 1071–74.

12. William C. C. Claiborne, *Official Letter Books*, 4:354, 364. Rebecca Scott, "Paper Thin," 1071–73, demonstrates that Cuba did not recognize the slave status of the people claimed as property by Dominguan refugees in 1809. The group passports issued to departing ship captains listed such individuals as *criados* (servants). The reports of refugee landings by officials in Orleans Territory classified the same individuals as "slaves," taking the first step in reinscribing bonded status on individuals declared free by the general emancipation of 1794.

13. Rebecca Scott, "Paper Thin," 1071–73.

14. Ibid., for a sense of how the deportation proceeded.

15. "City of New Orleans Mayor's Office: An Extract from the Lists of Passengers

reported at the Said Office by the Captains of Vessels who have Come to this Port from the Island of Cuba," July 8, 1809, Claiborne, *Official Letter Books*, 381–82.

16. Ibid., 352.

17. Ibid., 356.

18. Ibid., 365.

19. Ibid., 365–66.

20. Ibid., 354.

21. Ibid., 352.

22. Ibid., 381–82.

23. Ibid., 381–82, 414.

24. Ibid.

25. Testament of Sieur Jean Moreu, August 20, 1810, Acts of Marc Lafitte, NONA; Declaration by Sieur Jean Moreu, August 28, 1810, ibid.; Declaration of Paternity by Joseph Saint Victor, December 20, 1811, ibid.

26. Ashli White, *Encountering Revolution*, esp. 124–202.

27. Garrigus, *Before Haiti*, 111–14, 152–57.

28. Hilliard d'Auberteuil, *Considérations*, 40–45, quote on 45.

29. For an alternate view from that presented here, see Garraway, *Libertine Colony*, who proposes a different timeline and analysis for the discourse of libertinage and interracial desire, sex, and procreation, arguing for its establishment in the seventeenth century and its elaboration in the last third of the eighteenth century in response to rising anxiety over the threat of interracial progeny as a threat to moral order and the colonial project. See esp. 194–292.

30. Girod de Chantrans, *Voyage*, 180.

31. Garrigus, *Before Haiti*, 109–70.

32. Over the same period of time, the enslaved population of Saint-Domingue increased from 219,698 to 455,564. All figures from Rogers, "Les libres de couleur," 68.

33. Moreau de Saint-Méry, *Description Topographique*, 95. On historians who have shared this presumption, see, for example, Fick, *The Making of Haiti*, 18; and Geggus, "The Major Port Towns of Saint-Domingue in the Later Eighteenth Century."

34. Rogers, "Les libres de couleur," 68–72.

35. Girod de Chantrans, *Voyage*, 181. Garraway, *Libertine Colony*, 29, also charts this transition.

36. Moreau de Saint-Méry, *Description Topographique*, 92–93; Wimpffen, *A Voyage to Saint Domingo*, 111–13. The English version was published in French slightly later the same year as *A Saint-Domingue, pendant les années 1788, 1789 et 1790 par le Baron de Wimpffen* (Paris: Chez Cocheris, 1797), 1:147–48. Garraway, *Libertine Colony*, 249, contends however that Moreau de Saint-Méry's work was "never intended as a response to events in the colony."

37. Moreau de Saint-Méry, *Description Topographique*, 93.

38. Girod de Chantrans, *Voyage*, 184.

39. Moreau de Saint-Méry, *Voyage aux Etats Unis*, 335. The editor of the manu-

script of this work dates its final version, based upon Moreau's journal entries and correspondence from the 1790s, to 1815. Ibid., xxxii.

40. Hilliard d'Auberteuil, *Considérations*, 77.

41. Moreau de Saint-Méry, *Description Topographique*, 97.

42. Ibid.

43. Ashli White, *Encountering Revolution*, 166; Sansay, *Secret History*.

44. Sansay, *Secret History*, 78.

45. Ibid., 126–29.

46. The original French can be found in Berquin-Duvallon, *Vue de la Colonie Espagnole du Mississippi*, 354; for the English version, see Berquin-Duvallon, *Travels in Louisiana and the Floridas*, 80.

Another French commentator, Charles-César Robin, also echoes descriptions of the Dominguan *mûlatresse* in his brief discussion of the cohabitation of white men with free women of color in New Orleans in the early 1800s in *Voyages dans l'intérieur de la Louisiane*, 206–7.

47. Ashe, *Travels in America*, 343; Moreau de Saint-Méry, *Description Topographique*, 93; Wimpffen, *Voyage to Saint Domingo*, 114. Francis H. Herrick notes, "From Ashe's own account it is apparent that the *Travels* were composed a year after the journey took place, that his object was to produce an interesting and popular book rather than an accurate description of the country he visited, and that he was not the type of man to worry much about the accuracy of the reputed facts in his narrative," in Herrick, "Thomas Ashe and the Authenticity of His Travels in America," 50–57, quote 55.

48. Moreau de Saint-Méry, *Voyage aux Etats Unis de l'Amérique*, 335. The editor of the manuscript of this work dates its final version, based upon Moreau's journal entries and correspondence from the 1790s, to 1815. Ibid., xxxii.

49. Sansay, *Secret History*, 169–72.

50. Jan Lewis, "The Republican Wife," 689; quoting L., "Thoughts on Matrimony."

51. *Acts Passed at the First Session of the First Legislature of the Territory of Orleans,"* chapter 30, 126–29, quote 128.

52. Claiborne to Maurice Rogers, *Official Letter Books*, 2:401–2. See Ashli White, *Encountering Revolution*, 166–202, for an overview of the immigration to New Orleans.

53. Norton, *Liberty's Daughters*, 138–39; Perry, "'Lost Women,'" 195–214; van de Pol and Kuijpers, "Poor Women's Migration to the City," 44–60; Beswick, "'If You Leave Your Country You Have No Life!'" 69–98; Berstein, "Sex for Food in a Refugee Economy."

54. Baptism of Louis Marie Couvreur, September 13, 1810, born April 5, 1810, SLC B23, 145, AANO; Baptism of Jacques Couvreur, September 8, 1812, born August 22, 1812, SLC B26, 31, AANO.

55. Baptism of Luisa Trigg, October 9, 1810, born June 26, 1810, SLC B23, 155, AANO; Burial of Maria Luisa Peche, September 29, 1814, SLC F9, 212, AANO.

56. Baptism of Anna Harvey, August 8, 1810, SLC B23, 129, AANO; Baptism of Jean Harvey, December 2, 1814, SMNO B1, AANO. Baptism of Marie Magdelaine Haltt, December 29, 1812, born June 14, 1812, SLC B26, 61, AANO.

57. Baptism of Andre Joachim Miranda, November 15, 1812, at eleven months, SLC B26, 53, AANO.

58. Baptism of Maria Silvas [*sic*], February 20, 1812, born December 1, 1811, SLC B24, 129, AANO; Baptism of Rosa Silva, November 7, 1815, born March 16, 1814, SLC B27, 160, AANO; Baptism of Elizabeth Silva, November 19, 1819, born May 24, 1819, SLC B30, 154, AANO; Baptism of Amelie Silva, April 23, 1822, born March 9, 1821, SLC B32, 128, AANO; Burial of Amelie Silva, April 25, 1822, SLC F12, 93, AANO; Burial of Antoine Ignace Silvas [*sic*], October 29, 1821, SLC F15, 274, AANO.

59. Grossmann, *Jews, Germans, and Allies*, 184–235, offers a portrait of this phenomenon among Holocaust survivors in postwar displaced persons camps. In 2006, following the catastrophic devastation of Hurricane Katrina in New Orleans, there was a significant one-time increase of 43 per 1,000 in the number of babies born to women aged twenty to thirty-four. Willinger, *Katrina and the Women of New Orleans*, 7. Anecdotal evidence ascribed a motivation of renewal to some of these Katrina parents. Simmons, "Katrina babies march in," http://articles.chicagotribune.com/2006-08-16/news/0608160191_1_ochsner-health-system-newborns-touro-infirmary (accessed January 10, 2012); Porter, "New Orleans swelled by post-Katrina baby boom," http://www.nytimes.com/2006/12/11/world/americas/11iht-baby.3854640.html (accessed January 10, 2012).

60. Raimond, *Réponse aux considérations de M. Moreau, dit Saint-Méry*, 16; Garrigus, *Before Haiti*, 47, 68–69.

61. Hilliard d'Auberteuil, *Considérations* 79; Houdaille, "Trois Paroisses," 100, and Houdaille, "Le Métissage dans les Anciennes Colonies Françaises," 278.

62. For examples of marriages across the color line after 1778, see Rogers, "Les libres de couleur," 3:545–53.

63. Stewart R. King, *Blue Coat or Powdered Wig*, 182, 195; Garrigus, *Before Haiti*.

64. Marriage of Francisco Bosse and Rose Mignon, September 23, 1813, Libro primero, AANO.

65. Marriage of Pierre Durouleau and Marie Françoise Antoine, February 25, 1816, Libro primero, AANO.

66. Marriage of Michel Raymond and Marie Magdaleine Savournée, February 19, 1814, Libro primero, AANO.

67. Marriage of Jean Louis Denis and Marie Joseph Jessé, November 19, 1822; Marriage of Louis Henry and Antoinette Jessé, October 18, 1823, Libro primero, AANO.

68. One slightly later such intra-refugee marriage took place between Jacques

Tinchant and Rosalie Vincent, Marriage of Santiago Tinchan and Suzet Bayole (name of bride misrecorded), September 28, 1822; Marriage contract of Jacques Tinchant and Marie Dieudonné, September 26, 1822, Acts of Marc Lafitte, NONA. The family of Tinchant and Vincent form the subject of Scott and Hébrard's brilliant study, *Freedom Papers*.

69. Marriage of Jean Bartolomy and Isabel François, September 2, 1812, Libro primero, AANO; Marriage Contract of Joachin Poyra dit Vitry and Marie Joseph Chais, November 15, 1811, Acts of Marc Lafitte, NONA; Marriage Contract of François Olivier and Cecile Emmanuel, February 26, 1816, ibid.

70. Caryn Cossé Bell, *Revolution, Romanticism*, 60–63; Faye, *Privateers of the Gulf*, 301–53. According to the U.S. Census for 1830, there were 1,654 free men of color and 3,682 free women of color in New Orleans. See also the discussion of sex ratios in Chapter 4.

71. Marriage Contract of François Courreur and Rosalie Aldoin, December 6, 1817, Acts of Christoval de Armas, NONA; Marriage Contract of Louis Charles Ferant and Zacharine Rouzan, August 1, 1818, Acts of Narcisse Broutin, NONA; Marriage Contract of Marie (Laveau) and Santyague [sic] Paris, July 27, 1810, Acts of Hughes Lavergne, NONA.

72. Statistics calculated from Libro primero, AANO; SLC B22, SLC B23, and SLC B24, AANO.

73. Orleanian daughters who were baptized between 1810 and 1813 and married during the 1820s included Rosalie Helene Dupart, born September 4, 1810, baptized February 27, 1811, SLC B24, 10, AANO; married January 4, 1830, Libro primero, AANO; Lucia/Lucila Dupuis, baptized June 7, 1812, SLC B26, 6, AANO, married August 15, 1727, Libro primero, AANO; Felicite Galeau baptized October 13, 1812, SLC B26, AANO, married April 30, 1830, Libro primero, AANO; Marie Marthe Hardy, baptized June 2, 1812, SLC B26, 3, AANO, married May 22, 1830, Libro primero, AANO; Marie Magdaleine Narcisse, baptized October 6, 1810, SLC B23, 152, AANO; married July 27, 1830, Libro primero, AANO; Maria Josepha Olivier, baptized November 6, 1812, SLC B26, 51, AANO, married May 24, Libro primero, AANO; Marie Anne Pijeaux, baptized October 7, 1811, SLC B24, 97, AANO, married August 18, 1823, Libro primero, AANO; Maria Populus, baptized May 13, 1811, SLC B24, 43, AANO, married December 27, 1827, Libro primero, AANO; Rose Quinones, baptized March 30, 1812, SLC B24, 143, AANO, married April 22, 1828, Libro primero, AANO; Rosalie Simon, baptized June 28, 1811, SLC B24, 64, AANO, married February 21 or 22, 1830, Libro primero, AANO.

74. Orleanian daughters baptized between 1810 and 1812 who married 1830–1835 included Silvanie Brunetti, baptized March 26, 1811, SLC B24, 22, AANO, married April 12, 1831 (her second marriage following the death of her first husband), SLC M9, No 19, AANO; Marie Anne Antoinette Boisdoré, baptized June 10, 1811, SLC B24, 57, AANO; married November 12, 1831, SLC M9, AANO; Marie Stephanie Lorreins, baptized December 12, 1811, SLC B24, 114, AANO; married December 20,

1834, SLC M9, AANO; Eulalie Magdaleine Narcisse, baptized October 6, 1810, SLC B23, 152, AANO; married March 29, 1833, SLC M9, AANO; Marie Porée, baptized February 8, 1812, SLC B24, 126, AANO; married October 21, 1833, SLC M9, AANO; Adélaide Primpain, baptized December 22, 1812, SLC B26, 58, AANO, married April 30, 1834, SLC M9, AANO; Marie Angele Wale, baptized December 28, 1811, SLC B24, AANO, married April 17, 1831, SLC M9, AANO; Elisabeth Wiltz, baptized July 6, 1810, SLC B23, AANO, married February 21, 1832, SLC M9, AANO.

Girls born to Dominguan mothers and baptized between 1810 and 1812 who married between 1830 and 1835 included Rosalie Felix, baptized March 15, 1811, SLC B24, AANO, married March 19, 1831, at the age of twenty, SLC M9, AANO; Barbe Grenot, baptized February 4, 1810, SLC B23, AANO, married June 6, 1835, at the age of twenty-five, SLC M9, AANO; Marie Lajoie, baptized November 6, 1812, SLC B26, AANO, married October 28, 1833, at the age of twenty-one, SLC M9, AANO.

75. Girod de Chantrans, *Voyage*, 140.

76. Moreau de Saint-Méry, *Description Topographique*, 94–95.

77. Wimpffen, *Voyage*, 112.

78. In addition to the unparalleled work of Dominique Rogers on the *ménagère*, two recent studies in English provide briefer discussions of the practice, with several examples: Garrigus, *Before Haiti*, 56–60, 191; Stewart R. King, *Blue Coat or Powdered Wig*, 187, 191. King provides a list of the *ménagères* that he identified in his sample of notarial documents in an appendix, 280.

79. Rogers, "Les libres de couleur," 137,

80. Ibid., 3:137.

81. Ibid., 3:139.

82. Ibid., 3:10:566–67.

83. Stewart R. King, 191–93, xv.

84. Rogers, "Les libres de couleur," 3:137–38.

85. Ibid., 138, quoting from the contract at Centre des archives d'outre mer, Archives Nationales de France, Aix-en-Provence, Fonds Colonies, notsdom 1085, November 8, 1778.

86. *Marie Louise Tonnelier, et al. v. Paul Lanusse; Tonnelier v. Maurin's Executor*, http://www.lexisnexis.com.libproxy.tulane.edu:2048/hottopics/lnacademic/ (accessed January 3, 2012).

87. Moreau, *Description Topographique*, 466–67; Garrigus, *Before Haiti*, 141.

88. Wimpffen, *Voyage*, 110–11.

89. Moreau de Saint-Méry, *Danse*, 51–54.

90. Dessens, *From Saint-Domingue to New Orleans*, 23.

91. Quoting Berquin-Duvallon, *Vue de la Colonie*, 185–86.

92. The French of the original advertisement reads: "A[u]guste Tessier . . . se propose de donner Bal deux sois par semaine aux femmes de couleur libres, ou les hommes de cou[leur] ne seront pas admis; is a diffé [ ] faire l'ouverture des Bals jus[que] Samedi 23 du courant." *Moniteur* (New Orleans), November

23, 1805. See note 1 regarding Tessier's journey from France to New Orleans via Saint-Domingue.

93. Moreau de St-Méry, *Danse*, 39.

94. On balls in New Orleans before 1805, see Din, *New Orleans Cabildo*, 173. The most recent book on Saint-Domingue refugees in New Orleans cites secondary sources authored by popular historians in noting that the refugees are said "to have reinforced such practices as *plaçage* . . . and quadroon balls, especially the Bal des Cordons Bleus." Dessens, *From Saint-Domingue to New Orleans*, 104, 210, n. 154 and n. 155.

95. *Moniteur* (New Orleans), November 23, 1805; ibid., April 12, 1806; *Courier* (New Orleans), December 23, 1808.

96. Auguste Tessier was the father of two mixed-race daughters born to Francisca Besinon, Maria de los Dolores, born December 15, 1811, and baptized April 2, 1812, SLC B24, 144, AANO; and Rosa Leonor, born December 5, 1808, baptized April 2, 1812, SLC B24, 144, AANO. The baptismal records identified both Tessier and Besinon as natives of Port-au-Prince on Santo Domingo, but Tessier's 1817 burial record states that he was a native of Paris, interment of August Tessier, October 13, 1817, SLC F11, 83, AANO.

97. Bernhard, *Travels through North America*, 2:61–62.

98. His account differs very little, for example, from an 1820 account published in Rhode Island in 1820, discussed at greater length in Chapter 5. "Extract of a letter from a Gentleman at Mobile, to his friend in this county, dated Mobile Point, March 23, 1820," *Providence (R.I.) Gazette*, August 7, 1820, 1.

99. Ibid.

CHAPTER THREE

1. Marriage of Baltasar Noel Carriere and Maria Scipion Sarpy, July 22, 1822, Libro primero, AANO.

2. Délibérations du Conseil," UCANO, 57, identifies Joseph Leveillé as the nuns' overseer; "Emancipation of Joseph Leveillé," December 15, 1777, Acts of Jean Garic, NONA, provides his age.

3. Clark, *Masterless Mistresses*, 173–75.

4. Figures compiled from SLC B1, SLC B2, SLC B3, SLC B4, SLC B5, SLC B7, AANO. On marriage among the enslaved, see also Clark and Vidal, "Les familles d'esclaves à La Nouvelle-Orléans." Supression of the Jesuits in France and its colonies became effective in November 1764, "The Suppression of the Jesuits (1750–1773)," *The Catholic Encyclopedia*, http://www.newadvent.org/cathen/14096a .htm (accessed September 12, 2011).

5. Noel [Carriere]'s age is given as twenty-five in two notarial acts involving him in 1771, Sale of Noel, September 4, 1771, Acts of Andrés Almonester y Roxas, NONA; Manumission of Noel, December 30, 1771, ibid.

6. Gwendolyn Midlo Hall, *Africans in Colonial Louisiana*, 29–118; Labat, *Novelle relation de l'Afrique occidentale*, 2: 301–2, 208–9.

7. "Délibérations du Conseil," 64, UCANO; Acts of Raphael Perdomo, January 10, 1786, 7–8, NONA; "Délibérations du Conseil," 57, UCANO, identifies Joseph Leveillé as the nuns' plantation overseer; his act of emancipation, December 15, 1777, Acts of Jean Garic, NONA, states his age as fifty-five.

8. Dumont de Montigny, *Mémoires Historiques*, 2:225–26.

9. "Oath of Allegiance," September 20, 1769, RSCL 1769092001.

10. Baptism of Pierre Calpha, August 18, 1761, SLC B4, AANO; Baptism of Constance, April 24, 1764, SLC B5, AANO; Baptism of Genevieve, March 30, 1767, SLC B5, AANO; Baptism of Louis, May 30, 1771, SLC B6, AANO.

11. Noel Carriere was legally the slave of Madame Carriere at the time of her death in 1769. He was bought from her estate by Jacques Enoul Livaudais, who then sold him in 1771 to Basilio Antonio Ximenez, who, in turn, manumitted Carriere later that year.

12. Partition of Property, Succession of Veuve (Marguerite Trepagnier) Carriere, Colonial Documents 1769, February 5(1), Louisiana State Historical Center, New Orleans. Noel was valued at 3,000 livres in the act of partition, twice the amount of the next-highest-valued individual inventoried. Sale of Noel, September 4, 1771, Acts of Andrés Almonester y Roxas, NONA; Manumission of Noel, December 30, 1771, ibid.

13. "Liste de négres libres établis tant à 4 lieues de cette ville," AGI PC, Legajo Cuba 188-A6; Baptism of Baptiste, June 24, 1764, SLC B5, AANO; and Baptism of Françoise, November 18, 1764, SLC B5, AANO. Noel Carriere's name is denoted in the sacramental register without a title, a form reserved for people of African descent.

14. Marriage of Manuel [Noel] Carriere and Mariana [Marianne Thomas], November 16, 1778, Libro primero, AANO. The sanctuary where Noel and Marianne married was a parish church in 1777. It became St. Louis Cathedral in 1794 with the creation of a bishopric in New Orleans.

15. Hanger, *Bounded Lives*, 120–23, 128–30; McConnell, *Negro Troops of Antebellum Louisiana*, 18–19, 68.

16. McConnell, *Negro Troops of Antebellum Louisiana*, 18–19, 68.

17. Marriage of Joseph Leveillé and Marie Therese Carriere, May 14, 1786, Libro primero, AANO.

18. Pragmática Sanción para evitar el abuso de contraer matrimonios desiguales, El Pardo, March 23, 1776, in Konetzke, *Colección de documentos para la Historia de la Formación Social de Hispanoamerica*, 3:1, 406–13.

19. Saether, "Bourbon Absolutism," 475–509. I wish to thank Justin Wolfe for first suggesting the possible connection between Carriere's marriage and the colonial promulgation of the *Real Pragmática*.

20. Saether, "Bourbon Absolutism," 491.

21. Baptism of Marianne, négritte libre, June 9, 1757, SLC B3, AANO.

22. Twinam, *Public Lives, Private Secrets*, is an excellent study of the value of legitimacy in Spanish colonial America.

23. Calculated from Libro primero, AANO.

24. Baptisms of Carriere's children are recorded in SLC B8, SLC B10, SLC B12, SLC B13, SLC B15, and SLC B16, AANO. All marriages are recorded in Libro primero, AANO, beginning with Marriage of Noel Carriere and Luisa Gonzales, August 18, 1805.

25. Marriage Contract of Pierre Laviolette and Marie Arthemise Carriere, June 20, 1822, Acts of Christoval de Armas, NONA; Marriage Contract of Charles Pierre Mayoguin and Marie Deseada Carriere, Act 836 (1822), Acts of Philippe Pedesclaux, NONA; Marriage Contract of Jean Montfort and Anne Hermione Daquin, June 8, 1824, Acts of Marc Lafitte, NONA.

26. Marriage of Felipe Asur and Julia Boisdore," December 10, 1801, Libro primero, AANO.

27. Marriage of Mauricio Populus and Artemesa Celestin, March 22, 1804; Marriage of Luis Morin and Margarita Populus, July 16, 1821; Marriage of Agustin Alexandro and Maria Populus, December 27, 1827; Marriage of Hipolito Lafargue and Maria Martina Populus, July 1, 1815; Marriage of Manuel St. Martin and Dorothea Populus, October 24, 1815; Marriage of Carlos Populus and Marta Alexandrina, November 3, 1819; Marriage of Louis Valiere and Dorothée Populus, June 6, 1826, Libro primero, AANO.

28. Hanger, *Bounded Lives*, 15–16.

29. AGI PC, legajo 160 A, 353.

30. Figures derived from Libro primero, AANO.

31. Ibid. Marriage of Juan Pedro Claver and Celeste, October 8, 1794; Marriage of Mauricio Populus and Artemisa Celestin, March 22, 1804; Marriage of Noel Carriere and Luisa Gonzales, August 18, 1806, Libro primero, AANO.

32. Marriage of Joseph Leveillé and Marie Therese Carriere, May 14, 1786; Marriage of Santiago Apolon and Maria Magdalena, June 22, 1790, Libro primero, AANO.

33. Marriage of Pedro Sarpy and Catarina, March 8, 1804; Marriage of Carlos and Maria Juana, January 21, 1806; Marriage of Antoine Castor and Cecile Palus, July 9, 1823; Marriage of Jean Casimire and Felicité Abat, April 13, 1822; Marriage of Charles and Marie Jeanne, January 21, 1806; Marriage of Pierre Lange and Marie Françoise Lucile, September 23, 1811, Libro primero, AANO; Marriage contract of Antoine Castor and Cecile Palus, July 8, 1823, Acts of Christoval de Armas, NONA.

34. Marriage of Juan Bautista Pedro and Maria Dupart, November 16, 1803; Marriage of Julian Vienville and Maria Ricardo, February 7, 1804; Marriage of Carlos Pedro Vivant and Iris Lugar, October 4, 1823; Marriage of Manuel St. Martin and Dorothée Populus, October 24, 1815, Libro primero, AANO.

35. Ashe, *Travels in America*, 3:344–45.

36. See Libro primero, AANO; and chapter 2, above.

37. Hanger, *Bounded Lives*, 164–65.

38. *Acts Passed at the First Session of the First Legislature of the Territory of Orleans*, 128, 164, 188, 198, 200; *Acts Passed at the Second Session of the First Legislature of the Territory of Orleans*, 82–88, 180, 188.

39. Ibid.

40. Marriage of Francisco and Ignes, December 1, 1805, Libro primero, AANO; Book 1, Title IV, Chapter II, Article 8, and Book 1, Title VII, Chapter 1, Louisiana Civil Code of 1808, electronic version, http://www.law.lsu.edu/index.cfm?geaux=clo.maindigest (accessed September 1, 2011).

41. Marriage of Joseph Beaulieu and Josepha Jalió, April 24, 1811; Marriage of Juan Castelan and Juana Nivet, November 22, 1811; Marriage of Juan Luis Doliol and Hartanza Dussuau, February 15, 1818, Libro primero, AANO.

42. See chapter 2, above.

43. SLC B21; SLC B23; SLC B24; SLC B26; SLC B27; SLC B29; SLC B30, AANO.

44. Thrasher, *On to New Orleans*, is the best published account of the uprising.

45. Marriage of Hipolito Lafargue and Maria Martina Populus, July 1, 1815; Marriage of Carlos Pedro Marroguin and Maria Deseada Carriere, July 27, 1822; Marriage of Baltasar Noel Carriere and Maria Scipion Sarpy, July 29, 1822, Marriage of Marie Celeste Claver and Leandre Bijout, March 1, 1829, Libro primero, AANO; Clarke, *Lives of the Deceased Bishops*, 63.

46. Marriage of Maria Martina Populus and Hipolito Lafargue, July 1, 1815; and Marriage of Maria Populus and Agustin Alexandre, December 27, 1827, Libro primero, AANO.

Maria's father, Maurice Populus, was a slave owner. Bill of sale for a female slave named Louise Bougonneau to Maurice Populus by Victor Pognon, September 16, 1820, Acts of Hughes Lavergne, NONA; he sold a female slave and her three-year-old son in 1812, Bill of sale for a female slave named Eugenie and her son, Janvier, by Maurice Populus to Soly Caitana, June 16, 1812, Acts of Pedro Pedasclaux, NONA; Bill of sale for Joseph, shoemaker, to Maurice Populus by the estate of Louis Valiere, April 5, 1816, Acts of Michel de Armas, NONA. Maurice Populus was a lieutenant in the free black militia of New Orleans that was mobilized to fight under Andrew Jackson in the Battle of New Orleans, January 8, 1815, Caryn Cossé Bell, *Revolution, Romanticism*, 54.

Another of Maurice Populus's daughters may also have married a Saint-Domingue refugee. Margarita Populus married Luis Morin in 1821. Morin was described as a native of Philadelphia, which was a popular destination for the earlier wave of refugees in the 1790s. Marriage of Margarita Populus and Luis Morin, July 16, 1821, Libro primero, AANO; Lachance, "Three-Caste Society," 224, provides population figures and gender ratios.

47. Calculations are based on figures provided by Lachance, "Three-Caste Society," 224.

48. Will of Joseph Meunier, September 5, 1738, Document 1, Louisiana State Historical Center, New Orleans; Baptism of Marianne, negritte belonging to Sr. Meunier, August 5, 1731, SLC B1; Baptism of Marguerite, daughter of Marianne Pantalon, October 17, 1749, SLC B2; Burial of Marguerita Fontano Toutant, daughter of Mariana, cir. 60 yr., March 19, 1808, SLC F8, AANO.

49. Baptism of Andre Pantalon, July 31, 1746, SLC B2; Baptism of Marguerite Pantalon, October 17, 1749, SLC B2, AANO; Will of Martin Tomé Beauregard, Acts of Francisco Broutin, February 27, 1792, NONA.

50. Marriage of Honoré Rillieux and Victoria Dorville, March 21, 1819; Marriage of Adelaide Dorville and Cyril Arnoult, September 27, 1823; and Marriage of Honoré Toutant Beauregard and Maria Kernion, February 5, 1823, Libro primero, AANO.

51. Martineau, *Society in America*, 326.

52. Marriage of Jaquelin Meffre-Rouzan and Luis Ferand, September 28, 1818, Libro primero, AANO; Marriage Contract of Charles Louis Ferand and Zacharine Rouzan, Acts of Narcisse Broutin, August 1, 1818, NONA; Marriage of Juan Flemin and Maria Meffre-Rousan, November 9, 1826, Libro primero, AANO; Marriage Contract of Jean Fleming and Marie Meffre Rouzan, Acts of Hughes Lavergne, November 9, 1826, NONA; Marriage of Santiago Meff Rousan and Catarina Andre Cavalier, September 7, 1825, Libro primero, AANO.

53. Clark, "Atlantic Alliances."

54. Deborah Gray White, *Ar'n't I a Woman*, 27–61.

CHAPTER FOUR

1. Martineau, *Society in America*, 2:326–27.

2. Manumission of Agnes, December 16, 1779, Record Group 2, Spanish Judicial Records, Louisiana State Historical Center, New Orleans. Devaux's role in the Battle of Baton Rouge is described by historian Jason Wiese at http://www-tc.pbs .org/opb/historydetectives/static/media/transcripts/2011-05-23/810_galvezpapers .pdf.

The manumission of Agnes was the subject of a segment of "History Detectives," http://www.pbs.org/opb/historydetectives/investigation/galvez-papers/, which concluded that Devaux's role in the Battle of Baton Rouge moved Governor Galvez to find in favor of Devaux's final petition, ibid. This interpretation is debatable since the governor decided in favor of freedom in ten other contested *coartación* cases in 1779, all in Record Group 2, Spanish Judicial Records, Louisiana State Historical Center, New Orleans.

3. Testament of Mathieu Devaux, July 9, 1810, Acts of Narcisse Broutin, NONA.

4. Baptism of Maria Ester Mathieu, daughter of Ygnes Mathieu, godfather Santiago Mathieu, February 22, 1804, SLC B16, AANO; Marriage of Joseph Mateo and Maria Ignes, October 15, 1806, Libro primero, AANO. Maria Ignes (Marie Agnes) is identified as a native of St. Charles Parish on the German Coast in the

record. Mathieu's paternity is inferred from his appearance as godfather and subsequent marriage to Agnes.

5. Sale of Marianne by Agnes Mathieu to M. LaRose, March 21, 1806, Acts of Pedro Pedesclaux, NONA; Sale of Comba by Aquiles Dosobry to Ignes Mathieu, June 15, 1808, Acts of Estevan Quinones, NONA; Sale of Bimbi by Bernard Marigny to Agnes Mathieu, September 2, 1808, Acts of Narcisse Broutin, NONA.

6. Spear, *Race, Sex, and Social Order*, 100–54, provides the most recent and thorough investigation of the variety and nature of these circumstances.

7. As historian Cécile Vidal notes, "The word '*ménagère*' is even missing from the Louisianan documents" of the French colonial period. "The interethnic relations and the racial conceptions that developed in the colony," she notes, "were influenced by those of the West Indies, but they also differed from them." "French Louisiana and Saint-Domingue."

8. Hanger, *Bounded Lives*, 22.

9. Spear, *Race, Sex, and Social Order*, 138–40, provides an excellent summary of the factors that discouraged Orleanians of all races from contracting legal sacramental marriage in Spanish colonial New Orleans.

10. Hanger, *Bounded Lives*, 93; Spear, *Race, Sex, and Social Order*, 134–42, offers a thorough discussion of the legal and social climate for interracial unions in Spanish colonial New Orleans and documents the three marriages known to have taken place.

11. Hanger, *Bounded Lives*, 22.

12. Spear, *Race, Sex, and Social Order* is the most recent and best among them. Diana Williams's unpublished dissertation, "'They Call it Marriage,'" is a virtuosic exploration of quasi-marriage between white men and free women of color in antebellum New Orleans. See also Hanger, *Bounded Lives*, a pioneering, formidably detailed study; Ingersoll, *Mammon and Manon*; Thompson, *Exiles at Home*; and Schafer, *Brothels, Depravity and Abandoned Women*.

13. Will of Martin Tomé Toutant Beauregard, February 27, 1792, Acts of Francisco Broutin, NONA; Marriage of Honoré Toutan Beauregard and Maria Jaques Kernion, February 5, 1823, Libro primero, AANO; Baptism of Honoré Toutant Beauregard, February 16, 1824, SLC B34, AANO.

14. Surnames of elite families among the witnesses included Aubry, Lafreniere, Bernoudy, Dufossat, Huchet de Kernion, Fazende, and Dubreuil. Marriage of Pierre François Dreux and Marie Jeanne Constance Hazure, February 18, 1767, SLC M2, AANO.

15. Laussat, *Memoirs of My Life*, 52–53.

16. Baptism of Antonita Hazeur de Lorme, December 2, 1796, SLC B13, AANO. Antonia Celeste Dreux is identified as the daughter of François Dreux and Marie Hazeur in her wedding record, Marriage of Antonia Celeste Dreux and Juan Bautista Severino Latapie, February 1, 1813, SLC M6, AANO. She was eight years old at the time of her niece's baptism. Baptism of Maria Antonia Dreux, April 15, 1788, SLC B11; Baptism of Antonia Favre, October 5, 1792, SLC B13, AANO.

17. Marriage of Ortanse Pelagie Dreux to Pedro Robin La Coste, April 28, 1794, SLC M5; Marriage of Antonia Celeste Dreux to Juan Bautista Severina Latapie, February 1, 1813, SLC M6, AANO.

18. Marriage of Luis Marcos Tio and Matilde Hazeur, May 5, 1827; Manumission of Mauricio Dublet and Maria Antonia Hazur, September 6, 1828, Libro primero, AANO.

19. Marriage of Luis Severino Robert and Luisa Hazure, May 25, 1822, SLC M7; Marriage of Susana Felicité Hazur and Luis Augusto Savant Decoudreaux, February 7, 1825, SLC M7; Marriage of Antoinette Hazeur and Pierre Raphael Crocker, April 19, 1831, SLC M9, AANO.

20. Marriage of Prospero Hazeur and Felicité Monplessis Robert, October 3, 1812, Libro primero, AANO.

21. Marriage Contract of Louis Hazeur and Louise Mandeville, January 14, 1817, Acts of Philippe Pedesclaux, NONA; Marriage of Louis Hazeur and Louise Mandeville, January 11, 1817, Libro primero, AANO.

22. Baptism of Jean Pierre Cazelar, April 20, 1764, born May 28, 1764, SLC B5; Baptism of Adelaide Cazelar, September 15, 1787, SLC B12; Baptism of Marie Felice Cazelar, March 23, 1789, SLC B12; Baptism of Isabel Pompona Cazelar, May 5, 1791, SLC B12; Baptism of Marie Louise Cazelar, April 2, 1793, SLC B13; Baptism of Jean Pierre Cazelar, April 18, 1800, SLC B15, AANO.

23. Verification of holographic will of Jean Pierre Cazelar, dated April 11, 1829, Succession of Jean Pierre Cazelar, July 16, 1836, Acts of Felix de Armas, NONA.

24. Arthur, *Old New Orleans*, 129.

25. St. Gême Papers, HNOC, f. 175:5–6, f. 265:9.

26. The American troops at Cazelar plantation, under the command of General David B. Morgan, failed to hold the line and retreated just before Jackson's victory on the other side of the river. A few obscure military histories mention the action at Cazelar plantation, but none of them discuss the family who lived there and made their own contribution to the Battle of New Orleans. Latour, *Historical Memoire of the War in West Florida and Louisiana*, 127; Seymour, "General Jackson's Last Letter from Chalmette," 48.

27. Charlotte Wiltz disappears from the archival record after the baptism of her son in 1800. St. Gême Papers, HNOC, f. 175:5–6, f. 265:9; Succession of Jean Pierre Cazelar.

28. The U.S. Census for 1830 shows Emile Sainet residing with an adult free woman of color and five children; Baptism of Maria Luisa Emilia Sainet, December 16, 1822, SLC B33; Baptism of Juan Francisco Emilio Sainet, April 27, 1822, SLC B23; Baptism of Carlota Sainet, October 31, 1825, SLC B35; Baptism of Marie Sainet, April 22, 1830, SLC B31, AANO; Sale of Land by Emile Sainet to John McDonough, March 28, 1837, Acts of Felix de Armas, NONA; Sale of Slaves by Emile Sainet, April 7, 1837, Acts of Felix de Armas, NONA; Sale of Land by Emile Sainet to Jean Pierre Cazelar, 1838:15, Acts of Felix de Armas, NONA; Sale

of Land by Emile Sainet to Multiple Purchasers, March 28, 1837, Acts of Felix de Armas, NONA; Sale by Emile Sainet to Adelaide Cazelar, 1838:16, Acts of Felix de Armas, NONA; Sale of Land by Emile Sainet to Felicite Cazelar, 1838:18, Acts of Felix de Armas, NONA; Jean Pierre Cazelar's reported worth in 1860–61 was $41,000, Rankin, "The Origins of Black Leadership in New Orleans," 431, fn. 34; Jean Pierre Cazelar III owned twenty slaves in 1850, United States Census 1850 Slave Schedules.

29. 1808 Civil Code; *Civil Code of the State of Louisiana* (1825).

30. 1808 Civil Code, 1:7:1:4; 1:7:3:2:24; 1:7:3:2:30; 3:2:2:10; 3:2:2:12.

31. *Macarty et al. v. Mandeville*; Baptism of Artemise Emerlita Macarty, August 3, 1794, "Saint Bernard, New Galvez, Baptisms of Slaves and Free Persons of Color, 1787–1857," AANO; Baptism of Maria Macarty, February 13, 1792, SLC B12, AANO.

By 1794 Victoire Wiltz had entered into a relationship with Marcos Tio. Their first child was born in October of that year and baptized several months later. Baptism of Joseph Tio, January 12, 1795, SLC B13, AANO. Brigitte testified that she was the younger half-sister of Maria Macarty, *Marie L. Badillo et al. v. Francisco Tio*; Baptism of Françoise Birgette Macarty, April 11, 1752, SLC B2, AANO.

32. Baptism of Patrico [Patrice] Macarty, May 26, 1799, SLC B15, AANO; *Marie L. Badillo et al. v. Francisco Tio*.

33. *Marie L. Badillo et al. v. Francisco Tio*.

34. Ibid.

35. Ibid.

36. Ibid.

37. Ibid.

38. Ibid.

39. Ibid.

40. Ibid.

41. Ibid.

42. Ibid.

43. Ibid.

44. Ibid.

45. Ibid.

46. Ibid.

47. Ibid.

48. Ibid.

49. Ibid.

50. List of Tavernkeepers Licensed by the City of New Orleans, City Treasury Accounts, 1787, City Archives, Records and Deliberations of the Cabildo, vol. 3, no. 2, New Orleans Public Library; Kinzer, "The Tio Family," viii, 1–4.

Baptisms of the children born to Marcos Tio and Victoire Wiltz: Baptism of Joseph Tio, January 12, 1795, SLC B13; Baptism of Luis Tio, July 1, 1798, SLC B15; Baptism of Victoire Tio, May 12, 1800, SLC B15; Baptism of Lorenzo Tio, April 6,

1804, SLC B16; Baptism of Juan Tio, January 28, 1806, SLC B19; Baptism of Julie Tio, February 13, 1809, SLC B21; Baptism of Mariano Marcos Tio, August 22, 1811, SLC 24; Baptism of Leocadia Tio, April 4, 1815, SLC B27; Baptism of Magdeleine Tio, June 17, 1817, SLC B29; Baptism of Victoire Tio, February 13, 1809, SLC B21, AANO.

51. Robin, *Voyages dans l'Intérieur de la Louisiane*, 2:77–78, author's translation.

52. Joseph Pilié, "Plan de la Ville de la Nouvelle Orléans," HNOC, shows Wiltz as the owner of a lot at what is now 926–928 St. Philip Street; Act of Sale Rousette Roussere to Marie Madeline Wiltz, September 12, 1809, Acts of Pedro Pedesclaux, NONA; Baptism of Victoire Tio, February 13, 1809, SLC B21, AANO; Baptism of Julie Tio, February 13, 1809, SLC B21, AANO; Kinzer, "Tio Family," 3–4.

Although Marcos Tio is shown as residing at his place of business in the 1810 census with five slaves, two other adult white men, and no people of color, and Victoire Wiltz is shown residing on St. Phillip Street with no white men present, the testimony in *Badillo v. Tio* suggests that this official representation of their living arrangements did not match the reality of an openly shared household. Josephine lived with Francisco Tio continuously beginning in 1807. *Marie L. Badillo et al. v. Francisco Tio.*

53. *Marie L. Badillo et al. v. Francisco Tio.*

54. Corrections appear in the baptismal records of Lorenzo Tio, April 6, 1804, SLC B16; Juan Tio, January 28, 1806, SLC B19; Julie Tio, February 13, 1809, SLC B21; and Victoire Tio, February 13, 1809, SLC B21, AANO.

55. Marriage contract of Jean Baptiste Chon and Victoire Tio, August 23, 1827, Acts of Joseph Arnaud, NONA; Marriage of Jean Baptiste Chon and Victoire Tio, August 25, 1827, Libro primero, AANO.

56. Marriage contract of Louis Coussey and Julie Tio, September 15, 1827, Acts of Joseph Arnaud, NONA; Marriage of Louis Coussey and Julie Tio, September 15, 1827, Acts of Joseph Arnaud, NONA.

57. Marriage of Luis Marcos Tio and Matilde Hazeur, May 5, 1827, Libro primero, AANO.

58. Kinzer, "The Tio Family," 83.

59. Ibid., 99–109. The Tios remained in Mexico until 1877, returning to New Orleans at the end of Reconstruction to a racial landscape that would soon become as inhospitable as the one they had fled on the eve of the Civil War. The details of their odyssey have survived largely because the returned self-exiles formed one of the most influential musical families in the city during the gestation of jazz. Deeply steeped in the European musical tradition, the Tios taught classical music and technique to jazz great Sidney Bechet and trained Duke Ellington's clarinetist, Barney Bigard. Ibid., 124–25.

60. Ashe, *Travels in America*, 342.

61. Flint, *Recollections of the Last Ten Years*, 307.

62. *Western Christian Advocate* (1834–1883); February 10, 1837, 3, 42.

63. Tregle, "Creoles and Americans," 131–36.

64. Padget, "Minutes, First Session, West Florida Assembly," 317; Howard, "Colonial Pensacola," 247.

65. Natchez Court Records, Book d, 487, Historic Natchez Foundation, Natchez, Miss.

66. Sale of a Slave by Pedro Poulus to Alexander Moore, April 13, 1792, Acts of Pedro Pedesclaux, NONA. The interment record for Alexander Moore reads, in translation, "Alexandro Moore, native of Ireland, 72 yr Protestant who abjured his errors during his sickness, widower of Juana Escriven, buried June 2, 1795," SLC F4, AANO.

67. See, for example, Sale of a Slave to Samuel Moore by Joseph Favrot, June 16, 1795, Acts of Francisco Broutin, NONA; Sale of a Slave by Samuel Moore to Luis Terrier, June 28, 1796, Acts of Pedro Pedesclaux, NONA; Contract between Samuel Moore and Henry Bossler, February 13, 1797, ibid.; Sale of Land by Elena Soileau to Samuel Moore, March 21, 1797, ibid.; Sale of Land by Francisco Badillo for Pedro Godefroy to Samuel Moor, April 11, 1799, ibid.; Sale of Land by Samuel Moore to Gilberto Andry, November 9, 1799, ibid.; Sale of a House by Samuel Moore to Alejandro Norie, June 30, 1803, ibid.; Sale of Land by Samuel Moore to Cochran, July 17, 1802, ibid. The sale by Moore of a male slave skilled in construction confirms Moore's activity in property development and construction. Sale of Slaves by Samuel Moore to Francisco Caisegues, May 28, 1801, Acts of Pedro Pedesclaux, NONA. For additional slave sale transactions involving Moore, see Gwendolyn Midlo Hall, *Databases for the Study of Afro-Louisiana History and Genealogy.*

68. Baptism of Sara Virginia Moore, September 4, 1804, SLC B16, AANO.

69. Baptism of Samuel Moore, April 4, 1812 (born June 1, 1804), SLC B25; Baptism of Maria Antonia Moore, July 12, 1809 (born October 23, 1808), SLC B22; Baptism of Urania Moore, April 4, 1812 (born December 3, 1810), SLC B25; Baptism of Maria Adelaida Eugenia Moore, November 13, 1821 (born April 14, 1813) SLC B31; Baptism of Antonio Roberto Moore, November 12, 1821 (born February 25, 1814), SLC B31; Baptism of Maria Camille Moore, November 23, 1817 (born May 18, 1815), SLC B29; Baptism of Alexandro Santiago Moore, November 13, 1821 (born July 17, 1821), SLC B31, AANO. Lassize may also have borne Moore a daughter early in 1807, Josephina Lassis, daughter of Dorothée, was interred at age sixteen months in June 1808, Burial of Josephina Lassis, June 12, 1808, SLC F8, AANO.

70. Marriage records 146, 151, 152, 155, 158, 166, 180, 181, 184, 185, 210, 225, 227, 254, 261, 266, 268, 269, 272, 276, 286, 288, 290, 302, 318, 321, 324, 331, 337, 339, 357, Libro primero, AANO.

71. 1808 Civil Code, 1:4:2:8.

72. Baptism of Sara Virginia Moore, September 4, 1804, SLC B16; Baptism of Samuel Moore, April 4, 1812, SLC B25; Baptism of Urania Moore, April 4, 1812, SLC B25, AANO.

73. Baptism of Maria Camile Moore, November 23, 1817, SLC B29, AANO.

74. Baptism of Alexandro Moore, November 13, 1821, SLC B31; Baptism of Antonio Roberto Moore, November 12, 1821, SLC B31, AANO.

75. Baptism of Sara Virginia Moore, September 4, 1804, SLC B16; Burial of Sara Virginia Moore, SLC F5, AANO.

76. United States Census for 1810; Affidavit by Dorothée Lassize and Samuel P. Moore, October 4, 1816, Acts of Michel de Armas, NONA; Quittance by Dorothée Lassize to Samuel P. Moore, October 4, 1816, ibid.

77. Revocation of Contract between Nicolás María Vidal and Samuel Moore and Reassignment to Pedro Aparicio, February 29, 1796, Acts of Pedro Pedesclaux, NONA; Loan by Juan Noel Destrehan to Samuel Moore, April 12, 1802, ibid.

78. *Acts Passed at the First Session of the Seventh Legislature of the State of Louisiana*, 107–9; Act of Sale Dorothée Lassize from Marcelin Batigue, May 7, 1825, Acts of Marc Lafitte, NONA.

79. Marriage of Eulalie Allain and Pierre Dalcour, November 24, 1813; Marriage of Marie Antoinette Eufemie Moor and Juan Clay, November 17, 1825; Marriage of Samuel Moore and Maria Francisca Malvina Lowelle, December 23, 1826; Marriage of Charlotte Eugenie Moore and Eloy Valmont Mathieu, September 21, 1829, Libro primero, AANO; Marriage of Eurania Eulalia [Euranie Eulalie] Moore and Manuel Dalcour, December 1, 1828, SLC M7, 131, AANO.

80. Marriage of Marie Antoinette Eufemie Moore and Juan Clay, November 17, 1825, Libro primero, AANO.

81. In addition to these examples, Spear, *Race, Sex, and Social Order*, 146–47 provides two others that are similar.

82. Some thirty such New Orleans men have been located in colonial and early national sources by the three historians who have published most extensively on the city's free people of color in the past fifteen years, Hanger, *Bounded Lives*; Aslakson, "The 'Quadroon-*Plaçage*' Myth"; and Spear, *Race, Sex, and Social Order*.

83. *Macarty et al. v. Mandeville*. Eugene Macarty also fit the profile of a bachelor patriarch, but in his case it was his life partner, Eulalie Mandeville, who was the richer of the two. Eugene Macarty's collateral heirs claimed that Eulalie's assets, which amounted to more than $100,000, were not lawfully hers but had been illegally passed to her by Eugene. This would have contravened the prohibition against making donations to a concubine. The court found, however, that it was Eulalie who had amassed the fortune through her own successful labors as a dry-goods merchant, and that Eugene's collateral heirs could lawfully claim only a portion of his declared worth, which was a considerably smaller sum.

Macarty v. Mandeville has been discussed by several scholars, including Spear, *Race, Sex, and Social Order*, 178–79; and Thompson, *Exiles at Home*, 190–200.

84. See Chapter 2, above.

85. Baptism of Elisabeth Clay, July 16, 1803, SLC B16, AANO. When Elisabeth died in 1804, her surname was given as Raguet. Burial of Ysavel Raguet, July 30,

1804, SLC F5, AANO. Baptism of Juan Bautista Clay, January 7, 1806, (born April 16, 1805) SLC B19, AANO; Marginal notation on the record of the marriage of Jean Clay and Marie Antoinette Moore, December 22, 1825, SLC 16, AANO; Probate and succession file of John Clay, Louisiana Division, Records of the Louisiana Court of Probates, New Orleans Public Library.

Baptism of Maria Francisca Malvina Lowell, May 30, 1812, SLC B26, AANO. Raguet's first child by William Lowell was buried at age three in October, 1806, indicating that he was conceived shortly after the baptism of her son by John Clay. Burial of Carlos Lovel Raguet, October 5, 1809, SLC F8, AANO. No baptismal record for him can be found.

86. For population figures and sex ratios in late colonial New Orleans, see Hanger, *Bounded Lives*, 22. Population figures and sex ratios for 1810 and 1820 are based on the U.S. Federal Census for these years. The large Anglophone influx after the Louisiana Purchase has been often asserted but never systematically charted. See, for example, the seminal Tregle, "Early New Orleans Society," 21–36; and Lachance, "The Foreign French," 101–30.

87. Bernhard, *Travels through North America*, 55–65.

88. Ibid. Grymes moved to Louisiana in 1808, served as an aide to Jackson at the 1815 Battle of New Orleans, and later served as Jackson's chief counsel in the United States Bank case. In Louisiana he served as U.S. district attorney, state attorney general, state legislator, and delegate to the state constitutional convention. *The National Cyclopaedia of American Biography*, http://books.google.com/books?pg=PA420&dq =%22john+randolph+grymes%22+new+orleans&ei=ucbTTtqYAYXrtgfJvfmpDQ &ct=result&id=gawYAAAAIAAJ#v=onepage&q=%22john%20randolph%20grymes %22%20new%20orleans&f=false (accessed November 28, 2011).

89. Martineau, *Society in America*, 2:323–25. For a full account of this story, see Chapter 5, below.

90. Olmsted, *The Cotton Kingdom*, 306.

CHAPTER FIVE

1. Ingraham, *The Quadroone*, 141–42.

2. Ibid., 77–78. The seminal text on orientalism, a founding text of postcolonial studies is Said, *Orientalism*, which has generated a voluminous literature, for example, Bohrer, *Orientalism and Visual Culture*; Conant, *The Oriental Tale in England in the Eighteenth Century*; Irwin, *Dangerous Knowledge*; Jun, "Black Orientalism"; Kontje, *German Orientalisms*; Reina Lewis, *Gendering Orientalism*; Lowe, *Critical Terrains*; Macfie, *Orientalism*; Nochlin, "The Imaginary Orient"; Peltre, *Orientalism in Art*; Stevens, *The Orientalists*; Yoshihara, *Embracing the East*. On the application of postcolonial theory and approaches to U.S. history and the question of internal colonialism, see, for example, Gordon, "Internal Colonialism and Gender"; and Stoler, "Tense and Tender Ties."

3. Brown, "Negro Character as Seen by White Authors." See also Sollors, *Neither Black Nor White*, 220–25; and Zanger, "The 'Tragic Octoroon' in Pre-Civil War Fiction," 63–70.

4. Sollors, *Neither Black Nor White*, 361–94, provides an excellent, though not complete, chronology of interracial literature from the Classical age to the present.

5. Child, "The Quadroons," 115–41.

6. Ingraham, "The Quadroon of Orleans," quotes 267, 268, 270.

7. Ingraham, *The South-West*, 188–89.

8. Ingraham, "The Quadroon of Orleans," 258.

9. Ibid., 258–59. On the veil as a double marker of desirability and unattainability, see Behdad, "Orientalist Desire, Desire of the Orient," 37–51.

10. Ingraham, "The Quadroon of Orleans," 260.

11. Ingraham, *The Quadroone*, 81.

12. Oxford English Dictionary, online version, http://www.oed.com.libproxy. tulane.edu:2048/view/Entry/88879?redirectedFrom=houri#eid (accessed January 19, 2012); Rustomji, "American Visions of the *Houri*."

13. Delacroix, *The Women of Algiers*.

14. Ingraham, *The Quadroone*, 81–82. The loose slipper appears regularly in orientalist portraits of women. In addition to Delacroix's *Women of Algiers*, see also his *Death of Sardanopolis*.

15. Sir Walter Scott, *Ivanhoe*, 1:146–47.

16. Ibid.; Ingraham, *The Quadroone*, 82; Ingraham, "The Quadroon of Orleans," 258.

17. On the centrality of eyes in orientalist literary discourse, including that relating to Jews, see, for example, Behdad, *Belated Travelers*, 18; Bullock, *Rethinking Muslim Women and the Veil*, 12; Peleg, *Orientalism and the Hebrew Imagination*, 7.

18. Ingraham, "Quadroon of Orleans," 261; Ingraham, *The Quadroone*, ix.

19. Sir Walter Scott, *Ivanhoe*, 1:146; Ingraham, "The Quadroon of Orleans," 258.

20. Stedman, *Narrative, of a Five Years' Expedition*, 1:87. The same publisher issued reprints in 1806 and 1813. Child, "Joanna," 65–104.

21. Stedman, *Narrative of a Five Years' expedition*, 1:86–89, 99–100, 103–5, 129, 189, 193, 195–96, 208, 239, 283, 303, 306, 311, 319, 332, 334, 336, 343–44, 346, 352–53, 359, 363, 367, 373; 2:70–72, 81–84, 131, 150, 170, 179, 186, 194, 216, 223, 226, 235, 238, 240–41, 243, 300–301, 313, 323, 368, 373, 377–79, 382, 401.

22. Ibid.; Child, "Joanna."

23. Sollors, *Neither Black Nor White*, 193–95, relates the popular version of *Inkle and Yarico* in circulation in the eighteenth century, reprinting extensive passages from an influential version published in 1711.

24. "Harriet Martineau," *Encyclopedia of World Biography*.

25. Martineau, *Society in America*, 2:323–25.

26. Ibid., 2:114–16.

27. Child, "The Quadroons," 62.

28. Ibid., 63; "The Bridal of Andalla," in Warner, Mabie, Runkle, and Warner, *Library of the World's Best Literature, Ancient and Modern*, 40:16655.

29. Longfellow, "The Quadroon Girl," in *Poems on Slavery*, 26–29.

30. Stowe, *Uncle Tom's Cabin*, 204.

31. Reid, *The Quadroon*, 1:128.

32. Ibid., 125–26.

33. Peacocke, *Creole Orphans*, 10.

34. "Letters from Mr. Bourcicault," *New York Times*, February 9, 1860, http://chnm.gmu.edu/lostmuseum/lm/263/ (accessed January 25, 2012); "Pen Sketches for Sunday," *Daily True Delta* (New Orleans), December 11, 1859, 1; "The Last of Mr. Bourcicault," *Daily Picayune* (New Orleans), December 24, 1859, 15; "The 'Octoroon' at the Winter Garden," *New York Daily Tribune*, October 24, 1861, 8; "'The Octoroon' Director Withdraws," *New York Times*, June 18, 2010, Section C, 2.

35. See Figure 11 and Chapter 6, below.

36. Hildreth, *The Slave, or Memoirs of Archy Moore*; Pocahontas [Emily C. Preston], *Cousin Franck's Household*; Trowbridge, *Neighbor Jackwood*.

37. Ingraham, *The Quadroone*, ix, note 2.

38. Ingraham, "The Quadroon of Orleans," 265, suggests that many quadroons were actually enslaved, though they lived as free.

39. Ingraham, *The Quadroone*, ix.

40. See Chapter 2.

41. On the repetitious nature of descriptions of the *plaçage* complex, see Aslakson, "The 'Quadroon-*Plaçage*' Myth.

42. Ibid.

43. Ashe, *Travels in America*, 3:269–74.

44. Ibid.

45. Hubac, *Early Midwestern Travel Narratives*, 41; Schultz, *Travels on an Inland Voyage*, 1:iv-vi.

46. Schultz, *Travels on an Inland Voyage*, 2:193–95.

47. Ibid.

48. Stoddard, *Sketches, Historical and Descriptive*, v-vi.

49. Ibid., 321.

50. "Extract of a letter from a Gentleman at Mobile, to his friend in this county, dated Mobile Point, March 23, 1820," *Providence (R.I.) Gazette*, August 7, 1820, 1.

51. Bernhard, *Travels through North America*, 2:61–63

52. Ibid.

53. Ibid.

54. Ibid. Martineau also almost certainly drew on the description of quadroon women provided in Trollope, *Domestic Manners of the Americans*, 15.

55. Martineau, *Society in America*, 2:326–27.

56. A sample: Dunbar-Nelson, "People of Color in Louisiana, Part II," 51–78; Emery, *Black Dance*, 149; Mulvey, *Transatlantic Manners*, 100–102; Couch, "The

Public Masked Balls of Antebellum New Orleans," 403–31; Martin, "*Plaçage* and the Louisiana *Gens de Couleur Libre*"; Buonaventura, *Something in the Way She Moves*; Li, *Something Akin to Freedom*, 76; Smith, *Southern Queen: New Orleans in the Nineteenth Century*.

57. Stuart, *Three Years in North America*, 1:237–38.

58. Lanusse, "Un Marriage de Conscience."

59. Lanusse, "Epigramme," in *Les Cenelles*. English translation by Jennifer Gipson, http://www.centenary.edu/french/anglais/ang-epigram.html.

60. There is only one free family of color named Lanusse/Lanus documented in New Orleans between 1810 and 1842, when Armand Lanusse published his poem. Marie Marguerite Lanus, daughter of Pierre Lanusse of Cap Français and Marie Françoise Baudoin of Gonaïves was baptized October 9, 1811, SLC B24; Baptism of Marie Lanus, daughter of Jean Pierre and Marie Françoise, June 6, 1814, SLC B27; Baptism of Charles Lanusse, son of Jean Pierre and Marie Françoise Baudouin, March 4, 1819, SLC B30; Jean Pierre Lanus son of Jean, native of Port-au-Prince and Maria Rosa [o] native of Cap Français, SLC B32, No. 84, appears to be the son of the same Jean Lanus who fathered two children by Marie Françoise Baudouin; Baptism of Pierre Lanusse, son of Jean Pierre Lanusse and Marie Françoise, January 28, 1820, SLC B30, AANO.

61. Marriage of Hanrrieta Montreuil and Louis Fondal, August 17, 1727; marriage of Matilde Hazeur and Louis Tio, May 5, 1827, Libro primero, AANO. For more on the colonial families of these free black Orleanians, see Chapter 4.

62. Lanusse, *Les Cenelles*.

63. Baptism of Pierre Camille Thierry, son of J. B. Thierry and Elizabeth Phelis Lahogue, February 9, 1815, SLC B25, 149; Burial of Juan Bautista Simon Thierry, March 6, 1815, SLC F7, AANO; Dessens, *From Saint-Domingue to New Orleans*, 58, 87.

64. Duplantier, "Creole Louisiana's Haitian Exile(s)," 68.

65. Lanusse, "La Jeune Fille au Bal," in *Les Cenelles*; Hugo, "Fantomes," http://poetes.com/hugo/fantomes.htm (accessed January 28, 2012); Cheung, "*Les Cenelles* and Quadroon Balls," 12–13.

66. St. Pierre, "Deux Ans Après," in *Les Cenelles*. The dedication is to "A. Populus," probably Antoine Populus. Baptism of Antonio Augusto Maricio Populus, son of Mauricio Populus and Artemisa Celestin, March 1, 1813, SLC B26; Marriage of Mauricio Populus and Artemesa Celestin, March 22, 1804; Marriage of Augustin and Francisca Populus, January 29, 1808; Marriage of Hipolito Lafargue and Maria Martina Populus, July 1, 1815; Marriage of Manuel St. Martin and Dorotea Populus, October 24, 1815; Marriage of Carolos Populus and Marta Alexandrina, November 3, 1819; Marriage of Luis Morin and Margarita Populus, July 16, 1821; Marriage of Agustin Alexandro and Maria Populus, December 27, 1827, Libro Primero, AANO.

67. Séjour, "Le Mulâtre."

68. Caryn Cossé Bell, *Revolution, Romanticism*, 120.

69. Marriage of Jean François Louis Victor Séjour Marcou and Eloise Philippe Ferrand, January 13, 1825, Libro Primero, AANO; Marriage Contract of Jean François Louis Victor Séjour Marcou and Eloise Philippe Ferrand, January 6, 1825, Acts of Felix de Armas, NONA. Eloise is identified in her marriage contract as the natural daughter of free man of color Philippe Ferand and free woman of color Françoise Toutant.

70. Baptism of Juan Victor Sejour Marcou, October 1, 1817, SLC B29, 174, AANO; Marriage Contract of Jean François Louis Victor Séjour Marcou and Eloise Philippe Ferrand. Sollors, *Neither Black Nor White*, 164–66. "Le Mulâtre" was never published in New Orleans and was not translated into English until 1995. Although it anticipated the Anglophone tragic mulatto genre, its influence on it was probably negligible. Piacentino, "Seeds of Rebellion in Plantation Fiction."

71. Baptism of Carlos Hartur Nicolas Gayarré, May 5, 1826, SLC B36; Burial of Juan Theodoro Le Maitre, native of Cap Français, October 11, 1807, SLC F8; Burial of Marie Lefevre, native of Croix-des-Bouquets, October 21, 1817, SLC F11; Baptism of Marie Delphine Le Maitre, daughter of Charles Le Maitre, native of Saint-Domingue, May 4, 1831, SLC B40, AANO. This child may well have been the niece of the Delphina Le Maitre who bore Gayarré's child.

72. Socola, "Charles E. A. Gayarré," 320–23; Phillips, "Charles Etienne Arthur Gayarré."

73. Frazier, *The Negro Family in the United States*, 206–8. Frazier drew on Grace King, *New Orleans: The Place and the People*, long passages of an 1883 manuscript of Charles Gayarré printed therein, and on Olmsted, *A Journey in the Seaboard Slave States*. Frazier, *Negro Family*, 206 n. 74, n. 75, 207 n. 76.

74. Herskovits, *Life in a Haitian Valley*, 105.

75. St. John, *Hayti; or, the Black Republic*, 145.

76. There is also one piece of evidence that suggests that Haitian-descended residents of New Orleans used the word *placer* to refer to the relationships of enslaved women. Joseph Tinchant wrote to his mother from New Orleans in 1850 about several enslaved women he has just acquired from a succession. He comments that "Seulement Eveline vient de se placer et . . . Rosa ne tardera à en faire autant." Letter of Joseph Tinchant to Elizabeth Vincent, March 19, 1850, Archives of Philippe Struyf, Brussels. My thanks to Jean Hébrard for sharing this letter with me.

77. Olmsted, *Journey in the Seaboard Slave States*, 696, 698. Featherstonhaugh, *Excursion through the Slave States*, 2:268, is the first Anglophone author to use the term *placée* for New Orleans free women of color, but Olmsted's readership was probably considerably larger, since his essays were originally serialized in the *New York Times*.

78. Featherstonhaugh, *Excursion through the Slave States*, 2:267–69.

79. Houstoun, *Hesperos*, 2:74–75; Olmsted, *Journey in the Seaboard Slave States*.

80. Billington, *The Protestant Crusade*; Cohen, "Nativism and Western Myth,"

23–39; Cohn, "Nativism and the End of the Mass Migration"; Sernett, "Nativism and Slavery," 136–37.

CHAPTER SIX

1. Boucicault, "The Octoroon," 15.
2. Walter Johnson, *Soul by Soul*, 113.
3. Ibid., 155.
4. Landau, *"Spectacular Wickedness,"* 18.
5. *Maunsel White v. Hope H. Slatter.*
6. Johnson, *Soul by Soul*, 113.
7. *Maunsel White v. Hope H. Slatter; Alexina Morrison v. James White.*
8. The case of Alexina Morrison has been the subject of a good deal of scholarly attention, for example, Gross, *What Blood Won't Tell*, 1–4; 39–40; and Walter Johnson, "The Slave Trader, the White Slave, and the Politics of Racial Determination." The potential of her case and others similar to it to illuminate the evolving dynamics of the market in light-skinned women has not been fully exploited.
9. Watson, "Diary."
10. Ashe, *Travels in America*, 3:272–74.
11. For Ashe's reliability as a source, see Herrick, "Thomas Ashe and the Authenticity of His Travels in America," 50–57.
12. Ashe, *Travels in America*, 273–74; Watson, "Diary."
13. United States Census 1830. The refugee status of Labretonniere is documented in Baptism of Jean Honoré LaBretonniere, June 2, 1818, SLC B30, 18, AANO, in which the child's mother is identified as a native of Jacmel, Saint-Domingue.
14. Schultz, *Travels on an Inland Voyage*, 2:194.
15. Sparkle, "To the Honorable Mayor and City Council," *Louisiana Gazette* (New Orleans), September 18, 1810.
16. "Extract of a letter from a Gentleman at Mobile, to his friend in this county, dated Mobile Point, March 23, 1820," *Providence (R.I.) Gazette*, August 7, 1820, 1.
17. Holmes, *An Account of the United States of America*, 326.
18. Stuart, *Three Years in North America*, 2:237–38.
19. Bernhard, *Travels through North America*, 61–62.
20. See, for example, the case of the Cazelar family discussed in Chapter 4, above.
21. See, for example, the case of Marie Louise Tonnelier discussed in Chapter 2, above.
22. Voltaire, *Letters Concerning the English Nation*, http://www.fordham.edu/halsall/mod/1778voltaire-lettres.asp (accessed March 1, 2012); Twain, *Innocents Abroad*, 368–69.
23. Ingraham, "Quadroon of Orleans," 263–64.
24. Sullivan, *Rambles and Scrambles*, 223.
25. Ingraham, "Quadroon of Orleans," 265.

26. See Chapter 4. Olmsted, *Journey in the Seaboard Slave States*, 594–98. The informant was probably from the northeastern United States, or was at least familiar with life there, since he compares his New Orleans arrangement favorably with that of salaried bachelors in New York.

27. A Resident, *New Orleans as it is*, 34–42, discusses the surfeit of men in a bachelor state in New Orleans, either literally unmarried or living in New Orleans alone, having left their families for extended periods to work in the Crescent City. The tone of moral outrage and hyperbole of this work suggests that it was a reformist tract, perhaps based on hearsay.

28. Gayarré, "Historical Sketch: The Quadroons of Louisiana." Although Gayarré did not write this piece until 1890, he makes clear in it that he is describing antebellum New Orleans.

29. Watson, "Diary," 10.

30. Ibid.

31. "Petellat, Gillet & Co., No. 7 Chartres Street," *Louisiana Advertiser* (New Orleans), November 21, 1826, 3.

32. Ibid. Couch, "Public Masked Balls," 409 and fn. 30, notes that an attempt to reintroduce masking may have been made in the 1805–6 season, but on January 25, 1806, the New Orleans City Council explicitly prohibited masking.

33. Ibid., 411, 414–15; *L'Abeille*, January 1, 3, and 4, 1828.

34. Couch, "Public Masked Balls," 410.

35. Ibid., 418–19; Bernhard, *Travels through North America*, 2:62.

36. Bernhard, *Travels through North America*, 2:62.

37. Bernhard's visit to New Orleans was widely covered in the popular press. See, for example, "Saxe Weimar," *New York Daily Advertiser*, December 25, 1825; 3; "Saxe Weimar; N. Orleans; Indisposition," *Daily Georgian* (Savannah), December 31, 1825, 1; "Duke Saxe Weimar," *National Gazette* (Philadelphia), January 4, 1826, 2. Notices after the publication of his account appeared in, for example, "Review," *Newburyport Herald*, September 9, 1828, 2; "Saxe Weimar's Travels," *National Gazette and Literary Register*, October 16, 1828, 4; "New Works," *Baltimore Gazette and Daily Advertiser*, November 4, 1828, 3. Bernhard's attendance at a quadroon ball in New Orleans was mentioned in "Waltzing," *Baltimore Patriot & Mercantile Advertiser*, April 27, 1829, 2.

38. Semmes, *John H. B. Latrobe and His Times*, 313–14.

39. Kellar, "A Journey through the South in 1836," 361–62.

40. "Masquerades!" *Daily Picayune* (New Orleans), October 27, 1837, 2.

41. Semmes, *Latrobe*, 315; Boze to Ste. Gême, New Orleans, March 1, 1830, Ste. Gême Papers. Lachance, "Formation of a Three-Caste Society," 234–35.

42. Marriage of Henriette Joséphine Fortunée Saint-Gême and Joseph Firmin Perrault, February 4, 1833, SLC M9; Marriage Contract of Henriette Joséphine Fortunée Saint-Gême and Joseph Firmin Perrault, Act 58: 1833, Acts of Theodore Seghers, NONA.

43. Pickett, *Eight Days in New-Orleans*, 38.

44. Sullivan, *Rambles and Scrambles*, 223.

45. Olmsted, *Journey in the Seaboard Slave States*, 595–96 describes the *plaçage* complex and links quadroon balls to the Globe Ballroom in the 1850s.

46. Houstoun, *Hesperos*, 2:74–75, noted: "The Quadroon Balls are very much resorted to by *white* gentlemen, but neither *white* ladies, nor *black* men ever attend them: the reason for this is obvious, and need not be commented upon. I heard that the balls themselves were delightful, the young Quadroons generally doing the honours of their entertainments with great propriety and grace."

47. Tasistro, *Random Shots*, 2:19–20.

48. Ibid., 20.

49. Ibid., 20–21.

50. Duval, *The Adventures of Big-Foot Wallace*.

51. Ibid.

52. Bernhard, *Travels through North America*, 2:62.

53. Typical works of this type are William Wells Brown, *Clotel*; and Lydia Maria Child, *A Romance of the Republic*.

54. Long, *Great Southern Babylon*, 1.

55. Grant, *The Papers of Ulysses S. Grant*, 17–32, quotes 17, 20; Hawort, *Hayes-Tilden*, 95; King, "A Most Corrupt Election;" Tunnell, "The Negro, the Republican Party, and the Election of 1876," 101–16; Woodward, *Reunion and Reaction*.

56. Hawort, *Hayes-Tilden*, 81–121; 168–219; *New York Times*, February 10, 1877.

57. *New York Times*, February 10, 1877.

58. The Thirteenth Amendment abolished slavery in the United States. The text of the amendment reads:

> Section 1. Neither slavery nor involuntary servitude, except as a punishment for crime whereof the party shall have been duly convicted, shall exist within the United States, or any place subject to their jurisdiction.
>
> Section 2. Congress shall have power to enforce this article by appropriate legislation.

59. Horace White, *Life of Lyman Trumbull*, 224, 409–10.

60. "Latest Dispatches," *San Francisco Bulletin*, February 6, 1877, 3.

61. "The Dead Issue," *Philadelphia Inquirer*, February 21, 1877, 4; "The Festive Five," *Georgia Weekly Telegraph* (Macon), April 10, 1877, 6.

62. Among the best known of these is Woodward, *Reunion and Reaction*. See also Benedict, "Southern Democrats in the Crisis of 1876–1877," 489–524. The Louisiana election continued to be a matter of controversy, leading to a renewed Congressional investigation in 1878. Vazzano, "The Louisiana Question Resurrected," 39–57.

63. *Blue Book—Tenderloin 400*, HNOC acc. no. 1969.19.4; and "New Mahogany Hall," (New Orleans, c. 1900), HNOC acc. no. 56–15.

64. As Landau, *"Spectacular Wickedness,"* 151–52, demonstrates, Lulu White's actual birthplace is unknown. White told the census taker in 1900 that she was

born in Jamaica but claimed to be an Alabama native for the census of 1910 and Cuban born in 1920. In 1900 she was labeled "black," in 1910 "mulatto," in 1920 "octoroon." She was probably born in 1868. Bureau of the Census, *Twelfth Census of the United States (Louisiana), Schedule 1—Population*, Enumeration District 36, page 14; *Thirteenth Census of the United States (Louisiana), Schedule 1—Population*, Enumeration District 58, page 6; *Fourteenth Census of the United States (Louisiana), Schedule 1—Population*, 8.

65. Ibid.

66. Struve, *Blue Book, Sixth Edition*, HNOC acc. no. 1969.19.6.

67. Struve, *Blue Book, Seventh Edition*, HNOC acc. no 1969.19.7.

68. Landau, *"Spectacular Wickedness,"* 2; Long, *Great Southern Babylon*, 194–214.

EPILOGUE

1. Trouillot, *Silencing the Past*, 73.

2. Asbury, *The Gangs of New York*. On the Barnes & Noble website, *The French Quarter* ranks 175,815, compared to 186,410 for *Gangs of New York* in sales; http://www.barnesandnoble.com/w/french-quarter-herbert-asbury/1103267143; http://www.barnesandnoble.com/w/gangs-of-new-york-herbert-asbury/1103622011?ean=9780307388988 (accessed July 5, 2012).

3. Asbury, *The French Quarter*, 130; Featherstonhaugh, *Excursion through the Slave States*, 2:267–69; Houstoun, *Hesperos*, 2:74–75; Martineau, *Society in America*, 2:326–27.

4. See, for example, O'Rourke, "Secrets and Lies," 168–76; Payne, "New South Narratives of Freedom," and Pistacchi, "Reading Paula Morris in the Heart of Nepantla."

5. Cable, "Belles Demoiselles Plantation"; "'Tite Poulette"; "Jean-ah Poquelin"; "Madame Delicieuse"; "Cafe des Exiles"; "The Grandissimes."

On the circulation and popularity of *Scribner's Monthly*, see Scholnick, "Scribner's Monthly and the 'Pictorial Representation of Life and Truth,'" esp. 46.

6. On the power of Cable to influence both the memory and history of New Orleans in ways that preserved unreliable details of its past, see Sakakeeny, "New Orleans Music as a Circulatory System."

7. Cable's sources for his unpublished gloss on New Orleans quadroons were Berquin-Duvallon, Gayarré (quoting a bishop's report of 1795). Since he cites Bernhard in other contexts, his characterization of New Orleans free women of color was also undoubtedly influenced by this account as well. Cable, *The New Orleans of George Washington Cable*, fn. 35, 192; fn. 9, 194; fn. 35, 195.

8. Cable, "'Tite Poulette"; *Madame Delphine*, 7–8.

9. Cable, *Madame Delphine*, 7–8.

10. Cable, "'Tite Poulette"; and *Madame Delphine*.

11. King, *New Orleans: The Place and the People*, 347–48.

12. See Sollors, *Neither Black Nor White*, 361–94, for a catalogue of interracial literature through the late twentieth century.

13. Faulkner, *Absalom, Absalom!*; Ingraham, "The Quadroon of Orleans." See chapter 5 above for a discussion of the incest plot.

14. Allende, *Island Beneath the Sea*.

15. Dunbar-Nelson, "People of Color in Louisiana," Part I, 56–57, fn. 15.; Part II, 11, fn. 53.

16. Frazier, *The Negro Family*, 206–7.

17. Tregle, "Early New Orleans Society," 34.

18. Sterkx, *The Free Negro*, 250.

19. Early, *New Orleans Holiday*, 194, 198–99; Martin, "Plaçage and the Louisiana *Gens de Couleur Libre*," 67. Eleanor Early was a Boston journalist and travel writer active in the first half of the twentieth century. "Exhibit on the Life and Work of Best-Selling Travel Writer Eleanor Early—A Native of Newton—at BC's Burns Library through July 31 (2006), http://www.bc.edu/bc_org/rvp/pubaf/06/Early.pdf (accessed March 10, 2012).

20. Bernard Arthur Owen Williams, *Truth and Truthfulness*, 240.

21. Ignatieff, "The Broken Contract."

22. Walker, "Blood Brother."

23. Simpson, "New Orleans as a Literary Center: Some Problems," 88, observes that "the American literary imagination has insisted on the colonization of the exotic in this city—on making New Orleans, in the generic meaning of the term exotic, a place 'outside' the national 'cultural norm.'"

24. 44th Annual Conference & Technical Exhibition of the American Society for Healthcare Engineering (ASHE) of the American Hospital Association (AHA).

25. "Gabrielle, A New Orleans Quadroon," http://images.google.com/imgres? imgurl=http://www.southernelegance.net/gabrielle.jpg&imgrefurl=http://www .southernelegance.net/dolls-black-southern.html&h=400&w=278&sz=52&hl=en& start=1&um=1&tbnid=ETeFjZ_LBy8PXM:&tbnh=124&tbnw=86&prev=/images %3Fq%3Dquadroon%252Bnew%2Borleans%26svnum%3D10%26um%3D1%26hl%3 Den%26client%3Dsafari%26rls%3Den%26sa%3DG (accessed October 22, 2007).

26. Trouillot, *Silencing the Past*, 72.

27. Ibid., 95.

28. Ibid., 97.

29. Guillory, "Some Enchanted Evening on the Auction Block," 73–79; Thompson, *Exiles at Home*, 164–80.

30. Dawdy, *Building the Devil's Empire*; Landau, *"Spectacular Wickedness"*; Long, *The Great Southern Babylon*. See also, Schafer, *Brothels, Depravity, and Abandoned Women*; Spear, *Race, Sex, and Social Order in Early New Orleans*.

31. Trouillot, *Silencing the Past*, 106.

Bibliography

MANUSCRIPT PRIMARY SOURCES

Archives of the Archdiocese of New Orleans
St. Louis Cathedral Baptisms, 1731–1733
St. Louis Cathedral Baptisms, 1744–1753
St. Louis Cathedral Baptisms, 1753–1759
St. Louis Cathedral Baptisms and Marriages, 1759–1762
St. Louis Cathedral Baptisms and Marriages, 1763–1766
St. Louis Cathedral Baptisms, 1767–1771
St. Louis Cathedral Baptisms, 1772–1776
Libro donde se asientan las partidas de baptismos de negros esclavos y mulatos
    que se han celebr[a]do en esta Iglesia parroquial de Sr. San Luis de la ciudad
    de la Nueva Orleans desde el dia 1 de enero de 1777 que empezo hasta el ano
    de 1781 que es el corrente
St. Louis Cathedral Baptisms, 1777–1786
Libro donde se asientan las partidas de bautismos de negros y mulatos libres
    o esclavos el que dio principio en 17 de junio de 1783 para el Isso. de esta
    parroquial de San Luis de Nueva Orleans en la provincia de la Luisiana
St. Louis Cathedral Baptisms, 1786–1796
Libro de bautizados de negros y mulatos, [1786–1792]
Libro quinto de bautizados negros y mulatos de la parroquia de San Luis de esta
    ciudad de la Nueva Orleans: contiene doscientos trienta y sieta folios utiles,
    y da principia en primero de octubre de mil seteceintos noventa y dos, y acaba
    [en 1789]
St. Louis Cathedral Baptisms, 1796–1802
Baptisms of Slaves and Free Persons of Color, 1798–1801
St. Louis Cathedral Baptisms of Slaves and Free Persons of Color, 1801–1804
St. Louis Cathedral Baptisms, 1802–1806
St. Louis Cathedral Baptisms of Slaves and Free Persons of Color, 1804–1805
St. Louis Cathedral Baptisms of Slaves and Free Persons of Color, 1805–1807
St. Louis Cathedral Baptisms, 1806–1809
St. Louis Cathedral Baptisms of Slaves and Free Persons of Color, 1807–1809
St. Louis Cathedral Baptisms, 1809–1811
St. Louis Cathedral Baptisms of Slaves and Free Persons of Color, 1809–1811
St. Louis Cathedral Baptisms of Slaves and Free Persons of Color, 1811–1812
St. Louis Cathedral Baptisms, 1811–1815

St. Louis Cathedral Baptisms of Slaves and Free Persons of Color, 1812–1814

St. Louis Cathedral Baptisms of Slaves and Free Persons of Color, 1814–1816

St. Louis Cathedral Baptisms, 1815–1818

St. Louis Cathedral Baptisms of Slaves and Free Persons of Color, 1816–1818

St. Louis Cathedral registro o libro 16 de bautismos de gente de color, 1818–1820

St. Louis Cathedral Baptisms, 1818–1822

St. Louis Cathedral libro decimo septimo de bautismos de sola gente de color, 1820–1823

St. Louis Cathedral Baptisms, 1822–1825

St. Louis Cathedral Baptisms of Slaves and Free Persons of Color, 1823–1825

St. Louis Cathedral Baptisms of Slaves and Free Persons of Color, 1825–1826

St. Louis Cathedral Baptisms, 1825–1827

St. Louis Cathedral Baptisms of Slaves and Free Persons of Color, 1826–1827

St. Louis Cathedral Baptisms, 1827–1828

St. Louis Cathedral Baptisms of Slaves and Free Persons of Color, 1827–1829

St. Louis Cathedral Baptisms, 1828–1832

St. Louis Cathedral Baptisms of Slaves and Free Persons of Color, 1829–1831

St. Louis Cathedral Baptisms of Slaves and Free Persons of Color, 1831–1834

St. Louis Cathedral Marriages, 1720–1730

St. Louis Cathedral Marriages, 1764–1774

Libro primero de Matrimonios de Negros y Mulatos en la Parroquia de Sn. Luis de la Nueva-orleans; en 137 folios da principio en 20 de enero de 1777 y acaba en 1830

St. Louis Cathedral Marriages, 1777–1784

Libro de matrimonios celebrados en esta Inglesia parroq.l de San Luis de Nueva Orleans, provincia de la Luisiana, el que da principio en el mes de abril del año de mil setecientos ochenta y quatro en adelante

St. Louis Cathedral Marriages, 1806–1821

St. Louis Cathedral Marriages, 1821–1830

St. Louis Cathedral Marriages, 1830–1834

St. Louis Cathedral Second registre des Actes de celebrations de Mariages [couleurs libres]. Il commence en août 1830. Et Finit en octobre 1835, conenant 245 actes

St. Louis Cathedral Marriages, 1831–1833

St. Louis Cathedral Funerals, 1772–1790

Continuación de las partidas de blancos, muertos en esta parroquia de San Luis de la Nueva Orleans, desde el primero de 8.bre de año de 1784, hasta concluirse este libro [1793]

Libro de diffunctos. D[e negros y] mu[latos . . .]

Libro quarto de difuntos blancs de esta parroquia de San Luis de la Nueva Orleans, en 284 folios, da principio al primero folio, partida primera en treze de septiembre de mil setecientos noventa y tres; y acaba [1803]

Funerals of Free Persons of Color and Slaves, 1797–1806
St. Louis Cathedral Funerals, 1803–1807
St. Louis Cathedral Funerals, 1803–1815
St. Louis Cathedral Funerals of Slaves and Free Persons of Color, 1806–1810
St. Louis Cathedral Funerals of Slaves and Free Persons of Color, 1810–1815
St. Louis Cathedral Funerals of Slaves and Free Persons of Color, 1815–1819
St. Louis Cathedral Funerals, 1815–1820
St. Louis Cathedral Funerals of Slaves and Free Persons of Color, 1819–1825
St. Louis Cathedral Funerals, 1820–1824
St. Louis Cathedral Funerals, 1824–1828
St. Louis Cathedral Funerals, 1829–1831
St. Louis Cathedral Funerals of Slaves and Free Persons of Color, 1829–1832
Archivo General de Indias, Seville, Spain
Audiencia de Santo Domingo
Mapos y Planos
Papeles Procedentes de la Isla de Cuba
Centre des archives d'outre-mer, Archives Nationales de France, Aix-en-Provence
Fondes Colonies
Hill Memorial Library, Louisiana State University
Charles E. A. Gayarré, "Historical Sketch: The Quadroons of Louisiana" (1890),
Mss. 156, box 6, folder 87–88, Gayarré Papers 1720–1895
Historic Natchez Foundation, Natchez, Miss.
Natchez Court Records
Historic New Orleans Collection
Ste. Gême Papers
Joseph Pilié, "Plan de la Ville de la Nouvelle Orléans Avec les noms des
proprietaires," 1808.
Louisiana State Historical Center, New Orleans
Records of the Superior Council of Louisiana
Spanish Judicial Records
New Orleans Notarial Archives
Acts of Andrés Almonester y Roxas
Acts of Joseph Arnaud
Acts of Francisco Broutin
Acts of Narcisse Broutin
Acts of Christoval de Armas
Acts of Felix de Armas
Acts of Michel de Armas
Acts of Jean Garic
Acts of Marc Lafitte
Acts of Hughes Lavergne
Acts of Estevan Quinones

Acts of Pedro Pedesclaux
Acts of Philippe Pedesclaux
Acts of Raphael Perdomo
Acts of Theodore Seghers
New Orleans Public Library
    City Archives, Records and Deliberations of the Cabildo
    Louisiana Division, Records of the Louisiana Court of Probates
Ursuline Convent Archives, New Orleans
    Délibérations du Conseil

PUBLISHED PRIMARY SOURCES

Newspapers and Periodicals

American Citizen (New York)
Aurora (Philadelphia)
Aurora General Advertiser (Philadelphia)
Baltimore Gazette and Daily Advertiser
Baltimore Patriot & Mercantile Advertiser
Carlisle Gazette (Philadelphia)
Courier (New Orleans)
Daily Georgian (Savannah)
Daily Picayune (New Orleans)
Daily True Delta (New Orleans)
Democratic Press (Philadelphia)
Dunlap's American Daily Advertiser (Philadelphia)
Federal Gazette (Philadelphia)
Gazette of the United States (Philadelphia)
General Advertiser (Philadelphia)
Georgia Weekly Telegraph (Macon)
Independent Gazetteer (Philadelphia)
L'Abeille (New Orleans)
Louisiana Advertiser (New Orleans)
Louisiana Gazette (New Orleans)
Moniteur (New Orleans)
National Gazette (Philadelphia)
New York Daily Advertiser
New York Daily Tribune
New York Times
Pennsylvania Gazette (Philadelphia)
Pennsylvania Packet and Daily Advertiser (Philadelphia)

Portland (Maine) Gazette
Providence (R.I.) Gazette
San Francisco Bulletin
Scribner's Monthly
Spirit of the Press (Philadelphia)
Tickler (Philadelphia)
Times-Picayune (New Orleans)
Western Christian Advocate (Cincinnati)

Books and Pamphlets

Acts Passed at the First Session of the First Legislature of the Territory of Orleans.
New Orleans: Bradford & Anderson, 1806.

Acts Passed at the First Session of the Seventh Legislature of the State of Louisiana.
New Orleans: M. Cruzat, 1824 & 1825.

Acts Passed at the Second Session of the First Legislature of the Territory of Orleans.
New Orleans: Bradford & Anderson, 1807.

Adams, John. *The Works of John Adams, Second President of the United States.* Edited
by Charles Francis Adams. 10 vols. Boston: Little, Brown, 1853.

A. J. and R. A. *A Narrative of the Proceedings of the Black People During the Late
Awful Calamity in Philadelphia, in the Year 1793 and a Refutation of Some Censures,
Thrown upon Them in Some Late Publications.* Philadelphia: William W.
Woodward, 1794.

L'Album Littéraire: Journal des Jeunes Gens, Amateurs de Littérature 1 (August 15) 1843.
Electronic version, Bibliothèque Tintamarre: Oeuvres Louisianaises en ligne,
http://www.centenary.edu/french/textes/mariagedeconsc.html.

Alexina Morrison v. James White, 16 La. Ann. 100, 1861. DSpace at the University of
New Orleans, Earl K. Long Library, Historical Archives of the Supreme Court
of Louisiana, LASC Images, http://hdl.handle.net/123456789/15820 (accessed
March 1, 2012).

Ashe, Thomas. *Travels in America Performed in 1806, for the Purpose of Exploring the
Rivers Alleghany, Monongahela, Ohio, and Mississippi, and Ascertaining the Produce
and Condition of their Banks and Vicinity.* London: R. Phillips, 1808.

Bayard, James. *The Papers of James A. Bayard, 1796–1815. American Historical Association, Annual Report for the Year 1913.* Edited by Elizabeth Donnan. Washington:
American Historical Association, 1915.

Bernhard, Karl. *Travels through North America, during the Years 1825 and 1826.*
Philadelphia: Carey, Lea & Carey, 1828.

Berquin-Duvallon, Pierre-Louis. *Travels in Louisiana and the Floridas, in the Year
1802 Giving a Correct Picture of those Countries.* Edited by John Davis. New York:
I. Riley & Co, 1806.

———. *Vue de la Colonie Espagnole du Mississipp: Ou des Provinces de Louisiane et Floride Occidentale: En l'Année 1801: Par Un Observateur Résident Sur Les Lieux.* Paris: Imprimerie expéditive, 1803.

Blue Book—Tenderloin 400. New Orleans: n.p., c. 1893.

Boucicault, Dion. "The Octoroon; A play, in Four Acts." In *Dicks' London Acting Edition of Standard English Plays and Comic Dramas.* New York: De Witt Publishing House, n.d.

Cable, George Washington. "Belles Demoiselles Plantation." *Scribner's Monthly: An Illustrated Magazine for the People* 7, no. 6 (April 1874): 739–47.

———. "Cafe des Exiles," *Scribner's Monthly: An Illustrated Magazine for the People* 11, no. 5 (March 1876): 727–37.

———. "The Grandissimes," *Scribner's Monthly: An Illustrated Magazine for the People* 19, no. 1 (November 1879); 97–110; 19, no. 2 (December 1879): 251–65; 19, no. 3 (January 1880): 369–83; 19, no. 4 (February 1880): 582–92; 19, no. 5 (March 1880): 690–703; 19, no. 6 (April 1880): 841–59; 20, no. 1 (May 1880): 24–34; 20, no. 2 (June 1880): 194–205; 20, no. 3 (July 1880): 380–91; 20, no. 4 (August 1880): 527–36; 20, no. 5 (September 1880): 696–705; 20, no. 6 (October 1880): 812–24.

———. "The Grandissimes," *Scribner's Monthly: An Illustrated Magazine for the People* 20, no. 6 (October 1880): 812–24; 22, no. 1 (May 1881): 22–31; 22, no. 2 (June 1881): 191–99; 22, no. 3 (July 1881): 436–43.

———. "Jean-ah Poquelin." *Scribner's Monthly: An Illustrated Magazine for the People* 10, no. 1 (May 1875): 91–100.

———. "Madame Delicieuse," *Scribner's Monthly: An Illustrated Magazine for the People* 10, no. 4 (August 1875): 498–508.

———. *Madame Delphine.* New York: C. Scribner's sons, 1881.

———. *The New Orleans of George Washington Cable: The 1887 Census Office Report.* Edited by Lawrence N. Powell. Baton Rouge: Louisiana State University Press, 2008.

———. "'Tite Poulette." *Scribner's Monthly: An Illustrated Magazine for the People* 8, no. 6 (October 1874): 674–84.

Carey, Matthew. *A Short Account of the Plague or Malignant Fever Lately Prevalent in Philadelphia.* Philadelphia: Matthew Carey, 1794.

Child, Lydia Maria. "Joanna." *The Oasis.* Boston: Benjamin C. Bacon, 1834: 65–104.

———. "The Quadroons." In *Liberty Bell.* Boston: Massachusetts Anti-Slavery Fair, 1842: 115–41.

Civil Code of the State of Louisiana, Preceded by the Treaty of Cession with France, The Constitution of the United States of America, and of the State. N.p.: 1825. Google Books electronic version, http://books.google.com/ebooks/reader?id=HIU2AAAAMAAJ&printsec=frontcover&output=reader&pg=GBS.PA343 (accessed November 10, 2011).

Claiborne, William C. C. *Official Letter Books of W. C. C. Claiborne, 1801–1816.* Vol. 4.

Edited by Dunbar Rowland. Jackson, Miss.: State Department of Archives and History, 1917.

Dalmas, Antoine. *Histoire De La Revolution De Saint-Domingue, Depuis Le Commencement Des Troubles, Jusqu'a La Prise De Jeremie Et Du Mole S. Nicolas Par Les Anglais; Suivie d'Un Memoire Sur Le Retablissement De Cette Colonie.* Vol 2. Paris: Mame freres, 1814.

Debien, Gabriel, ed. "Documents aux origines de l'abolition de l'esclavage." *Revue d'histoire des colonies* 36 (1er trimestre, 1949): 24–55, and 36 (3ème trimestre, 1949): 348–423.

A Digest of the Civil Laws Now in Force in the Territory of Orleans, with Alterations and Amendments Adapted to its Present System of Government. New Orleans: Bradford & Anderson, 1808. Electronic version, http://www.law.lsu.edu/index .cfm?geaux=digestof1808.home (accessed November 10, 2011).

Dumont de Montigny, Jean-François-Benjamin. *Mémoires Historiques Sur La Louisiane, Contenant Ce Qui y Est Arrivé De Plus mémorable Depuis l'année 1687 Jusqu'à présent: Avec l'établissement De La Colonie françoise Dans Cette Province De l'Amérique Septentrionale Sous La Direction De La Compagnie Des Indes: Le Climat, La Natur & Les Productions De Ce Pays: L'Origine Et La Religion Des Sauvages Qui l'Habitent: Leurs Mœurs & Leurs Coutumes, & c.* Edited by Jean Baptiste Le Mascrier. Paris: C. J. B. Bauche, 1753.

Duval, John C. *The Adventures of Big-Foot Wallace, the Texas Ranger and Hunter.* Macon, Ga.: J. W. Burke & Company, 1885.

Featherstonhaugh, George William. *Excursion through the Slave States: From Washington on the Potomac to the Frontier of Mexico; with Sketches of Popular Manners and Geological Notices.* London: John Murray, 1844.

Flint, Timothy. *Recollections of the Last Ten Years, Passed in Occasional Residences and Journeyings in the Valley of the Mississippi, from Pittsburgh and the Missouri to the Gulf of Mexico, and from Florida to the Spanish Frontier; in a Series of Letters to the Rev. James Flint, of Salem, Massachusetts.* Boston: Cummings, Hilliard, and Company, 1826.

Girod de Chantrans, Justin. *Voyage d'un Suisse dans Différentes Colonies D'Amérique pendant la Derniere Guerre.* Paris: Neuchatel, 1785.

Grant, Ulysses S. *The Papers of Ulysses S. Grant.* Edited by John Y. Simon. Carbondale: Southern Illinois University Press, 1967.

Hall, Edward Hepple. *Appletons' Hand-book of American travel: The Southern Tour; Being a Guide through Maryland, District of Columbia, Virginia, North Carolina, Georgia and Kentucky. . . .* New York: D. Appelton & Co., 1866. Electronic version, http://quod.lib.umich.edu/m/moa/AFJ8846.0001.001?rgn=main;view=fulltext, University of Michigan Digital Library (accessed March 15, 2012).

Hildreth, Richard. *The Slave, or Memoirs of Archy Moore.* Boston: Whipple and Damred, 1840.

Hilliard d'Auberteuil, Michel-René. *Considérations sur l'état présent de la colonie française de Saint-Domingue. Ouvrage politique et législatif, présenté au ministre de la marine.* Paris: Grangé, 1776.

Holmes, Isaac. *An Account of the United States of America: Derived from Actual Observation, during Residence of Four Years in that Republic, Including Original Communications.* London: Printed at the Caxton Press, by H. Fisher, 1823.

Houstoun, Matilda Charlotte. *Hesperos, Or, Travels in the West.* Edited by John McDonogh. London: J. W. Parker, 1850.

Ingraham, Joseph Holt. "The Quadroon of Orleans." In *The American Lounger, or Tales, Sketches and Legends Gathered in Sundry Journeyings.* Philadelphia: Lea and Blanchard, Successors to Carey & Co., 1839: 255–71.

———. *The Quadroone; or, St. Michael's Day.* New York: Harper & Brothers, 1841.

———. *The South-West by a Yankee, in Two Volumes.* Vol. 1. New York: Harper & Brothers, 1933.

Jefferson, Thomas. "Jefferson's Draft of a Constitution for Virginia," [May-June 1783]. In *The Papers of Thomas Jefferson.* Edited by Julian P. Boyd et al. 25 vols. to date. Princeton: Princeton University Press, 1950).

———. *Notes on the State of Virginia.* Electronic Text Center, University of Virginia Library, http://etext.virginia.edu/etcbin/toccernew2?id=JefVirg .sgm&images=imagesmodeng&data=/texts/english/modeng/parsed&tag= public&part=14&division=div1 (accessed March 12, 2012).

———. *The Papers of Thomas Jefferson, Vol. 6: 21 May 1781 to 1 March 1784.* Edited by Julian P. Boyd. Princeton: Princeton University Press, 1952.

———. *The Papers of Thomas Jefferson Digital Edition.* Edited by Barbara B. Oberg and J. Jefferson Looney. Charlottesville: University of Virginia Press, Rotunda, 2008. http://rotunda.upress.virginia.edu/founders/TSJN.html.

———. *The Writings of Thomas Jefferson.* Edited by Andrew Adgate Lipscomb, Albert Ellery Bergh, Richard Holland Johnston, Albert Ellery Bergh, and Thomas Jefferson Memorial Association of the United States. Washington, D.C.: Thomas Jefferson Memorial Association of the United States, 1903.

King, Grace Elizabeth. *New Orleans: The Place and the People.* New York: Macmillan, 1917.

Labat, Jean Baptiste. *Nouvelle relation de l'Afrique occidentale.* Vol. 2. Paris: Chez G. Cavelier, 1728.

Lanusse, Armand. "Un Marriage de Conscience." Electronic version; Bibliothèque Tintamarre: Oeuvres Louisianaises en Ligne, http://www.centenary.edu/french/ textes/mariagedeconsc.html (accessed February 1, 2012).

———, ed. *Les Cenelles: choix de poésies indigènes.* New Orleans: H. Lauve, 1845. Electronic version; Bibliothèque Tintamarre: Oeuvres Louisianaises en Ligne, http:// www.centenary.edu/french/textes/cenelles1.htm (accessed February 1, 2012).

Latour, A. Lacarriere. *Historical Memoire of the War in West Florida and Louisiana in 1814–1815.* Translated by H. P. Nugent. Philadelphia: John Conrad and Col, 1816.

Laussat, Pierre-Clément de. *Memoirs of My Life to My Son during the Years 1803 and After, which I Spent in Public Service in Louisiana as Commissioner of the French Government for the Retrocession to France of that Colony and for its Transfer to the United States.* Baton Rouge: Published for the Historic New Orleans Collection by the Louisiana State University Press, 1978.

Longfellow, Henry Wadsworth. *Poems on Slavery.* Cambridge, Mass.: J. Owen, 1842.

Louisiana Civil Code of 1808. Electronic version, http://www.law.lsu.edu/index.cfm?geaux=clo.maindigest.

Louverture, Toussaint, and Edward Stevens. "Letters of Toussaint Louverture and of Edward Stevens, 1798–1800." *American Historical Review* 16, no. 1 (October 1910): 64–101.

Macarty et al. v. Mandeville. Supreme Court of Louisiana, New Orleans, 3 La. Ann 239; 1848 La. Lexis 128.

Madison, James. *The Papers of James Madison.* Secretary of State Series. 2 vols. Edited by Robert J. Brugger and Mary A. Hackett. Charlottesville: University Press of Virginia, 1986.

Marie L. Badillo et al. v. Francisco Tio. Supreme Court of Louisiana, New Orleans, 6 La. Ann. 129; 1851 La. Lexis 77.

Marie Louise Tonnelier et al. v. Paul Lanusse, Francois Benetaud, executors of John Baptiste Maurin, Territory of Orleans, Superior Court, Case No. 2929, New Orleans Public Library; *Tonnelier v. Maurin's Executor,* Superior Court of the State of Louisiana, First District, 2 Mart. (l.s.) 206; 1812 La. Lexis 38. http://www.lexisnexis.com.libproxy.tulane.edu:2048/hottopics/lnacademic/ (accessed January 3, 2012).

Martineau, Harriet. *Society in America.* Vol. 2. London: Saunders and Otley, 1837.

Maunsel White v. Hope H. Slatter, 5 La. Ann. 29, 1849; 1850. DSpace at the University of New Orleans, Earl K. Long Library, Historical Archives of the Supreme court of Louisiana, LASC Images, http://hdl.handle.net/123456789/2060 (accessed March 1, 2012).

Mavidal, Jérôme, and Emile Laurent, eds. *Archives Parlementaires de 1787 à 1860.* 96 Vols. Paris: Paul Dupont, 1867–1990.

Moreau de Saint-Méry, Médéric Louis Élie. *Danse Article: Extrait d'un Ouvrage de M. L. E. Moreau de St. Mery, ayant pour titre: Répertoire des Notions Coloniales.* Philadelphia: published by the author, 1796.

———. *Description Topographique, Physique, Civile, Politique Et Historique De La Partie Francaise De l'Isle Saint-Domingue. Avec Des Observations Generales Sur Sa Population, Sur Le Caractere & Les Murs De Ses Divers Habitans; Sur Son Climat, Sa Culture, Ses Productions, Son Administration, &c.* Philadelphia: published by the author, 1797.

———. *Moreau de St. Méry's American Journey.* Edited by Kenneth Lewis Roberts, Anna S. Mosser, and Stewart Lea Mims. Garden City, N.Y.: Doubleday & Company, 1947.

————. *Voyage Aux États-Unis De l'Amérique, 1793–1798*. Edited by Stewart Lea Mims. New Haven: Yale University Press, 1913.

Murdock, John. *The Triumphs of Love, Or, Happy Reconciliation*. Electronic version; Cambridge: Proquest LLC, 2003, accessed via Howard-Tilton Memorial Library, Tulane University.

Olmsted, Frederick Law. *The Cotton Kingdom: A Traveller's Observations on Cotton and Slavery in the American Slave States, 1853–1861*. Edited and introduction by Arthur M. Schlesinger. New York: Alfred A. Knopf, 1963.

————. *A Journey in the Seaboard Slave States, with Remarks on their Economy*. New York: Dix & Edwards, 1856.

Padget, James A. "Minutes, First Session, West Florida Assembly 1766–7." *Louisiana Historical Quarterly* 22 (April 1939): 311–84.

Pickett, Albert James. *Eight Days in New-Orleans in February, 1847*. Montgomery, Ala.: A. J. Pickett, 1847.

Pocahontas [Emily C. Preston]. *Cousin Franck's Household; or, Scenes in the Old Dominion*. Boston: Upham, Ford and Olmstead, 1853.

The Quid Mirror: The First Part. Philadelphia: George Helmbold, 1806.

Raimond, Julien. *Réponse aux considérations de M. Moreau, dit Saint-Méry, sur les colonies, par M. Raymond, citoyen de couleur de Saint-Domingue*. Paris: Imprimerie du Patriote Françoise, 1791.

Reid, Mayne. *The Quadroon; or, A Lover's Adventures in Louisiana*. London: G. W. Hyde, 1856.

A Resident, *New Orleans as it is. its Manners and Customs—Morals—Fashionable Life—Profanation of the Sabbath—Prostitution—Licentiousness—Slave Markets and Slavery, &c., &c., &c*. Utica, N.Y.: DeWitt C. Grove, Printer, 1849.

Robin, Charles-César. *Voyages dans l'intérieur de la Louisiane, de la Floride Occidentale, et dans les Isles de la Martinique et de Saint-Domingue, Pendant Les années 1802, 1803, 1804, 1805 Et 1806 . . . En Outre, Contenant Ce Qui s'Est Passé De Plus intéresssant, Relativement à l'établissement Des Anglo-Américains à La Louisiane. Suivis De La Flore Louisianaise. Avec Une Carte Nouvelle, gravée En Taille-Douce.* Vol. 3. Paris: F. Buisson, 1807.

Sansay, Leonora. *Secret History; or, the Horrors of St. Domingo, in a Series of Letters, Written by a Lady at Cape Francois, to Colonel Burr, Late Vice-President of the United States, Principally during the Command of General Rochambeau*. Edited by Aaron Burr. Philadelphia: Bradford & Inskeep, 1808. Electronic version, North American Women's Letters and Diaries: Colonial to 1950, accessed via Howard-Tilton Memorial Library, Tulane University.

Schultz, Christian. *Travels on an Inland Voyage through the States of New-York, Pennsylvania, Virginia, Ohio, Kentucky and Tennessee, and through the Territories of Indiana, Louisiana, Mississippi and New-Orleans; Performed in the Years 1807 and 1808; Including a Tour of nearly Six Thousand Miles*. New York: Isaac Riley, 1810.

Scott, Sir Walter. *Ivanhoe; A Romance*. Edinburgh: Archibald Constable and Co., 1820.

Séjour, Victor. "Le Mulâtre." *Revue des Colonies* (March 1837): 376–92. Electronic version; Bibliothèque Tintamarre: Oeuvres Louisianaises en Ligne, http://www.centenary.edu/french/textes/mulatre.html (accessed January 27, 2012).

Semmes, John Edward. *John H. B. Latrobe and His Times, 1803–1891*. Baltimore: Norman, Remington Co, 1917.

Sloane, Hans. *A Voyage to the Islands Madera, Barbados, Nieves, S. Christophers and Jamaica, with the Natural History of the Herbs and Trees, Four-Footed Beasts, Fishes, Birds, Insects, Reptiles, &c. of the Last of those Islands; to which is Prefix'd an Intro-duction, Wherein is an Account of the Inhabitants, Air, Waters, Diseases, Trade, &c. of that Place, with some Relations Concerning the Neighbouring Continent, and Islands of America. Illustrated with Figures of the Things Described, which have Not been Heretofore Engraved; in Large Copper-Plates as Big as the Life*. London: Printed by B. M. for the author, 1707.

Stedman, John Gabriel et al. *Narrative, of a Five Years' Expedition, against the Re-volted Negroes of Surinam, in Guiana, on the Wild Coast of South America, from the Year 1772, to 1777: Elucidating the History of That Country, and Describing Its Productions, Viz. Quadrupedes, Birds, Fishes, Reptiles, Trees, Shrubs, Fruits, & Roots; with an Account of the Indians of Guiana, & Negroes of Guinea*. London: Printed for J. Johnson, 1796.

Stoddard, Amos. *Sketches, Historical and Descriptive, of Louisiana*. Philadelphia: Published by Mathew Carey. A. Small, 1812.

Stowe, Harriet Beecher. *Uncle Tom's Cabin, Or, Life among the Lowly*. Boston: J. P. Jewett; Cleveland: Jewett, Proctor & Worthington, 1852.

Struve, Billy. *Blue Book, Sixth Edition*. New Orleans: n.p., 1905.

———. *Blue Book, Seventh Edition*. New Orleans: n.p., 1906.

Stuart, James. *Three Years in North America*. Edinburgh: Robert Cadell, 1833.

Sullivan, Edward Robert. *Rambles and Scrambles in North and South America*. London: Richard Bentley, 1852.

Tasistro, Louis Fitzgerald. *Random Shots and Southern Breezes: Containing Critical Remarks on the Southern States and Southern Institutions, with Semi-Serious Observations on Men and Manners*. New York: Harper & Brothers, 1842.

Trollope, Frances Milton. *Domestic Manners of the Americans*. London: Whittaker, Treacher, & Co., 1832.

Trowbridge, John Townsend. *Neighbor Jackwood*. Boston: J. E. Tilton and Company, 1856.

Twain, Mark. *The Innocents Abroad*. Edited by Brander Matthews. New York: Harper & Brothers, 1911.

United States Census 1810

United States Census 1820

United States Census 1830

United States Census 1840

United States Census 1850

United States Census 1860

[Vermont] Constitution of 1777. Vermont State Archives & Records Administration, http://vermont-archives.org/govhistory/constitut/con77.htm (accessed June 30, 2012).

Voltaire. *Letters Concerning the English Nation*. Edited by John Lockman. London: Printed for C. Davis and A. Lyon, 1733.

Warner, Charles Dudley, Hamilton Wright Mabie, Lucia Isabella Gilbert Runkle, and George Henry Warner, eds. *Library of the World's Best Literature, Ancient and Modern*. New York: International Society, 1896.

Watson, John F. "Diary of John F. Watson's trip to New Orleans, Observations there in 1804–1805." http://www.winterthur.org/html/research/Gateway_to_the_South/Watson.html (accessed February 7, 2012).

Wimpffen, François Alexandre Stanislaus. *Voyage a Saint-Domingue, Pendant Les Annees 1788, 1789 et 1790*. Paris: Cocheris, 1797.

———. *A Voyage to Saint Domingo, in the Years 1788, 1789, and 1790*. Edited by J. Wright. London: T. Cadell Jr. and W. Davies, 1797.

Paintings

Delacroix, Eugene. *Death of Sardanopolis*, 1827–28. Musée Louvre, Paris.

———. *The Women of Algiers*, 1834. Musée Louvre, Paris.

SECONDARY SOURCES

44th Annual Conference & Technical Exhibition of the American Society for Healthcare Engineering (ASHE) of the American Hospital Association (AHA), (2007) http://www.ashe.org/ashe/education/annual2007/index.html (accessed September 1, 2007).

Allende, Isabel. *Island Beneath the Sea: A Novel*. New York: Harper, 2010.

Arthur, Stanley Clisby. *Old New Orleans, a History of the Vieux Carré, its Ancient and Historical Buildings*. New Orleans: Harmanson, 1936.

Asbury, Herbert. *The Gangs of New York*. 1928. Reprint, New York: Capricorn Books, 1970.

———. *The French Quarter: An Informal History of the New Orleans Underworld*. New York: Alfred A. Knopf, 1936.

Aslakson, Kenneth. "The 'Quadroon-*Plaçage*' Myth of Antebellum New Orleans: Anglo-American (Mis)interpretations of a French-Caribbean Phenomenon." *Journal of Social History* (2011): 1–26.

Behdad, Ali. *Belated Travelers: Orientalism in the Age of Colonial Dissolution.* Durham N.C.: Duke University Press, 1994.

———. "Orientalist Desire, Desire of the Orient." *French Forum* 15, no. 1 (January 1990): 37–51.

Bell, Caryn Cossé. *Revolution, Romanticism, and the Afro-Creole Protest Tradition in Louisiana, 1718–1868.* Baton Rouge: Louisiana State University Press, 1997.

Bell, Madison Smartt. *Toussaint Louverture: A Biography.* New York: Pantheon Books, 2007.

Benedict, Michael Les. "Southern Democrats in the Crisis of 1876–1877: A Reconsideration of Reunion and Reaction." *Journal of Southern History* 46, no. 4 (November 1980): 489–524.

Bennett, Herman L. *Africans in Colonial Mexico: Absolutism, Christianity, and Afro-Creole Consciousness, 1570–1640.* Bloomington: Indiana University Press, 2003.

[Bernard, Joanne] "Gabrielle, A New Orleans Quadroon," <http://images.google .com/imgres?imgurl=http://www.southernelegance.net/gabrielle.jpg&imgrefurl= http://www.southernelegance.net/dolls-black-southern.html&h=400&w=278& sz=52&hl=en&start=1&um=1&tbnid=ETeFjZ_LBy8PXM:&tbnh=124&tbnw=86 &prev=/images%3Fq%3Dquadroon%252Bnew%2Borleans%26svnum%3D10%26 um%3D1%26hl%3Den%26client%3Dsafari%26rls%3Den%26sa%3DG> (accessed October 22, 2007).

Berstein, Murray Royce. "Sex for Food in a Refugee Economy: Human Rights Implications and Accountability." *Georgetown Immigration Law Journal* 14 (1999–2000), HeinOnline (http://heinonline.org) (accessed January 5, 2012).

Beswick, Stephanie. "'If You Leave Your Country You Have No Life!' Rape, Suicide, and Violence: The Voices of Ethiopian, Somali, and Sudanese Female Refugees in Kenyan Refugee Camps." *Northeast African Studies* 8, no. 3 (2001): 69–98.

Billington, Ray Allen. *The Protestant Crusade, 1800–1860; a Study of the Origins of American Nativism.* New York: Macmillan, 1938.

Bohrer, Frederick Nathaniel. *Orientalism and Visual Culture: Imagining Mesopotamia in Nineteenth-Century Europe.* New York: Cambridge University Press, 2003.

Brasseaux, Carl A., Glenn R. Conrad, and David Cheramie, eds. *The Road to Louisiana: The Saint-Domingue Refugees, 1792–1809.* Lafayette: Center for Louisiana Studies, University of Southwestern Louisiana, 1992.

Brown, Sterling A. "Negro Character as Seen by White Authors." *Journal of Negro Education* 2 (1933): 179–203.

Bullock, Katherine. *Rethinking Muslim Women and the Veil: Challenging Historical and Modern Stereotypes.* Herndon, Va.: International Institute of Muslim Thought, 2002.

Buonaventura, Wendy. *Something in the Way She Moves: Dancing Women from Salome to Madonna.* Cambridge, Mass.: DaCapo Press, 2004.

Catholic Encyclopedia. http://www.newadvent.org/cathen/

Cheung, F. D. "*Les Cenelles* and Quadroon Balls: 'Hidden Transcripts' of Resistance and Domination in New Orleans, 1803–1845." *Southern Literary Journal* 29, no. 2 (Spring 1997): 5–16.

Childs, Frances Sergeant. *French Refugee Life in the United States, 1790–1800*. Baltimore: Johns Hopkins University Press, 1940.

Clark, Emily. "Atlantic Alliances: Marriage among People of African Descent in New Orleans, 1759–1830." In *Louisiana: Crossroads of the Atlantic World*, edited by Cécile Vidal. Philadelphia: University of Pennsylvania Press, forthcoming 2013.

———. *Masterless Mistresses: The New Orleans Ursulines and the Development of a New World Society, 1727–1834*. Chapel Hill: Omohundro Institute of Early American History and Culture by University of North Carolina Press, 2007.

Clark, Emily, and Cécile Vidal. "Les familles d'esclaves à La Nouvelle-Orléans et sur les plantations environnantes sous le Régime français (1699–1769)." *Annales de Demographie* 2 (2011): 99–126.

Clarke, Richard Henry. *Lives of the Deceased Bishops of the Catholic Church in the United States*. Vol. 2. New York: P. O'Shea, Publisher, 1872.

Cohen, Bronwen J. "Nativism and Western Myth: The Influence of Nativist Ideas on the American Self-Image." *Journal of American Studies* 8, no. 1 (April 1974): 23–39.

Cohn, Raymond L. "Nativism and the End of the Mass Migration of the 1840s and 1850s." *Journal of Economic History* 60, no. 2 (June 2000): 361–83.

Conant, Martha Pike. *The Oriental Tale in England in the Eighteenth Century*. New York: Columbia University Press, 1908.

Couch, R. Randall. "The Public Masked Balls of Antebellum New Orleans: A Custom of Masque Outside the Mardi Gras Tradition." *Louisiana History* 35 (Fall 1994): 403–31.

Dawdy, Shannon Lee. *Building the Devil's Empire: French Colonial New Orleans*. Chicago: University of Chicago Press, 2008.

Debien, Gabriel. "The Saint-Domingue Refugees in Cuba, 1793–1815." In *The Road to Louisiana: The Saint-Domingue Refugees, 1792–1809*, edited by Carl A. Brasseaux, Glenn R. Conrad, and David Cheramie, 31–112. Lafayette: Center for Louisiana Studies, University of Southwestern Louisiana, 1992.

Debien, Gabriel, and René J. Le Gardeur. "The Saint-Domingue Refugees in Louisiana, 1792–1804." In *The Road to Louisiana: The Saint-Domingue Refugees, 1792–1809*, edited by Carl A. Brasseaux, Glenn R. Conrad, and David Cheramie, 113–243. Lafayette: Center for Louisiana Studies, University of Southwestern Louisiana, 1992.

Dessens, Nathalie. *From Saint-Domingue to New Orleans: Migration and Influences*. Gainesville: University Press of Florida, 2007.

Din, Gilbert C. *The New Orleans Cabildo: Colonial Louisiana's First City Government, 1769–1803*. Edited by John E. Harkins. Baton Rouge: Louisiana State University Press, 1996.

Dubois, Laurent. *Avengers of the New World: The Story of the Haitian Revolution.*
  Cambridge: Belknap Press of Harvard University Press, 2004.

Dun, James Alexander. "Dangerous Intelligence: Slavery, Race, and St. Domingue in
  the Early American Republic." Ph.D. diss., Princeton University, 2004.

———. "'What Avenues of Commerce Will You Americans Not Explore!': Commercial Philadelphia's Vantage Onto the Early Haitian Revolution." *William and
  Mary Quarterly* 62, no. 3 (July 2005): 473–504.

Dunbar-Nelson, Alice Moore. "People of Color in Louisiana, Part II." *Journal of
  Negro History* 2, no. 1 (January 1917): 51–78.

Duplantier, Jean-Marc Allard. "Creole Louisiana's Haitian Exile(s)." *Southern
  Quarterly: A Journal of the Arts in the South* 44, no. 3 (April 2007): 68–84.

Early, Eleanor. *New Orleans Holiday.* New York: Rinehart, 1947.

Egerton, Douglas R. *Death or Liberty: African Americans and Revolutionary America.*
  Oxford: Oxford University Press, 2009.

———. *Gabriel's Rebellion: The Virginia Slave Conspiracies of 1800 and 1802.* Chapel
  Hill: University of North Carolina Press, 1993.

———. *He Shall Go Out Free: The Lives of Denmark Vesey.* Madison, Wis.: Madison
  House, 1999.

Elkins, Stanley, and Eric McKitrick. *The Age of Federalism: The Early American
  Republic, 1788–1800.* New York: Oxford University Press, 1995.

Emery, Lynne Fauley. *Black Dance: From 1619 to Today.* Princeton: Princeton Book
  Company, 1989.

Encyclopedia of World Biography. 1st ed., 1998. Gale Biography in Context, online
  edition, (accessed January 22, 2012).

Faye, Stanley. *Privateers of the Gulf.* Hemphill, Tex.: Dogwood Press, 2001.

Faulkner, William. *Absalom, Absalom!* New York: Random House, 1936.

Ferguson, Thomas. *Golden Rule: The Investment Theory of Party Competition and the
  Logic of Money-Driven Political Systems.* Chicago: University of Chicago Press,
  1995.

Fick, Carolyn E. *The Making of Haiti: The Saint Domingue Revolution from Below.*
  Knoxville: University of Tennessee Press, 1990.

Frazier, Edward Franklin. *The Negro Family in the United States.* Chicago: University
  of Chicago Press, 1939.

"The Galvez Papers." *History Detectives.* http://www-tc.pbs.org/opb/history
  detectives/static/media/transcripts/2011–05–23/810_galvezpapers.pdf.

Garraway, Doris Lorraine. *The Libertine Colony: Creolization in the Early French
  Caribbean.* Durham, N.C.: Duke University Press, 2005.

Garrigus, John D. *Before Haiti: Race and Citizenship in French Saint-Domingue.*
  New York: Palgrave Macmillan, 2006.

Geggus, David. "The Major Port Towns of Saint-Domingue in the Later
  Eighteenth Century." In *Atlantic Port Cities: Economy, Culture, and Society in the*

Atlantic World, 1650–1850, edited by Franklin W. Knight and Peggy K. Liss, 87–116. Knoxville: University of Tennessee Press, 1990.

Girard, Philippe R. "Trading Races: Joseph and Marie Bunel, a Diplomat and a Merchant in Revolutionary Saint-Domingue and Philadelphia." *Journal of the Early Republic* 30, no. 3 (2010): 351–76.

Gordon, Linda. "Internal Colonialism and Gender." In *Haunted by Empire: Geographies of Intimacy in North American History*, edited by Ann Laura Stoler, 427–51. Durham, N.C.: Duke University Press, 2006.

Gordon-Reed, Annette. *The Hemingses of Monticello: An American Family*. New York: W. W. Norton & Co, 2008.

———. *Thomas Jefferson and Sally Hemings: An American Controversy*. Charlottesville: University Press of Virginia, 1997.

Gross, Ariela Julie. *What Blood Won't Tell: A History of Race on Trial in America*. Cambridge: Harvard University Press, 2008.

Grossmann, Atina. *Jews, Germans, and Allies: Close Encounters in Occupied Germany*. Princeton: Princeton University Press, 2007.

Guillory, Monique. "Some Enchanted Evening on the Auction Block: The Cultural Legacy of the New Orleans Quaroon Balls." Ph.D. diss., New York University, 1999.

Hall, Gwendolyn Midlo. *Africans in Colonial Louisiana: The Development of Afro-Creole Culture in the Eighteenth Century*. Baton Rouge: Louisiana State University Press, 1992.

———. *Databases for the Study of Afro-Louisiana History and Genealogy*. Baton Rouge: Louisiana State University Press, 2000.

Hanger, Kimberly S. *Bounded Lives, Bounded Places: Free Black Society in Colonial New Orleans, 1769–1803*. Durham, N.C.: Duke University Press, 1997.

Hawort, Paul Leland. *The Hayes-Tilden Disputed Presidential Election of 1876*. Cleveland: Burrows Brothers Company, 1906.

Herrick, Francis H. "Thomas Ashe and the Authenticity of His Travels in America." *Mississippi Valley Historical Review* 13, no. 1 (1926): 50–57.

Herskovits, Melville J. *Life in a Haitian Valley*. New York: Octagon Books, 1937.

Hirsch, Arnold R., and Joseph Logsdon, eds. *Creole New Orleans: Race and Americanization*. Baton Rouge: Louisiana State University Press, 1992.

Houdaille, Jacques. "Le Métissage dans les Anciennes Colonies Françaises." *Population (French Edition)* 36, no. 2 (1981): 267–86.

———. "Trois Paroisses de Saint-Domingue au XVIIIe Siècle. Étude Démographique." *Population (French Edition)* 18, no. 1 (1963): 93–110.

Howard, Clinton N. "Colonial Pensacola: The British Period. Part II." *Florida Historical Quarterly*, 19, no. 3 (January 1941): 246–69.

Hubac, Robert Rogers. *Early Midwestern Travel Narratives: An Annotated Bibliography, 1634–1850*. Detroit: Wayne State University Press, 1998.

Ignatieff, Michael. "The Broken Contract: Mismanagement of Assistance to Victims of Hurricane Katrina." *New York Times Magazine*, September 25, 2005, 15.

Ingersoll, Thomas N. *Mammon and Manon in Early New Orleans: The First Slave Society in the Deep South, 1718–1819.* Knoxville: University of Tennessee Press, 1999.

Irwin, Robert. *Dangerous Knowledge: Orientalism and Its Discontents.* Woodstock, N.Y.: Overlook Press, 2006.

James, Cyril Lionel Robert. *The Black Jacobins; Toussaint L'Ouverture and the San Domingo Revolution.* New York: Vintage Books, 1963.

Johnson, Ronald Angelo. "A Revolutionary Dinner: U.S. Diplomacy Toward Saint Domingue, 1798–1801." *Early American Studies* 9, no. 1 (Winter 2011): 141–68.

Johnson, Walter. "The Slave Trader, the White Slave, and the Politics of Racial Determination in the 1850s (*Morrison v. White*)." *Journal of American History* 87, no. 1 (June 2000): 13–38.

———. *Soul by Soul: Life Inside the Antebellum Slave Market.* Cambridge: Harvard University Press, 1999.

Jun, Helen H. "Black Orientalism: Nineteenth-Century Narratives of Race and U.S. Citizenship." *American Quarterly* 58, no. 4 (December 2006): 1047–66.

Katzew, Ilona. *Casta Painting: Images of Race in Eighteenth-Century Mexico.* New Haven: Yale University Press, 2004.

Kein, Sybil, ed. *Creole: The History and Legacy of Louisiana's Free People of Color.* Baton Rouge: Louisiana State University Press, 2000.

Kellar, Herbert A. "A Journey through the South in 1836: Diary of James D. Davidson." *Journal of Southern History* 1, no. 3 (August 1935): 345–77.

Kennedy, Richard S., ed. *Literary New Orleans: Essays and Meditations.* Baton Rouge: Louisiana State University Press, 1992.

King, Ronald F. "A Most Corrupt Election: Louisiana in 1876." *Studies in American Political Development* 15, no. 2 (2001): 123–37.

King, Stewart R. *Blue Coat or Powdered Wig: Free People of Color in Pre-Revolutionary Saint Domingue.* Athens: University of Georgia Press, 2001.

Kinzer, Charles E. "The Tio Family: Four Generations of New Orleans Musicians, 1814–1933. Ph.D. diss., Louisiana State University, 1993.

Kmen, Henry Arnold. "Singing and Dancing in New Orleans: A Social History of the Birth of Balls and Opera, 1791–1841." Ph.D. diss., Tulane University, 1961.

Knight, Franklin W., and Peggy K. Liss, eds. *Atlantic Port Cities: Economy, Culture, and Society in the Atlantic World 1650–1850.* Knoxville: University of Tennessee Press, 1990.

Konetzke, Richard, ed. *Colección de Documentos para la Historia de la Formación Social de Hispanoamerica, 1493–1810.* Madrid: Consejo Superior de Investigaciones Cientificas, 1953.

Kontje, Todd. *German Orientalisms.* Ann Arbor: University of Michigan Press, 2004.

Lachance, Paul. "The 1809 Immigration of Saint-Domingue Refugees to New

Orleans: Reception, Integration and Impact." *Louisiana History* 29, no. 2 (1988): 109–41.

———. "The Foreign French." In *Creole New Orleans: Race and Americanization*, edited by Arnold R. Hirsch and Joseph Logsdon, 101–30. Baton Rouge: Louisiana State University Press, 1992.

———. "The Formation of a Three-Caste Society: Evidence from Wills in Antebellum New Orleans." *Social Science History* 18, no. 2 (Summer 1994): 211–42.

Landau, Emily Epstein. *"Spectacular Wickedness": New Orleans, Prostitution, and the Politics of Sex, 1897–1917*. Baton Rouge: Louisiana State University Press, 2013.

Lewis, Jan. "The Republican Wife: Virtue and Seduction in the Early Republic." *William and Mary Quarterly: A Magazine of Early American History and Culture* 44, no. 4 (October 1997): 689–721.

Lewis, Reina. *Gendering Orientalism: Race, Femininity, and Representation*. New York: Routledge, 1996.

Li, Stephanie. *Something Akin to Freedom: The Choice of Bondage in Narratives by African American Women*. Albany: State University of New York Press, 2010.

Lloyd, William H. "The Courts from the Revolution to the Revision of the Civil Code." *University of Pennsyvania Law Review and American Law Register* 56 (1908): 88–115.

Long, Alecia P. *The Great Southern Babylon: Sex, Race, and Respectability in New Orleans, 1865–1920*. Baton Rouge: Louisiana State University Press, 2004.

Lowe, Lisa. *Critical Terrains: French and British Orientalisms*. Ithaca: Cornell University Press, 1991.

Lyons, Clare A. *Sex among the Rabble: An Intimate History of Gender & Power in the Age of Revolution, Philadelphia, 1730–1830*. Chapel Hill: Published for the Omohundro Institute of Early American History and Culture, Williamsburg, Virginia, by the University of North Carolina Press, 2006.

Macfie, A. L., ed. *Orientalism: A Reader*. New York: New York University Press, 2000.

Martin, Joan M. "Plaçage and the Louisiana *Gens de Couleur Libre.*" In *Creole: The History and Legacy of Louisiana's Free People of Color*, edited by Sybil Kein, 57–70. Baton Rouge: Louisiana State University Press, 2000.

Matthewson, Tim. "Jefferson and Haiti." *Journal of Southern History* 61, no. 2 (May 1995): 209–48.

McConnell, Roland C. *Negro Troops of Antebellum Louisiana; a History of the Battalion of Free Men of Color*. Baton Rouge: Louisiana State University Press, 1968.

Meigs, William M. "Pennsylvania Politics Early in This Century." *Pennsylvania Magazine of History and Biography* 17, no. 4 (1893): 462–90.

Melish, Joanne Pope. *Disowning Slavery: Gradual Emancipation and 'Race' in New England 1780–1860*. Ithaca, N.Y.: Cornell University Press, 1998.

Morazan, Ronald R. "'Quadroon' Balls in the Spanish Period." *Louisiana History* 14, no. 3 (Summer 1973): 310–15.

Morris, Thomas D. *Southern Slavery and the Law, 1619–1860*. Chapel Hill: University of North Carolina Press, 1996.

Mulvey, Christopher. *Transatlantic Manners: Social Patterns in Nineteenth-Century Anglo-American Travel Literature*. New York: Cambridge University Press, 1990.

Nash, Gary B. *Forging Freedom: The Formation of Philadelphia's Black Community, 1720–1840*. Cambridge: Harvard University Press, 1988.

National Cyclopaedia of American Biography. Vol. 12. New York: James T. White, & Company, 1904. Electronic edition, Google Books, http://books.google.com/books?pg=PA420&dq=%22john+randolph+grymes%22+new+orleans&ei=ucbTTtqYAYXrtgfJvfmpDQ&ct=result&id=gawYAAAAIAAJ#v=onepage&q=%22john%20randolph%20grymes%22%20new%20orleans&f=false (accessed November 28, 2011).

"New Orleans Sights: Quadroon Ballroom." *Fodors Travel Intelligence*, http://www.fodors.com/world/north-america/usa/louisiana/new-orleans/review-194020.html (accessed March 14, 2012).

Nochlin, Linda. "The Imaginary Orient." *Art in America* (May 1986): 118–31, 187–91.

Norton, Mary Beth. *Liberty's Daughters: The Revolutionary Experience of American Women, 1750–1800*. Boston: Little, Brown, 1980.

Oberholtzer, Ellis Paxson. *Robert Morris: Patriot and Financier*. New York: Macmillan, 1903.

O'Rourke, James. "Secrets and Lies: Race and Sex in *The Awakening*." *Legacy* 16, no. 2 (1999): 168–76.

Oxford English Dictionary, online version.

Pascoe, Peggy. *What Comes Naturally: Miscegenation Law and the Making of Race in America*. New York: Oxford University Press, 2009.

Payne, James Robert. "New South Narratives of Freedom: Rereading George Washington Cable's "'Tite Poulette' and *Madame Delphine*." *Melus* 27, no. 1 (Spring 2002): 3–23.

Peacocke, James S. *The Creole Orphans, Or, Lights and Shadows of Southern Life a Tale of Louisiana*. New York: Derby & Jackson, 1856.

Peeling, James Hedley. "Governor McKean and the Pennsylvania Jacobins (1799–1808)." *Pennsylvania Magazine of History and Biography* 54, no. 4 (1930): 320–54.

Peleg, Yaron. *Orientalism and the Hebrew Imagination*. Ithaca, N.Y.: Cornell University Press, 2005.

Peltre, Christine. *Orientalism in Art*. New York: Abbeville Press, 1998.

Pernick, Martin S. "Politics, Parties, and Pestilence: Epidemic Yellow Fever in Philadelphia and the Rise of the First Party System." *William and Mary Quarterly* 29, no. 4 (October 1972): 559–86.

Perry, Mary Elizabeth. "'Lost Women' in Early Modern Seville: The Politics of Prostitution." *Feminist Studies* 4, no. 1 (February 1978): 195–214.

Phillips, V. Faye. "Charles Etienne Arthur Gayarré." *KnowLA: Encyclopedia of Louisiana*, http://www.knowla.org/entry.php?rec=744 (accessed January 30, 2012).

Piacentino, Ed. "Seeds of Rebellion in Plantation Fiction: Victor Séjour's 'The Mulatto.'" *Southern Spaces*, August 28, 2007, <http://www.southernspaces.org/2007/seeds-rebellion-plantation-fiction-victor-séjours-mulatto> (accessed January 29, 2012).

Pistacchi, Ann. "Reading Paula Morris in the Heart of Nepantla." *Journal of New Zealand Literature: JNZL* 24 (2007): 98–116.

Popkin, Jeremy D. *You Are All Free: The Haitian Revolution and the Abolition of Slavery*. New York: Cambridge University Press, 2010.

Powell, John Harvey. *Bring Out Your Dead; the Great Plague of Yellow Fever in Philadelphia in 1793*. New York: Arno Press, 1970.

Powell, Richard E. "Coachmaking in Philadelphia: George and William Hunter's Factory of the Early Federal Period." *Winterthur Portfolio* 28, no. 4 (Winter 1993): 247–77.

Rankin, David C. "The Origins of Black Leadership in New Orleans during Reconstruction." *Journal of Southern History* 40, no. 3 (August 1974): 417–40.

Rogers, Dominique. "Les libres de couleur dans les capitales de Saint-Domingue: fortune, mentalités et intégration à la fin de l'Ancien Régime (1776–1789)." Ph.D. diss., L'université Michel de Montaigne, Bordeaux III, 1999.

Rustomji, N. "American Visions of the *Houri*." *Muslim World* 97, no. 1 (January 2007): 79–92.

Saether, Steinar A. "Bourbon Absolutism and Marriage Reform in Late Colonial Spanish America." *The Americas* 59, no. 4 (April 2003): 475–509.

Said, Edward W. *Orientalism*. New York: Pantheon Books, 1978.

St. John, Spenser. *Hayti; or, the Black Republic*. London: Smith, Elder, & Co, 1884.

Sakakeeny, Matt. "New Orleans Music as a Circulatory System." *Black Music Research Journal* 31, no. 2 (Fall 2011): 291–325.

Schafer, Judith Kelleher. *Brothels, Depravity, and Abandoned Women: Illegal Sex in Antebellum New Orleans*. Baton Rouge: Louisiana State University Press, 2011.

Scharf, J. Thomas, and Thompson Westcot. *History of Philadelphia, 1609–1884*. Vol. 3. Philadelphia: L. H. Everts & Co., 1884.

Scholnick, Robert J. "Scribner's Monthly and 'The Pictorial Representation of Life and Truth' in Post-Civil War America." *American Periodicals: A Journal of History, Criticism, and Bibliography* 1, no. 1 (Fall 1991): 46–69.

Scott, Rebecca J. "Paper Thin: Freedom and Re-Enslavement in the Diaspora of the Haitian Revolution. (Law, Slavery, and Justice: A Special Issue)." *Law and History Review* 29, no. 4 (November 2011): 1061–87.

Scott, Rebecca J., and Jean M. Hébrard. *Freedom Papers: An Atlantic Odyssey in the Age of Emancipation*. Cambridge: Harvard University Press, 2012.

Scoville, Joseph A. *The Old Merchants of New York City*. New York: Carleton, 1863.

Sernett, Milton C. "Nativism and Slavery: The Northern Know Nothings and the Politics of the 1850s." *Church History: Studies in Christianity and Culture* 63, no. 1 (1994): 136–37.

Seymour, William H. "General Jackson's Last Letter from Chalmette, Prior to the Battle of New Orleans." Publications of the Louisiana Historical Society. New Orleans: L. Graham & Son., Ltd., 1895.

Shankman, Andrew. "Democracy in Pennsylvania: Political, Social, and Economic Arguments in the Jeffersonian Party, 1790–1820." Ph.D. diss., Princeton University, 1997.

———. "Malcontents and Tertium Quids: The Battle to Define Democracy in Jeffersonian Philadelphia." *Journal of the Early Republic* 19, no. 1 (Spring 1999): 43–72.

Sidbury, James. *Ploughshares into Swords: Race, Rebellion, and Identity in Gabriel's Virginia, 1730–1810.* New York: Cambridge University Press, 1997.

Simpson, Louis P. "New Orleans as a Literary Center: Some Problems." In *Literary New Orleans: Essays and Meditations,* edited by Richard S. Kennedy, 76–88. Baton Rouge: Louisiana State University Press, 1998.

Smith, Thomas Ruys. *Southern Queen: New Orleans in the Nineteenth Century.* New York: Continuum International Pub. Group, 2011.

Socola, Edward M. "Charles E. A. Gayarré, A Biography." Ph.D. diss., University of Pennsylvania, 1954.

Sollors, Werner. *Neither Black Nor White Yet Both: Thematic Explorations of Interracial Literature.* New York: Oxford University Press, 1997.

Spear, Jennifer M. *Race, Sex, and Social Order in Early New Orleans.* Baltimore: Johns Hopkins University Press, 2009.

Sterkx, H. E. *The Free Negro in Ante-Bellum Louisiana.* Rutherford, N.J.: Fairleigh Dickinson University Press, 1972.

Sterling, David L. "A Federalist Opposes the Jay Treaty: The Letters of Samuel Bayard." *William and Mary Quarterly* 3rd series, vol. 18, no. 3 (July 1961): 408–24.

Stevens, Mary Anne, ed. *The Orientalists, Delacroix to Matisse: The Allure of North Africa and the Near East,* edited by National Gallery of Art (U.S.). Washington, D.C.: National Gallery of Art, 1984.

Stoler, Ann Laura, ed. *Haunted by Empire: Geographies of Intimacy in North American History.* Durham, N.C.: Duke University Press, 2006.

———. "Tense and Tender Ties: The Politics of Comparison in North American History and (Post) Colonial Studies." In *Haunted by Empire: Geographies of Intimacy in North American History,* edited by Ann Laura Stoler, 23–67. Durham, N.C.: Duke University Press, 2006.

Summers, John H. "What Happened to Sex Scandals? Politics and Peccadilloes, Jefferson to Kennedy. (Thomas Jefferson)." *Journal of American History* 87, no. 3 (December 2000): 825–54.

Thomas Jefferson Foundation. "Research Committee Report on Thomas Jefferson and Sally Hemings." Electronic version; http://www.monticello.org/site/plantation-and-slavery/report-research-committee-thomas-jefferson-and-sally-hemings (accessed March 14, 2012).

Thompson, Shirley Elizabeth. *Exiles at Home: The Struggle to Become American in Creole New Orleans.* Cambridge: Harvard University Press, 2009.

Thrasher, Albert. *On to New Orleans! Louisiana's Heroic 1811 Slave Revolt.* New Orleans: Cypress Press, 1996.

Tregle, Joseph G., Jr. "Creoles and Americans." In *Creole New Orleans: Race and Americanization,* edited by Arnold R. Hirsch and Joseph Logsdon, 131–88. Baton Rouge: Louisiana State University Press, 1992.

———. "Early New Orleans Society: A Reappraisal." *Journal of Southern History* 18, no. 1 (1952): 20–36.

Trouillot, Michel-Rolph. *Silencing the Past: Power and the Production of History.* Boston: Beacon Press, 1995.

Tunnell, T. B., Jr. "The Negro, the Republican Party, and the Election of 1876 in Louisiana." *Louisiana History* 7, no. 2 (Spring 1966): 101–16.

Twinam, Ann. *Public Lives, Private Secrets: Gender, Honor, Sexuality, and Illegitimacy in Colonial Spanish America.* Stanford, Calif.: Stanford University Press, 1999.

Van de Pol, Lotte, and Erika Kuijpers. "Poor Women's Migration to the City: The Attraction of Amsterdam Health Care and Social Assistance in Early Modern Times." *Journal of Urban History* 32, no. 44 (2005): 44–60.

Vazzano, Frank P. "The Louisiana Question Resurrected: The Potter Commission and the Election of 1876." *Louisiana History* 16, no. 1 (Winter 1975): 39–57.

Vidal, Cécile. "French Louisiana and Saint-Domingue: The Dependent Servant of an Island Master—in Short, the Colony of a Colony?" In *Louisiana: Crossroads of the Atlantic World,* edited by Cécile Vidal. Philadelphia: University of Pennsylvania Press, 2013.

Walker, Dave. "Blood Brother." *New Orleans Times-Picayune,* September 6, 2006.

White, Ashli. *Encountering Revolution: Haiti and the Making of the Early Republic.* Baltimore: Johns Hopkins University Press, 2010.

White, Deborah Gray. *Ar'n't I a Woman? Female Slaves in the Plantation South.* New York: Norton, 1985.

White, Horace. *The Life of Lyman Trumbull.* Boston, New York: Houghton Mifflin Company, 1913.

Williams, Bernard Arthur Owen. *Truth and Truthfulness: An Essay in Genealogy.* Princeton: Princeton University Press, 2002.

Williams, Diana. "'They Call it Marriage': The Interracial Louisiana Family and the Making of American Legitimacy." Ph.D. diss., Harvard University, 2007.

Williams, Greg H. *The French Assault on American Shipping, 1793–1813: A History and Comprehensive Record of Merchant Marine Losses.* Jefferson, N.C.: McFarland, 2009.

Willinger, Beth, ed. *Katrina and the Women of New Orleans.* New Orleans: Newcomb College Center for Research on Women, 2008.

Woodward, Comer Vann. *Reunion and Reaction: The Compromise of 1877 and the End of Reconstruction.* Boston: Little, Brown, 1951.

———. *The Strange Career of Jim Crow*. New York: Oxford University Press, 1955.

Wright, Robert E. "Artisans, Banks, Credit, and the Election of 1800." *Pennsylvania Magazine of History and* Biography 122, no. 3 (1998): 211–39.

Yoshihara, Mari. *Embracing the East: White Women and American Orientalism*. Oxford: Oxford University Press, 2002.

Zanger, Jules. "The 'Tragic Octoroon' in Pre–Civil War Fiction." *American Quarterly* 18, no. 1 (Spring 1966): 63–70.

Acknowledgments

The debts that I have accumulated in researching and writing this book are many. They will never be discharged, but I am very happy to recognize them here.

Cécile Vidal is known to all who labor in the vineyard of Louisiana history as much for her commitment to its collective advancement as for her own brilliant scholarship. Her organization of a workshop in Paris in 2007 gave me the opportunity I needed to try to make sense of the marriage records of late colonial New Orleans, and is one more example among many of the way she contributes to the field. The critiques and comments of the historians who participated in that meeting were key to persuading me that there was a larger story to be told about the figure of the quadroon and the women on whom it was modeled, and it's my pleasure now to thank Guillaume Aubert, Shannon Dawdy, Alexandre Dubé, Sylvia Frey, Sylvia Hilton, Jean-Pierre LeGlaunec, Rebecca Scott, François Weil, Sophie White, and Mary Williams. Cécile pushed me and the project along again three years later by inviting me to spend a month as a visiting professor at the Center for North American Studies at the École des Hautes Études en Sciences Sociales in Paris, where my work in progress was tested by the fire of debate around the seminar table and over endless cups of strong coffee. In addition to Cécile, Camille Amat, Nicolas Barreyre, Jean Hébrard, Martha Jones, and Sara Le Menestrel were especially welcoming and generous colleagues there.

Tony Badger's invitation to present this project at an early stage to the American History Seminar at the University of Cambridge gave it momentum at a critical stage. I thank him and Ruth Badger for their continued support as the book took shape. As the project drew to a close, Laurent Dubois gave me an opportunity to run part of the manuscript past a formidable collection of historians at a workshop at Duke's Haiti Lab. For this, for his remarkable scholarship on Haiti, and for his generous responses to my innumerable research questions, my deep thanks.

Colleagues who have read part of this manuscript in various versions include Laurent Dubois, Susan Klepp, Jean Hébrard, Rosalind Hinton, Martha Jones, Sue Peabody, and Rebecca Scott. The Delta Women Writers group read several chapters and offered commentary on three different occasions. Thanks especially to Elizabeth Jacoway and Elizabeth Payne for organizing the group. Glenda Gilmore offered critical advice and encouragement for the project at its conception. Jane Daily, Sylvia Frey, and Daniel Usner provided close and careful readings of the entire manuscript and offered invaluable corrections, critiques, and encouragement in the later stages. I count myself beyond fortunate to have had such distinguished and demanding readers. They did their best to save me from mistakes and my worst instincts. The errors of fact, judgment, and interpretation that remain are mine alone.

At Tulane, George Bernstein, Donna Denneen, Patrice Downes, Marline Otte, Linda Pollock, Larry Powell, Judy Schafer, Randy Sparks, Justin Wolfe, and Trudy Yeager in the History Department each offered help and support in ways large and small. Nathalie Dessens at the University of Toulouse came through with crucial cites when I'd reached a dead end. Michael Henderson shared his research on his family with me, and although he and I imagine somewhat different pasts for his ancestor Agnes Mathieu, we share a passion for making her history visible. Among the many others who supported me intellectually, materially, and emotionally, I want especially to thank Barbara Clark, Tamara Kreinin, Jude, Don, and Jessie Woodman, John Pope, and the late Diana Pinckley.

As every historian knows, no undertaking of this kind succeeds without the expertise and patience of a small army of archivists and librarians who track down elusive documents and illustrations and steer us toward sources we would otherwise have missed. I wish to thank especially Emilie Leumas of the Office of Archives of the Archdiocese of New Orleans and the members of her staff, as well as her predecessor, Charles Nolan, who have made it possible for me to work so productively in the remarkable records in their care. At the New Orleans Public Library, Irene Wainwright and Greg Osborn assisted me with their customary, unflappable expertise. Sybil Thomas and Juliet Pazera at the New Orleans Notarial Archives Research Center and Pamela D. Arceneaux, Mary Lou Eichhorn, Daniel Hammer, Alfred Lemmon, Howard Margot, John McGill, Jennifer Navarre, and Eric Seiferth at the Historic New Orleans Collection were welcoming and responsive whenever I darkened the doors of their collections. At Tulane, Leon Miller of Special Collections at the Howard-Tilton Memorial Library and Hortensia Calvo, Christine Hernandez, and Rachel Roberts of the Latin American Library bent over backward to help me locate obscure items. Greg Lambousy, Tony Lewis, Elizabeth Sherwood, and Michael Leathem at the Louisiana State Museum all deserve medals for helping me find and decide upon the beautiful image used on the cover. Antonio Rueda was positively heroic in his efforts to obtain permission for me to use an image in Seville.

This book would have taken much longer to finish without grants that supported its research, writing, and publication. A Phase II Research Enhancement Grant from Tulane University and a Dianne Woest Fellowship in the Arts and Humanities from the Historic New Orleans Collection funded initial research. A fellowship from the American Council of Learned Societies, a grant from the Louisiana Board of Regents Awards to Louisiana Artists and Scholars, and a sabbatical leave from Tulane University provided time away from teaching that allowed me to draft and complete the manuscript. A subvention from the Tulane University School of Liberal Arts supported the publication of this book.

Kate Douglas Torrey retired after more than twenty years as executive director of the University of North Carolina Press in 2012, but not before she took hold of this project, nurtured it to maturity, and flawlessly oversaw its transfer into the extraordinarily capable hands of Chuck Grench. Kate is a legend in the academic publishing business with a well-deserved reputation for excellence in all things. Authors who have had the great privilege and gift of working with her as an editor know that her professionalism is organic. Her brilliance and poise are rooted in a generosity of spirit that lifts authors above their limits to produce the books she knows they can write. It's a special honor to be among the authors who can thank her for bringing their books into print.

My special callout to Kate is not intended to overshadow in any way the other phenomenal staff it has been my pleasure to work with at the Press. Chuck Grench has been a wise, energetic, and efficient editor. Together with Dino Battista, Kim Bryant, Sara Cohen, Gina Mahalek, Ron Maner, and Mark Simpson-Vos, he has made sure that my manuscript progressed through the publication process without a hitch. Liz Gray was the most thoughtful and thorough copyeditor an author could wish for and has made me look far better than I deserve.

This book came into being because of and despite the trauma of Hurricane Katrina in 2005. I had just returned to my hometown to join the history department at Tulane when the storm swept through and upended the plans and certainties of an entire city full of people. Historical certainties were among the casualties of that awful calamity. I am not the only historian who laid aside a scholarly project that suddenly seemed far less compelling in order to embark on a new one once the floodwaters abated. Though I felt impelled to realign my research in the wake of the hurricane, I fell victim to the exhaustion and pessimism that befell most Orleanians at the time. Three people made it possible for me to remain a historian and take on the daunting challenge of trying to write a new history for the New Orleans quadroon. My husband, Ron Biava, is the best life partner anyone could ever have. He gives me space, he gives me encouragement, he gives me abundant love, and he never, ever, lets me believe that I can't finish what I start. Two wise and generous women played special roles in getting this book out of my head and onto the page. Callie Winn Crawford used her pulpit to help heal my storm-struck soul and persuaded me, along with many others, that the impossible was possible. Sylvia Frey has taught me what it is not just to be a historian, but to live as one, guiding me in more ways than she can ever know. To Callie and Sylvia I dedicate this book with gratitude and love.

Index

Dunbar-Nelson, Alice, 191
Dunlap's American Daily Advertiser, 20
Dupart, Joseph, 84
Dupart, Marie, 84
Duralde, Julie, 128
Durouleau, Charles, 60
Durouleau, Pierre, 60
Dussuau, Hortanza, 88

Early, Eleanor, 193, 236 (n. 19)
"Épigramme" (poem; Lanusse), 156, 160
Eureka Colony, Mexico, 121, 224 (n. 59)
Exclusif, 14

"Fantomes" (poem; Hugo), 157
Faulkner, William, 134, 190, 191
Favre, Jeanette, 104, 106
Featherstonhaugh, George, 160, 188, 231 (n. 77)
Federalists, 26–27, 29, 30–31, 32, 33, 36, 207 (n. 48)
Felicité (slave), 105, 106
Ferant, Louis Charles, 62
Ferber, Edna, 134
First Battle of Bull Run, 104
Fleming, Jean, 95
Flint, Timothy, 121
Fort Sumter, 104
France: French Revolution, 13–15, 18, 24; Louisiana as colony of, 28, 40, 72, 73, 75, 82, 104, 204 (n. 12); *métissage* and colonies of, 46–47, 211 (n. 29); U.S. commerce banned with, 24–25, 34. *See also* Saint-Domingue
Francisca, Maria, 83
Frazier, E. Franklin, 159, 191, 231 (n. 73)
Free black militia of Louisiana: American Revolution and, 76; companies of, organized by racial ancestry, 81, 82; constraints on, by new territorial code of law, 87–88; as free citizens of Louisiana in new American republic,

86–90; under French colonial rule, 75; marriage and, 78–81, *80*, 83, 84–85, 90, 91; as proponents of marriage, 72, 90–91; service for United States, 62, 89–90, 197, 219 (n. 47); under Spain, 75, 76, 77, 82. *See also* Free men of color
Freedmen's Bureau, 182
Free men of color: African origin of, 74, 75, 83; balls and, 38, 66–67, 68–69; as godparents, 74, 75; scarcity of in New Orleans for free women of color, 62, 91, 93–94, 100–110, 128–29, 131, 214 (n. 70), 227 (n. 86); owning slaves, 60, 61, 62, 75–76, 91, 110, 219 (n. 47), 222–23 (n. 28); planters in Saint-Domingue, 40, 60–61, 65; Revolutionary War and, 71, 72, 76; from Saint-Domingue to Louisiana, 37, 41–45, 59–60, 62, 86–87, 90–91, 120; from slavery to freedom, 75, 76, 217 (nn. 12–13); whites prohibiting arrival of in New Orleans, 54, 57, 62; writings of, 155–57, 160, 230 (n. 60). *See also* Free black militia of Louisiana; Haiti; Marriage—New Orleans; Saint-Dominguan refugees; Saint-Dominguan refugees in New Orleans; Saint-Domingue
Free women of color: of African descent, 87, 92–93, 96, 101; Anglophone Protestants vs. Francophone Catholics in New Orleans and, 57–58, 102, 121, 122, 126–27, 129–31, 165–66; bi-racial partnerships broken by white wife and, 97, 126–27, 153–54; cohabitation with white men in New Orleans, 97–98, 101–9, 123; scarcity of free men of color in New Orleans and, 62, 91, 93–94, 100–101, 128–29, 131, 214 (n. 70), 227 (n. 86); as *ménagères*, 59, 63–66, 70, 100, 156, 166, 167, 168, 171–72, 215 (n. 78); notaries used by, 95, 103, 120; known as *placées* in New Orleans, 66, 70, 148–49,

Laussat, Pierre Clement de, 105, 121
Laveau, Marie, 62
Laviolette, Pierre, 79, 83, 90
Leclerc, Charles, 27–28, 39, 86
Leib, Michael, 11, 29–30, 31, 32, 33, 36–37
Le Maitre, Delphina, 158–59
"Le Mulâtre" (Séjour), 158, 231 (n. 70)
Le Patriotism américain (Petit), 47
"Le Retour de Napoleon" (poem, Séjour), 158
Les Cenelles (poetry; compiled by Lanusse), 157–58
Leveillé (slave), 93, 94
Leveille, Jean-François, 65
Leveillé, Joseph, 72–73, 74, 76–77, 83, 217 (n. 7)
Leveillé, Louis, 74, 77
Lewis, Jan, 54
Lewis and Clark expedition, 33
"Libertinage," 46, 48, 211 (n. 29)
Libres de fait, 75
Life in a Haitian Valley (Herskovits), 159
Logan, George, 35
Loi Municipal, 101
Longfellow, Henry Wadsworth, 146
Louisiana: Civil Code of 1808, 87–88, 110–11, 113, 117, 123–24, 126, 131; as French colony, 28, 40, 72, 73, 75, 82, 104, 204 (n. 12); as Spanish colony, 72, 73, 75–76, 77–78, 82, 93, 98, 101, 111, 123, 138; sugar production in, 40–41, 108; transfer to United States, 83, 86, 105, 121. *See also* New Orleans
Louisiana Purchase, 89, 121, 122, 127, 129, 227 (n. 86)
Louisiana Supreme Court: denying inheritance to colored progeny of white men and, 113–14; ruling on recognition of mixed-race partnerships, 127–28
Louverture, François-Dominique Toussaint. *See* Toussaint Louverture, François-Dominique

Lowell, Marie Françoise, 96
Lowell, William, 128, 226–27 (n. 85)
Lucile, Marie François, 83–84
Lugar, Iris, 84–85

Macarty, Augustin, 111–18, 121, 124, 127
Macarty, Brigitte, 111, 115, 223 (n. 31)
Macarty, Eugene, 111, 127–28, 226 (n. 83)
Macarty, Jean, 111
Macarty, Josephine, 95, 113, 114, 115–16, 117, 118, 119, 224 (n. 52)
Macarty, Patrice, 111–12
Madame Delphine (Cable), 189–90
Madison, James, 27, 33, 86
Mahogany Hall, 185
Mandeville, Eulalie, 111, 127, 128, 226 (n. 83)
Manumission, 74, 75, 93, 217 (n. 12); under Louisiana territorial law, 87; in Saint-Domingue, 47–48; under Spanish law, 98–99, 220 (n. 2)
Marie (slave), 75
Marquis, Edouard, *196*
Marriage: ideals of, in early U.S. republic, 54; mixed-race, 1770s to early 1800s, 34–35, 46, 101, 124; rarity of among French men, in Saint-Domingue, 46, 47
—New Orleans: African-born men and women and, 83–84; family members at, of free men and women of color, 84–85; of free black Orleanians vs. Saint-Dominguan refugees, 63, 72, 88–89, 90–92, 119–20, 156–57, 214–15 (n. 74); free black Saint-Dominguan refugees and, 60–63, 91–92, 106, 119–20; free men and women of color legitimizing children through, 72, 77, 83–84, 88–89, 95, 123–24, 158; free Orleanian men and women of color and, 71–72, 76–86, 87–96, 97, 99, 100, 106, 126, 217 (n. 15), 219 (n. 47), 220–21

(n. 4); honor and, 78, 85; Louisiana law forbidding, between slave and free, 87–88; Louisiana law forbidding, between white and free black, 88, 114, 124, 131, 148; mixed-race, under Spanish law, 101, 124; *Real Pragmática* during Spanish colonial time and, 77–78; slaves and, 72, 73, 74, 87–88, 93; terms for racial mixture and, 82, 83

Martin, Joan M., 191, 193

Martineau, Harriet, 98, 131, 189, 193, 195, 229 (n. 54); disapproval of quadroons by, 1, 188, 191; New Hampshire story of quadroons, 130, 143–45; quadroons and white men and, 94, 97, 118, 126, 153–54

Masks at balls, 69, 152, 173–75, 233 (n. 32)

Mathieu, Agnes, 97, 98–100, 220 (n. 2), 220–21 (n. 4)

Mathieu, Eloy Valmont, 96

Mathieu, Joseph, 99, 100, 220–21 (n. 4)

Maurin, Jean Baptiste, 66

Maurin, Theresa, 60

Mayeux, Maria Francisca, 85

McKean, Elizabeth, 30, 208 (n. 74)

McKean, Thomas, 30, 31, 33, 35, 208 (n. 74)

Meffre-Rouzan, Jacqueline, 95

Meffre-Rouzan, Jacques, 95

Meffre-Rouzan, Michel, 95

Ménagères, 59, 63–66, 215 (n. 78); New Orleans and, 70, 100, 156, 166, 167, 168, 171–72, 221 (n. 7)

Mestizo, 82

Métissage, 46–47, 211 (n. 29)

Meunier, Joseph, 93

Mexico, 121, 224 (n. 59)

Mifflin, Thomas, 28, 33

Mignon, Basille, 60

Mignon, Rose, 60

Miranda, Charlotte, 58

Moni, Aloysius, 90

Monroe, James, 5

Moore, Alexander, 122, 123, 124, 225 (n. 66)

Moore, Alexander James, 124

Moore, Antoine Robert, 124

Moore, Charlotte Eugenie, 96, 126

Moore, Euranie Eulalie, 96, 124, 126

Moore, James, 123

Moore, Marie Antoinette, 96, 126

Moore, Marie Camille, 124

Moore, Samuel, Jr., 96, 124, 125, 126

Moore, Samuel P., 96, 122–26, 127–28, 130, 225 (nn. 67, 69)

Moore, Sara Virginia, 123, 124

Moreau de Saint-Méry, Médéric Louis Élie: Chica dancing and, 67–68; descriptions of *ménagères*, 64, 65; observations about race in Saint-Domingue, 47, 81, 211 (n. 36); quadroon balls and, 69; quadroon racial combinations and racial terms by, 6, *8*; writings portraying dangers of beautiful quadroons/*mûlatresses*, 6, 23, 48–50, 51, 52, 60, 67, 128, 132

Moreno, 82

Moreu, Jean, 45

Morris, Phillip, 33

Morris, Robert, 21–22, 25

Morrison, Alexina, 164–65, 232 (n. 8)

Mortis causa donations, 110

"Mouers coloniales: le Mulâtre" (Séjour), 134

Moultrie, William, 5

Mouton, Marie Françoise, 34

Mulato/mulata, 81, 82, 83, 85

Mûlatresses, 48–54, *56*, 59, 63–64, 65, 67, 69, 70, 85, 88, 137, *140*, 149

Mulatten: originalt romantisk Drama i Fem Akter (Andersen), 134

Mulatto (Hughes), 134

Murdock, John, 23, 28, 51

Napoleon, 27, 39

National Gazette, 20–21, 206 (n. 35)

Natural children, Louisiana law and, 110, 112–18. *See also* Bachelor patriarchs of New Orleans; Baptisms

Navarre, Marianne, 81

Nègre, 47

Négresse, 65, 94

Negritte, 94

Negro, 82, 83, 85

Negro Family in the United States, The (Frazier), 159, 191, 231 (n. 73)

Neighbor Jackwood (Townsend), 147

New Hampshire, 130, 143–44

New Orleans: bachelor businessmen setting up house with free women of color in, 130–31, 160, 171–72, 233 (nn. 26–27); balls of 1790s, 38, 68; Battle of New Orleans, 62, 89–90, 109, 197, 219 (n. 47), 222 (n. 26), 227 (n. 88); disapproval of mixed-race liaisons in, mid-nineteenth century, 121–22, 127; as exception to common U.S. history, 9–10, 146, 161, 181, 193–94, 195, 197, 236 (n. 23); free people of color as citizens of United States and, 86–90; French colonial elite, 104, 108, 221 (n. 14); Hurricane Katrina and, 193, 213 (n. 59); scarcity of free men of color for free women of color, 100–101, 128–29, 214 (n. 70), 227 (n. 86); scarcity of white women for white men, 100–101, 102, 128–29, 227 (n. 86); literary quadroons affecting demand in slave markets of, 161, *163*, 164–65, 169–71, 184–87; masks at balls in, 69, 152, 173–75, 233 (n. 32); *placées* and, 66; postbellum red light district, 180, 181, 184–87; quadroon stories and, 132, 133–34, 135–39, 141–42, 143–49, 155–59, 162, 188–90, 235 (n. 7); racism against free people of color in, 120–21; Reconstruction politics and,

181–84, *184*, 234 (n. 62); religious orders in, French colonial period, 72–74; slave trade in, 40, 41, 72, 73, 145, 147, 162–65, *163*, 232 (n. 8); tourism and, 2, 193–94; travel book portrayals of quadroons in, 1–2, 136, 149–55, 158, 160–61, 165–66, 167, 170, 171–73, 229 (n. 54); white fears of free black rebellion in, 37, 44, 45, 53, 54, 86, 120; women of the levee, 149–50, 154, 166, 167, 168. *See also* Africa; Anglophone Protestants vs. Francophone Catholics in New Orleans; Bachelor patriarchs of New Orleans; Marriage—New Orleans; Quadroon balls in New Orleans

Nicholls, Francis T., 181, 183

Nicholson, John, 18, 21–22

Nivet, Juana, 88

Noleau, Hortense, 61, 62, 160

Notaries, 45, 95, 98, 103, 108, 109, 120, 125, 168–69

Notes on the State of Virginia (Jefferson), 3

Nuestra Señora Del Carmen (ship), 44, 45

Oasis, The, 142

"Octoroon; or, Life in Louisiana, The" (play; Boucicault), 134, 147, 162, *163*

Octoroons, 133, 185, *186*

Odalisque with Slave (painting; Ingres), *140*

Oger, Marie Catherine, 58

Oldner, Prudence, 58

Olmsted, Frederick Law, 1, 130–31, 160, 161, 171, 172, 181, 191, 195, 231 (n. 77), 234 (n. 45)

Oneida Indians, 21

O'Reilly, Alexander, 75

Orientalism, 137, 138–42, 145, 146, 169, 228 (n. 14); in paintings, *140*

Packard, Stephen B., 181

Palmer, John, 182

174–76, 177, *177*, 178, 185, 234 (n. 45); Dominguan free women of color and, 67, 68–70, 154–55, 158, 159, 216 (n. 94); excluding free men of color, 38, 66–67, 68–69; as low-life tourist attractions, 176–80; masks at, 173–75; poetry describing, 157, 176; pricing of, 153, 174, 178; Reconstruction politics and, 181–84, 234 (n. 62); travel book portrayals of, 129–30, 150–53, 154–55, 160–61, 164, 172–73, 174–76, 177, 178–80, 233 (n. 37), 234 (n. 46); twenty-first-century scholarship and, 191, 193; twenty-first-century tourism and, 194

Quadroone, The; or, St. Michael's Day (Ingraham), 132, 138–39, 141

"Quadroon Girl, The" (poem; Longfellow), 134, 146

"Quadroon of Orleans, The" (Ingraham), 135–38, 141, 169, 170, 190

Quadroon, The; or, a Lover's Adventures in Louisiana (Reid), 146

Quadroons: as commercial sex partners for white men, 166–72, 176–78, 180–81, 233 (n. 26); descriptions of their beauty, 6, 132, 137–38, 139, 142, 151; descriptions of their eyes, 137, 141, 142, 146, 147–48; extent of, in United States, 2, 7–8, 9; fictionalized to highlight horrors of slavery, 133, 134, 143–45; Jefferson's "algebra" and, 1, 2–3, *4*, 10; literary imagination vs. reality of, 131, 133, 154, 161, 162–64, *163*, 169, *196*; literary accounts of, affecting demand for slaves in New Orleans, 161, *163*, 164–65, 169–71, 184–87; living free, but actually slaves, 148, 170, 229 (n. 38); mixed-race combinations producing, 5–6, *8*; mothers described as agents of, 152, 153, 155–56, 160–61, 165–66, 167, 169–70, 171, 191, 193; myth of, twentieth-century, 188; naming of, New Orleans,

69–70, 81, 111, 129, 131, 136; notaries used for drawing up partnerships and, 168–69; orientalized through fiction, 132–48, 169, 228 (n. 14); pejorative paintings of, 6, *7*; as pejorative term for Philadelphian political faction, 11, 35–37, *37*, 209 (n. 95); *plaçage* and, 148–49, 193, 195, 216 (n. 94), 234 (n. 45); sexual insatiability ascribed to, in postbellum New Orleans, 180–81, 191; as stereotype of black woman with white man, 129, 190, 191, *192*; stereotype of mothers of bringing up girls to be with white men and, 1, 118, 153, 160–61; stories of, and New Orleans, 132, 133–34, 135–39, 141–42, 143–49, 155–59, 162, 188–90, 235 (n. 7); travel book portrayals of, in New Orleans, 1–2, 136, 149–55, 158, 160–61, 165–66, 167, 170, 171–73, 229 (n. 54); twenty-first-century scholarship and, 195, 197; twenty-first-century tourism of New Orleans and, 2, 194; understanding and use of term, in eighteenth century, 5–6, 204 (n. 12); wearing of veils, 137–38. *See also* Free women of color; Quadroon balls in New Orleans

"Quadroons, The" (Child), 134, 135, 145

Quid Mirror, The, 35

Quids, 35, 36

Racial ideas: Jefferson and, 3, 5, 35, 202–3 (n. 10); racial equality and Haitian Revolution, 12

Racism, 9; in antebellum New Orleans, 120–21; free women of color from Saint-Domingue in Philadelphia and, 49–50; Haitian Revolution obscured by, 195; Philadelphia, early 1800s, 28–29, 35, 36; "Quadroon" political faction in Philadelphia and, 35–37, *37*, 209 (n. 95)